Religious Understandings of a Good Death in Hospice Palliative Care

SUNY series in Religious Studies

Harold Coward, editor

Religious Understandings of a Good Death in Hospice Palliative Care

Edited by

Harold Coward

and

Kelli I. Stajduhar

SUNY
PRESS

Cover art by Susan Coward

Published by State University of New York Press, Albany

© 2012 State University of New York

For information, contact State University of New York Press, Albany, NY
www.sunypress.edu

Production by Eileen Meehan
Marketing by Michael Campochiaro

Library of Congress Cataloging-in-Publication Data

Religious understandings of a good death in hospice palliative care / edited by
    Harold Coward and Kelli I. Stajduhar.
        p. cm. — (SUNY series in religious studies)
    Includes bibliographical references and index.
    ISBN 978-1-4384-4273-0 (hardcover : alk. paper)
    1. Terminal care—Religious aspects. I. Coward, Harold G. II. Stajduhar,
Kelli I.

    R726.8.R437 2012
    362.17'5—dc23   2011032337

10 9 8 7 6 5 4 3 2 1

Contents

Acknowledgments

This book is a joint project of the Centre for Studies in Religion and Society and the Centre on Aging at the University of Victoria, Canada. Authors were recruited and then met to present first drafts of their chapters at a seminar hosted by the Centre for Studies in Religion and Society in November 2009. Faculty, graduate students, and hospice palliative care clinicians (Dr. Michael Downing and Ms. Kathy Bodell) in Victoria and Vancouver attended and helped with the critique of draft chapters. Authors then revised their chapter for presentation in this volume.

Funding for this research and book project was provided by the Canadian Institutes of Health Research, Ottawa. Special thanks are due to June Thomson for her assistance with library research and to Leslie Kenny (administrator) and Rina Langford-Kimmett (secretary) of the Centre for Studies in Religion and Society for organizing the project meeting and preparing the manuscript for publication. The editors are grateful to Michael Hadley for editing help he provided with one of the chapters. At the Centre on Aging Shelly Waskiewich gave valuable assistance in preparing and submitting our grant application. We also thank Julie Lachance, senior policy analyst at Health Canada, Ottawa, for her encouragement and critical advice throughout the research and writing process.

The drawing on the cover of the book is by Susan Coward, who, in addition to being Harold Coward's daughter, is an artist, a longtime hospice volunteer, and now a hospice nurse. She is to be thanked for having sparked Harold's interest in hospice palliative care, which has resulted in this book.

Harold Coward and Kelli I. Stajduhar

Introduction

Harold Coward
Kelli I. Stajduhar

In the 1960s in London, England, Cicely Saunders introduced a new way of treating the terminally ill, which she called "hospice care." Saunders, a trained nurse, social worker, and medical doctor, held that humans should be able to die with dignity and at peace. This viewpoint originated from her medical experience as well as her religious commitment as a Christian. The religious basis of hospice care permeates Saunders's whole approach to the terminally ill, and her vision resulted in the founding of St. Christopher's Hospice in 1967 in London. There, Saunders developed a program of care for the dying based on three key principles: pain control; a family or community environment; and an engagement with the dying person's most deeply rooted spirituality. Although the hospice movement began in a Christian context, it was clear from the start that there was to be no "forcing of religion," and openness to all religious traditions was encouraged. While the first two of Saunders's principles have been well studied, the third, engagement with a person's most deeply rooted spirituality or religion, has not been. Thus, the focus of this book is on the religious understandings of a "good death" in hospice care. Leading scholars of the major religious traditions will formulate their own understanding of a good death, specifically with regard to the "spiritual pain" that often parallels and accompanies "physical pain" in hospice care. These understandings are formulated in terms accessible to people from different intellectual, social, and religious traditions. To ensure that our answers go beyond the theoretical level, a series of real-life case studies from different cultures, religions, and medical challenges are included.

1

Saunders's biographer (du Boulay 2007) notes that the hospice movement, which Saunders founded, combines the best care that medicine can provide together with an engagement with the dying person's most deeply held spiritual understandings. Saunders uses the term *spirituality* to refer to a person's individual experience within a religious tradition such as Christianity or Buddhism, taking into account its various denominations and institutionalized forms. In this study, we will follow Saunders's approach. "Religious tradition" includes the institutional forms of a religion, as well as an individual's experience within that religious tradition. A person's spirituality is therefore shaped by the interplay between the institutional vehicle and a particular, individual experience. Throughout, we prefer the term *religious tradition* rather than *religion* to signal our recognition that the major religious traditions do not have a single theological, cultural, or institutional identity. Rather, they are highly diverse, and their variety and internal differences will be taken into account throughout. We do not assume that an atheist, agnostic, or someone practicing spirituality outside a religious tradition cannot die "with dignity and peace." This increasingly large group of people (especially in North America; Garces-Foley 2003) also needs to be dealt with in regard to hospice care—which we have planned as a second volume. This book focuses on followers of religious traditions such as Buddhism, Judaism, and Christianity and their understanding of a good death in hospice care—a large enough project in and of itself. The issue of atheist/agnostic/secular spirituality is also a large and important project and needs to be dealt with separately.

The hospice movement began in an Anglo-Christian context and subsequently spread to North America and around the world. In the process, much attention was given to the medical and community requirements for hospice care. Since the early 1980s however, little has been written about the religious dimension, even though this continues to be important in practice. The most effective study of how death is treated by the major religious traditions is *Facing Death: Where Culture, Religion, and Medicine Meet* (Spiro, McCrea Curnen, and Wandel 1996). Part 2 of the volume, "Framing Death: Cultural and Religious Responses," contains excellent chapters on a good death in the Hindu, Jewish, Chinese, Islamic, and Roman Catholic traditions, yet these interesting chapters do not consider hospice care. Within the hospice movement itself, the survey by Saunders and Kastenbaum (1997) of the "state of the art" of hospice development in various cultures and countries around the world barely mentions religion. In summary, our literature review shows that there is no systematic analysis of how to resolve spiritual pain in the achievement of a good death in hospice care.[1] This, then, is our research question: *What are the religious understandings of a good death in hospice palliative care?* This study fills a significant gap in knowledge and will be an essential tool for the training of doctors, nurses, social workers, psychologists, chaplains, and volunteers for work in hospice care in Canada and worldwide.

The Place of Religion in the Modern Hospice Movement and the Concept of "Total Pain"

Writings during the 1970s and 1980s on the formation of the modern hospice movement tended to describe its religious dimension exclusively with reference to Christianity, with the Church of England as a major player (du Boulay 2007). Although she was open to whatever religious tradition a hospice patient might practice, Cicely Saunders was a deeply committed Christian and a member of the Church of England. In her own writings on the religious dimension of hospice care, Saunders commonly evokes Christian concepts and makes frequent reference to the Bible (Saunders 1988). Yet Saunders held also that hospice should be a place of spiritual growth for both patients and staff, and this growth could occur not only in a Christian context but also in religious traditions other than Christianity, and even in the absence of any religious commitment. As Saunders states: "We are ourselves a community of the unlike, coming from different faiths and denominations or the absence of any commitment of this kind. What we have in common is concern for each individual . . . and our hope is that each person will think as deeply as he can in his own way" (Saunders 2006, 227). Saunders clearly sees how the science of medicine and the wisdom of religion are inextricably related in hospice care. As the Yale University citation for an honorary degree given to Saunders in 1969 says: "You have combined the learning of science and the insight of religion to relieve physical pain and mental anguish and have advanced the humanistic aspects of patient care in all states of illness" (Saunders 2007, 184). In Saunders's view a good death honors the whole of life—material affairs, human relationships, and spiritual needs (Saunders 2006, 266). She further defines a good death as "attention to the achievements that a patient could still make in the face of his physical deterioration and awareness of the spiritual dimension of his final search for meaning" (Saunders 1981, ix).

Spiritual needs are defined by Saunders as follows: "'Spiritual' concerns the spirit or higher moral qualities, especially as regarded in a religious aspect with beliefs and practices held to more or less faithfully. But 'spiritual' also covers much more than that—the meaning of life at its deepest levels as understood through our patients' different religions." As Saunders puts it, "The realization that life is likely to end soon may well stimulate a desire to put first things first and to reach out to what is seen as true and valuable—and give rise to feelings of being unable or unworthy to do so. There may be bitter anger at the unfairness of what is happening, and at much of what has gone before, and above all a desolate feeling of meaninglessness. Herein lies, I believe, the essence of spiritual pain" (Saunders 1988, 218). In Saunders's understanding, "spiritual pain" is parallel and interpenetrates with "physical pain." Indeed, Saunders coined the term *total pain* to take into account a broader conceptualization of pain to include physical, psychological, social, emotional, and spiritual components (Clark 1999). Our research, then, is theoretically guided by Saunders's conceptualization of "total pain," but with a focus on spiritual pain and an acknowledgment that religious needs have to be addressed in hospice palliative care for a good death to be realized.

Hospice Palliative Care as a "Philosophy of Care"

Definitions of hospice and palliative care have continued to evolve since the inception of the modern hospice movement. Currently, there is no single agreed-upon definition. The diversity of meanings associated with the terms *hospice* and *palliative care* and the lack of agreement among scholars and clinicians has resulted in conceptual confusion in the field (Billings 1998). Hospice has been closely linked with grassroots volunteer movements, whereas palliative care has been more commonly associated with medical and professional care (Downing and Wainwright 2006). For some, hospice is equated with respite and care provision in free-standing facilities, or with care in the community. Palliative care has most typically been associated with care in hospital-based settings (Downing and Wainwright 2006). Twycross (1980), a leading physician scholar contends, however, that "hospice is a concept of care rather than a particular type of institution" (36), and the World Health Organization (2002) refers to palliative care as an "approach" to care. While multiple connotations of the terms *hospice* and *palliative care* exist, it is now commonly understood that hospice and palliative care are not institutions or "places" of care. Rather, hospice palliative care is a *philosophy of care* that "embodies the active total care of an individual" (Daaleman and VandeCreek 2000) and their family members (Doyle, Hanks, and MacDonald 1999; Ferrell and Coyle 2006). It is this philosophical approach to defining hospice palliative care that guides our research.

Use of the Term Modern Biomedicine Rather Than Western

We use the term *modern biomedicine* rather than *Western biomedicine* (with its European scientific worldview) to acknowledge that various worldviews and belief systems exist within the religious traditions. We contend that Westernized beliefs and approaches alone are inadequate to helping us gain religious understandings of a good death in hospice palliative care. We also recognize that the approach of modern biomedicine has been exported around the world, and now functions side by side with alternative medical approaches such as that of the traditional Buddhist monk healers who offer much of the hospice palliative care in Thailand (see chapter 9).

Overview of the Book

Today, many of those involved in the hospice palliative care movement worldwide may know little of the details of Cicely Saunders's life and the early development of hospice care in England from the 1950s forward. For those who would like to know more, chapter 1, written by Michael Wright and David Clark, offers a more detailed recounting of Cicely Saunders's life, her vision for the founding of St. Christopher's Hospice in London in the 1960s, and the subsequent spread of hospice palliative care around the world in the 1970s and 1980s. Although founded by Saunders essentially within an interdenominational Christian context, Wright and Clark recount how by the 1990s the religious dimension of the hospice movement was being newly described in Jewish, Buddhist, and Indigenous (Australian Aboriginal) terms.

The purpose of this book is to expand and make more inclusive the religious understandings of a good death in hospice care. In part 1, leading scholars of Hinduism, Buddhism, Islam, Judaism, Christianity, and Chinese religion examine how Cicely Saunders's conception of a good death in hospice palliative care may be understood within each religious tradition. Each of these chapters includes a brief introduction to the religious tradition, the concept of a good death latent in this religious tradition's texts and practices relevant to hospice care, narrative case studies exemplifying the approach of the particular religion, and the identification of special issues such as the position of women and children. A response of each religious tradition to the question of how to treat persons who are suffering from dementia or Alzheimer's disease (a rapidly increasing problem in hospice palliative care) is included in each chapter of part 1. Our goal, in each of these chapters, is to offer to hospice and palliative care clinicians an understanding of how Cicely Saunders's goal of a good death may be realized within each religious tradition. These chapters in part 1 also make a contribution to religious studies of dying and life after death (e.g., Coward 1997). The new knowledge presented in these chapters is a clear understanding of how a good death is to be conceived and practiced in palliative situations. For many of the religious traditions, this specific focus on the good death in hospice care is new knowledge and thus is a contribution to the self-understanding of the process of living and dying well in each religion.

Part 2 contains six case studies of real-life hospice palliative care examples involving Thailand's Buddhist monks, the Ugandan way of living and dying (with HIV/AIDS), Punjabi (Sikh and Hindu) extended-family hospice care, caring for children in hospice palliative care, and interfaith chaplaincy in hospice palliative care.

A glossary and index have been provided to aid a busy reader who may want to read about one religion or one case at a time. For example, a reader who wanted to focus on Buddhism could choose to read chapter 3, part 1, on Buddhist perspectives of a good death, followed by chapter 8 on Buddhist hospice care in Thailand, which includes a case study from a Thai hospice centre. Likewise, someone interested in Hinduism could focus on part 1 of chapter 2 on as well as the Punjabi case study described in part 2 of chapter 10. But our hope is that the contents are sufficiently interesting that most readers will want to read right through the whole book. And, as we mentioned earlier in our introduction, for those wondering why we have left out atheists/agnostics and those who follow some form of spirituality rather than a religious tradition, our second volume (forthcoming) will explore understandings of a good death in atheist/agnostic and spirituality-based hospice palliative care.

Note

1. The Association for Clinical Pastoral Education has been a leading organization for clinical counseling and chaplaincy teaching in the United States since 1967. However, a review of its publications and programs indicates no particular attention given to the topic of a good death in hospice or palliative care.

References

Billings, J. A. 1998. What is palliative care? *Journal of Palliative Medicine* 1(1): 73–81.

Bowlby, J. 1961. Processes of mourning. *International Journal of Psycho-analysis* 42: 317–40.

Bradshaw, A. 1996. The spiritual dimension of hospice: The secularization of an ideal. *Social Science & Medicine* 43: 409–19.

Branson, R. 1975, May 7. Is acceptance a denial of death? Another look at Kubler-Ross. *The Christian Century*, 464–68.

Clark, D. 1999. "Total pain," disciplinary power and the body in the work of Cicely Saunders, 1958–1967. *Social Science & Medicine* 49: 727–36.

Coward, H., ed. 1997. *Life after death in world religions.* Maryknoll, NY: Orbis Books.

Copp, G. 1998. A review of current theories of death and dying. *Journal of Advanced Nursing* 28(2): 382–90.

du Boulay, S. 2007. *Cicely Saunders: Founder of the modern hospice movement.* London: SPCK.

Daaleman, T. P., and L. VandeCreek. 2000. Placing religion and spirituality in end-of-life care. *Journal of the American Medical Association* 284(19): 2514–17.

Downing, G. M., and W. Wainwright. 2006. *Medical care of the dying.* Victoria, BC: Victoria Hospice Society.

Doyle, D., G. Hanks, and N. MacDonald. 1999. *Oxford textbook of palliative medicine.* Oxford: Oxford University Press.

Ferrell, B. R., and N. Coyle. 2006. *Textbook of palliative nursing* (second ed.). Oxford: Oxford University Press.

Garces-Foley, K. 2003. Buddhism, hospice, and the American way of dying. *Review of Religious Research* 44(4): 341–53.

Germain, C. P. 1980. Nursing the dying: Implications of Kubler-Ross' staging theory. *The ANNALS of the American Academy of Political and Social Science* 447: 46–58.

Golden, F., et al. 1999, March 29. Cranks . . . villains . . . and unsung heroes. *Time* 153(12). www.time.com. (Accessed Aug. 28, 2009).

Hinton, J. 1967. *Dying.* Baltimore and Middlesex: Penguin Books.

Maciejewski, P. K. et al. 2007. An empirical examination of the stage theory of grief. *Journal of the American Medical Association* 297(7): 716–24.

Munley, A. 1983. *The hospice alternative: A new context for death and dying.* New York: Basic Books.

Parkes, C. M. 1972. *Bereavement: Studies of grief in adult life.* New York: International Universities Press.

Saunders, C. 2006. *Cicely Saunders: Selected writings 1958–2004.* Oxford: Oxford University Press.

———. 1990. *Beyond the horizon.* London: Darton, Longman, and Todd.

———. 1988. Spiritual pain. *Journal of Palliative Care* 4(3): 29–32. (Reprinted from *Cicely Saunders: Selected writings 1958–2004,* ed. C. Saunders, 217–21. Oxford: Oxford University Press, 2006).

———. 1981. Foreword. In *Hospice: Complete care for the terminally ill,* ed. J. M. Zimmerman, ix–x. Baltimore: Urban and Schwarzenberg.

———, and R. Kastenbaum, eds. 1997. *Hospice care on the international scene.* New York: Springer.

Spiro, H. M., M. G. McCrea Curner, and L. F. Wandel. 1996. *Facing death: Where culture, religion, and medicine meet.* New Haven: Yale University Press.

Twycross, R. 1980. Foreword. In *The Royal Victoria Hospital manual on palliative/hospice care,* ed. I. Ajemian and B. Mount. Montreal, QC: The Ayer Company.

World Health Organization 2002. Definition of palliative care. World Health Organization www.who.int/cancer/palliative (accessed Aug. 19, 2009).

Part I

Religious Understandings of a Good Death

1

Cicely Saunders and the
Development of Hospice Palliative Care

Michael Wright
David Clark

Religion has had a profound role in shaping the development of the international hospice movement. It remains a vibrant force in informing the philosophy, organization, and day-to-day delivery of hospice care in many settings. It all goes back to the London-based Cicely Saunders, who by the late 1950s was well established in the intention of dedicating the rest of her life to developing a modern approach to the care of the dying. She viewed this work as a matter of personal calling. She was singularly qualified for it, having read social sciences as an undergraduate, trained as a nurse and almoner (or medical social worker), and then qualified as a physician. She had studied medicine as a third profession specifically to do something about the problem of pain in patients dying of cancer. In 1959 she was forty years old, unmarried, and a committed Christian whose evangelical orientation was beginning to broaden. One year earlier she had published the first of what would become many papers setting out her ideas on care at the end of life (Saunders 1958). She had gained experience in the care of the dying as a nurse volunteer at St. Luke's Hospital and then as a research fellow at St. Joseph's Hospice, both in London. At St. Luke's she saw demonstrated some of the principles of pain relief that she would later do much to promulgate. In particular, she became interested in the regular giving of analgesics. In St. Joseph's she had an opportunity not only to put these ideas into practice but also

11

to develop a wider view of pain in the context of the whole person's suffering (Clark 1999). Here she also experienced a culture of religious solicitude, which fostered her belief in the dignity of dying and the care of both body and soul.

The inspiration for this work went back to 1948, when in a London hospital she had cared for David Tasma, a dying Jewish émigré from Warsaw. Together they had discussed the possibility that one day she might found a special place more suited to those in his condition (Saunders 1981). As he had told her: "I only want what is in your mind and in your heart." His words served immediately as a fount of inspiration and later became emblematic of Cicely Saunders's wider philosophy of care, both intellectual and spiritual. Later, her links with Jewish friends and colleagues—particularly in the United States (Clark 2001)—would grow and strengthen. Her increasing knowledge of Judaism would contribute to a broadening in her own personal sense of spirituality. Likewise, the telling and retelling of the story of David Tasma would constitute a foundation myth for the hospice movement that would capture the imagination of people of many faiths and no faith at all, around the world. But as the 1950s came to a close Cicely Saunders still sought to clarify her initial ideas, striving to create a program for action and laboring to realise her vision for St. Christopher's Hospice (Clark 1998).

Absolutely central to this process was the question of the religious and spiritual foundation of the institution she was to establish. The issue had come early on to the agenda. She had first raised it in 1959 while on a retreat at the Mother House of the Church of England order of St. Mary the Virgin, at Wantage, Berkshire, in southern England. Subsequently, she gathered a group of friends and associates who might help in her quest to found a new home for dying people; she tackled them in turn on the question of religious priorities. This led to numerous meetings and extended correspondence with a clutch of evangelically inclined Anglican friends. By the end of 1960 a certain clarity had emerged sufficient to take the project forward. Though the protagonists were likely unaware of it, their deliberations were also to have a profound influence upon the later development of what became known as the hospice movement.

A good deal of initial thinking centered around the involvement in St. Christopher's of those of different "churchmanship." Some of her associates advised her against bringing in those inclined towards the "higher" (more Anglo-Catholic) wing of the Anglican Church. Some of her close friends also held the view that the practical management of the home and the clinical work conducted within it should be undertaken by the same group of committed Christians. Indeed, there was a growing sense that this was to be both a medical unit *and* a Christian community. At this point the vision for St. Christopher's was something akin to that of a dedicated spiritual order, with its own discipline and rule. Evangelical friends were nervous about this, feeling that it sat more easily within an Anglo-Catholic tradition. Cicely Saunders herself recognized that this was not the case, however, and pointed to examples such as the Lutheran deaconesses and the Iona Community on the west coast of Scotland. She was aware, too, of a move within the Church of England toward the formation of intentional communities and saw this as a "work of the spirit." Yet she did not see herself as being in the vanguard of a new spiritual movement. This, she believed, lay outside her "own spiritual capacity" at that time (Saunders 1960a).

Nevertheless, some pressed her as to which aspect of her vision was most important: the spiritual or the medical. She took the view that the medical and spiritual are inextricably mingled. "I long to bring patients to know the Lord and to do something towards helping many of them to hear of him before they die, but I also long to raise standards of terminal care throughout the country from a medical point of view at least, even where I can do nothing about the spiritual part of the work" (Saunders 1960b). There was, in fact, a sense in these discussions that it was easier to conceive of the "medical unit" than the notion of a religious community. A certain cautiousness about the latter was to become a persistent feature.

Significantly, her association with Dr. Olive Wyon, then a retired theologian living in Cambridge, did much to clarify the issue (du Boulay 1994). Olive Wyon had studied the new religious movements and communities that were developing across Western Europe (Wyon 1963), and this knowledge was to prove helpful in resolving the issues that Saunders brought to her. Cicely Saunders first wrote to Olive Wyon in spring 1960:

> The problem . . . is the question of the "Community" which some people seem to see envisaged in my plan. I am tremendously impressed by the love and care with which the Irish Sisters give to our patients—something more than an ordinary group of professional women could ever give, I think. But I was not really thinking of anything nearly so definite as a real new Community, I think I was using the term in a much less technical way. . . . I

had not been thinking of going any further than pray for the right people to come, and wait for the leading of the Spirit should He want us to draw together more definitely. (Saunders 1960c)

Two issues now required resolution. First was the question of the precise religious character of the hospice. The debate initially had focused on which wing of the Church of England it should be located. Yet, ecumenical ideas and the influence of discussions about Christian unity became quickly apparent. This was the extent of interfaith considerations. In these years Britain was still some way from addressing multicultural issues and the question of non-Christian religions was not given any acknowledgment. That would come later. To a considerable extent, the issue was resolved pragmatically. A major source of charitable funds, the City Parochial Foundation, was showing an interest in the project, but under its terms of trust the foundation was unable to give to a purely Anglican venture. This provided hospice with a strong reason for adopting an interdenominational orientation. Months earlier, and in a different way, the mother of a friend from medical school had captured this in theological terms. In a letter encouraging her not to be too dismayed by the apparent diversity of Christian influences that were helping to form St. Christopher's she wrote: "Could it be do you think, that in heaven our ways don't seem quite so different as they appear to us—and who knows that the edges might well melt away or not matter so much" (West 1960).

By the end of 1960 the issue was settled and Cicely Saunders could write to Olive Wyon:

We have decided that it shall be an interdenominational foundation, although we will have something in the documents stating as firmly as possible that it must be carried out as a Christian work as well as a medical one. . . . I found that I just couldn't think it was right to be exclusive. First of all, I could not be exclusively evangelical and thought that perhaps it would therefore have to be Anglican to keep it safe from heresy or secularisation. But then it didn't seem right to be that either, and in our legal Memorandum stands the statement: "there shall be a chapel available for Christian worship," and I do not think that really we could be much broader than that! (Saunders 1960c)

On the second question however—that of St. Christopher's as some form of community—no such categorical statement appeared. Indeed there was a sense that this issue remained something to be explored and encountered, even as the work of the hospice got under way. In the midst of debate about denominational identity one supporter insisted:

> To the outside world you must be first and foremost a medical concern. . . . You are a Christian doctor not a spiritual leader with a medical vision. You have lots of experience of working with others on a professional basis but God has never given you the experience of being a member of a Community. Don't you think he would if that were to loom large in his plan? (Burch 1960)

So it was that Cicely Saunders was able to write to Olive Wyon in December 1960: "It does not seem to have been right to think much more along the lines of a Community for this Home at the moment. I think that if we are to be drawn together in this work, that it will happen when we get there" (Saunders 1960c).

It is now clear that 1960 was an intensely formative year for Cicely Saunders. It was one of deep reflection and consultation with others on the precise nature of her vision for St. Christopher's Hospice. The issues that she had explored at such length with her friends and associates during that year would continue to tax her imagination and energy, but a clear and pragmatic turn had occurred which enabled the purposes of St. Christopher's to be explained succinctly to the wider public, including potential donors.

A few years later, the supporters of St. Christopher's, who had been meeting from 1962 under the guidance of the Bishop of Stepney, sought to formulate the basic principles of their work. They called themselves "a community of the unalike." At a meeting in June 1964, Olive Wyon, in Cicely Saunders's words, "made an excellent digest of my woolly thoughts" (Saunders 1964). The resulting document, *Aim and Basis*, was to have currency at the hospice for many years in the future (St. Christopher's Hospice 1964). It defined St. Christopher's Hospice as a religious foundation based on the full Christian faith in God. It listed five underlying convictions: (1) all persons who serve in the hospice will give their own contribution in their own way; (2) dying people must find peace and be found by God, without being subjected to special pressures; (3) "love is the way through," given in care, thoughtfulness, prayer, and silence; (4) such service must be group work, led by the Holy Spirit, perhaps in unexpected ways; (5) the foundation must give patients a sense of security and support, which will come through a faith radiating out from the chapel into every aspect of the corporate life.

Aim and Basis, therefore, provided St. Christopher's with a statement of underpinning motivation, which has been reviewed from time to time in the intervening years. The discussions that preceded it, however, were to shape the work of the hospice for many years to come. They reveal a profound sense of purpose coupled with a rigorous approach to debate and discussion, which were essential in establishing the dominant themes in the life and work of the world's first modern hospice. They largely agreed on three themes about the aim and basis of the work of St. Christopher's Hospice: religion, medicine, and the notion of "community." The key issue was how these could in some way be harmonized.

It is clear that Cicely Saunders did not see her vision as bounded solely by the discipline of medicine. The concept of "total pain," ideas about the multidisciplinary team and the involvement of families, and the creation of a charitable foundation outside the parameters of the British National Health Service all display a skepticism about the ability of the mainstream health care system to foster her ambitions. Significantly, the real importance of the early thinking that led to St. Christopher's lies in what was decided *against.* The ideas that were not pursued or which were allowed to recede are themselves significant.

In particular, it was decided that hospice would not be located in a narrow evangelical wing of the Church of England, whose primary purpose would be to proselytize. Nor was it to be a new religious community in which a dedicated few—operating outside of the secular world—would care for the dying in their own special way. Instead, it became a foundation underpinned by the Christian religion, but which fostered the contributions of various disciplines, facilitated research and teaching, and where others came to develop their own ideas and skills. So defined, the vision could be successfully emulated or elaborated, thereby enabling its spread both nationally and internationally in the following years.

Within a decade of the opening of St. Christopher's (1967), another fourteen hospices were established in the United Kingdom. Meanwhile, other services had opened in Europe (Oslo, Norway; Motola, Sweden), western Asia (Nicosia, Cyprus), and North America (Winnipeg and Montreal, Canada; New Haven and New York, U.S.A.). As the 1970s drew to a close, hospices were also operating in Africa (South Africa and Zimbabwe) and Oceania (New Zealand). Within a thirteen-year period, hospice services had become available to local populations on five continents. Latin America followed in the 1980s (Stjernswärd and Clark 2003).

Influenced by Cicely Saunders, an international network of people has emerged to become hospice champions and to drive forward palliative care innovation in many places. Testimonials and adaptive models in countries as disparate as Japan, Zimbabwe, and Australia are a matter of record.

Many of the early pioneers who were influenced by Saunders drew on a common spirituality that was informed by the Christian tradition (Wright 2004). The Canadian Balfour Mount, for example, acknowledges his "Christian background," while the English physician David Allbrook, working in Australia, states that he "gave his life to Christ" at an early age. A succinct articulation of the interrelationship between hospice and faith comes from the Polish anesthesiologist Tomasz Dangel, founder of the Warsaw Hospice for Children: "When I was working at the hospital, I felt that my professional life and my personal life were two different lives. . . . Working in a hospice, I really feel I can follow my Christian values; so now my life is not divided into two parts, it's one whole life" (Dangel 2001).

But as the hospice ideal gained ground, questions came to be asked about its religious foundation. Was the Christian perspective part of the essence of hospice, or did it merely provide a motivating force among like-minded pioneers? In the United Kingdom, as the National Health Service opened its doors to palliative medicine, shifts in perspective occurred. One came to view religiously based principles encapsulated within the "Aim and Basis" statements of hospices such as St. Christopher's as institution-specific rather than generalizable. Alongside these changing perceptions, a universal register acknowledging "human dignity" and "quality of life" began to replace the religiously invested language of "sympathy," "love," and "sanctity of life" (ten Have and Clark 2002, 6). In the international setting—especially where populations are multiethnic, multicultural, and multifaith—questions relating to religiously imbued practices concerning death and the dying process are particularly important.

Attitudes toward human suffering provide a key to understanding the religious dimensions of a good death. For the Christian, for example, suffering may be regarded as a means of transformation, linked somehow to the suffering and redemptive mission of Jesus. Saunders's own view toward the end of her life as a resident of hospice resonates with the perception of palliative medicine pioneer Robert Twycross: "Many of our patients . . . are going through their own agony before their death, their own Garden of Gethsemane" (Twycross 1996). However, Sam Klagsbrun, for many years the "visitor" at St. Christopher's, takes a different, Judaic view and recalls the time he met with hospice leaders at Windsor Castle in England. According to Klagsbrun, the conference leader was "holding forth on suffering" and he felt a need to respond:

> I finally spoke up and said, "Look, you all know who I am, and I'm a heretic in this system. You know, I'm against suffering. I don't like it. Religiously I'm opposed to it." And people started laughing. But what we got into was a fascinating, very intense discussion on the views of suffering from a Christian point of view, and its role in history/ philosophy/ theology, and from a Judaic point of view. And the gap was really enormous. (Klagsbrun 1996)

Buddhist physician Sumalee Nimmannit, retired professor of medicine from Siriraj Hospital, Mahidol University, Bangkok, Thailand, sets suffering in another light. As a person living with cancer and coming toward the end of her life, she put it this way:

> Suffering does not exist in nature, you build it up. The body has pain, but not suffering. Suffering is in the heart and mind. People tell me to fight the cancer and I say, "I don't have to fight, I just accept it and live with it." As I told you, I'm going to die, just let go of the body. I accept that death is coming to me. I experienced death in meditation, and that's why I'm not afraid of death. It's something that's very peaceful, very, very peaceful if you have mindfulness. And that's why I'm trying to tell people who are afraid of death to just let go and be relaxed. Nothing is frightening. Just accept what is coming on to you. (Nimmannit 2007)

These different approaches to suffering point in turn to a bigger issue: the relationship between hospice and culture.

Since the early 1990s the relationship between culture and health care has assumed a greater prominence in debate and commentary. This is due to a number of factors, not the least of which is international migration and a growing awareness of Indigenous peoples and of their unequal access to the benefits and services of their homelands.

Against this complex background of migration and discrimination, a complicating factor for health workers is the contrasting approach to issues of autonomy and the disclosure of diagnosis which are to be found in Western and Eastern societies (Wright 2009). The culture of individualism found in the West promotes the belief that respect for patient autonomy includes disclosure of the diagnosis. Yet in Africa and the East—where to be is to belong—an individual exists within embedded networks and structures as a member of a family, clan, or ethnic group. This collectivist culture highlights the leading roles of family members, many of whom may be parties to the diagnosis—though this may not necessarily include the patient. Here, a higher value is placed on beneficence rather than autonomy. Importantly, such autonomy is not respected if the community believes that a person is not acting in his or her best interests (Kasenene 1994). Temsak Phungrassami, a radiologist and palliative care leader in Hat Yai, Thailand, is familiar with this standpoint and explains:

> Thailand is not like a Western country where autonomy is the first priority. We have to evaluate both the patient and the family, and there are still some patients that don't want to know their diagnosis. Yet these patients cooperate in their treatment; they plan for their future; they prepare themselves for their funeral. So they accept their approaching death; they just don't know they have cancer. The Lord Buddha said that the truth we have to tell needs to be told at the proper time, when it will benefit the person who receives it. So we can use this principle in handling this kind of cancer disclosure. (Phungrassami 2007)

A heightened awareness among practitioners and researchers of the cultural implications of hospice care has led to a small but growing body of literature to assist health professionals in meeting the cultural and religious needs of their patients. We highlight here a few key examples from contrasting regions of the world.

In Australia, for example, hospice-palliative care providers are mirroring the efforts of federal and state governments to make their services more accessible to 517,000 Indigenous people (463,900 Aboriginal, 33,100 Torres Strait Islanders). But increasing the number of Aboriginal and Torres Straight Islanders in hospice-palliative care services presents significant challenges. This is partly due partly to their distribution across remote areas. Equally significant, however, is the fact that their spiritual worldview is at odds with the majority population. In the past, a lack of understanding and cultural-religious sensitivity has caused deep and prolonged hurt. Helen Guyula, an Aboriginal interpreter connected to the Royal Darwin Hospice in the Northern Territory, tells of the importance of singing and dancing to her people; of storytelling and ceremonies around a dying person; of preparation for the journey to ancestors and continuing life in The Dreamtime; and of the fundamental connection with homeland. Sadly for her and other family members, these ceremonies did not happen for her father, who died in an enclosed hospital room, dislocated from his family and land. She recalls:

> We had to grieve ourselves because we didn't see our father. We were very angry because we were going to have our father die in front of us. And our sorrows and everything made us bad. It took us six/ten years to think of him. Our sadness was for us, because he wasn't with us. And now we believe, maybe he found his land. And with my belief I can still think of him, that he's on homeland. When I'm going out into the bush, I can sit and think of him, and listen to the birds that are related to me and my father, and our totem as well. When I'm sitting with the wind blowing, I can still think of him, that we are together, talking together or yes sitting under the trees like way back when I was nine or ten years old and he used to sit and tell the stories. So with all those memories I believe his spirit is still with us. (Guyula 2008)

In order to raise awareness of the spiritual and cultural needs of Aboriginal people at the end of life, Darwin Hospice's Aboriginal health worker, Beverley Derschow, created the Northern Territory Aboriginal palliative care model. What is striking is that its concentric circles contrast with those linear models familiar to Western eyes. It is a pattern in keeping with the cyclical perception of Aboriginal life: an existence that has its origins in The Dreamtime and, after time spent on earth, returns to The Dreamtime. The dying person and the family are at the center of the model, surrounded by culture, kinship, and country.

This approach is reflected in the labyrinth in the garden of the Royal Darwin Hospice, which opened in 2005. It is the Northern Territory's first purpose-built palliative care unit. Recognized in the 2006 Royal Australasian Architect Society Awards, it has been constructed to suit both Indigenous and non-Indigenous patients. Gardens surround the buildings, which incorporate glass doors that lead from bedrooms to plant-surrounded patios, each giving a sense of openness together with a blending of inside and outside space. Warpole highlights the special nature of hospice gardens, which draw "as much upon a rich history of religious associations with gardens . . . as places of retreat, meditation and containers of *memento mori* (artefacts designed to allow people to reflect on their own mortality) as they do upon herbal gardens and naturalistic gardens designed to emphasize the health-giving properties of the natural world" (Warpole 2009, 80). Darwin's hospice garden includes a centerpiece found in many religious traditions: a labyrinth. Its circular shape resonates with the Aboriginal palliative care model and, perhaps unsurprisingly, has found favor in the local community. As the patient walks the path—a journey in what may be considered sacred space—there is the opportunity to pause, reflect, and explore one's inner, spiritual life confronted by the challenges of illness and mortality.

Pastoral coordinator Amanda Cox, who conceptualized and led the project, comments:

> One way of walking a labyrinth path is to see it as having three stages: the walking in, being in the centre and the walking back out. When a person walks in they may symbolically take in whatever is happening for them at that time—the burdens, sorrows and decisions. When they arrive in the centre of the labyrinth it's a place where they can stop, rest, wait and be quiet for as long as they need to. . . . The walk is a very symbolic act. For some, the labyrinth is a place where they pray, for others it's a place where they have an opportunity to think through the decisions or emotions they are encountering. For many it is just having some space where they are alone. (Cox 2008)

By contrast, hospice care in the postcommunist countries of Eastern Europe and Central Asia raises radically different questions about the place of religion in palliative care. In particular, how is the spiritual dimension of hospice care shaped and delivered in countries that experienced an ideological repression of religion during the major part of the twentieth century? Significantly, since the collapse of communism during the last decade of the twentieth century, hospice services have sprung up across Central and Eastern Europe and in the Commonwealth of Independent States. Only in Poland did hospice care in these countries pre-date the 1990s.

The change in emphasis post-1989 is striking. Those who experienced communist-era oppression have vivid recollections: "When I joined the [religious] order I lost my right to vote, I couldn't go to a doctor, I lost my social card. I didn't have rights that everybody else had" (Sr. Ruža Andlar 2004, Croatia). "For my first communion, I was in the church alone. Only my family and priest were there. It was a secret until 1990 because my parents were afraid that if it became known, I wouldn't go to high school" (Patricia Porubčanová 2004, Slovakia). "It was terrible. They said to us 'You don't need religion, you need only to be a member of the Communist Party'" (Rema Gvamichava 2003, Georgia). When the communist era passed, however, each of these individuals contributed to the development of end-of-life care within their country, sustained by their religious faith. Sr. Ruža became coordinator of the hospice home care service in Zagreb; Patricia Porubčanová, a psychologist, academic, and deputy chair of the national hospice association, was instrumental in opening a hospice facility at Trnava University Hospital, dedicated to Blessed Zdenka, who died there; and Rema Gvamichava, a surgeon, was a founder of Georgia's first hospice-palliative care service, which opened in 2003, strongly associated with the Georgian Orthodox Church.

Despite the formal repression of religion, a spiritual pulse continued to beat throughout the region until a more open expression of faith could become reestablished in social and public life. Two countries exemplify the point: Poland in the West and Mongolia, on Russia's Asian border, in the East. Poland is a special case in that the hospice movement had its origins in the 1970s and soon flourished as an example of emblematic resistance to a communist philosophy that placed little value on human worth unless the individual was a member of the workforce and contributing to the economy. In the context of a debate about the nature of Christian love, a group of parishioners from the Lord's Ark Church in Nowa Huta (Cracow) began to visit the dying in a local hospital—an initiative that came to be regarded as Poland's first informal hospice service. In Gdansk, a home care team was founded in 1984 by the Catholic priest

Fr. Eugeniusz Dutkiewicz, which became a model for other groups that started to be operational across the country. The first hospice palliative care service within Poland's national health structure opened in Poznan in 1987, led by Jacek Łuczak. He became the country's first national hospice palliative care consultant and subsequently opened a freestanding unit in Poznan, Hospice Pallium (Clark and Wright 2003). Łuczak typifies the religious perspective of many Polish hospice staff when he says, "My faith has played a very important role. I never expected I would be so deeply immersed in life, in suffering, and also happiness; almost every day you find God in your connections" (Łuczak 2003).

Farther east, the twentieth-century "Great Purge" in Mongolia resulted in the deaths of thousands of Buddhist lamas (an estimated one hundred thousand existed in a then population of around seven hundred thousand), together with the destruction of more than one thousand temples and monasteries (Byrne et al. 2005). Yet Buddhism has remained part of the fabric of Mongolian society and returned to prominence during the 1990s. Odontuya Davaasuren, who opened the first palliative care service at the National Cancer Centre in Ulaanbaatar, describes the importance of spiritual support for patients at the end of life in Mongolia:

> 90 per cent of the Mongolian population are Buddhists and spiritual support is very important for the dying patient. The lama comes near to the bed to pray, to meditate, and this meditation spiritually frees them from depression or anxiety. After this the patient accepts death and dies very quietly, because they feel spiritually free. (Davaasuren 2003)

Hospice care in Russia began in Lakhta (St. Petersburg) in 1990 when a social hospital was transformed into a hospice under the leadership of Victor Zorza (an émigré Polish journalist based in the United Kingdom) and the Russian psychiatrist Andrei Vladimirovich Gnezdilov, a deeply religious man. The hospice fulfilled Gnezdilov's dream. Prior to becoming the hospice medical director, he had used role play, shadow figures, and an array of bells, keys, and dolls to address symbolically the taboo issue of death with his dying patients. As his dream became reality, it was no surprise that strong links were established with the Church—reemerging as communism crumbled. Orthodox Patriarch Alexei II became a founder of the hospice. A chapel was created in the Russian Orthodox tradition with the inclusion of relics. Close links were established with Lakhta's Fr. Georgy and his local congregation. Then, a religious order, the Sisterhood of St. Elizabeth, extended the hospice's remit to include the care of orphans: an innovation that was welcomed by lone parents as they approached the end of life (Wright 2006, 42). When asked where the sisters come from, Elena Kabakova, the head sister, replied simply: "God sends them to us; they are all believing people" (Kabakova 2001).

But what of the patients who spend their last days in an organization with an overt religious perspective? Hospice doctor Galina Moskalenko comments: "People in the Communist Party were Christians in childhood. Towards the end, they come, they want to pray, they want the sacrament and they remember what they were taught as children" (Moskalenko 2003). Gnezdilov expanded this insight when he was awarded an honorary doctorate by Essex University (UK) in 2001:

> More than ten years working in the hospice has meant a great deal for me personally. . . . It has revealed the existence of an inner life, in which suffering may be transformed into a positive experience for the individual, and into a treasure of the human spirit. . . . Sooner or later death reveals to us more than does life itself. For many, it reveals the existence of one's own soul; order in the chaos of human life; beauty, in the thick of ugliness, and finally and above all, the smile of God in the midst of endlessly changing life. (Gnezdilov 2001)

These varied life experiences, found across cultures and continents, take us into fascinating areas in a search for greater understanding. On an individual level, Denzin sheds light on the rediscovery of past practices by his use of the term *pentimento*: something painted out of a picture that later becomes visible again. Applying this notion to human beings, he considers that "lives and their experiences are . . . like pictures that have been painted over and, when the paint is scraped off, something new becomes visible . . . displacing what was certain and seen" (Denzin 1989, 81). In terms of end-of-life care—as medicine runs out of options, as hopes for a cure have passed and the old certainties fade away—religious memories resurface to claim a newfound significance of transcendence and hope in the face of death and bereavement.

Yet this memory has a collective as well as an individual dimension. Addressing this notion, Hervieu-Léger (2000) posits that in traditional societies—where religious symbolism is structured by a myth of creation that accounts for the origin of both the world and the group—collective memory is contained within the structures and observances of the society. Yet where established religions are found in differentiated and multicultural societies, collective religious memory is subject to a constantly recurring construction. Hence, the past, which has its source in the religious events that are at its core, can be grasped at any moment.

This reconstruction—seen as a religious chain of memory that connects past, present, and future members of a community—is reinforced by a group defining itself as "a *lineage* of belief" (Hervieu-Léger 2000, 125). This is poignantly exemplified by Ruža Andlar when speaking of the relevance of funeral ceremonies in Croatia:

> I would say there is a historical tradition; it's in our memory, even if some didn't practise in communist time. But in our history, in our literature, and in our identity, we have described and remembered rituals and a tradition of lamentation. . . . Sometimes, cemeteries will be lit during the night with lots of candles. It's a place of light; a light that reminds us of connectedness, reminds us of being connected with them [the departed], and reminds us of eternal life. (Andlar 2004)

Through such beliefs, we begin to see the challenging and widespread character of faith and culture as they interrelate with issues of mortality and the care of those dying and bereaved.

In conclusion, this chapter has offered a recounting of the life of Cicely Saunders, her founding of St. Christopher's Hospice in London, and the subsequent development of hospice palliative care from an essentially Christian vision to its reconception in Jewish, Buddhist, and Australian Aboriginal terms as it began to spread around the world. We now turn to the chapters of part 1 of this volume in which leading scholars of Hinduism, Buddhism, Islam, Judaism, Christianity, and Chinese religion examine how Cicely Saunders's conception of a good death in hospice palliative care may be understood within each religious tradition.

References

Andlar, R. 2004. Hospice history interview. Nov. 16.

du Boulay, S. 1994. *Cicely Saunders: The founder of the modern hospice movement*, revised edition. London: Hodder and Stoughton.

Bradshaw, A. 1996. The spiritual dimension of hospice: The secularisation of an ideal. *Social Science and Medicine* 43(3): 409–19.

Burch, R. 1960. Letter to Cicely Saunders. June 16.

Butterfield, Maureen. 2003. Hospice history interview. June 7.

Byrne, S., R. Franken, and G. Verboom. 2005. *Documentation of Mongolian Buddhist temples: Report of a pilot project conducted in 2004.* Arts Council of Mongolia. http://www.mongoliantemples.net/english.php (Accessed Aug. 2009).

Clark, D. 2004. History, gender, and culture in the rise of palliative care. In *Palliative care nursing. Principles and evidence for practice*, ed. S. Payne, J. Seymour, and C. Ingleton, 39–54. Maidenhead: Open University Press.

——— 1998. Originating a movement: Cicely Saunders and the development of St Christopher's Hospice, 1957–67. *Mortality* 3(1): 43–63.

———. 2001. A special relationship: Cicely Saunders, the United States, and the early foundations of the modern hospice movement. *Illness, Crisis and Loss* 9(1): 15–30.

———. 1999. "Total pain," disciplinary power, and the body in the work of Cicely Saunders, 1958–67. *Social Science and Medicine* 49: 727–36.

———, and M. Wright. 2003. *Transitions in end of life care: Hospice and related developments in Eastern Europe and Central Asia.* Buckingham: Open University Press.

Council of Europe. Recommendation Rec. 2003. 24 of the Committee of Minister to member states on the organization of palliative care. http://www.coe.int/t/dg3/health/Source/Rec(2003)24_en.pdf (Accessed Aug. 2009).

Dangel, T. 2001. Hospice history interview. Nov. 15.

Davaasuren, O. 2003. Hospice history interview. Oct. 16.

Denzin, N. K. 1989. *Interpretive biography.* London: Sage.

Dufour, Prue. 1999. Hospice history interview. Dec. 15.

Ekblad, S., A. Marttila, and M. Emilsson. 2000. Cultural challenges in end of life care: Reflections from focus groups' interviews with hospice staff in Stockholm. *Journal of Advanced Nursing* 31(3): 623–30.

Gnezdilov, A. V. 2001. On being awarded an honorary doctorate by Essex University. April 5.

Gvamichava, R. 2003. Hospice history interview. Oct. 18.

Hedayat, K. 2006. When the spirit leaves: Childhood death, grieving, and bereavement in Islam. *Journal of Palliative Medicine* 9(6): 1282–91.

Hervieu-Léger, D. 2000. *Religion as a chain of memory.* Translated by S. Lee. New Brunswick, NJ: Rutgers University Press. First published as *La Religion pour Mémoire.* Éditions du Cerf, Paris, 1993.

Hospice 23. 2008. Newsletter 42 (Winter).

International Observatory on End of Life Care. http://eolc-observatory.net/. (Accessed Aug. 30, 2009).

James, N., and D. Field. 1992. The routinization of hospice: Charisma and bureaucratisation. *Social Science and Medicine* 34(12): 1363–75.

Kabakova, E. 2001. Hospice history interview. Sept. 26.

Kasenene, P. 1994. African ethical theory and the four principles. In *Principles of health care ethics*, ed. R. Gillon, 183–92. Chichester: John Wiley and Sons.

Klagsbrun, S. 1996. Hospice history interview. Feb. 27.

Łuczak, J. 2003. Hospice history interview. Oct. 18.

McElvaine, D. 1997. Zimbabwe: The Island Hospice experience. In *Hospice care on the international scene*, ed. C. Saunders and R. Kastenbaum, 55–58. New York: Springer.

McQuillan, R., and O. an Doorlsaer. 2007. Indigenous ethnic minorities and palliative care: Exploring the views of Irish travellers and palliative care staff. *Palliative Medicine* 21(7): 635–41.

Moskalenko, G. 2003. Hospice history interview. Oct. 5.

Mount, B. 1995. Hospice history interview. Oct. 16.

Mui Hing Mak, J. 2002. Accepting the timing of one's death: An experience of Chinese hospice patients. *Omega: Journal of Death and Dying* 45(3): 245–60.

Murray, S. et al. 2003. Dying from cancer in developed and developing countries: Lessons from two qualitative interview studies of patients and their carers. *British Medical Journal* 7385: 362–68.

Nimmannit, S. 2007. Hospice history interview. March 9.

Phungrassami. 2007. Hospice history interview. March 10.

Porubčanová, P. 2004. Hospice history interview. Oct. 14.

St. Christopher's Hospice. 1964. *Aim and basis*, mimeograph, revised.

Saunders, C. 1960a. Letter to Jack Wallace. Feb. 10.

———. 1960b. Letter to Bruce Reed. March 14.

———. 1960c. Letters to Olive Wyon. March 4, March 16, December 6.

———. 1958 Dying of cancer. *St Thomas's Hospital Gazette* 56(2): 37–47.

———. 1964. Letter to Olive Wyon. June 11.

———. 1981. The founding philosophy. In *Hospice: The living idea*, ed. C. Saunders, D. Summers, and N. Teller, 4. London: Edward Arnold.

———. 1997. Hospices worldwide: A mission statement. In *Hospice care on the international scene*, ed. C. Saunders and R. Kastenbaum. New York: Springer.

Shaw, R. 2005. Hospice history interview. Feb. 12.

St. Columba's Fellowship. 2006. http://www.stcolumbasfellowship.com/newsletter9.htm. (Accessed Oct. 19, 2009).

Staudenmaier, J. M. 2000. Sensual prayer—electronic context: Ignatian prayer for Internet users. *The Way* 40(3): 209–21.

Stjernswärd, J., and D. Clark. 2003. Palliative medicine: A global perspective. In *Oxford textbook of palliative medicine*, ed. D. Doyle et al. Oxford: Oxford University Press.

Taxis, J. C., T. Keller, and V. Cruz. 2008. Mexican Americans and hospice care. *Journal of Hospice and Palliative Nursing* 10(3): 133–41.

ten Have, H., and D. Clark. 2002. *The ethics of palliative care: European perspectives.* Buckingham: Open University Press.

Thomson, N. et al. 2008. *Overview of Australian Indigenous health status 2008.* http://www.healthinfonet.ecu.edu.au/health-facts/overviews. (Accessed Aug. 30, 2009).

Twycross, R. 1996. Hospice history interview. June 4.

United Nations, Department of Economic and Social Affairs, Population Division. 2009. International Migration Report 2005: A Global Assessment. http://www.un.org/esa/population/publications/2006_MigrationRep/report.htm. (Accessed Aug. 30, 2009).

United Nations. 2007. *Declaration on the rights of Indigenous Peoples.* United Nations. http://www.un.org/esa/socdev/unpfii/documents/DRIPS_en.pdf. (Accessed Aug. 30, 2009).

Vanstone, W. H. 1982. *The stature of waiting.* London: Darton, Longman, and Todd.

Wald, F. 1996. Hospice history interview. Feb. 29.

West, B. 1960. Letter to Cicely Saunders. Feb. 11.

Worpole, K. 2009. *Modern hospice design: The architecture of palliative care.* London: Routledge, Taylor, and Francis Group.

Wright, M. 2004. Hospice care and models of spirituality. *European Journal of Palliative Care* 11(2): 75–78.

———. 2006. *Victor Zorza: A life amid loss.* Lancaster: Observatory Publications.

———, et al. 2008. Mapping levels of palliative care development: A global perspective. *Journal of Pain and Symptom Management* 35(5): 469–85.

———, and D. Clark. 2006. *Hospice and palliative care in Africa: A review of developments and challenges.* Oxford: Oxford University Press.

———, et al. 2009. *Hospice and palliative care in Southeast Asia: A review of developments and challenges in Malaysia, Thailand and the Philippines.* Oxford: Oxford University Press, 2010.

Wyon, O. 1963. *Living springs: New religious movements in Western Europe.* London: SCM Press.

2

"Like a Ripe Fruit Separating Effortlessly from Its Vine"

Religious Understandings of a Good Death: Hinduism

Anantanand Rambachan

Introduction

Hinduism is an astonishingly diverse religious tradition, perhaps more so than other major religions. "Hindu" is not a founder's personal name and does not give any suggestions about beliefs and practices. It is the Iranian version of the name of a river that the Indo-Europeans referred to as the Sindhu, the Greeks as the Indos, and the British as the Indus. Those who lived on the lands neighboring were derivatively called Hindus. Today, the Hindu tradition reflects the rich and complex variation in geography, culture, and language across the Indian subcontinent and in places such as the Caribbean, North America, the United Kingdom, Africa, Malaysia, and Singapore. It is helpful to think of the Hindu tradition as an ancient and large extended family sharing common features but also reflecting unique traits in its individual members.

Organizationally, the Hindu tradition has never been centralized. There is no founder and single person or institution speaking authoritatively for all Hindus. While there are widely prevalent teachings and practices, doctrinal and ritual uniformity are not sought or demanded. The Hindu tradition is a dynamic flow of the forces of unity and diversity.

Hindus look to a vast array of sacred texts, and oral traditions, some in Sanskrit, others in the vernacular languages of India, for guidance.

Most Hindus, however, recognize the four Vedas (*Rg, Sama, Yajur, Atharva*), which include the Upanishads, as an authoritative and foundational revelation. Other important texts include the Bhagavadgita, the Mahabharata, the Ramayana in its various regional versions, and the Bhagavata Purana.

The Hindu tradition is neither life denying nor otherworldly. Wealth (*artha*) and pleasure (*kama*) are among the four legitimate goals of life, but these must be sought in religiously and ethically approved ways (*dharma*). The fourth and highest goal of Hindu life is liberation (*moksha*), understood, in different ways, as the overcoming of ignorance about the reality and nature of God and living a life that is centered in the knowledge of God.

The Hindu belief in freedom and moral responsibility is affirmed, in particular, through the interrelated doctrines of *karma* and *samsara*. Hindus understand the doctrine of *karma* to mean that all actions, good and bad, produce appropriate results in the life of the performer, while also fundamentally shaping our characters. In the Hindu understanding, however, the moral consequences of our actions may not always manifest in the course of the life in which we perform the action. Life is a journey of experience and learning through many different births toward the ultimate goal of liberation (*moksha*). The journey through a continuous and connected series of lives is referred to as *samsara*.

Although shared beliefs may be identified across Hindu traditions, shared practices are much more common. The most popular one, referred to as *puja*, is a ritual of hospitality offerings performed in honor of God in Hindu temples and homes. These offerings, which include water, flowers, food, incense, and light, are made to the accompaniment of sacred verses (*mantras*) and before the consecrated icon (*murti*). *Puja* always concludes with the distribution of a food item (*prasada*) offered to God. The particular icon that is the object of *puja* is usually the individual's or family's favorite form of God (*ishtadeva*), determined by region in India, ancestral traditions, or even personal preference. The icon is usually a form of Vishnu, Shiva, or the Mother-Goddess (*Devi*). Hindus generally think of God as one and as having multiple names and forms. Many Hindus visit temples only for the purpose of seeing (*darshana*) the sacred icon, believed to be special form in which God makes Godself accessible for worship. *Darshana* is a special experience of seeing and of being seen by God. Other popular temple and home practices include the repeated recitation of short prayers or sacred texts (*mantras*), chanting the names of God (*japa* or *kirtana*), and the singing of hymns of devotion (*bhajana*).

Hindu Theological Streams

Hindu understandings of a good death in hospice care are deeply informed by the particular theology that shapes the meaning of life and the after-life. With the risks of generalization, we may identify three interwoven theological streams, often difficult to separate in practice (Hopkins 1992). The first stream emphasizes the power of ritual action (*karma marga*) in life and in postmortem ceremonies designed to ensure eternal life in the world of the ancestors (*pitri loka*). This stream is sustained by priestly interpretations of the first or ritual sections of the Vedas. Attainment and residence in the world of the ancestors requires not only faithful observance of obligatory rituals in life, but regular ritual offerings on the part of one's descendants.

The second stream draws from the teachings of the Upanishads, the final section of the Vedas, and puts the salvific emphasis on wisdom (*jnana marga*). The Upanishads do not question the existence of the world of the ancestors, but propose that this is transient and is followed by rebirth. Ritual actions, performed as these are in place and time, cannot lead to a result that is eternal. The Upanishads teach that the highest reality is the infinite (*brahman*), the source, ground, and end of all created realities. *Brahman* is identical with the human self (*atma*). Knowledge of the identity between *brahman* and *atma* constitutes liberation and brings an end to *karma* and to the cycle of birth, death, and rebirth. Liberation, after death, is not characterized in spatial or temporal language; one exists as identical with the limitless *brahman*.

The third stream (*bhakti marga*) places the emphasis on love and devotion to God and on divine grace. It draws from the Vedas and Vedic traditions but more from later traditions centered on texts such as the Bhagavadgita, Bhagavata Purana, and the Ramayana commending the love of God who is personalized as Vishnu and his incarnations, Rama and Krishna, Shiva and the Goddess. This devotion finds expression in temple ritual centered on icons, pilgrimage, acts of piety, and in fervent singing and chanting. Liberation is a gift of grace, and the devotee anticipates eternal life in the heavenly world (*svarga*), thought of as the abode of the particular form of God to which the person has devoted herself. This ensures freedom from the bonds of *karma* and *samsara*. The promise of Krishna in Bhagavadgita (9:34) is quite typical of this stream.

> Be mindful of me
> with love offered to me;

> sacrificing for me,
> act out of reverence for me.
> Surely you shall
> come to me,
> thus having absorbed
> your self in yoga with
> me as the supreme goal.

Although one's location in a particular stream of the Hindu tradition informs understanding of a good death and choices in hospice care, it would be wrong to think of these streams as flowing exclusively. In practice, they blend and flow in and out of each other. The Hindu tendency to think of these ways as personal preferences makes for porous boundaries. It is not, for example, unusual for a person who stands in the devotional stream to make annual offerings on behalf of departed parents as though they existed in the world of the fathers. Hindus are more than likely to honor the religious wishes and needs of a terminally ill family member even when these are different from their own. Family members consider the fulfillment of these as a vital and sacred obligation.

Overcoming the Fear of Dying

The good life, as conceived in Hinduism, provides opportunities for satisfying decently one's material needs, is full of sensual and aesthetic delight, is guided by virtue, and culminates in liberation. The four sequential stages (*ashramas*) of life, student, householder, forest-dweller, and renunciant, are conceived to facilitate the progressive focus on life's four goals. In the final two stages, attention shifts to liberation and there is detachment from material acquisition. The two stages are characterized usually by greater attentiveness to religious practices that include study and recitation of sacred texts, repetition of the names of one's favorite form of God, fasting, pilgrimage to temples and other sacred places, the practice of *yoga*, and various forms of contemplation as prescribed by one's teacher (*guru*) or specific tradition.

For those who follow such a structured course of life, the general Hindu expectation is that such persons will overcome the fear of death and look to its approach peacefully by understanding its inevitability and seeing it as a normal and universal feature of existence. Death, in other words, is not an aberration in the stream of life. Hindus often cite Krishna's words in the Bhagavadgita (2:27), teaching about death's naturalness:

> Indeed, for one who is born
> death is certain,
> and for one who has died
> birth is certain.
> You ought not to grieve.

At the same time, Hindus are realistic in acknowledging that most may not achieve such a desirable mental and emotional condition of fearless peace through wise living and preparation for dying. Recognizing that fear and anguish are not desirable states of mind when dying, Hindu family members make a special effort to help the dying overcome such conditions by exposure to those core teachings that emphasize the self's (*atma*) immortality and its continuing existence even when the body dies. This is accomplished by the practice of chanting sacred texts in the presence of the dying. Although this is most effectively done when there is still the possibility of comprehension, the loss of sight or speech does not imply the absence of understanding, and sacred texts may still be read. According to the Brhadaranyaka Upanishad (4.4.2), the sense of hearing is lost only after sight, smell, taste, and speech. Although dementia may be present in an elderly dying, this does not alter the religious practices that Hindus are likely to perform as death approaches. Hindus believe that such actions, like all actions, will produce results and will benefit the person for whose sake the ritual actions are performed.

The text to which Hindus turn often to provide wisdom and comfort to the dying and their families is the Bhagavadgita and especially to those verses (2:20–25) that proclaim immortality and the continuity of life beyond bodily death and end with the plea not to be overwhelmed by grief. The following two verses (2:22–23) are at the heart of this sequence likening dying to the familiar daily process of changing clothing and ruling out all commonly known methods of destroying the self.

> As a person abandoning
> worn out garments
> acquires other new ones,
> So the embodied,

> abandoning worn-out bodies
> enters other new ones.
> Weapons do not pierce it,
> fire does not burn it,
> And water does not moisten it;
> nor does wind wither it.

Dying with the certain knowledge of one's undying nature is an important characteristic of a good death for a Hindu.

Another text read for the dying, especially in north India, is the *Ramacharitmanas,* the Hindi version of the Ramayana authored by the poet Tulasidasa (ca. sixteenth century). Justice (1997, 100) describes the scene in Muktibhavan, a home for the dying, in Varanasi:

> Once a day, for instance, one of the priest-workers goes from room to room carrying the huge book which contains the *Ramcharitmanas.* The hearing of religious stories is another way of gaining spiritual benefit. So the priest-worker spends twenty minutes or so in each room reading and didactically explaining passages. The priest-worker often will be sitting cross-legged up on the wooden cot, while the family sits listening on the floor. The readings are done for and are directed toward the dying person but it is usually the family who are the most interested.

A small text, especially popular among Hindus from north and central India, is the *Hanuman Chalisa.* Attributed also to the poet Tulasidasa, it is a forty-verse poem in praise of Hanuman, the most famous devotee and servant of Rama in the Ramayana. The *Hanuman Chalisa* is commonly recited in times of illness and as death approaches. It promises relief from all pain and the attainment of the abode of Rama after death.

Many Hindus also choose to recite or hear the *Gayatri Mantra* or the *Mahamrtunjaya Mantra,* or both, as death draws close. The *Gayatri Mantra,* from the Rg Veda, is a prayer for mental illumination and guidance.

> Om, the Lord is most worshipful. We meditate on that all-knowing Lord.
> May he illumine and rightly guide our minds.

The *Mahamrityunjaya Mantra* is a prayer to God as Shiva, the One who overcomes death. The words are a specific request for immortality and a painless freedom from body as a ripe fruit falls away from its vine.

> We worship the fragrant, three-eyed Lord Shiva, who enhances prosperity. May He liberate us from death like a ripe fruit separating effortlessly from its vine and not withhold immortality.

The Significance of One's Mental State at the Time of Death

The concern for overcoming the fear of death in the dying person expresses the more fundamental Hindu teaching, articulated in Bhagavadgita (8:6), that one's state of mind at the time of death significantly determines one's destiny after death.

> Furthermore,
> Whatever state of being
> one remembers upon
> giving up the body
> at the end [of life],
> To that very state
> one always goes,
> O Kaunteya,
> being conditioned
> by that state of being.

This belief is particularly important when deciding whether to disclose a terminal illness to the patient, since the knowledge of approaching death may act as the incentive to cultivate a proper mental state. As Firth (2005) reminds us, such a decision may be complicated by information received from the hospital staff or by the fear of relatives that disclosure may hasten death:

> The Hindu practitioner warned Ramesh that his father [Suresh] was terminally ill with prostate cancer and tuberculosis. Ramesh did not want his father informed of the prognosis. Unfortunately, the hospital staff repeatedly assured Ramesh that Suresh would

recover, and his impending death was never discussed with Suresh. As often happens, he was clearly aware that he was dying, as he gave his books away, talked about dying, and obtained a gold chain for his granddaughter's marriage, but he colluded with his son's silence. When he died unexpectedly in his son's absence, Ramesh was racked with guilt because he had not been present to give him the last rites or to say goodbye.

Keeping in view the importance of the religious needs of the patient, the Hindu tradition favors disclosure and honesty. The potential religious benefits outweigh concerns about the pains of disclosure and any potential discomforts in family relationships.

The religious needs of the patient will also inform measures taken in hospice care to control and alleviate pain, one of the three key principles of Cicely Saunders, founder of the modern hospice movement. Hindus welcome the administering of medication and other palliative measures that alleviate pain. It is preferable, however, if such measures do not impair significantly the patient's awareness and ability to control mental processes. The Hindu patient should be consulted about such decisions and may choose the experience of some pain in favor of retaining clarity of mind. We should not assume that the elimination of pain is the only or the most important concern of the dying. Here again, we are reminded that the basic principles of modern hospice care, articulated by Saunders, pain control, and attentiveness to social, emotional, and spiritual needs, speak about a balance that may be determined differently by persons in various religious traditions.

The fact that one's state of mind while dying is likely to be in continuity with one's central preoccupations while living does not diminish the importance given to it in Hindu considerations of a good death. The possibility of religious growth, for the Hindu, exists until the final moment of life, a fact recognized by Saunders when she wrote of a good death as "attention to the achievements that a patient could still make in the face of his physical deterioration and awareness of the spiritual dimension of his final search for meaning" (Saunders 1981, ix). The reality of death has always been recognized as a powerful awakener to that which is of ultimate significance and value. Nothing reminds us more intensely of life's transient character than the certainty of death, and this can grant extraordinary clarity about the meaning of life. Dying offers a unique opportunity for us to cultivate detachment from the finite and to appreciate the ultimate value of the enduring infinite. Contemplating our mortality can be enlightening, but this presupposes an awareness of the fact and process of dying.

The Desirability of Centering the Mind and Heart in God

Having noted the importance that Hindus give to one's mental state at the time of dying, we can now comment more specifically on desirable states of mind and on the measures that may be conducive in hospice care to enter into these. A good death, in the Hindu tradition, is clearly one that is synonymous with liberation or the attainment of God that follows from centering oneself in God in life and death. This is the explicit promise of Krishna in the Bhagavadgita (8:5;7) where he gives the assurance that he is attained by those who remember him while departing from the body and urging also that we offer him all actions and remember him throughout life:

> And at the time of one's end,
> remembering me alone
> while giving up the body—
> One who thus goes forth,
> Goes to my state of being;
> about this there is no doubt. (5)
> Therefore, at all times
> Remember me
> and fight!
> With your mind and
> discernment offered to me,
> certainly you shall come to me—
> of this there is no doubt. (7)

The Hindu belief that centering one's mind in God at the time of dying leads to attainment of God after death expresses, in reality, a profound theology of divine grace and forgiveness. To emphasize God's boundless compassion, there are many popular accounts of the redeeming results of even unintentionally repeating God's name at the time of dying.

One of the well-known tales from the Bhagavata Purana (614–615) tells the story of Ajamila, a pious priest who abandoned his wife and family for a life with a prostitute. He became a social outcast and took to a life of stealing and drinking. Ajamila fathered many children, naming his youngest and favorite Narayana (one of the names of God as Vishnu). As he lay on his deathbed, Ajamila experienced great fear and called on his son, Narayana. The power of God's name, even unintentionally, was effective in warding off the messengers of Death (Yama) and in securing for the sinner, Ajamila, freedom from sin and a place in the abode of Vishnu. One of the practices at Muktibhavan is the musical chanting of the names of God twenty-four hours a day. This ensures that no resident dies without the opportunity to hear the name of God (Justice 1997, 98). Family members deeply appreciate this religious offering.

In the Hindu belief, religious effort is never futile or without results. The Bhagavadgita (2:40) encourages with the promise that "even a little of this *dharma* frees one from great fear" (my translation). The faith of the Hindu is that if the journey toward God does not end in liberation, there is continuity in the subsequent birth where the conditions for religious growth will be favorable. Anxious about death before the attainment of liberation, Arjuna, in the Bhagavadgita (6:37–39), asks Krishna if he will simply dissipate like a cloud. Krishna gives the assurance that

> neither in this world
> nor in the next
> is the destruction of such
> a person to be found.
> For no one who acts
> In virtuous ways
> ever goes to
> an unfortunate
> destiny, my dear friend.

One gains a rare rebirth in a family of wise practitioners, and continues the religious journey toward God initiated in the previous life.

The Case of Pariksit in Srimad Bhagavata Purana

One of the archetypal Hindu accounts of choosing a good death is narrated in the Bhagavata Purana (Book One) about King Pariksit. It exemplifies the preferences of the Hindu when there is certainty of impending death. Out on a hunting expedition, Pariksit grew tired and thirsty. He approached the hermitage of a sage who was, at the time, deeply absorbed in meditation and did not hear the king's request for a drink of water. Misunderstanding the sage's indifference to his presence as disrespect, Pariksit became angry and, in a state of rage, threw a dead serpent around the neck of the sage. While the sage remained unperturbed by the king's action, his young son felt that the king had not honored his father's dignity and pronounced a curse upon the king that he would die from the venom of a snake on the seventh day. Upon awakening from his meditation, the sage was distressed to learn of his son's actions but was unable, however, to undo his son's curse.

When Pariksit learned of his impending death, he accepted its inevitability, seeing it as an opportunity to free himself from attachment to the finite and impermanent. He gave up this throne and wealth and retired to the bank of the River Ganges to turn his attention to God, and practice religious discipline. He implored the teachers who visited him to speak to him of God and to instruct him about the duties of a person about to die. His request for instruction was most specifically addressed to a young, radiant teacher, Sukadeva. "When the hour of death comes," Sukadeva instructed, "one should shake off all fear and cut with the sword of non-attachment the tie of affection for one's body as well for those that are connected with it. Full of self-control, he should quit the house, bathe in the holy waters of some sacred stream or lake and, squatting on a seat, made according to the scriptural ordinance, in a clean and secluded spot, should repeat with his mind the holy Pranava, [name of God] consisting of three parts (AUM)" (Srimad Bhagavata Purana, 96–97). The dialogue between teacher and student endured for the next seven days until the passing of Pariksit, free from fear and peacefully united with God.

The seminal narrative of King Pariksit provides us with important insights about the Hindu understanding of a good death in hospice care. Like a hospice patient in our times, Pariksit received the news of his terminal condition. He set about immediately to prepare himself for departure from this world. First, he settled his worldly affairs by relinquishing power and wealth, loosening his ties to the finite. Unresolved issues relating to such matters should not anxiously consume the energy of our minds as death approaches. He made the effort, in other words, to adopt the lifestyle of a renunciant or a person in the fourth stage of Hindu life. Second, Pariksit welcomed the visits of religious teachers and requested instruction about God. Although aware of the importance of such a turning to God, the closeness of death acts as the incentive to intensify his focus. Settling worldly affairs and detachment from the finite freed his mind for absorption in God. Pariksit did not spend his limited time raging against dying. He saw in his condition the opportunity to grow spiritually and committed himself to this challenge. He was oriented to the positive possibilities in his situation. Third, Pariksit moved to a sacred place, the bank of the Ganges, to spend his final days. Sacred places are referred to, in Sanskrit, as *tirthas* (places of crossing). Filled as they are with centers of worship, sacred chanting, and pilgrims, they are conducive to God-centeredness. We will return to the importance of sacred space later. Fourth, Pariksit surrounded himself with those who recognized his wish for a good death and who were helpful and supportive to him throughout the process. He did not have to struggle with those whose intentions were contrary to his own or who distracted him from his religious purpose. The four features of Pariksit's response to his condition, although important to our understanding of a good death in hospice care, will require creative adaptation in our contemporary contexts.

A Hindu Prayer for a Good Death

The religious hopes of a Hindu at the time of death are beautifully expressed in a prayerful Hindi song that I hear often at funeral (*antyeshti*) ceremonies. I have never, until now, thought of this anonymous hymn composition as helping us to understand the wishes and needs of the Hindu in hospice care, but it is obvious that few available sources do so with such heartfelt passion. The prayer is addressed to God as Krishna, but one could just as easy substitute any other chosen God (*ishtadevata*), with a different name, form, and attributes. The hopes will be similar. A translation of this song will help us identify these hopes.

> (1) I pray, O lord, that when the breath of life departs my body
> You enable me to utter Your name, Govind
> (2) Whether this occurs on the shore of the Ganges, or the
>   shore of the Yamuna
> I ask only that my Beloved be near.
> (3) Whether this occurs on the soil of Vrindaban
> or near the water flowing from Vishnu's feet

I ask only that a leaf of the sacred tulasi [basil] be on my lips.
(4) May my Beloved stand next to me with folded feet
and may the air be filled with the enchanting sounds of His
   flute.
(5) May I contemplate Him with a crown on His head
and lock of black hair on His face
when the breath of life departs my body.
(6) In my final moment
when the breath of life ascends to my throat
May I be free from pain and from the fear of death.
(6) This is my prayer, O Lord
What do you lose by granting my wish?
Is it not your obligation as my Beloved
when the breath of life departs my body? (My translation)

This prayer to Krishna confirms, clarifies, and adds to the details of our understanding of the religious requirements for a good death in the Hindu tradition. First, we must note the desire to recite and/or hear sacred sounds. In this case, the preference is for the names of God as Krishna, but other Hindus may express a preference for the names of God as Rama, Shiva, or the Goddess Durga, depending on family traditions or personal preference. Family members and friends regularly chanting scripture selections and the names of God may meet this need. We noted earlier the twenty-four-hour chanting of God's names that is done at the Muktibhavan in Varanasi. In the absence of family members or friends to chant, appropriate recordings may be a suitable substitute, and hospice institutions ought to keep a collection of sacred Hindu chants. It is important that hospice caregivers understand, support, and facilitate this desire for sacred sounds and ascertain the particular form of God (*ishtadevata*) to which the patient is devoted. Gandhi's death with the name of God as Rama ("Ram, Ram") on his lips is inspirational for Hindus as the last words of a dying person whose heart and mind are fixed on God. Hindus may wish also to have copies of sacred texts, favorite hymns, and prayers.

Second, we must note the desire for a good death in a sacred space. Traditionally, many Hindus journeyed to special pilgrimage places such as Varanasi or Vrindaban hoping that death in such sanctified locations would ensure liberation. Although this practice is declining in India and rare among the growing numbers of Hindus in the diaspora, the desire to die in a sacred space is still a strong preference. Keeping in mind that most Hindu homes have a room or part of a room that serves as a place of worship, the desire for sacred space at the time of dying may take the form of transforming the hospice room by the addition of an icon (*murti*) of one's favorite form of God. This *murti* should be located in the room where it is easily visible since it is the seeing (*darshana*) of the *murti* that constitutes one of the very important acts of Hindu worship. Hindus visit temples to see the consecrated *murti*, an act that facilitates the experience of seeing and being seen by God. Having a *murti* in the hospice room is one of the ways the dying Hindu receives the comfort of knowing that God is close through a visual presence. Sacred sound is complemented by sacred sight.

Third, we must note the desire for a good death in the midst of sacred ritual expressed in the desire for the *tulasi* leaf. *Tulasi* leaves are offered to God as Vishnu (Krishna is a form of Vishnu) and returned to the worshipper as a consecrated gift (*prasada*). Along with a *murti*, a dying Hindu may wish to have other items that are used in daily worship (*puja*), such as flowers (*pushpa*), incense (*dhupa*), and light (*dipa*), a rosary (*mala*), and sandalwood paste (*chandana*). These may be used in acts of worship performed by the dying or by the family members. Hindu worship always concludes with the receiving of some item, usually edible, that has been offered to God and now received as God's gift (*prasada*). This may be a leaf, a fruit, a flower, or drops of water. At the Varanasi Muktbhavan, *puja* is performed twice daily in the central hall that serves as the temple. At the end of the worship, ritual priests visit each room with a dying person, carrying a tray on which is kept the flame used in honoring God (*arati*) and a small vessel containing red powder. Reciting *mantras*, the flame is waved over the patient and the red powder applied to his or her forehead.

Priests also visit the dying person every two hours, between eight in the morning and six at night, with the tray, for a special ritual of administering sacred water.

> On the tray is a small bottle of *charanamrit*—water from the river Ganga which has been used to wash the feet of an image of Vishnu—infused with some dried leaves of the holy *tulsi* plant. In the midst of the family, the priest-worker bends over the dying person and, with a hand full of densely smoking sticks of incense, inscribes the sound "Aum" in the air while reciting a mantra. . . . Next a little *charanamrit* is spooned up by the priest

worker and poured into the mouth of the dying person and a second mantra is recited. (Justice 1997, 100–101)

Again, the particular ritual objects needed and the forms of worship that a person will desire to perform or have performed on his or her behalf will depend on the specific Hindu tradition followed. We should note, also, the devotee's desire to be free from fear and pain, although the consciousness of God hoped for presupposes mental control. Hindus do not hold that the pain of the dying must not be alleviated as a way of diminishing the burden of *karma*. Such a position is in conflict with the importance of practicing compassion and reducing suffering. They affirm, with Saunders, the value of pain management.

Many Hindus follow the ritual practice, noted above, of offering drops of Ganges water to the dying regularly or when death is imminent, based on the belief in the spiritual potency of the river. Lack of communication between caregivers and family members on this issue can be a source of misunderstanding and distress, as the following account of a British Hindu family demonstrates (Firth 1997, 117).

> An aunt was dying; everybody knew she was dying. The doctors told the family, and the whole family was present at the death, but when the doctors switched off the life-support machine, they would not let the family give Ganges water or perform the last rites on this woman. The reason the doctors gave was that she would live a little longer, but there was no point, she was dying anyway. They switched off the machine, and they said they must not give her anything that would give her a shock and kill her straight away, that would choke her. But it did not matter anyway, because she was dying, even today, ten years afterwards, it still affects the family that they weren't able to do this.

Although the doctors may have believed wrongly that a large quantity of water would be poured down the aunt's throat, the family lived with the anxiety that they were unable to fulfill a necessary obligation to a dying member and that generations would be affected adversely by this omission. Some Hindus will prefer also to be placed on the ground as death approaches. Lying on the ground is symbolic of a return to the earth, the source of life. Many believe that it promotes detachment and eases the process of dying.

The traditions—the placing of the dying on the floor, the offering of Ganges water and a basil (*tulasi*) leaf, as well as the gathering of relatives—are followed easily when hospice care is offered at home. When death occurs in institutions, these procedures may become difficult. Institutions may not be willing to allow the dying to be placed on the ground and, unless the room is a private one, may be reluctant to allow large numbers of relatives to gather for chanting and singing (Rambachan 2003). Laungani (1997) suggests that "there is no reason why a thoughtful hospital chaplain might not keep a supply of Ganges water and offer some to the relatives of dying patients." Such a gesture may inspire feelings of gratitude. With growing numbers of Hindus settled outside of India and ending their life journeys in hospice institutions, mutual understanding is needed so that the obligations of medical personnel and family are fulfilled without conflict.

The Need for Cultural Sensitivity

One of the important characteristics of the Hindu tradition is the unity or rather difficulty of separating religion and culture. There is no Sanskrit equivalent for "religion," and the often-used term *dharma* is far more comprehensive than what may be suggested by religion. It embraces theology, law, ethics, dietary habits, ritual, and the arts. That which appears, in the eyes of the outsider, to be a matter of cultural preference, and consequently not given significance, may have deep religious meaning for the Hindu patient. Let me illustrate with a few relevant examples.

Hindus view the physical body as a temple of God and look upon human birth as a rare and precious opportunity for religious growth and the attainment of liberation (*moksha*). There is a very strong emphasis on divine immanence. The Bhagavadgita (16:18) condemns attitudes and behavior that are abusive of one's own or the body of another caused by ignorance of God's indwelling presence. Such reverence for the body is expressed in modest dress choices and in the preference for caregivers of the same sex. Scanty gowns, designed with different cultural assumptions, cause considerable distress and discomfort to many Hindus who are not offered an alternative. Hindu reverence for the body is expressed particularly in specific markings and symbols. Married Hindu women apply a red vermilion dot (*bindi*) to the forehead or where the hair is parted to signify faithfulness to their husbands. Some also wear an auspicious necklace (*mangala sutra*), indicating marriage and devotion to spouse. Other body markings signify the particular form of God to which the Hindu devotes herself or himself. Worshippers of God as Vishnu may wear a vertical V-shaped mark made of sandalpaste or clay on the forehead. Worshippers of Shiva apply three horizontal lines made of ash, while those who worship God as Mother wear a red dot. These markings may be made on other parts of the body. Many Hindus wear rosaries of various kinds, and males who have been religiously initiated wear a thread (*upavita*) of three strands across the left shoulder and around the torso. While performing ritual worship (*puja*), many Hindus tie a red string on the wrist. It continues to be worn until it naturally disintegrates. It is important to understand the meaning of such body markings and objects since their removal may be a source of pain if done without permission and without proper ritual. Caregivers must respect the right of the Hindu patient to wear and use such items and understand the fact that improper handing or contact with other objects may pollute these.

Notions of purity/impurity and auspiciousness/inauspiciousness are important to Hindu religious practice, and these often run parallel. Hindus are generally scrupulous about cleanliness and purity, understanding these as religious requirements. The observance of cleanliness norms in a hospice context becomes particularly important when the hospice room becomes a sacred space. Traditionally, Hindus prefer flowing water for the purpose of purification and will choose a shower over a bathtub. Some will wish to bathe before offering worship or wash after using the toilet. Others will find it difficult to use a commode in the same room where an icon and ritual objects are kept.

A Hindu in hospice care may choose to continue with regular religious fasts based on the religious calendar. Some who abstain from meat on religious occasions may choose to live the last period of life following a vegetarian diet, considering such a diet to be more conducive to the deepening of their religious lives. The large number of Hindus who are vegetarians are lacto-vegetarians. Few are vegans, and so milk and milk-derived products are acceptable. Some follow a more restrictive vegetarian diet that excludes the use of onion and garlic, foods that are believed to arouse passion and desire at a time when there is an effort to cultivate detachment. There are very conservative Hindus who will be concerned that meat has not been cooked in the utensils used to prepare their meals or who will eat only food that is offered first to God (*prasada*). Such patients may express a desire for home-prepared meals.

The Role of the Family

Cultural sensitivity education becomes very important, particularly in Hindu communities outside of India, where the family structure is changing. The traditional Hindu family has a joint structure with several generations sharing a common roof. Elderly family members and children, especially sons and daughters-in-law, were available to provide hospice care, to be with the dying, to read or recite sacred texts, chant *mantras*, and sing devotional songs. Such persons will also be familiar with the special religious preferences of the dying. Since they were related to the dying by ties of family, friendship, or community, they could provide both emotional and physical support and solace.

Today, in urban areas of India and especially in Hindu communities outside of India, the joint family structure is giving way to nuclear families, making it difficult for the family to provide hospice care. Datta (2008) has noted significant changes, in India, affecting the traditional role of the family in caring for elderly members. Among these are the changing status of women and their desire for nuclear families, and immigration from rural to urban centers as well as to foreign countries. Increasing numbers of Hindus will receive institutional hospice care, underlining the need for professional caregivers to be familiar with Hindu religious preferences.

The movement toward nuclear families, however, does not mean the disappearance of the commitment and a profound sense of obligation to care for elderly members, although one study in Delhi notes the increase in elder abuse and neglect (Datta 2008). Children will do all that is possible to be with and to care for dying parents, and suffer tremendously if circumstances do not allow such service to the parent or if opportunities, for some reason, are denied. As death approaches, relatives will want to gather to say good-bye, to speak farewell words, to pray, and to receive and extend forgiveness. Forgiving and receiving forgiveness is believed to liberate from and lighten the burdens of *karma*. The family priest may be asked also to be present and to begin the rituals that will be performed both before and after death. Institutions will have to be flexible in the numbers of family members allowed to be with the dying.

Grief is intensified if a family member is not afforded the opportunity to be present with the dying at the moment of death. Mahatma Gandhi, in his autobiography (1927, 26), writes of what he describes as an unforgettable "blot" of being with his wife and not with his father at the moment of his death. Dying is as much a family as it is an individual event, and the needs of each must be recognized and balanced.

The Significance of Gender in Hospice Care

In addition to being an individual and family event, dying is also a social event, and the process is not exempt from the influence of those sociocultural factors that shape and influence human behavioral patterns. In the case of Hindu society, in spite of the ideal of spiritual equality rooted in the teaching about God's equal and identical presence in all, the reality is a culture of patriarchy in which women are accorded value and significance only in relation to men. They are regarded with the highest esteem in their roles as wives and mothers. Patriarchy manifests itself in the preference for a male child, and statistics consistently reveal that the girl child in India is disadvantaged in terms of access to health care and education.

The tragic consequence of perceiving the significance of women only in relation to men is seen most clearly in Hindu attitudes to widows. Widows are widely regarded as inauspicious. The widow not only mourned the loss of her husband, but also suffered the guilt of living longer than he. In some conservative communities, she was required to shave her head and avoid all forms of personal adornment. With the death of her husband, she had lost the most important reasons for living. Her problems include economic deprivation, limited mobility, loss of self-worth, poor health, and loneliness. Many are condemned to lives of poverty and begging in the pilgrimage cities of Varanasi and Vrindaban where they await death (Giri and Khanna 2002). They are not residing in those cities by choice. Although the status of the widow has been improving, they are still not always accorded the privileges and honor extended to wedded women (Rambachan 2001).

The Delhi study cited above (Datta 2008) notes that elderly women, especially the widowed and economically dependent, were vulnerable to neglect, isolation, loneliness, and deprivation of medical care. One must assume less concern for ensuring a good death. Increasing numbers of elderly women end their lives in old age homes (Bagga 2008).

In most Hindu families, women are the caregivers, and this responsibility, because of longevity, often lasts into old age. The same longevity factor, however, deprives women of the care that a spouse may offer, and they often have to look to other family members or institutions (Bagga 2008). Gender disparity in access to health care and, specifically, to hospice care is a larger issue of religious and cultural value that needs to be addressed. We need also to study this issue in relation to caste and the underprivileged.

Conclusion

No discussion of religious understandings of a good death in Hinduism can claim to be exhaustive and to treat the tradition in its splendid diversity. The regional and oral traditions of marginalized communities, such as the Dalits, will have resources and perspectives to contribute. Although I have focused here on Sanskrit/Hindu sources and traditions, much of what is discussed is widely shared. Hindu understandings of a good death are deeply informed by the central *telos* of the tradition that is centered on the attainment of liberation (*moksha*), conceived as eternal life in the presence of God or identity with the infinite (*brahman*). *Moksha* is the fulfillment of life and the end toward which the Hindu life is oriented.

Although not neglecting the importance of pain control and physical comfort, the Hindu emphasis is clearly centered on addressing the religious needs of the dying. Recognizing with Saunders the learning and growth opportunities present at the time of dying and the importance that is given in Hinduism to being in a proper state of mind, a good death is characterized by turning away attention from the finite and fixing one's mind and heart on God. Practices to foster this state include the creation of a sacred space, usually by the installation of an icon (*murti*) of the Hindu's favorite God-form (*ishtadeva*), the regular recitation of sacred sounds (*mantras*), and arrangements for the performance of religious ritual (*puja*). In light of the internal diversity of the Hindu tradition, it is important that hospice caregivers ascertain the specific religious traditions that are followed by the individual and, in particular, his or her chosen God-form. Hindus will welcome hospice institutions having at hand some of the standard ritual objects and materials used in worship. Dying, for the Hindu, should be an experience of peaceful exit from the vehicle that is the physical body.

Hindu understandings of a good death in hospice care are informed also by attitudes to the physical body and by norms of purity and cleanliness. The view of the body as a temple of God expresses itself in attitudes of modesty in dress and in a preference for caregivers of the same sex. Sacred markings and jewelry must be honored and properly handled. Purity practices in a room that has been transformed into sacred space must be observed and special dietary habits supported.

Hindu family members traditionally provide physical and spiritual care for the dying, and Hindus hope to have their company at the time of departure from this world. Family members long to be with loved ones to express gratitude and love and to extend and receive forgiveness. Hospice institutions will have to exercise flexibility in accommodating family members during the dying process, recognizing the lasting pain caused by exclusion.

Preparations for a good death in the Hindu tradition involve cultivating detachment from finite and transient things through understanding their transitory character. Many Hindus use the approach of death to resolve personal conflicts and resentments. Detachment from the finite and resolving interpersonal conflicts enable the dying to focus mental and emotional energy on God as the moment of death approaches. Hindus may be willing to accept some physical pain for the freedom of a conscious death.

References

Bagga, A. 2008. Gender issues in care giving. In *Discourses on aging and dying*, ed. S. C. Chatterjee, P. Patnaik, and V. M. Chariar, 171–85. New Delhi: Sage.

Datta, A. 2008. Socio-ethical issues in the existing paradigm of care for the older persons: Emerging challenges and possible responses. In *Discourses on aging and dying*, ed. S. C. Chatterjee, P. Patnaik, and V. M. Chariar, 149–70. New Delhi: Sage.

Firth, S. 1997. *Dying, death, and bereavement in the British Hindu community.* Leuven: Utigeverji Peeters.

———. 2005. End-of-life: A Hindu view. *Lancet* 682(6).

Gandhi, M. K. 1927. *The story of my experiments with truth.* Ahmedabad: Navajivan.

Giri, M. V., and K. Meera. 2002. Status of widows of Vrindavan and Varanasi: A comparative study. http://griefandrenewal.com/widows study.htm. (Accessed July 23, 2009).

Goswami. C. L., trans. 1971. *Srimad Bhagavata Mahapurana.* Gorakhpur: Gita Press.

Hopkins, T. J. 1992. Hindu views of death and afterlife. In *Death and afterlife: Perspectives of world religions*, ed. Hiroshi Obayashi, 143–55. New York: Greenwood Press.

Justice, Christopher. 1997. *Dying the good death: The pilgrimage to die in India's holy city.* Albany: State University of New York Press.

Laungani, P. 1997. Death in a Hindu family. In *Death and bereavement across cultures,* ed. C. M. Parkes, P. Laungani, and B. Young, 52–72. London: Routledge.

Prasad, R. C., trans. 1991. *Sri Ramacaritamanasa.* Delhi: Motilal Banarsidass.

Rambachan, A. 2001. A Hindu perspective. In *What men owe to women,* ed. John C. Raines and Daniel C. Maguire, 17–40. Albany: State University of New York Press.

Schweig, Graham M., trans. 2007. *Bhagavad Gita: The beloved Lord's secret song.* New York: HarperCollins.

3

Welcoming an Old Friend

Buddhist Perspectives on Good Death

Anne Bruce

> When death finally comes you will welcome it like an old friend,
> being aware of how dreamlike and impermanent the phenomenal
> world really is.
>
> —Dilgo Khyentse Rinpoche

Christina was an artist, a mother, and a Buddhist who had been living
with cancer for most of her adult life. She had been diagnosed with
cancer shortly after her daughter, now seventeen, was born, and accepted
the inevitability of it one day returning. At thirty-seven, she expressed
surprise and delight about living so long and spoke openly and humor-
ously of her life with cancer. Then, approximately two years later, she
learned the cancer had returned and spread.

Christina was a devoted meditator and volunteer within her various
communities. She had a strong network of friends and a close-knit *sangha*
(Buddhist community). When she learned that her death was inevitable
she invited a small group of *sangha* members to be a support team to
help her during the months leading up to her dying. She arranged to have
a friend who was a professional caregiver attend to her physical needs
and another friend, a *sangha* friend, assist with her spiritual needs. She
graciously introduced everyone over coffee, indicating her wishes—to be
in her home, surrounded by her close friends, to have her pain managed,

and to remember the Buddhist teachings in maintaining a compassionate mind as she passed.

Christina also had several specific requests. First, she wanted to die in her one-bedroom apartment where she lived with her daughter, and expressed a wish to change the color of her walls. Ever the artist, she had once painted her walls burgundy and brown giving quite a dark yet dignified tone to the room. She now requested the colors be changed to bright yellow and cream. Her *sangha* worked to make that happen— brightening her world.

Christina also had the benefit of Changling Rinpoche visiting her twice. Changling Rinpoche is a renowned Buddhist teacher; he heads a monastery in India devoted to the support of those who are dying. It was fortuitous that he happened to visit her city twice before she died. The first time, a year and a half before her death, he gave her instructions for how to prepare for dying using specific meditations. The second time, only months before her death, he told her she would now find it difficult to meditate and so she should visualize her spiritual teacher (guru) topmost in her mind.

She requested that sections of the *Tibetan Book of the Dead* be read over and over as she was dying and following her death. She was surrounded by many friends and admirers. They listened in a sacred silence and took turns reading the instructions for dying as requested next to Christina's head while she was dying and continuously for twenty-four hours afterward.

On the forty-ninth day following Christina's death, her family and *sangha* performed a ceremony to acknowledge her new journey and rebirth. She had come so far in the two years since the rediagnosis, and with her devotion, determination, and compassion it was believed that she was now fine.[1]

Buddhism has been and continues to be a religion that is concerned about dying, death, and the dead. Meditative practices and doctrines are linked to recognizing and accepting death as natural and inevitable. For Buddhists, dying itself is an opportunity for spiritual practice and liberation. In its broadest sense, death is understood as happening in each moment as one thought passes away and the next arises. Death is also the inevitable end of human life and a spiritual opening. Dzogchen Ponlop (2006) describes it this way:

> Though we do not wish to confront death or the fear it inspires, running away from this inconvenient truth will not help us. Real-

ity will catch up to us in the end. If we have ignored death all of our lives then it will come as a big surprise. There will be no time to learn how to handle the situation, no time to develop the wisdom and compassion that could guide us skillfully through death's terrain. . . . If we choose to look into the face of death directly, then we can be certain of transforming that meeting into a profound experience that will bring untold benefit to our spiritual journey. (3)

According to Buddhist teachings, if people are prepared and willing to engage death directly, it comes as a "most glorious moment of life" (Sogyal 1993, 14). Christina's story opening this chapter conveys her willingness to engage with dying directly, and her death would be considered a good death by many. While Christina's story may not reflect death rituals and practices for all Buddhists, it does point to key elements of a good death in a Buddhist context. Notably, these are not that different from many of the goals of palliative care: (1) having a peaceful and clear mind at the moment of death; (2) having pain managed in order to pay attention to the experience of dying; (3) being surrounded by family and spiritual friends; and (4) recognizing the continuity of living, dying, and future rebirth.

The centrality of compassion and the relief of suffering in Buddhism align smoothly with the core principles of palliative care. This may account, in part, for the growing interest in Buddhism within hospice and palliative care. The Zen Hospice Project in San Francisco offers a spiritual care program (ZHP 2009), and the Being with Dying: Professional Training Program in Integral End-of-Life Care (Upaya 2009) incorporates mindfulness meditation and Buddhist teachings in the psychological and spiritual aspects of care of the dying. In addition, Naropa University, a Buddhist university in Colorado, offers a contemplative end-of-life care program for health care professionals bringing together the spiritual tradition of Buddhism and the knowledge, skills, and best practices of hospice palliative care.

The interest in Buddhism and end-of-life care may also be reflective of the growing number of Buddhists in North America. In Canada, Buddhists are found in all provinces and regions, including northern areas such as Nunavut (Matthews 2006). In the 2001 census, 345,000 Canadians identified their religious affiliation as Buddhist (Canada 2001). Similarly, in the United States, 1.0–2.1 million adults and 1.4–2.8 million of the total population identify as Buddhist (Smith 2002). These numbers also reflect the large-scale immigration from Asia after World War II and the Vietnamese, Cambodian, and Tibetan refugees who found havens in North America (Bramadat 2006). In addition to what have been called ethnic Buddhists, there are now second generations of European and North American Buddhists.[2]

In this chapter, I will introduce the central tenets of Buddhism that shape how a good death is understood within Buddhist perspectives. The chapter is organized as follows: (1) the historical background of Buddhism, (2) three Buddhist traditions and corresponding case examples of preparing for death, (3) Buddhist doctrines (four truths, rebirth, self/no-self), (4) creating conditions for a good death, and (5) doctrinal and generational tensions concerning end-of-life rituals. The case examples are interspersed to illustrate both commonalities and diversity within Buddhist perspectives of dying. These examples are composites using pseudonyms developed from my experience as a nurse and student of Buddhism, conversations with Buddhist caregivers, and scholarly writings from the literature.

Historical Background of Buddhism

Unlike theistic traditions such as Christianity, Islam, or Judaism, Buddhism does not posit an Ultimate Being or divine source. Buddhism is often described as a philosophy, a religion, and an Asian psychology. What is interpreted here as introductory Buddhism is drawn from texts written by Buddhist scholars, meditation masters, and a generation of Westerners trained in Buddhist doctrine and meditative practices. In addition, I draw on work done for my doctoral nursing research at a Buddhist hospice in the United States (Bruce 2002).

Historically, Buddhism originated in the life and words of Siddhartha Gautama, who was born in approximately 600 BCE in what is known today as Nepal. Siddhartha was the son of a king of the *Shakya* clan and was destined to rule his father's kingdom. However, instead of becoming a monarch, he left home at age twenty-nine in search of answers about the nature of human action (*karma*) and how to relieve suffering in the cycle of rebirth, old age, sickness, and death. After six years of study and meditation, Siddhartha sat in deep meditation and realized how karma functioned to keep people trapped in suffering, and discovered a method for liberation; he became a Buddha or an awakened or "enlightened one" (Seager 1999; see ch. 3). Siddhartha's realizations included the understanding that passionate attachments to illusions about self and reality keep humans trapped in suffering. His teachings instruct how to obtain liberation (*nirvana*) from suffering. Both the Buddha's teachings and a way of life that leads toward a lasting state of happiness free from suffering and discontent are known as *dharma* or *Buddhadharma* (Wallace 2003).

Three Denominations of Buddhism

Buddhism includes a number of doctrines, ideologies, and practices that are distinct within cultures and regions. Challenges arise in trying to generalize Buddhist views across cultures and traditions. The complexity of understanding Buddhist denominations is akin to the diversity found in Christian traditions that vary across ethnic and linguistic lines. While Roman Catholics, Protestants, Anglicans, Greek Orthodox, and members of the Church of Jesus Christ of Latter-day Saints all belong under the larger umbrella of Christianity, many of their practices and traditions are separate. Likewise, Buddhism—or perhaps it is more accurate to say Buddhism(s)—also vary greatly across ethnic and linguistic lines. Nevertheless, just as foundational tenets based on the life and teachings of Jesus of Nazareth underpin a breadth of Christian traditions, there are shared doctrines among the denominations of Buddhism, and some of these are presented later.

For health care providers interested in understanding the complexity of Buddhist traditions in the context of end-of-life care, three major denominations of Buddhism are commonly identified: Theravada, Mahayana, and Vajrayana Buddhism. All three traditions, Theravada (practiced in India, Sri Lanka, Thailand, Cambodia, Laos, Burma, Korea, China), Mahayana (Japanese and Vietnamese Zen, Chinese Chan, and Indo-Tibetan), and Vajrayana (practiced in Tibet and Japan), have growing numbers of adherents in North America and Europe. As Buddhism is taking root in the West through immigration and Westerners becoming Buddhist, the practices and interpretation of doctrine are also being adapted. Some of the significant changes as Buddhism has come to the West include democratization (the rise of women in membership and leadership and the emphasis on lay practice); pragmatism (an emphasis on ritual practice, including meditation and chanting); and engagement (broadening spiritual practice to benefit society and all people; promotion of politicization and engaged Buddhism) (Ryuken Williams and Queen, 1999). These changes mark all three traditions of Buddhism within North America and Europe.

Theravada

The first tradition of Theravada means "the way of the elders" and refers to the oldest denomination. Theravada is based on Buddhist scripture written in Pali. The Pali texts, an ancient Indian language, are thought to be the closest textual sources to the teachings of Shakyamuni Buddha (Seager 1999). This denomination emphasizes the Eightfold path (see below) and monastic codes with lay practitioners often deferring to the monastic community or *sangha*. Theravada Buddhists in Thailand, for example, rely on monks to perform rituals and devotional practices at the end of life (see chapter 8). Offerings and support to monks or nuns for death, marriage, and birth rituals are seen as meritorious actions. Theravada Buddhism emphasizes the Buddha's teachings of the truth of suffering and its cessation along with a distinctive form of meditation—*vipassana*, or insight meditation (Seager 1999). While insight meditation practice has been embraced and adopted in North America, the strict, hierarchical monastic community and traditional practices of merit-making through offerings have not flourished. Unfortunately, due to warfare in the tenth century CE, the women's Theravada monastic lineage was destroyed, and there has not been a women's order since then (Seager). This curtails the role women play in religious and death rituals in traditional Theravada Buddhism. The central meditation practices of Theravada are well known in all other denominations and include mindfulness, loving-kindness, and generosity practices. Like most Buddhists, the state of mind of the dying person and those around him or her at the time of death is vitally important. Theravada monks and priests may be invited to instruct a dying person on meditations such as mindfulness and loving-kindness to help the person stabilize and cultivate a positive state of mind in preparing for dying. While not always the case, the more ritualized chanting and devotional practices at the end of life are not as prominent in Theravada as they are in Mahayana and Vajrayana Buddhism.

CASE EXAMPLE

Mrs. Nu-ai Bi is an eighty-seven-year-old Chinese elder who immigrated to Vancouver, Canada, in the 1960s.[3] She married a Chinese immigrant from her home village in China and had two daughters. Even though Mrs. Bi has lived in Canada for almost fifty years she never mastered the English language. When Mrs. Bi entered palliative care her daughters invited local Chinese Theravada monks to visit their mother's bedside. While Mrs. Bi was a devout Buddhist, neither of her daughters is observant. When the monks arrived on the palliative care unit the nurses provided privacy, posting a "Do not Disturb" sign, which allowed the monks to give a dharma discourse (teachings of the Buddha), to chant Buddhist sutras, and to give the refuge vows and precepts. The monks encouraged Mrs. Bi to try to keep her mind calm, peaceful, and mindful as she approached death. Her daughters were encouraged to reflect on the good deeds their mother has done and to help her to rouse confidence that these deeds will give her a good rebirth and support her in her next life.

The monks also suggested that although there are many Chinese funereal rituals and taboos, there was no doctrinal need for Theravada Buddhists such as Mrs. Bi to have a basin of water and towel placed under the casket, or to place a bowl of rice with chopsticks in front of the casket, or to burn joss sticks or candles before the casket. Mrs. Bi's daughters were both relieved by this instruction as they knew that these rituals were not in keeping with their mother's religion, but they also suspected that their relatives arriving from China for the funeral would probably disapprove and interpret these postmortem rituals differently.

Mahayana

The second tradition is Mahayana Buddhism known as the "great vehicle." The origins of the Mahayana are obscure, but scholars believe the teachings arose around 100 C.E. in India in response to the aloofness of the elders' monastic denominations (Nakasone 2000). Mahayana Buddhism developed as it moved to Korea (*Zen*), China (*Chan, Pure Land*), and Japan (*Zen, True Pure Land-Jodo Shin Shu, Nichiren Shoshu,* and *Soka Gakkai*). A central difference between Mahayana and Theravada is the emphasis on compassionate communication and relating compassionately with each other (Chodron 1997). This is exemplified in the Mahayana figure of the *bodhisattva* (enlightened being), who does not seek freedom from suffering for him or herself alone. Through compassion for others, the bodhisattva forgoes self-liberation until all beings are free from suffering. The central role of bodhisattvas in Mahayana introduces cosmic realms and devotional practices of chanting, prayer, and offerings to these compassionate beings who can be called upon for assistance or protection. In some traditions such as Pure Land Buddhism, including Jodo Shin Shu, practitioners may aspire to be reborn in a higher realm or pure land of Buddhas and bodhisattvas. This shift in cosmology from a simplicity of Theravada to the cosmic realms of Buddhas in Mahayana denominations also brought new philosophical perspectives emphasizing wisdom and compassion:

> Mahayana Buddhists expressed [a] unified view of reality in terms of *nonduality*. There was neither nirvana nor samsara, this world or another, all such distinctions rested on concepts, ideas, and discriminations considered illusory. Philosophers expressed this nondualism in terms of *shunyata* or emptiness. . . . The idea that beyond illusory distinctions is the blissful clarity of universal wisdom and compassion. (Seager 1998, 24–25; italics in original)

Mahayana Buddhism emphasizes the universality of awakened mind or basic goodness so that all beings regardless of gender, caste, or education can attain freedom. These teachings highlight that all phenomena, including mind, bodhisattvas, and the universe, are intrinsically empty of inherent existence. In addition to the Theravada practices, Mahayana religious practices emphasize developing wisdom and compassion such as *tonglen*, the practice of breathing in the suffering of others and breathing out peace and ease (Chodron 1997). Sometimes referred to as "taking in and sending out," this practice is often used when dying or attending to someone who is dying. Traditionally, women have not played central roles in Mahayana religious rituals; however, this is changing within Western countries.

CASE EXAMPLE

Maiko Aki's father emigrated from Japan to Alberta in the 1930s, and, like his father, Maiko is a traditional Jodo Shin Shu or True Pure Land Buddhist.[4] When Maiko was infected with hepatitis C (along with thousands of Canadians who received blood and blood products between 1980 and 1985), he was surprised by the intensity of his loneliness and his fear of dying. Given his religious beliefs in impermanence and the inevitability of death, he realized that he was also attached to his reputation within the community and the expectations of others. Since his diagnosis, he has been living with an increasingly debilitating liver disease from which he is expected to die. Relying on his religious community he has taken the opportunity of knowing that he will die from this disease to prepare more fully for his death. When asked, Maiko now interprets his infection and impending death in a matter-of-fact manner as resulting from causes and conditions from lifetimes of actions. His past actions that were both virtuous and nonvirtuous have contributed to his current situation, and since living and dying are nothing more than the fruition of causes and conditions, he sees his impending death as taking place in its proper time.

As a Jodo Shin Shu Buddhist, Maiko prays that he will take birth in the Pure Land and in his daily prayers formulates a great aspiration to be born there. He firmly believes that if he prays with single-pointed concentration and great fervent faith he will be born in the Pure Land in the presence of the Buddha of Boundless Light, Amitabha. He also knows that it is very important to formulate the proper aspiration for rebirth at the moment of death. As a result, he has contacted a Buddhist priest who will be present at the deathbed and will recite prayers and chants to assist him in making the proper aspiration at the moment of death. Then, once he has died, the priest will perform a pillow service by reciting a short sutra, saying a few words of condolence, and reinforcing for the family members that he is deceased. Maiko knows that his role through death is to teach the truth of impermanence, especially when the bereaved family may be unwilling to concede to his death. Also in accordance with the Jodo Shin Shu tradition, he has made arrangements for members of the Buddhist church to help the family prepare for the funeral service. Church members will offer envelopes of donations to assist with the funeral costs. He will be cremated, and the funeral services will include a short sutra chanting and teaching on impermanence. The family will follow the custom of meeting every seven days for forty-nine days, and Maiko takes comfort in knowing that his family and friends will find support and solace in their bereavement through these weekly meetings.

Vajrayana

The third tradition is Vajrayana Buddhism, also known as Tibetan Buddhism or Tantra Buddhism. *Vajra* means "diamond-like" or "indestructible" and refers to mind beyond all levels of conceptualization (Ponlop 2006). Tibetan Buddhism emphasizes the essential purity of mind that can be realized through assiduous practice; that is, "infinite purity, fathomless joy, power, wisdom, and compassion; right here, right now" (Wallace and Wilhelm 1993, 186). Practitioners use elaborate meditative practices including visualizations, repetition of sacred sounds (*mantras*), and ritual hand gestures to realize the nature of mind and awaken from suffering. The central role of the teacher as spiritual guide or guru is emphasized more in Vajrayana than in the other traditions. Teachers are called *rinpoche*, which is an honorific title meaning "precious one" (Seager 1998). While most teachers are men, there are also Tibetan women rinpoches.[5] Although Buddhism in general has followed a patriarchal norm throughout its history, women authorized to teach and conduct rituals (such as women rinpoches) do perform these roles. In Tibet, householders or lay practitioners rarely performed the more intensive tantric practices, which were left for monastic yogis and yoginis. However, over the years many Tibetan teachers have taught Western students these practices and established meditation centers across North America and Europe. In addition, the popularization of the ancient text the *Tibetan Book of the Dead* and Sogyal Rinpoche's (1993) *The Tibetan Book of Living and Dying* has highlighted Tibetan Buddhist death practices in the Western world and is explained in more detail here.

TIBETAN BOOK OF THE DEAD

In Vajrayana Buddhism, descriptions of the dying process are based on an elaborate theory of winds, or energetic currents, that serve as foundations for the various levels of consciousness. Dying is envisaged as a process of dissolution of elements and is described with intricate detail in the *Bardo Thotrol*, written by Padmasambhava around 750 CE.[6] The English title, the *Tibetan Book of the Dead*, was given to this text by W. Y. Evans-Wentz, an Oxford anthropologist, in his 1927 translation. Subsequent English translations use titles such as *Attaining Liberation in the Bardo through Hearing* (Fremantle and Trungpa 1975), which more clearly demonstrate the nature of dying from a Vajrayana view. For example, *bar* means "in between" and *do* means "suspended," with *bardo* inferring an in-between space often translated as "transition" (Sogyal 1993, 102). *Bardos* are seen as states of mind or realities characterized by deep uncertainty or groundlessness that arise in everyday experiences and in the transition at the end of life. *Bardos* in the *Tibetan Book of the Dead* refer to several states of transitioning between birth and death, from moment to moment, and in the transition of dying.

> [I]t is not only the interval of suspension after we die but also suspension in the living situation; death happens in the living situation as well. The *bardo* experience is part of our basic psychological make-up. There are all kinds of *bardo* experiences happening to us all the time, experiences of paranoia and uncertainty in everyday life; it is like not being sure of our ground, not knowing quite what we have asked for or what we are getting into. So, . . . [it is] not only a message for those who are going to die and those who are already dead, but it is also a message for those who are already born; birth and death apply to everybody constantly, at this very moment. (Fremantle and Trungpa 1975, 2)

The detailed description of the dissolving of elements during dying and the intermediate state between death and rebirth is not taught in Theravada or Mahayana traditions. Even so, there does not appear to be conflict because the basic principles of element dissolution are shared by all traditions, albeit in varying degrees of specificity (Sogyal 1993). The three Buddhist traditions discussed here contain some version of the following. The universe and human mind-body experience is constituted into four elements of earth, water, fire, and air. While dying is viewed as a gradual "development of ever more subtle levels of consciousness" (Sogyal 256), Vajrayana teachers describe specific stages of dissolution for each element (or level of consciousness), which are accompanied by particular physical signs, inner experiences, and visual appearances. The clearly identified stages provide guidance for those who are dying and their families.

Specifically, the *Tibetan Book of the Dead (Bardo Thodrol)* describes what a dying person experiences as each element dissolves sequentially into finer levels of consciousness.[7] In brief, at first a feeling of heaviness overwhelms the dying person *as earth elements dissolve into water* and a mirage vision arises; the energy level and blood circulation decreases as the *water element dissolves into fire* and visions of cloudiness or smoke arise; we feel cool and are no longer aware of what is going on around us *as fire dissolves into air* and appearances of sparks arise in our mind's eye; the last feeling of contact with the physical world disappears as the *air element dissolves into space*; finally, a sense of intense white, red, and then black light arises and the dying person is unconscious. When the blackness dissolves into the mind of clear light, then death has occurred. Rather than death linked to the last exhalation, the appearance of clear light indicates death and the departure of consciousness (Fremantle and Trungpa 1975; Lati Rinpoche and Hopkins 1979). This usually occurs up to three days after breathing has ceased and is the beginning of the *bardo* or in-between transition. For Tibetan Buddhists, there is an emphasis on being aware of what is happening as the elements and consciousnesses are dissolving. As the Dalai Lama recommends, one level of practice is to be calm and not think too much, just observe what is happening (Bainbridge and Baines 2001). During this period the dying person may wish someone to read the explicit instructions provided in the *Bardo Thodrol* out loud or softly in their ear as they transition through the in-between state from death to rebirth. This may take up to three days. While hospitals cannot usually accommodate families' requests to leave the deceased undisturbed for long periods, efforts can be made to not move or jostle the body until family or *sangha* members arrive. If the body must be moved or touched, it's encouraged to first touch the body at the crown of the head to allow the consciousness to leave from the crown, fostering a good rebirth.

CASE EXAMPLE

Marcus was a forty-seven-year-old film director living in San Francisco, California, who had been diagnosed with the human immune deficiency virus in the early 1980s.[8] He had recently become a Vajrayana Tibetan Buddhist, following the teachings of Sakyong Mipham Rinpoche. In particular, Marcus was drawn to the art-based meditative practices of calligraphy and flower arranging (ikebana). Marcus quickly became a devoted student of Sakyong Mipham Rinpoche and immersed himself in the teachings and meditation practices. However, over an eight-month period his health declined, and as he became weaker he was no longer able to practice the more active art-based meditations. He received teachings about preparing for death and knew that the most important thing was to have his mind clear of negative thoughts. At the time of dissolution when he was actively dying, he would try to rest his mind with thoughts of his teacher Sakyong Mipham Rinpoche. He knew that when the dissolution began his mind would become more out of control. In order to help maintain his devotion he would bring a picture of his teacher to the hospital and keep it in view, trying to visualize him as best he could. He was also aware that after inner dissolution the mind becomes very, very clear. He was prepared to see lights, bright as sun shining directly in his eyes, and visualized this in his meditations so that he wouldn't panic when it occurred. He was ready to hear loud thunder coming into his ears, and not to panic—knowing it would be none other than his own thoughts; whatever he saw, whatever he heard, he would try to remain open and calm. To help him realize that the nature of mind is inherently compassionate and luminous, he asked a *sangha* friend to whisper instructions from the *Tibetan Book of the Dead* into his ear as he was dying. He requested his caregivers to do the well-known compassion meditation of visualizing breathing in his fear and sending him ease and calm. Unfortunately, Marcus had massive pulmonary emboli, and was rushed to the emergency room where he died.

As per his request, his body was brought to the meditation center and placed on dry ice for three days. During that time, members of his Buddhist community sat in meditation with his body around the clock. At the end of the three days, Marcus's consciousness was thought to have entered the *bardo,* and at that time his body was taken for cremation.

Buddhist Doctrines (Four Truths, Rebirth, Self/No-Self)

Four Truths

If Buddhism can be said to have a goal, it is to understand the nature of mind so that we can be free from suffering and be of benefit to others in the quest for happiness (Nyima 1987). This achievement is based on four assumptions: (1) the truth of suffering; (2) that the cause of suffering is a mind that clings, resulting in negative emotions; (3) that there is an antidote; and (4) if one follows a path consisting of eight steps, the result will be cessation of suffering.

First is the truth of suffering, or a repeated sense of lack or "dissatisfaction" in one's life; there is always something not quite right or not quite enough (Loy 1996). From a Buddhist view, to acknowledge and confront this sense of dissatisfaction in our experience is the first step toward relieving it. Buddhism can also be seen as pragmatic. The four truths not only acknowledge human suffering as a natural, inevitable occurrence, but the remaining "truths" also suggest a rationale for the cause of suffering and propose a way out.

The second truth addresses the question of why and how such dissatisfaction and anxiety arise. Recognizing impermanence, one can see how trying to hold on and clinging to that which is always changing is a source of suffering (e.g., clinging to our youth). Although moments of satisfaction and joy arise and pass away, clinging to experience often leads to fear of losing what we have or hoping conditions will not change. In Buddhism, the most problematic attachment is said to be our holding on to a fixed sense of "I." This holding becomes particularly painful as existentialist questions such as "Who am I?" and "Has my life been meaningful?" and "What happens when I die?" arise.

The third truth is that to let go of struggling for permanence and a secure sense of "I" is a way to free ourselves from suffering. Through insight into the constantly changing nature of phenomena, we can let go of trying to make things other than they are and learn to ride with the constantly changing flow of human experience.

And finally, the fourth truth is a prescription or way out; how to experience constant change in life without solidifying experience into a sense of separating "self" from "other," and therefore being able to decrease suffering. Conventional Buddhist teachings propose an eight-step training in meditation, wisdom, ethics, and action, and together these make up the Eightfold Path (Rothberg 1999). Meditation training includes cultivating (1) effort, (2) mindfulness, and (3) concentration. Wisdom training includes (4) understanding the four truths and (5) working with thoughts; and ethical training consists of fostering appropriate (6) conduct, (7) livelihood, and (8) speech. In summary, the four truths provide logic for why human beings experience suffering, seek lasting relief from suffering, and suggest an approach toward attaining such relief.

Rebirth

An understanding of the nature of consciousness and rebirth are central to Buddhism and understanding death rituals and the postmortem period. Rebirth is an often misunderstood concept in the West, where the implication is that someone will literally "come back" as another person, or parrot, or insect, etc. While from a Buddhist view there is no soul or tangible continuity that moves from one life to another, as T. R. Murti explains, "Rebirth does not mean the bodily transportation of an individual essence from one place to another. It only means that a new series of states arises, conditioned by the previous states" (cited in

Kapleau 1989, 185). Therefore, just as the body decomposes into hydrogen, nitrogen, and various gases at a rate and manner determined by the condition of the body at the time of death, so too does psychic energy or consciousness transform into more subtle states that are determined by the condition (and conditioning) of the mind at the time of death. Analogies often used for rebirth are the transference of a flame from one candle to another—are they the same flame? Or, another example used by Kapleau is how a billiard ball hits a second ball and thereby determines the direction of the second ball. What is transferred from one ball (life) to the other is the *momentum* of the ball (its conditioning or karma) and not a new movement that is reborn in the second ball. Limited as all analogies are, the question is not "what is reborn," which is perhaps a misguided question, but rather the notion of momentum in what is happening at every moment of consciousness better conveys the notion of rebirth.[9] Therefore, the state of mind of the dying person is important in determining the next rebirth. While sustaining a positive frame of mind during times of duress and fear is a lifelong practice of preparation and conditioning, great efforts are made at the time of death to support a virtuous mind for the dying person.

Self/No-self

The concept of *anatta* (Pali), often translated as no-self, is also a challenging concept integral to understanding death and dying in Buddhism. After all, if there is no self, who dies and what is reborn? The notion of *anatta* assumes there is no fixed, independent self (see chapter 2). That is, there is no inherently separate, autonomous substance-self, and yet it is also recognized that humans have agency and are process-selves that come into existence moment to moment (Gowans 2003). Unfortunately, daily experience is often "so permeated by our attachments that we perceive everything in terms of what is 'mine' and 'not mine,' and hence we do not see the world as it really is" (Gowans 2003, 91). As one Buddhist volunteer at Zen Hospice states,

> So there's the Buddhist teaching of not grasping onto beliefs and thoughts like, "this is my life and I shouldn't be dying; I don't want this experience." . . . But if I can have some experience where I'm free from grabbing after concepts, if I am able to really . . . I don't want to say "live it," but at least live it sometimes

> where I am not attached to me being a certain way or having
> control . . . if I can have at least a few moments of not holding
> on so tightly to everything . . . then maybe I can be of help to
> someone else who is afraid. (Bruce 2002, 171)

SELF-FORMATION

The importance of understanding the process of self-formation and how we construct our experience of reality is key within Buddhism and in understanding what may seem like a matter-of-fact attitude toward death by patients or families. Specifically, threats to our sense of self and self-dissolution are integral to the dying process (Ponlop 2006). Buddhist teachings maintain that the practice of meditation provides a way to see the process of self coming into being and dissolving away. Such realization allows the meditator to see the relative existence of a self that functions in the world yet does not exist independent of causes and conditions. During dying, this process is said to become clear and painfully more obvious if the dying meditator is able to pay attention (Ponlop).

Although the process of self-development continues from moment to moment, we have glimpses of the open spaces between thoughts (Welwood 1996). Through careful attention to thought processes using meditation, it is said that meditators learn to "see" an ever-changing matrix of self-constituting-self.

> Self, it turns out, is a metaphor for a process that we do not
> understand, a metaphor for that which *knows*. The insight practices
> [mindfulness] reveal that such a metaphor is unnecessary, even
> disruptive. It is enough, these practices reveal, to open to the
> ongoing process of knowing without imputing some*one* behind
> it all. (Welwood 1996, 155)

From a Buddhist view, if we are attached and grasp tightly to our sense of self and its stories, any threat to this identity will certainly result in some form of suffering. Therefore, although we can't eradicate the inevitability of death, we have a prescriptive approach such as meditation, to understand and work with the fear and anxiety of impermanence. Moreover, experiencing the constructed nature of self can be both fearful and liberating (see chapter 2).

Instead of thinking of oneself as a fixed nugget in a shifting current of mental and physical processes, we might consider ourself as a narrative that transforms these processes into an unfolding story. Our life is a story being continuously related to others through every detail of our being. (Batchelor 1997, 104)

While Buddhists may accept theoretically that there is no inherently separate self, the actualization of this view is not easy. As one Buddhist meditator shared, "Getting close to the mystery of death, it happens to me in my meditation practice, especially in my concentration practice where the fear of my own death comes up very strongly" (Bruce 2002, 171).

Creating Conditions for a Good Death

The idea that death may be viewed as an opportunity rather than a tragedy, or possibly a tragic opportunity, has been taken up among Western Buddhists, leading to a strong emphasis on meditation practices at the end of life. However, this is not always borne out in the cultural practices and attitudes of Asian Buddhists. With this in mind, the following general conditions for a good death are considered.

As seen in the earlier case examples, dying well in Buddhism means approaching the end of life and final moments with a calm and virtuous mind. During the dying process, the body loses its ability to support human consciousness and if the dying person is well trained and has created the causes and conditions, they may be able to rest in the natural state of mind at the moment of death and be liberated (*nirvana*). If not, the dying person's state of mind—whether fearful, afraid, or peaceful and calm—will determine their transition and next rebirth. Therefore, the end of life and final moments are ideally supported by an atmosphere that is calm and peaceful without loud noises and distractions. Family, friends, and caregivers are encouraged to generate mental and emotional states that will support the dying person's ability to meditate and generate compassion. Likewise, medications such as opiates may also be refused due to their impact on lucid awareness and the person's ability to generate virtuous thoughts. However, relieving severe pain with finely titrated medication may also allow the dying person to work with their meditation practices, and therefore patients may also request analgesia

(Barham 2003). Reminding the person of the positive things they have done in their life and mentally letting them go so they can move calmly and peacefully into the next stage is encouraged (Wallace and Wilhelm 1993).

Having lay persons and monastics recite prayers or mantras may assist the person to not be afraid or confused and help generate a serene and still mind. Having an altar or image of the Buddha at eye level, or placing a picture of the person's spiritual teacher in his or her hand may help to invoke ease and comfort. Meditations to let go of thoughts and concentrate on the movement of the breath are said to develop calmness, decrease fear, assist with pain control and ease at the time of dying (see chapter 8; Sogyal 1993). This can also be done through reading the *Bardo Thotrol* quietly to the dying person over and over again when requested. The opening paragraphs begin:

> My friend you are dying
> You are feeling heavy
> You can no longer open or close your eyes
> Blue, yellow, red and green, all are turning white,
> Logic, and the chair and the table, are dissolving
> The earth element in your body is dissolving.
> My friend your mind is losing its hold
> You grab at this, you grab at that
> Your blood is slowing
> You feel faint.
> No more internal sounds, no more external sounds . . . it's all
>   quiet
> You have no more saliva, no more sweat
> Everything is drying
> The water element is dissolving into fire. (Glin-pa and Van
>   Italie 1998)

However, if the person becomes agitated by recitations or rituals, it is recommended to stop in order to allow their mind freedom from irritation and restlessness (Dalai Lama 2002). Placing the person in a prescribed position (lying on the right side), like that of the dying Gautama Buddha, may be requested.

With the importance of a lucid mind at the end of life and the prevalence of dementia in end-of-life situations, it may be helpful to consider the impact of these cognitive deteriorations for dying Buddhists. In an online discussion about what happens for those who develop Alzheimer's disease or dementia in later years, Narayan Lieberson Grady (2006) shares firsthand knowledge and overall advice. First, she reminds people that, in Buddhist teachings, illness of any kind is a wake-up call and reminder to use one's precious life wisely. Grady recounts experience with a senior meditation teacher who developed dementia in the last years of his life. In the beginning stages of the illness he would become anxious as he progressively forgot what he was going to say. Then, because of his many years of meditation he began to shift his awareness to the anxiety itself and he learned to be less afraid of the forgetting; in the more advanced stages this capacity also diminished.

From a Buddhist view, what is important in living with cognitive deterioration such as dementia is "not to hold on to idealized ways of how things should be but to practice surrendering to how things are. For example, if you are frightened or angry, be aware that fear and anger are happening" (Grady 2006, 5). Having love and support from those who are patient and experienced in meditation can be very helpful. Grady also speculates that great meditation practitioners may be able to experience a deeper place even when the brain deteriorates before death. A great Hindu teacher is said to have "observed himself becoming senile and was not at all bothered by it because he knew so clearly that he was neither his body nor his mind" (7).

What happens after death is interpreted differently by different traditions of Buddhism. In speaking with North American Zen Buddhists the focus is often on the current moment rather than an afterlife. Whatever happens in the moment after death will be met with the same open, "unknowing" mind that is cultivated in meditation. A Soto Zen priest I spoke with exemplifies this perspective:

> I have no idea what is going to happen after I am dead. I haven't thought about it much and I don't think we can know that much about it. Maybe some people feel that they do, and that's fine, that's their belief, but . . . I have to say . . . I don't know what's going to happen. It's not something that I particularly want to know. I'll find out when I get there (laughs). I'm just focusing on my life here, as long as it lasts. And when it's over, we'll see what happens then. (Bruce 2002)

Another Soto Zen priest in Oregon spoke of how as a community they are now preparing for the inevitable death of aging *sangha* members.

They have developed several kits containing a simple cotton kimono to clothe the washed corpse, a white *mala* (beads strung like a rosary) to place around the deceased's hands, and well-known chants and prayers for recitation. As a community they are developing their own rites and rituals in accordance with the community's culture and Zen practices. In contrast, for conventional Japanese Pure Land Buddhists, rituals of *raigo* (welcoming descent) are performed at the deathbed and refer to a Buddha descending to welcome the dying person and escorting him or her to the Pure Land (Stone 2008). These practices are usually performed by Buddhist priests in Japan and, according to Stone, may be the only time for many modern Japanese to learn much about Buddhism.

In keeping with notions of karma and rebirth, some Buddhists believe that the deceased's consciousness can wander for forty-nine days before rebirth. In some Chinese and Tibetan communities services are performed on the seventh day for seven weeks over this period (Nakasone 2000). Through memorials the deceased's consciousness is supported and eventually will be reborn into a realm determined by his or her moral and accumulated merit. On the forty-ninth day family observances are performed, and on the first, third, and seventh year memorial services are often offered (Nakasone).

Deathbed and postmortem practices are diverse and varied and may be contested or redefined according to particular cultural specifics. With respect to children, no unique rituals are used when attending to dying children, and the meditation practices of mindfulness and loving-kindness are also taught to dying children (see chapter 8).

Doctrinal and Generational Tensions Concerning End of Life

While rituals during the dying process vary among traditions and their respective cultural contexts, there is also a history of criticism of deathbed rites usually based on doctrinal grounds. For example, Stone (2008) cites Japanese monk Kakukai's (1142–1223) criticism of Japanese medieval deathbed instructions that relied on a sort of deathbed expert, called a *zenchishiki*, to assist the dying person in reaching the Pure Land. Kakukai takes the position that, "for Buddhists, who should understand the emptiness and nonduality of all things, there is something improperly self-obsessed about fixing one's aspirations on a particular postmortem destination" (81). Similarly, Cuevas and Stone (2007) claim that contemporary Western Buddhists and second- or third-generation Buddhists brought up in the West are also more skeptical of death rites and afterlife rituals that suggest spirit realms and particular destinations.

While some death-related practices of ethnically diverse Buddhists may be at odds with doctrine or deemed superstitious by younger generations brought up within a scientific worldview, these tensions rarely seem to pose obstacles in providing end-of-life care. For example, the Buddhist ideal of lack of attachment to worldly materials is in tension with Chinese family obligations to bury the dead with money and paid rituals to ease their transitions through the afterlife. However, in Chinese and Japanese communities where this is done, the emphasis on ancestor worship remains strong and offers a clear example of the syncretism within Buddhist practices. The case example of Mrs. Bi, where the attending monks refuted the custom of leaving a bowl of rice for the departed as a waste of rice, provides another example of tensions between what might be called the theory of Buddhism and how living Buddhists around the world enact their beliefs.

Conclusion

Buddhism is not a monolithic entity but contains a number of doctrines, ideologies, and practices related to death and dying well. Challenges arise in trying to distinguish among Buddhist death rituals and views of good death that can be applied across cultures, geography, and schools of thought. Nevertheless, the importance of death as a spiritual practice, the reality of impermanence, and compassion in the face of change are considerations for most Buddhists. In this chapter, an overview of key religious doctrines that contribute to Buddhist notions of good death have been presented with an eye to avoiding essentializing these traditions and religious practices. As in good palliative care as espoused by Cicely Saunders, each person's/family's beliefs should be explored in their unique context in order to prevent oversimplifying or misunderstanding religious, and in this case Buddhist, interpretations and practices at the time of death. In closing, the attitude of welcoming death as an old friend is widely held by many Buddhists. Living and dying are intertwined like breathing in and breathing out.

So many veils and illusions separate us from the stark knowledge that we are dying. When we finally know we are dying, and all other sentient beings are dying with us, we start to have a burning, almost heartbreaking sense of the fragility and preciousness of each moment and each being, and from this can grow a deep, clear, limitless compassion for all beings.

Sir Thomas More, I heard, wrote these words just before his beheading: "We are all in the same cart, going to execution; how can I hate anyone or wish anyone harm?" To feel the full force of your mortality, and to open your heart entirely to it, is to allow to grow in you that all-encompassing, fearless compassion that fuels the lives of all those who wish truly to be of help to others. (Sogyal Rinpoche 2009)

Notes

1. I would like to acknowledge and thank Kim Kelso, a long-time Shambhala Buddhist practitioner for sharing this story.

2. See K. Garces-Foley, "Buddhism, Hospice, and the American Way of Dying," *Review of Religious Research* 44(4) (2003): 341–53 for a thorough discussion of the impact of Buddhism on hospice care in the United States.

3. This case is compiled from Venerable Suvanno's *How a Theravadin Buddhist Chinese Funeral May be Conducted,* accessed Dec. 20, 2009, from www.buddhanet.net.

4. This case draws on the chapter by Leslie Kawamura, "Facing Life and Death: A Buddhist's Understanding of Palliative Care and Bereavement," in *Meeting the Needs of Our Clients Creatively: The Impact of Art and Culture on Caregiving,* ed. John D. Morgan (Amityville, NY: Baywood, 2000).

5. Venerable Jetsun Kusho-la Rinpoche and Khandro Rinpoche are two well-known woman teachers.

6. The translation and spelling varies, with Fremantle and Trungpa (1975) using *Bardo Thotrol* and Sogyal (1993) using *Bardo Todrol Chenmo.*

7. See Lati Rinbochay and Hopkins 1979, 17–19 for detailed explanation.

8. This case is based on my experience with a friend and draws on teachings received from Changling Rinpoche.

9. See *Sleeping, Dreaming, and Dying* (Varela, 1997) for an in-depth discussion of this topic based on dialogues between the Dalai Lama and Western scientists during the fourth Mind and Life Conference. The previous three Mind

and Life Conferences addressed topics of cognitive science, neuroscience, and the relationship between emotions and health. Proceedings from all four conferences have been produced in published monographs.

References

Bainbridge, W., and E. Baines. 2001. Insight into palliative care: An audience with the Dalai Lama. *European Journal of Palliative Care* 8(2): 66–69.

Barham, D. 2003. The last 48 hours of life: A case study of symptom control for a patient taking a Buddhist approach to dying. *International Journal of Palliative Nursing* 9(6): 245–51.

Batchelor, S. 1997. *Buddhism without beliefs: A contemporary guide to awakening.* New York: Berkley Publishing Group.

Bramadat, P. 2006. Introduction. In *Buddhism in Canada,* ed. Bruce Mathew. London: Routledge.

Bruce, A. 2002. *Abiding in liminal spaces: Inscribing mindful living/dying in end-of-life care.* Unpublished manuscript, University of British Columbia, Vancouver.

Canada, 2001. Statistics Canada http://www40.statcan.gc.ca/l01/cst01/demo30a-eng.htm.

Chodron, P. 1997. *When things fall apart: Heart advice for difficult times.* Boston: Shambhala.

Cuevas, B., and J. Stone. 2007. *The Buddhist dead: Practices, discourses, representations.* Kuroda Institute: University of Hawaii Press.

Dalai Lama. 2002. *Advice on dying and living a better life.* Edited and translated by Jeffrey Hopkins. New York: Atria Books.

Epstein, M. 1995. *Thoughts without a thinker: Psychotherapy from a Buddhist perspective.* New York: Basic Books.

Fremantle, F., and C. Trungpa. 1975. *The Tibetan book of the dead.* Berkeley: Shambhala.

Fronsdal, G. 1998. Insight meditation in the United States: Life, liberty, and the pursuit of happiness. In *The faces of Buddhism in America,* ed. Charles Prebish and Kenneth Tanaka, 163–80. Berkeley: University of California Press.

Glin-pa, K., and J. C. Van Italie. 1998. *The Tibetan Book of the Dead for reading aloud.* Berkeley: North Atlantic Books.

Goldstein, J. 1987. *The experience of insight: A simple and direct guide to Buddhist meditation.* Boston: Shambhala.

Gowans, C. 2003. *Philosophy of the Buddha.* London: Routledge.

Grady, N. L. 2006. *Winter 2006: Is it possible to practice with dementia?* www.cimc.info/PDF/Narayan_Winter06.pdf?

Humphreys, C. 1985. *Zen: A way of life.* Sevenoaks, UK: Hodder and Stoughton.

Kabat-Zinn, J., et al. 1987. Four-year follow-up of a meditation-based program for the self-regulation of chronic pain: Treatment outcomes and compliance. *Clinical Journal of Pain* 2: 159–73.

Kawamura, L. 2000. Facing life and death: A Buddhist's understanding of palliative care and bereavement. In *Meeting the needs of our clients creatively: The impact of art and culture on caregiving*, ed. John D. Morgan, 105–21. Amityville, NY: Baywood.

Kapleau, R. P. 1989. *Zen: Merging of East and West.* New York: Doubleday.

Kornfield, J. 1979. Intensive insight meditation: A phenomenological study. *The Journal of Transpersonal Psychology* 11(1): 41–58.

Lati R., and J. Hopkins. 1979. *Death, intermediate state and rebirth in Tibetan Buddhism.* New York: Snow Lion.

Levine, S. 1989. *A gradual awakening.* New York: Doubleday.

Loy, D. 1996. *Lack and transcendence: The problem of death and life in psychotherapy, existentialism, and Buddhism.* New Jersey: Humanities Press International.

Matthews, B. 2006. *Buddhism in Canada.* London: Routledge.

Nagasone, R. 2000. Buddhist issues in end-of-life decision making. In *Cultural issues in end-of-life decision making*, ed. Kathryn Braun, James Pietsch, Patricia Blanchette, 213–28. Thousand Oaks, CA: Sage.

Ponlop, D. 2006. *Mind beyond death.* Ithaca: Snow Lion.

Ray, R. 2002. *Secret of the vajra world: The tantric Buddhism of Tibet.* Boston: Shambhala.

Rothberg, D. 1999. Transpersonal issues at the millennium. *Journal of Transpersonal Psychology* 31(1): 41–67.

Ryuken Williams, D., and C. Queen, eds. 1999. *American Buddhism: Methods and findings in recent scholarship.* Richmond: Curzon Press.

Seager, R. H. 1999. *Buddhism in America.* New York: Columbia University Press.

Smith, T. W. 2002. Religious diversity in America: The emergence of Muslims, Buddhists, Hindus, and others. *Journal for the Scientific Study of Religion*, 41(3): 577–85.

Sogyal, R. 1993. *The Tibetan book of living and dying.* San Francisco: HarperCollins.

———. 2009. *Rigpa glimpse of the day.* Glimpse.rigpaus.org. (Accessed November 2009).

Stone, J. 2008. With the help of "good friends": Deathbed ritual practices in early medieval Japan. In *Death and the afterlife in Japanese Buddhism*, ed. Jacqueline Stone and Mariko Walter. Honolulu: University of Hawaii Press.

Upaya Institute and Zen Center. www.upaya.org/training.

Vanderkooi, L. 1997. Buddhist teachers' experience with extreme mental states in Western meditators. *Journal of Transpersonal Psychology* 29(1): 31–46.

Varela, F. 1997. *Sleeping, dreaming, and dying: An exploration of consciousness with the Dalai Lama.* Boston: Wisdom.

Wallace, A. 1999. *Boundless heart: The cultivation of the four immeasurable.* Ithaca: Snow Lion.

———. 2003. *Buddhism and science: Breaking new ground.* New York: Columbia University Press.

———, and S. Wilhelm. 1993. *Tibetan Buddhism from the ground up: A practical approach for modern life.* Boston: Wisdom.

———, and B. Hodel. 2008. *Embracing mind: The common ground of science and spirituality.* Boston: Shambhala.

Welwood, J. 1996. Reflection and presence: The dialectic of self-knowledge. *Journal of Transpersonal Psychology* 28(2): 107–28.

Zenhospice. Zen Hospice Project. www.zenhopsice.org.

4

Muslim Perspectives on a Good Death in Hospice and End-of-Life Care

Earle Waugh

General Religious Perspectives on a Good Death

Recent studies have highlighted the importance of spiritual care as a fundamental component in palliative care, advocating extensive training and skill development for health care professionals (Marr et al. 2007). If this conclusion can be drawn for the population at large, it must doubly apply to Muslims, many of whom have to struggle valiantly to affirm their beliefs in institutions little sensitized to Islamic end-of-life teachings. Health care professionals can increase their skill level by trying to step outside the standard cultural assumptions of North American training, and engage the Muslim community in ways of acceptance and religious fulfillment (Kobeisy 2004). Exploring the notion of the good death in Islam will help considerably in that enterprise.[1]

The concept of a good death in Islam arises from several inter-related aspects: first, from specific religious sources of doctrine, such as Qur'an and hadith; second, from the dictates of Sharia[2] (Islamic law); third, from cultural sources influenced by Islamic values, and finally, from local or folk traditions that are interwoven into Muslim practice. The result is a multilayered cultural environment that, in addition, will reflect regional norms and tastes. This chapter will explore limited but trenchant aspects of this Islamic environment by exploring Islamic doctrinal and religious views on death and dying, then by describing the distinctive

Muslim community in Canada, finally by indicating issues of interaction between health care and Islamic values through selected case studies. A summary statement will attempt to provide the key elements of this exploration.

Good Death: God's Role in Both Time and Type of Death

Islamic attitudes to death and dying are difficult to disentangle from theology, for the role of God in determining both the time and nature of death is stated in scripture. The Qur'an explicitly states that divinity not only shapes our end, but determines the moment and type of our demise (Qur'an 56: 57–62; Welch 1977). While some have interpreted this to privilege a kind of individual fatalism in Islamic beliefs, this has scarcely been the standard Muslim view (this idea is related more to a philosophical school called Mu`tazilism, which was rejected by the developing Muslim community [Martin et al. 1997]). The result has been that Islam respects the individual's pathway to God and does not wish to intrude on a relationship that is ultimately controlled by divinity. The Qur'an makes very clear that the afterlife is more important than this life, at least in terms of one's eternal destiny, for one will be judged and rewarded there according to one's deeds in this life. Therefore post-death existence influences end-of-life perceptions and can be the source of some agitation. Preparation for death is therefore a critical element in the life course of Muslims, and Muslims wish to be in the proper religious frame of mind when they pass on. Furthermore, the attitude has been that, once death has taken an individual, that person belongs to God and the other world. In Islam, human society must acknowledge the primacy of God in these matters. Hence, in all evaluations of death the question of whether religious norms have been observed is key.

Furthermore, God plays a role in the experience of sickness. Popular notions of God's workings will often pointedly refer to sickness as a test (Al-Jibaly 1998), whose ultimate aim is to make the person more religious. Hence, even quite ordinary Muslims will view a life-limiting illness through the prism of their personal relationship to God. This has certain direct behavioral results: a sick person should not complain about illness; whatever suffering there is should be borne with fortitude, since clearly God is addressing eternal matters through it; negotiations with God often entail a "learning experience," and the patience demonstrated indicates the quality of one's evolving spiritual state. Indeed, the manner and the severity of the illness are understood to reflect God's concern for one's spiritual welfare. Its object is to offer the patient a deepening knowledge of deity. End of life is also the occasion for life review, and pain may be interpreted as directly related to the notion of atonement for past sins. Most believers scan their relationships with kin and neighbors to confirm that there is nothing hindering their mutual love and appreciation. For example, dying with enmity against another Muslim would be subject to judgment in the next life.

Good Death and the Sharia's View on "Ownership" of the Person

Still, dying is not just a personal matter. There is a social responsibility/ Sharia component attendant upon individual death. This is expressed in a number of ways, some of which also have legal and political ramifications: The body must remain inviolate, since the person's body, in some sense, belongs to God. It is the community's responsibility to see that this is the case. This has ramifications for organ harvesting, and for autopsies. Moreover, scripture has several directives regarding the disposition of one's estate, and these are all subsumed under the proper treatment of the dead, a matter that raises the issue of whether all protocols were faithfully carried out. Such a question brings Islamic law into play, and hence the judicial arm of the community. These cannot be ignored in any definition of a good death. God has instructed in the Qur'an that these matters are of consequence to Him, so they have to be part of the negotiations that provide the individual with a good death. Clearing up such matters is part of the "labor" of dying.

Good Death: The Role of the Spiritual in Human Health

Contemporary Western medical ideology is founded upon the distinction developed by the ancient Greeks concerning separate spheres of influence in human makeup. Generally known as the mind-body distinction, this concept affirms that two quite different components make up the human, a sphere of the mind that is largely unknown and relates poorly to causality, and the sphere of the body, governed by quantifiable elements that are subject to cause-effect analysis. In this schema, illness has an identifiable cause. Modern medicine's *modus operandi* is to determine the cause(s) and propose a solution. Chemical interference is a preferred method of altering the impact of an illness on the body.

In contrast, some Muslims continue to be influenced by traditional Islamic medicine (TIM). That tradition rejects the bifurcation of the human; rather, it holds that a human being is far more integrated, with no duality between mind and body. At the same time, it affirms that human existence has a spiritual component that underlies and controls all other elements. TIM is variously known by Muslims as "the Prophet's Medicine"; as *hikmat* (wisdom/knowledge) based on a practitioner called a *hakim* who prescribes therapies based on spiritual or "commonsense" notions; or as *unani* (i.e., Ionian), deriving from a system developed by the Greek physician Hippocrates. The *hakim*'s procedure was to determine what was causing the imbalance and prescribe an antidote. Chief among these "causes" would be religious violations, resulting in spiritual pain. The belief was that if spiritual "pain" was correctly diagnosed, then physical pain would naturally dissipate. While there may not be much of the traditional Islamic approach to health continuing among today's Muslims, still, spiritual tranquility is regarded as essential for the healthy person. A key element in a good death is, therefore, that one ought to avoid anything that will cause spiritual pain (i.e., is a religious violation).

Good Death: Providing the Context for Muslim Life

Muslim rituals are essential for living a Muslim life (Yosef 2008). It follows, then, that religious acts will be of the highest concern for a good death. All Muslim rituals will impact on the institutional situation of the believer. The most important daily ritual is prayer (called *salat* by Arabic speakers, *namaz* by Pakistanis). There are five daily prayers at designated times, and the pious will want to observe them even when prone in bed. Friday is especially prized in Muslim life, for the midday prayer is enjoined upon the whole community as a common prayer. It is customary for believers to gather at a *masjid* (mosque). Families may want to gather with the sick to pray in their room at this time. Before one can pray, he/she must perform *wudu*`, which is a ritual washing to signal that one is prepared to encounter God. Health care professionals may be asked to assist in this process, which involves washing the face and hands up to the elbows, cleansing the body's orifices, and rinsing the private parts. If no water is available, there is provision for a dry *wudu`*. If the individual is unable to bow, the process may be mimicked as much as one is able, for instance by bowing the head and attempting to reflect the submissive movements. These are moments of direct connection with God and are highly auspicious. Hospital protocol should be suspended during that period of time, and even the physician's rounds should be altered to allow for prayers. Careful attention to this will aid in the patient's experience of a good death.

An annual ritual that directly affects believers is the fast of Ramadan (*Ramzan* in South Asia). It takes place during the ninth month of the Muslim lunar calendar, so it rotates throughout the months. Since one is not to take food or drink, smoke, or have sexual relations during daylight hours, Ramadan can be a stressful time for the ill. Islamic law allows patients not to participate, but many do, especially those who sense they are near the end of life. It greatly stresses the sick person's physical and mental resources, but it is often regarded as spiritually powerful, even purifying, so some form of fasting may be attempted in hospital. Clearly, some negotiation will have to be undertaken with those who suffer from threatening diseases, such as diabetes. Ramadan is officially broken at sundown, when salt and a date may be ingested, and a meal, called *iftar*, is served. Scheduling meals according to the breaking of the fast will reduce Muslim tensions with hospital protocols. Ramadan is regarded as a visitation month, and relatives and friends often go well out of their way to visit and spend time with the ill. Hospitals may wish to alter visitation limits during this period. Hospice caregivers will also need to treat the Muslim frail with some deference during this period and make every effort to offset the physical impacts of loss of mobility.

Ramadan ends with a special feast, called *Eid*, at which the community gathers to celebrate the salutory effects of the fast and to rejoice that another year of spiritual achievement is upon them. It is a heightened moment of special community solidarity, and families will want to include the dying in that celebration. It will likely entail special foods and many visitations. Protocols may have to be relaxed during this time in order for the dying to continue to feel part of the community.

Iftar raises the additional issue of institutional food and Sharia. All Muslims, even those classified as secular, may be reluctant to eat some kind of foods. Food and eating have long been hallmarks of Muslim hospitality and conviviality, and they are significant indicators of Muslim values. *Halal* (lawfully killed meats) are widely available in the West now, but they may not be present in rural areas or in institutions. Muslims, like their Jewish neighbors, do not eat pork or its products; there are other types of meat that are also forbidden. It would be a source of much agitation to have these served to someone too ill to object.

Modesty is an important aspect of Muslim values. There is great reluctance to accept nudity, even in the cause of health. Women in particular may express great reluctance to undress for an examination, and even the normal bathroom visits can be a time of extreme stress. It is not unusual for women to request a female doctor for internal examinations, and if none is available, then a woman attendant must be there at all times. Men likewise will feel uncomfortable in the presence of women and may even prefer privacy for occasions such as bathing and examinations. In public, Muslim gender distinctions may be rigidly maintained, and health care professionals should be aware that "mainstream" Canadian perspectives on gender can be a source of distress.

Health care professionals sometimes are unsure of religious authorities in Muslim communities. In the West, the imam functions as a spiritual representative of spiritual verities to believers, but he does not have the same authority accorded to rabbis, priests, and ministers in Judaism and Christianity. Nevertheless, he often is the person to whom to refer an ill Muslim. Additionally, some Sunnis, particularly those from Pakistan or Afghanistan, may rely on the spiritual guidance of a special religious person called a *pir* or a *fakir*. These are deemed to have special spiritual insight; if they or their representative is available, they may provide spiritual comfort for the dying. Some *pirs* are believed to have curative powers over mental and serious physical diseases such as cancer. On occasion they may provide holy water from the tomb of the originator of the spiritual discipline, which may be drunk or rubbed on the body. They may also provide amulets, normally with special Quranic phrases printed thereon; these comfort the believers and should be understood as spiritual helps. The elderly immigrant sometimes is very much oriented toward this form of Islam, and will want pictures of shrines or other reminders to be present in the hospital room. Health care professionals and families unfamiliar with these requirements would do well to encourage them for they provide much comfort and assurance for the sick.

Good Death: Legal Responsibility of Community in Death

When one is dying, the community is very much part of the process. A family's oldest males are responsible for funeral arrangements and must involve the individual's social network in the mourning activities. They must properly wash and dress the body, and must arrange for the burial site and the proper grave construction. They should accompany the body to prayers in the local mosque, after which the males are responsible for taking the body to the cemetery, placing it on its side facing Mecca, and supervising burial. A good death cannot be achieved without the proper social actions implied by these requirements. Postburial rites also include such things as Qur'an recitals in honor of the deceased, family visitations, as well as public offerings of alms, and the dying will want to arrange these affairs if at all possible. Once the estate has been duly settled according to Sharia, the individual ceases to play a role in the human world, other than through normal memories and reminiscences on anniversaries of the death.

Good Death: Paucity of Public Display

In effect, personal mourning structures in Islam involve a tangle of theological, personal, social, and political beliefs, rights, and responsibilities with a decided focus on the impact within the living community. These assure the Islamic community that the deceased is righteously presented before God, and they signal the interweaving of the personal and the corporate in Islam.[3] Obviously, a number of factors will mediate how any particular death will be mourned, and family connections, economic status, and nature of the death will play a role. It follows, then, that, in every death within the community, a complex range of requirements and norms come into play, each of them nuanced by cultural and local traditions. All of them are deemed necessary for the social cohesion of the Muslim environment. Awareness of these distinctions is necessary if one is to provide culturally competent care for elderly Muslim immigrants. While no one could be aware of all the values and beliefs that the rich tapestry of Islam has formed, the main outlines as presented here will assist health care professionals to provide better, more sensitive care.

Who Are the Muslims in Canada?

According to recent estimates, there are 800,000 or more Muslims in Canada, with more than half of them in Ontario (Pew Forum on Religion and Public Life 2011; Statistics Canada 2001). They are now more numerous than Jews and Orthodox Christians. Because Muslims are a very visible minority, they may well have experienced some form of prejudice; A 2003 Statistics Canada study found, for example, that 24 percent of those surveyed felt out of place or uncomfortable in Canada, a figure that is three times higher than that reported by nonvisible minorities. Of those who immigrated to Canada between 1991 and 2001, 29 percent were especially vulnerable. For many Muslims, 9/11 was a personal and community disaster for it placed them in a situation over which they had no control and for which they bore no responsibility. The elderly in particular were vulnerable (Statistics Canada 2003).

In Canada, almost all the basic growth of the Muslim tradition has come from immigration. There is no equivalent to the Black Muslim movement in the United States. Immigrant Muslims have intense pride in their countries of origin because they appreciate the cultural achievements of their homelands. Their cultures are far older than those they encounter here; some immigrants experience a disconnect between the relative cultural wealth of their homeland in contrast to its financial poverty when compared to the West—for many, the West is culturally inferior. Muslim immigrants come from dozens of nations, and these national distinctions do not exhaust the variety. The Lebanese Arab community built the first Canadian mosque in 1938 in Edmonton, Alberta, and they remain a vibrant element in the Islamic mosaic. Their numbers, however, have now been eclipsed by those from other parts of the Islamic world, in particular from South Asia.

Even when the major ethnic divisions are noted, the Islam followed by Muslim immigrants to Canada may not coincide with that of similar ethnic groups in other regions of the world, because the tradition takes on national and ethnic coloration as it develops. For example, the ancient division in Islam between Sunnism and Shi'ism is retained fairly rigorously. For health care professionals, it would be a significant breach of protocol to call or refer a Sunni believer to a Shi'a official. At the same time, there are believers who belong to the Ahmadiyya tradition who are regarded by some Sunnis as "not true Muslims." Many of these come from Pakistan and have had to deal with the resistance posed by other Muslims to their presence here, as well as to being a religious minority within Canadian culture.

Distinctions are also to be found between various types of Shi'a believers (e.g., Twelvers [Iran], Isma`ilis [India, Pakistan, Afghanistan, Africa], and Ibadis [Yemen]). Immigrant believers from these groups have not moved uniformly into Western society. For example, Isma`ilis have been extraordinarily successful in Canada and have developed strong connections to Canadian public life. Their influence is really disproportionate to their numbers vis-à-vis Sunnis. In terms of aggregate numbers, though, Sunnis remain the largest Muslim group in the world, comprising at least 85 percent of all believers; hence, Sunnis predominate in "the countries of origin" of most Canadian immigrants. Still, health care professionals should not assume that patients are likely to be from this group, since immigration has not drawn equally from Muslim groups.

Modernity has introduced additional differentiations that were not part of Islamic identity in its original configuration; one of these differentiations relates to the rise of reformist and radical Islam in the last century that is still very much alive today. It arose in response to Western domination and colonialism. While it has not been institutionalized officially, some believers have been strongly influenced by its views. Adherents to Islam are very much aware of the contemporary divisions this movement has fostered. Its tendencies can be described, at the very least, as conservative. In some cases it can even be termed as radical. While the number espousing this viewpoint is rather small—some authorities suggest fewer than 2 percent of the Muslim world's population are active members of the movement—it is nevertheless the case that traditional and conservative views have dominated discussions under its pressure. Interestingly, those self-identifying as Muslims have increased since 9/11, and membership in North American mosque communities rose after the attacks. While there may be no overt sympathy for radical views among patients, their presence has made Muslims aware that Western culture is likely antagonistic to traditional Islam. Health care professionals must be aware of the implicit criticism these views have of all things Western, including medicine, regardless of the individual views of their patients. Indeed, one may find the younger generation more conservative than elder parents.

This information points to a cultural matrix that is important for health care professionals. In public discourse, Muslims may be reluctant to say much about the radical wing of Islam because they do not want to clash with conservatives within their community. They may also be fearful. In hospital situations, they are more apt to hew to a conservative line because of peer pressure within the community, where they may not wish to be known as anything less than a "true" Muslim. Health care professionals should be aware that the social context of discussions around death may privilege the more conservative viewpoints.

Case Studies: Culturally Appropriate Protocols for the Health Care Professional

Hospice Care and Islamic Values

CULTURAL CONFLICT IN HOSPICE CARE BETWEEN ISLAMIC
AND CANADIAN VALUES

Mrs. al-S[4] was first brought to the emergency room when she had gone for a walk and was found confused in another part of Edmonton from the community in which she lived. She was sixty-eight, and the mother of four well-known professional sons and wife of a prominent, wealthy Arab Muslim leader. Following tests, she was sent to a geriatric assessment unit for further workup. When the diagnosis was second-stage Alzheimer's, the attending physician called a family meeting at the hospital. It was attended by Mr. al-S, his four sons, and their wives. None of the wives was raised as a Muslim. The prognosis was outlined to the family, with the question as to where Mrs. al-S would be cared for as a key element. The doctor, at the suggestion of Mr. al-S, proposed that one of the sons care for her until she no longer recognized anyone, at which time she would be institutionalized. In the ensuing discussion, all the wives refused the task, citing their own careers and families. Mr. al-S pleaded with his eldest son to take them both into his large home and care for them together, until no longer possible. He pointed out that caring for one's parents was the Islamic way, required in the Qur'an. After much debate, Mr. al-S became angry that none of the wives wished the responsibility and, in a heated scene, denounced his sons and their wives for abandoning their faith for money. He indicated that he would write all of them out of his will, take his wife to Arizona, and hire someone to care for her. He told his sons never to expect to contact him again.

COMMENTARY

Certain elements in Muslim culture give every indication of severe tension with Canadian values, and this case reflects one of them. The issue is not exclusive to Muslims, as Fielo and Degazon's study points out (Fielo and Degazon 1997). Some health care professionals chose to argue for a pragmatic approach to these issues (Shapiro and Lenahan 1996), but it is difficult to see how such an approach could have solved this case's problem. In the Islamic tradition, care for elderly parents is not a matter left to happenstance. It is directly laid upon families in the Qur'an (26:23; 29:8; 31:14; 46:15–18) where the responsibility is explicitly regarded as a debt owing from the travails of childbirth. In most Islamic countries it is held to be the task of the eldest son's wife if at all possible; if not, then it falls to the youngest unwed daughter. This is obviously a cultural decision, but it bears the stamp of ancient Arab culture, which puts special emphasis on lineage and birthright. In some cases the treatment of parents is the litmus test for commitment to Islamic values, and it holds a rich vein in Islamic law (Brockopp and Eich 2004). It is a feature of debates about whom sons should marry, and in traditional cultures a discussion about the care of the elderly will figure in the evaluation of prospective mates. The tragedy in this case is that the issue had not been decided long before Mrs. al-S required assistance, for the ramifications were far-reaching and the destruction of family solidarity permanent and heartbreaking. It would appear that the sons have assimilated into the Canadian value system, causing a rift that apparently cannot be repaired. This is a critical matter that will need addressing by Muslim families in Canada, for caregiving will become quite common as the aged population grows to 25 percent of the total over the next two decades.

Health care professionals who deal with Muslim hospice patients will find it helpful to remember that the Qur'an itself recognizes the frailties of the aged; in fact, it notes that "you will get so old that you will not remember anything" (16:70). Thus, in the Qur'an, dementia-like symptoms are part of the trajectory of aging. Such knowledge can be an important tool when dealing with relatives of the patient. At the same time, professionals should be aware that there may well be diverse interpretations of mental illness, psychiatric ailments, and even of various dementias (Lukoff et al.). For example, based on other verses, Muslims often see these illnesses as tests or trials sent by God, or even resulting from violations of God's laws. Illness can be understood as disciplinary at the end of life. Moreover, popular interpretation can also attribute mental illnesses to spiritual beings called *jinn* (see Q. 6:100; and ch. 72); more modern sources accept various kinds of imbalance as the root of such problems. One can even find descriptions of madness arising from frustrated love. Professionals would do well to be aware of these variations, for determining the "root cause" of the illness is a negotiation the Muslim undertakes as soon as the problem appears. It is well to keep in mind that, traditionally, psychological and psychiatric problems had a social opprobrium attached to them, such that their presence in a family line could influence the choice of marriage partner. Health care professionals should expect to find echoes of these views in contemporary Muslim communities and be ready to discuss them. However, the responsibility for the aged appears to apply to whatever condition may be present, so diseases such as Alzheimer's do not absolve families either from the respect required for the elderly or from the duty of care.

Issues of Communication and Cultural Attitudes

SLIGHTS IN ADDRESSING THE MUSLIM AGED

Mr. V was a recent immigrant to Canada from Pakistan. He and his wife spoke mostly Urdu in their son's home, where they resided. His son sent him to his family doctor, himself an immigrant doctor of Hindu origin, when he complained of a chronic stomach pain. The doctor's nursing assistant, a Canadian, could not understand him very well, and elected to call him by his first name because of the difficulty in pronouncing his family name. Mr. V did not recognize his name being called, and after waiting for more than an hour, went home. He complained bitterly of the lack of respect shown by the female assistant. The doctor indicated he was dismayed by Mr. V's condescending attitude toward his assistant and, already overloaded, refused to take him as a patient.

COMMENTARY

In most Muslim countries, the elderly play an important role as the head of the family. Everything from respectful language to deference in seating is accorded to them, and in most Muslim countries it is not respectful to look an elder directly in the eye. Even in home situations, a formal system of greeting is used, and certainly someone outside the family would not refer to an elderly person by his/her first name. Health care professionals will note that the elderly person, already stressed by the situation, assumed some sort of bias from the doctor had been conveyed to the assistant. The background concerns perceived strained relations between Muslims and their Hindu counterparts in Southeast Asia; for example, the partition of Pakistan still rankles the elderly (Neuberger 2004, 30–31). Sometimes these tensions are transmitted to North America. It is also the case that some Muslim elders in Western countries find it difficult to adapt to women having roles of status and power—some female doctors complain about Muslim men refusing to regard them as physicians.

ILLNESS NARRATIVES AND MATTERS OF DELICACY

Mrs. Al-R was a sixty-year-old Afghani who recently joined her son and his family in a rural area outside Montreal. She does not speak either English or French, and she is usually accompanied by her son to the doctor. When she collapsed one day while he was at work, her daughter-in-law, who did not speak Farsi, had to take her to the ER. She was dressed in a full-length abaya and hijab. She refused to change into a paper gown for X-rays. Doctors were eventually able to find a man who worked in hospital maintenance who spoke Farsi, but she would not converse with him, saying it was none of his business. So they did preliminary blood tests and placed her in a geriatric ward. When her son came, he spoke with the doctor, also a male, and it became apparent that Mrs. Al-R may have had some severe vaginal problems. She refused to speak to her son or the doctor about the matter, however, and the doctor, while having medical suspicions, had no female physicians on call and elected to discharge her.

COMMENTARY

Most traditional Muslims are reluctant to discuss any matters having to deal with genitalia, and especially not with someone of the opposite sex. Nor are they likely to converse, even with a doctor, about sex or sexual matters. Questions about sexuality are considered an extremely delicate and personal issue. Therefore, questions about sexuality should be asked with great sensitivity. Asking a widowed woman about her sex life is a cultural *faux pas* and can be taken as an extreme insult. Older women prefer not to change into a gown even with the same-sex provider unless absolutely needed. Almost always, the elderly population will reject a physician or health care professional of the opposite sex in a delicate medical situation, and some Canadian doctors now inform young mothers-to-be that they cannot guarantee a female obstetrician were they to require a caesarian section, and that they should be prepared for a male doctor to perform any operation that is required (Maqsood 2009).

DISCUSSION PROTOCOLS

Mr. P is eighty-three and is now in an extended care facility. He is visited every day by his wife, who lovingly cleans and feeds him. He has an advanced case of Alzheimer's disease. He is a Sunni Muslim, originally from Lebanon. Various health care professionals have asked Mrs. P for guidance on what her husband was like and what should be done for him throughout this illness, but they have found her almost always unresponsive because she speaks very little English, and refers questions to her son, who lives in the city and will make any decisions. On occasion, health care professionals have been irritated by this, because she would seem to have a greater stake in her husband's health than her son, and it sometimes takes several phone calls to get one decision made. The doctor has taken to keeping a list of issues so he can discuss them all at once. One issue he has discussed is family attitude toward the feeding tube, since Mr. P. has problems swallowing.

COMMENTARY

Surrogate decision making in Lebanese Muslim families follows traditional pathways; all public aspects of a family's health decisions reside with the immediate male authority. It is known that 73 percent of surrogate decision makers experience anxiety, and 35 percent display depression. In the light of these figures, the wife's response is quite normal—nor will she breach Muslim protocols by taking over public decision making. That would only cause greater problems within the family. For most critical issues, then, the closest male blood relative will have the final say. If the closest relative is not available, in this case, the son, then the man's brother or uncle should be sought out. Retaining this protocol for decision making will avert some of the potential conflicts and disagreements over care that can arise. Furthermore, Muslims would not deny the use of the feeling tube, because the giving of food is founded on Islamic values. Removing it would cause considerable distress among Muslim family members. The case also highlights related issues of end-of-life discussion. While health care professionals would like to initiate the discussion, both from a personal care and an administrative perspective, Muslims are averse to the discussion. Nor, according to Valente, are professionals immune from tensions involved in exploring how to handle end-of-life discussions (Valente 2001), and this may impact on how they handle a situation.

Advance Directives and End-of-life Issues

ON WHEN GOD IS SAID TO HAVE TAKEN LIFE

Mr. H was on life support after a serious heart attack, but there was no evidence of brain activity. Still, his son was upset about removing the tubes. "My father never talked about his death . . . he thought there was nothing to do but wait for God to send the angel of death," said the son of an immigrant from Africa. "One shouldn't discuss it . . . discussing it will speed it up!" Moreover, the round-the-clock caregivers indicated that Mr. H did not want to discuss the matter with them because he said he had no confidence that the hospital would do what he asked anyway—he thought they would take orders from the medical people, leaving him with no real choice. "My father doubted that physicians would act on his behalf . . . he thought doctors always obeyed hospital protocols despite what patients wanted. In addition, my father said once that Muslims believed that God controlled the fate of every believer, so planning what to do was like telling God how to do His job. He was plenty miffed one time when his family doctor asked him if he had made a decision about advance directives. He figured the doctor was telling him that he was seriously ill, maybe even dying. So we have no idea what he would want."

COMMENTARY

In our study of the Lac La Biche Muslims, we found an antipathy to advance directives (Waugh et al. 2010). Because the moment of death was deemed to be in the hands of the deity, planning ahead seemed to run counter to the belief in God's beneficence at the end of life. Moreover, a critical time for the application of an advance directive is in an intensive care unit (ICU), likely when a patient has just been placed under hospital care. Gries and his team found that ICU decisions had little to do with providing a good death for frail patients, but was more related to disease treatment models (Gries et al. 2008). For Muslim patients, Muhammad's views on death are more important for end-of-life issues than even what the West's medical fraternity might call "a good death." Rather, a death that embraces the Prophet's view of death will be considered a good death (O'Shaughnessy 1969), and hence it likely will have little to do with the medical situation. Furthermore, Neuberger argues that there can hardly be one notion of a good death, since both medicine and culture are too diverse for such homologizing (Neuberger 2004). Still, to prevent medicine prolonging some form of life when God has already decreed the end of this lifetime seems an affront to the tradition. Muslims generally, then, argue for intervention only if the individual has a reasonable chance of having a conscious life again. They tend not to argue for the continuation of interventions when the individual will never be the same again.

Caring for the Dying

HANDLING THE DYING

Mr. A, a Muslim originally from Lebanon, eighty, has lived and worked in the Yukon most of this life. His wife predeceased him. He is now in poor health and lives by himself in a small community outside Whitehorse. There are no other Muslims in the village. He was diagnosed with prostate cancer in the city, but he returned home, having decided against any treatment. The physician gave him a prescription for MS Contin, but he is reluctant to use it because he knows it is morphine and he is ambiguous about the meaning of his pain vis-à-vis his religion. He has no relatives or close friends in the village, although he has been befriended by the head nurse in the local health care clinic where there are a few beds for overnight stays; she told him to come by to see her if he gets too ill. A neighbor brought him by yesterday, and he obviously was in great pain. He said he was dying. She sedated him to ease the pain, but before he lapsed into semiconsciousness, he asked her to turn his face to the *qibla* if he died. In fact, he died that evening, and it immediately threw her into a panic. She had no idea which way Muslims pray, and she did not know what he meant by the *qibla*. She didn't know if she would violate some Islamic law if she moved him incorrectly. She did not want to do nothing at all, because she liked the old man, and wanted to treat him with respect. She decided to turn his face northeast, since a friend she called said that was the direction that Muslims pray, but she was still very much concerned if she did the right thing. She is now worried about handling his body because she knows there are taboos about the opposite sex and the dead.

COMMENTARY

There are several important issues in this case. The first is the obvious role that religion played in his end-of-life situation, a role that is not well recognized in professional discussions of issues (Koeing 2002; Heyland et al. 2006). Despite the fact that he did not live in a supporting Muslim environment, Mr. A continued to the end to place faith in his religion. Religious culture, then, plays an important role in how illness will be perceived and whether a "cure" is necessary (Kleinman 1978; Davies et al. 2002). The second issue is pain and symptom management. There are controversies within the tradition, and even in the general literature about opioid use (Jovey 2002). Most Muslims acknowledge that there is a risk involved in psychopharmacology, because different individuals have a different pain threshold, and some claim they are mentally prepared through religious discipline to handle pain. In addition, a cross-cultural study has found considerable differences in mental health at the end of life arising from cultural factors (Albert et al. 2007), and end-of-life mental health has recently been the focus of curriculum development in Massachusetts (Foti et al. 2003). Athar argues that the action of a Muslim who does not seek treatment is equivalent to suicide, because it is against Sharia to hasten one's death. He believes they are in deep depression (Athar 2001). Furthermore, some studies show that psychosocial determinants and beliefs predominate in the terminally ill (Suarez-Almazor et al. 2002). Al-Shahri et al. have argued that Islam provides fairly consistent norms for care at this end-of-life spectrum—preparation for eternity—that should shift the emphasis from pain control to religious therapeutics (al-Shahri, Fadul, and Elsayem 2007).

Third, the case entails how much palliation should be introduced at the end of life (Byock 2000). The supportive care standards model has been adopted in Canada by the hospice palliative care nursing association, and it stresses the notion of meaning in life, and the integrity of the person. Standard 5 notes, "The hospice palliative care nurse assists the person and family to find meaning in their lives and their experience of illness," while standard 6 indicates that "the hospice palliative care nurse preserves the integrity of self, person and family" (Peden, Grantham, and Paquin 2005, 2–3). These standards have spawned discussions on their practical application in Canada (Peden et al. 2005). In the United States, specialty training has been introduced for this aspect of health care (Ferris et al. 2002). This activity suggests an arena of discourse still under development.

The case also raises the issue of last-resort pain management. Health care professionals are themselves not necessarily equipped to understand a patient's pain (JME 2009). Muslim families may be more wary than others of hospital environments precisely because of the discussions now going on in medicine about the use of painkillers for frail elders. There is, after all, a long antipathy to the medicalization of death, at least from the perspective of Arab and Jewish medicine (Smith 2000). As sensitive as Islam is about the line between life and death and the lack of human ownership over the moment of death, there is bound to be greater stress at that time among the faithful. There may well be raw emotional issues around this problem that have not been studied. We know that Courtemanche explores this issue in a novelistic representation of a family in Africa, but we do not know its relevance for Muslims in Canada (Courtemanche 2007). Finally, while the nurse tried valiantly to assist him, it is evident that she needed training in cultural competence (Purnell and Paulanka 2005), particularly in handling religious minorities at the time of death.

Summary Conclusions

This study indicates some important differences in Muslim attitudes, values, and culture concerning the good death. It also questions whether any one system can embrace the diversity offered by Islamic tradition concerning hospice and end-of-life care, for the simple reason that Muslims interact with local cultures in a sophisticated manner, creating hybrid forms. However, we have found that religious beliefs and values operate to produce a framework for the good death, the knowledge of which will aid greatly the caregivers in their professional activities. Awareness of conceptions such as "pain as God's discipline," or the norms of Sharia in shaping the end of life, are essential to providing sensitive care. In addition, we have found that Islamic culture shapes the perceptions of roles for patient supporters and caregivers, so when decisions have to be made, institutional protocols should factor in and promote religious affirmations. Being mindful of the way that Muslims address this critical time in life can provide the foundation for fulfillment for Muslims. Hence, rather than increasing tensions, then, health care professionals can be the means for Muslims to address religious verities held to reside in the auspicious moment of transition to the next life. Based on this study, the most compelling summary argument seems to be for special cultural competence training for health personnel around the Islamic notion of the good death, and its processes in health institutions.

Notes

1. "Hospice palliative care is more focused than end-of-life care and can be provided along the disease trajectory where people need help with suffering and symptom management. End-of-life care refers to the reliable, skilled and supportive care of people with advanced, potentially fatal illness and those close to them" (Peden et al. 2005: 7–8).

2. Sharia is usually translated as Muslim law, but it incorporates so many aspects of living that most of life falls within its purview. Thus, it is not strictly law in the Western sense of a code of rules that are then applied and defined through judgments and decisions of the judiciary. For a good overview see Coulson 1964.

3. Obviously, there are nuanced differences in the significance of funeral rites deriving from the cultural context. The socioreligious dimensions, however, are found in all such situations (Turner 1977, 24ff).

4. These examples are constructed from real cases, but the names and circumstances have been changed.

References

Albert, S. M. et al. 2007. Cross-cultural variation in mental health at end of life in patients with ALS. *Neurology* 68: 1058–61.

Ali, Z. A., S. H. Hussain, and A. H. Sakr. 1981. *Natural therapeutics of medicine in Islam.* Springfield, IL: UIS Press.

Al-Jibaly. 1998. *Sickness: Regulations and exhortations (the inevitable journey): Part I: Al-Kitaab.* Arlington: as-Sunnah Publishing.

Al-Shahri, M. Z., N. Fadul, and A. Elsayem. 2007. Death, dying, and burial rites in Islam. *European Journal of Palliative Care* 13(4): 164–67.

Athar, S. 1995. Health concerns for believers: Contemporary issues. In *Ethical decision-making in patient care: An Islamic perspective.* Chicago: Kazi Publications.

———. 1999. *Information for health care providers when dealing with a Muslim patient.* Lombard, IL: Islamic Medical Association of North America.

Byock, I. 2000. Completing the continuum of cancer care: Integrating life-prolongation and palliation. *CA: A Cancer Journal for Clinicians* 50(2): 123–32.

Brockopp, J. E. 2004. The "good death" in Islamic theology. In *Difficult conversations in medicine,* ed. Elisabeth Macdonald. New York: Oxford University Press.

———, and T. Eich, eds. 2004. *Muslim medical ethics.* Columbia: University of South Carolina Press.

Collins, K. S. et al. 2000. Diverse communities, common concerns: Assessing health care quality for minority Americans. Findings from the Commonwealth Fund 2001 Health Care Quality Survey. http://www.cmwf.org/publications/publications_show.htm?doc_id=221257.

Coulson, Noel J. 1964. *A history of Islamic law.* Edinburgh: University of Edinburgh.

Courtemanche, G. 2007. *A good death.* Trans. Wayne Grady. London: Douglas and McIntyre.

Davies, B., P. Brenner, S. Orloff et al. 2002. Addressing spirituality in paediatric and palliative care. *Journal of Palliative Care* 18: 59–67.

Debate of the age health and care study group. 1999. *The future of health and care of older people: The best is yet to come.* London: Age Concern.

Ethnic Diversity Survey: Portrait of a multicultural society. 2003. http://dsp-psi.tpsgc.gc.ca/Collection/Statcan/89-593-X/89-593-XIE2003001.pdf. (Accessed Oct. 16, 2009).

Ferris, F. et al. 2002. *A model to guide hospice care: Based on national principles and norms of practice.* Ottawa, ON: Canadian Hospice Palliative Care Association.

Fielo, S. B., and C. E. Degazon. 1997. When cultures collide: Decision-making in a multicultural environment. *Nursing and Health Care Perspectives* 18(50): 238–43.

Foti, M. E. et al. 2003. The curriculum for mental health providers: End-of-life care for persons with serious mental illness. Metro Suburban Area: Massachusetts Dept. of Mental Health.

Gries, C. J. et al. 2008, July 18. Family member satisfaction with end-of-life decision making in the ICU. *CHEST* 133(3): 704–12.

Heyland, D. K., P. Dodek, G. Rocker et al. 2006. What matters most in end-of-life care: Perceptions of seriously ill patients and their family members. *Canadian Medical Association Journal* 174: 627–36.

Jovey, R. D. 2002. Opioids, pain, and addiction. In *Managing pain: The Canadian healthcare,* ed. R. D. Jovey, 63–77. (Professional's reference). Toronto: Healthcare and Financial Publishing.

Kobeisy, A. 2004. *Counseling American Muslims: Understanding faith and helping the people.* Santa Barbara, CA: Praeger.

Koeing, H. 2002. The role of religion and spirituality at the end of life. *Gerontologist* 42: 20–23.

Kleinman, A. 1978. Culture, illness, and cure. *Clinic* 88: 251–58.

Lukoff, D. F. Lu, and R. Turner. 1992. Toward a more culturally sensitive DSM-IV. Psychoreligious and psychospiritual problems. *Journal of Nervous and Mental Disease* 180(11): 673–81.

MacPherson, C. 2009. Undertreating pain violates ethical principles. *Journal of Medical Ethics* 35(10): 603–606.

Maqsood, Ruqaiyyah Waris. Thoughts on modesty. *Islam for Today.* http://www.islamfortoday.com/ruqaiyyah05.htm. (Accessed Oct. 16, 2009).

Marr, L., J. A. Billings, and D. E. Weissman. 2007. Spiritual training for palliative care fellows. *Journal of Palliative Medicine* 10(1) (Feb.): 169–77.

Martin, R. C., M. R. Woodward, and D. S. Atmaja. 1997. *Defenders of reason in Islam.* Oxford: One World.

Mull, J. D., et al. 1989. Culture and compliance among leprosy patients in Pakistan. *Social Science and Medicine* 29(7): 799–811.

Mull, J. D., and D. S. Mull. 1988. Mothers' concepts of childhood diarrhea in rural Pakistan: What ORT program planners should know. *Social Science Medicine* 27(1): 53–67.

Neuberger, J. 1987. *Caring for dying people of different faiths.* London: Hochland and Hochland.

———. 2004. *Dying well: A guide to enabling a good death.* London: Austin Cornish.

O'Shaughnessy, T. 1969. *Muhammad's thoughts on death.* Leiden: E. J. Brill.

Peden, J., D. Grantham, and M-J. Paquin. 2005. Hospice palliative care nursing standards: How do these apply to our practice? *Perspectives in hospice palliative care: Nursing* 3–6. Edmonton: Pallium Project.

Periyakoil, V. S., J. C. Mendez, and A. B. Buttar. 2008. Health and health care for Pakistani American elders. http://www.stanford.edu/group/ethnoger/pakistani.html. (Accessed Oct. 16, 2009).

Pew Forum on Religion and Public Life. 2011. The future of the global Muslim population. http://features.pewforum.org/muslim-population/?sort=Pop2010.

Purnell, L. D., and B. J. Paulanka. 2005. *Guide to culturally competent health care.* Philadelphia: F. A. Davis.

Reynolds, S., A. B. Cooper, and M. McKneally. 2005. Withdrawing the sustaining treatment: Ethical considerations. *Thorac Surg Clin* 15: 469–80.

Satcher, D., and R. J. Pamies, eds. 2006. *Multicultural medicine and health disparities.* New York: McGraw-Hill Professional.

Shapiro, J., and P. Lenahan. 1996. Family medicine in a culturally diverse world: A solutions-oriented approach to common cross-cultural problems in medical encounters. *Family Medicine* 28(4): 249–55.

Sheikh, A., and A. R. Gatrad. 2000. *Caring for Muslim patients.* Abingdon, UK: Radcliff Medical Press.

Smith, R. 2000. A good death. *BMJ* 320 (January 15): 129–30.

Spirituality in palliative care. 2009. *Journal of Palliative Medicine* 12(10): 885–904. http:www.liebertonline.com/doi/10.1089/jpm.2009.01.42. (Accessed Oct. 15, 2009).

Statistics Canada. 2001. 2001 Census. Population by religion, by province and territory. Quebec, Ontario, Manitoba, Saskatchewan. http://www40.statcan.gc.ca/l01/cst01/demo30b-eng.htm.

Statistics Canada: Housing Family and Social Statistics. 2003. *Ethnic diversity survey: Portrait of a multicultural society.* Ottawa: Minister of Industry. http://dsp-psd.tpsgc.gc.ca/Collection/Statcan/89-593-X/89-593-X IE2003001.pdf.

Suarez-Almazor, M. E. et al. 2002. Attitudes of terminally ill cancer patients about euthanasia and assisted suicide: Predominance of psychosocial determinants and beliefs over symptom distress and subsequent survival. *Clinical Oncology* 20: 2134–41.

Turner, V. 1977. Death and the dead in the pilgrimage process. In *Religious encounters with death,* ed. F. Reynolds and E. H. Waugh, 24ff. University Park and London: Pennsylvania State University Press.

Valente, S. M. 2001. End-of-life issues. *Geriatric Nursing* 22(6): 294–98.

Waugh, E. H., O. Szafran, and J. Triscott, J. 2011. Culturally responsive care in the community. In *At the interface of culture and medicine,* ed. E. H. Waugh, O. Szafran, and J. Triscott. Edmonton: University of Alberta Press.

Welch, A. 1977. Death and dying in the Qur'an. In *Religious encounters with death,* ed. F. Reynolds and E. H. Waugh, 183–99. University Park and London: Pennsylvania State University Press.

Welch, L. C., J. M. Teno, and V. Mor. 2006. End-of-life care in black and white: Race matters for medical care of dying patients and their families. *Journal of the American Geriatric Society* 53: 1145–53.

Yosef, A. R. 2008. Health beliefs, practice, and priorities for health care of Arab Muslims in the United States. *Journal of Transcultural Nursing* 19: 284–91.

Zweifler, J., and A. M. Ginzalez. 1998. Teaching residents to care for culturally diverse populations. *Academic Medicine* 73(10): 1056–61.

5

Tradition and Change in Jewish Ideals Regarding a "Good" Death

Norman Ravvin

For much of 2008 the issue of a good death as it related to Jewish religious life made news, first in Canada and then abroad, by way of the media and the Canadian courts. This interest was motivated by the case of an eighty-four-year-old Winnipeg man named Samuel Golubchuk, whose final months in what doctors sometimes referred to as a persistent vegetative state became a focus of disagreement over questions of medical ethics and the responsibilities of Jewish belief and custom. In an editorial published in the *Canadian Medical Association Journal*, the case was described as making "religion a factor in allocating a hospital bed," while the patient's children were derided for "using their religion to privilege their father" (Attaran 2008). These views of the situation reflected unwillingness on the part of some doctors and their professional organizations to appreciate the way that religious traditions can influence decision making in end-of-life care. But, ironically, the Golubchuk case did not present—in the medical, legal, or media contexts where it was discussed—a detailed examination of Jewish notions of a good death. Rather, discussion focused upon the extreme positions expressed by each of the main stakeholders: the patient's children, who refused cessation of care based on their understanding of orthodox religious responsibilities, a response that should not be seen as normative in Jewish contexts, whether orthodox or not; the rabbi, who took a personal interest in the case and claimed misleadingly that Jews "have the obligation to do whatever we can even if it's only to live one day longer" (Neufeld 2008); the doctors at Winnipeg Grace Hospital, who overstepped their professional roles by telling the patient's children they would "unhook" their father from respirator and feeding tube without their agreement (Solomon 2008); and the media, who exerted little effort to examine the variety and particularities of Jewish ideas regarding the end of life.

Interest in the case confirmed a limited understanding of what Jews think and do in pursuit of a good death in hospice or palliative care. But it revealed, as well, the fact of widely divergent outlooks within Jewish communities regarding end-of-life decisions. In this chapter, I will strive to do two things: examine key traditions and sources, while highlighting the importance of originality and creativity in the ongoing Jewish response to challenges associated with the end-of-life decisions. Coverage of the Golubchuk case repeatedly described the patient as "orthodox" without defining the variety of meanings this term can take. Some key religious terms are useful here, including notions of personal autonomy as it relates to faith, and those used in rabbinic discussions of the final stages of life.

The Particulars: The Dying Body, Law, and Denominational Difference

Consideration of Jewish ideas of the end of life is framed by the laws of the Torah, by the commentary associated with these laws found in the Talmud,[1] and in ongoing discussions by rabbinic courts. Discussions of Jewish law, or *halacha*, have both a case-oriented approach as well as a method that relies on storytelling, or argument by allegorical narrative. The body of rabbinic decisions associated with a subject such as end-of-life care might be understood as part of the "case law of Judaism" (Mackler 2003, 49). Written outcomes of contemporary rabbinic decisions are known as *responsa*. These decisions guide a rabbi's notion of proper response in specific situations; but as the reader will see below, rabbis will not necessarily agree on the outcome of rabbinic debates, and the approaches of major North American Jewish denominational groups—Orthodox, Conservative, and Reform—disagree over how Jewish tradition should respond to the end of life. In an Orthodox context it can generally be assumed that an individual will be guided by a rabbi's interpretation of a situation as it relates to law and paradigmatic biblical and Talmudic narratives. But one physician active in end-of-life care writes that one can expect that an individual associated with Conservative or Reform congregations "do[es] not feel compelled to necessarily follow that advice" (Kinzbrunner 2004, 560). Canadian sociologist Morton Weinfeld asserts that in Canada,

> [m]ost of the members of Orthodox, Reform, Conservative, and Reconstructionist congregations have not studied the theological writings of their respective rabbinic authorities. . . . Many, perhaps most, do not know the "official" denominational position on various issues. (Weinfeld 2001, 295)

Weinfeld highlights the specific cultural and religious background of each denomination and tells us the following about the particularities of Canadian Jewish denominational life:

> The Judaism of Canadian Ashkenazi Jews can be divided into four formal denominations: Orthodoxy, Conservatism, Reform, and Reconstructionism. The progressive, avant-garde Jewish Renewal Movement could become a fifth. Secular Judaism, or secular humanist Judaism, enjoying a bit of a revival, could almost be considered a sixth. This ordering supposedly reflects the degrees of religiosity; the Orthodox are more likely to observe more of the precepts of traditional religious Judaism, followed by the other denominations in descending order. Yet each of these denominations is in turn diverse, none more so than the Orthodox. And none is static. (Weinfeld 2001, 36)[2]

In the case of each denomination's organizational and religious leaders, the response to questions associated with end-of-life care has been substantial, detailed, and varied. In 1995 the American leadership of Reform Judaism adopted a set of "Resolutions and Bylaws" with regard to "Compassionate and Comfort Care at the End of Life." Citing the notion of *pikuach nefesh*—an injunction allowing one to break laws related to the Sabbath and other forms of observance in order to save a life—the bylaws are introduced as follows:

> [W]e must strive toward an achievable goal, to provide a quality of life that is at least tolerable for each one whose journey

ends in pain and suffering. . . . We assert that most of the tragic choices to end life can be avoided through the combined efforts of caring doctors, clergy, providers, family, and community. By providing caring support for families and assisting in the development of hospices and similar environments where spiritual and physical needs are met, our congregations can help to preserve the meaning and purpose of our lives as we approach the end of the journey. (Union for Reform Judaism 1995)

The argument against euthanasia at the outset of this passage is representative of a prohibition found across most Jewish communal lines against active euthanasia or mercy killing. Conservative Judaism, its associated leaders, and responsa literature tend to view Reform Judaism's approach as being overweighted in the direction of the autonomy of the individual, and argue for a different balance between individual autonomy and rabbinic authority (Mackler 2003, 52). One writer in the Conservative tradition recognizes the importance of reasoning "analogically from a variety of [rabbinic] precedents," but insists as well that when basing decisions regarding end-of-life care on traditional story or legal debate one not ignore the "significant differences between the medical circumstances of our time and those of the past" (Dorff 1991, 8, 12). Elliot Dorff, whose essay "A Jewish Approach to End-stage Medical Care" is written from a Conservative standpoint, introduces key terms associated with end-of-life questions and decisions that derive from centuries of rabbinic commentary. The Hebrew word *treifah* is used to refer to a terminally ill person. Other sources define the term as relating to a prognosis of one year or less to live, noting its use in the writings of Maimonides, a twelfth-century physician and religious thinker, to describe an illness that "does not have any remedy for humans, and it will surely cause death" (Kinzbrunner 2004, 561–62). A more pressing term for these discussions is that of *goses*, which refers to when a patient is actively dying. Dorff refers to this as being "in the very last stages of life" (Dorff 1991, 4), while others limit it to the last three days of life, or to the time when death is "recognizable by the heavy, laboured, erratic breathing that a patient experiences when death is considered imminent" (Kinzbrunner 2004, 563). A broadly held Jewish view of this time is that nothing should be done to hasten death. On the other hand, impediments to the natural progress of death are to be removed. One encounters this latter notion in a variety of sources, often with reference to Talmudic lore. The most evocative of these accounts has to do with Talmudic figure Rabbi Yehudah Hanasi, whose students pray ceaselessly for his recovery, while a maidservant, accepting the imminent end and recognizing his suffering, causes a disturbance so the students' praying is interrupted and the rabbi, no longer distracted by them, dies. Certainly, this narrative helps us interpret situations where a patient is near death while being sustained by a respirator or other technologies, which most Jews would agree to remove.

Any effort to present a general portrait of Orthodox attitudes to end-of-life care must fail. One has, as a foundation, the assumption that decisions will be underwritten, concretely, by rabbinic law. In Orthodox responsa, Dorff tells us, "all life is sacred and must be preserved under all circumstances" (Dorff 1991, 15). This seems to promote the "do anything at all costs" approach in medical contexts, which is neither founded in Jewish texts or supported throughout the rabbinic writings of Orthodox figures. The Talmudic anecdote of the disturbing servant—validated in its original context and related interpretive discussion—confirms the importance of traditional Jewish texts and ideals that seek "to allow death . . . to occur 'naturally,' neither postponed nor brought on prematurely by active intervention" (Golbert 2006, 54).

Discussions of the viability of hospice in Orthodox Jewish circles often turn, however, on an assumption that by choosing hospice over active medical care one has in some way given up, or contravened the injunction to preserve life. One senses this discomfort in community literature addressing hospice care, as well as in certain academic articles that struggle with these assumptions. A good example of the latter is the essay "*Halacha* and Hospice," which appeared in the American *Journal of Halacha and Contemporary Society*. Its author, Marc Angel, who is a rabbi, introduces his discussion with a rhetorical query: "Does participating in a hospice program demonstrate a lack of *bitachon* in God, since the person seems to be admitting that death is inevitable and that prayers for the restoration of health are valueless?" (Angel 1986, 19 [*bitachon* in Hebrew means faith]). Angel's response to this is, in part, not unlike my own efforts in this chapter to broaden the impression of traditional precedent and story. He offers the examples of biblical patriarchs who accepted "their death without difficulty" (Angel 1986, 23), raising, in Angel's view, the possibility of returning, "at least in some measure, to [an] old style of dying" (Angel 1986, 18, 23). His effort to attend to both traditional

example and modern medical possibilities and excesses lead him to offer
a credo associated with the options for end-of-life care:

> I am very ill. It appears that I will die soon. I do not want to
> die in a hospital. I want to be in a comfortable setting. I want
> to be with family and friends. I am ill, but I am still a person
> and I want my humanity respected. While I understand that the
> odds are very much against my surviving, I know that the power
> over life and death is in God's hands. If he decides to grant me
> life, well and good. If not, I prefer to die in a hospice setting.
> (Angel 1986, 23–24)

One recognizes similar anxieties raised in community materials
addressing hospice and palliative care. In the New York–based newsletter of the American Orthodox Union, the author lays out efforts being
made by major American Jewish health care and social service providers
to initiate rabbi-doctor training programs that will increase awareness
of patients' anxieties, in particular, in relation to pain management and
the possibility that the drugs associated with it can have the effect of
hastening death (Borowski 2000, n.p.).[3] But the article's overall effort is
to argue in favor of hospice and to offer advice on how "proper sensitivity
to both the 'spirit' and the 'letter' of Jewish law" can assure that "services
can be designed to serve Jewish patients, even when the program is not
under formal Jewish or halachic auspices" (Borowski 2000, n.p.).

Biblical and Related Sources

Certain biblical narratives are ever-present and instructive in an effort
understand the Jewish worldview in relation to death. The conclusion of
Genesis, with its portrait of the death of the patriarch Jacob, is often
raised as a model of a good death and as a prototypic narrative regarding
end-of-life care. The onset of Jacob's illness, his ability to call his sons to
him to offer his "charge" to Joseph, including prophecies for the future of
his descendants, is a central Jewish scenario of familial love in the shadow
of death (*Soncino* 1971, Gen. 47, n.2). Though Jacob lies in bed, sick, he
is able to "strengthen himself" in order to sit "upon the bed" and place
his feet on the floor (48, 2). This ideal of intimacy, of self-consciousness,
even willfulness to the end, runs through discussions of death in Jewish

contexts and bears some similarity to the focus on mindfulness in the Buddhist and Hindu traditions. In the denouement to this scene the reader is given to understand that Jacob recognized the moment of his own passing: "And when Jacob made an end of charging his sons, he gathered up his feet into the bed, and expired, and was gathered unto his people" (49, 33). The narrative of Jacob's death is notable for its lack of attention to ritual activities; Jacob's final activities include intimacy with children and grandchildren, an account of his tribal past, and prophecy regarding filial duty and fortune. Unlike some of the other traditions presented in this volume, neither sacred space in the final days of the dying, nor attention to specific decoration and chanted devotional texts are central in the conclusion of Genesis. The narrative is one of simple intimacy and retains an uncanny relevance to contemporary Jewish imaginings of the end of life.

   With no authoritative theological doctrine associated with questions of the afterlife and the ultimate meaning of death, it is not possible to define an authoritative Jewish view of them. One must, to an extent, revert to anecdotal evidence, to a gathering of enough historical detail that a thick description of the past as it relates to contemporary views takes shape. To this end, I offer the following personal account: I have been steeped in a concern with death since my youth, being a grandchild of Old World Eastern European Jews, whose family was largely destroyed during the Holocaust. Death was part of my recent ancestral and cultural experience in the most direct and difficult way. The events that brought about my ancestors' death were brutal and entangled with the major political and historical collapse of our era. They were also a part of a continent-wide war over which cultural tradition would exist on European soil. My appreciation of such things has been tempered, naturally, by personal experience of death. When I was a child, a Calgary rabbi advised my parents not to bring me to my paternal grandmother's funeral, while I knew that decades before, in my grandmother's middle-class Polish existence, family members had been nursed and died at home, never in hospitals or the hospices associated with the poor and indigent, and that at funerals before World War II a remarkable presence was that of paid mourners whose specialty was wailing, an expression of grief largely unheard of in our time. One knew, too, even as a child, that heaven and hell were not important concerns, did not figure in literary or folkloric tradition in any substantial way, and were not part of the child's induction into an immature version of the tradition. One noticed, too, as one reached adolescence or had the ill-fortune to say *Kaddish* over a parent's grave, that the prayer for the dead extolled not the deceased, did not even mention them, or death, or the grave, or the possibility of resurrection and life after death, but instead the prayer was a statement of faith, a magnification of the divine, and a recognition, to quote the *Kaddish*, of the divine power's will to "make peace in the heavens" and "for us."

The gap between prewar Polish-Jewish traditions in connection with death and those maintained in postwar North America is substantial. There have been important incursions by the mainstream culture, alongside a covering over of specific practice by assimilationist and syncretistic trends. This includes the introduction of the eulogy in a chapel that now almost always precedes the saying of *Kaddish* at the burial site. But such syncretism is not new. The memorial candles, so central to Jewish mourning practice, imitate the Polish Catholic custom of candle lighting in churches and on grave sites at key times. And biblical scholars and archaeologists remind us that the Hebrew word for death—*mavet*—is borrowed from the name of the Canaanite god Mot, ruler of the underworld (Kashani 2007, 510).

In scholarly discussions regarding death in the Jewish tradition one reads that, as one author puts it, the "Jewish orientations toward death and its meaning" were "not elaborated either in formal doctrine or in theological treatises" (Abramovitch 1987, 132). Guides devoted to Jewish rituals of mourning and burial focus on the "specific ritual and halakhic context of mourning" (Abramowitch 1987, 132)—the laws associated with a dying man or woman, with treatment of the body, with prayers associated with burial and mourning. One writer has called this approach a "ritualized theology in action" (Abramovitch 1987, 132). But we can say more, in order to understand the trend in Jewish thought to evade or downplay doctrinal claims regarding death. As well, we can characterize key shifts in this approach that have taken place since biblical times.

In James P. Carse's *Death and Existence: A Conceptual History of Human Mortality*, a comparative effort to trace the uniqueness of Jewish ideas alongside those of other religious traditions, the author's frame is historical, as he traces important shifts in authoritative Jewish views since biblical times. Carse points to influential biblical narratives that provide the foundation for understanding and lived response to death. He reminds us that the narrative of the Tree of Knowledge in Genesis links mortality with "the uncovering of consciousness" and "the knowledge of good and evil" (Carse 1980, 172). Included in the punishment of being driven from the Garden is the ambiguous result of Adam and Eve's entry into history, that is, human time. Carse reminds us, too, of the absence in biblical narrative of "agents of death independent of God." Death in the Hebrew Bible, he writes, "comes from the hand of God" and "has no power of its own" (Carse 1980, 176). In the Bible the dead are not replaced or recovered; there is an absence of compensation, even of words of comfort in response to the most painful of losses, and the biblical notion of an afterlife is at best inchoate. *Sheol*, the place where the dead are said to go, is represented as a state of formlessness, even nothingness. "Rather than exciting the imagination it seems to confound it, binding one's reflections about death to thoughts of vanishing without a trace into the dust" (Carse 1980, 179). The books of the Hebrew Bible that offer sustained responses to death—Lamentations, Job, Ecclesiastes, and Proverbs—are alike in their unwillingness to "look for a continuation of life after death" (Carse 1980, 182). Carse summarizes the uniqueness of the Jewish response to death as a recognition that "the future is not something that will happen to us, but what will come of the way we are currently living" (Carse 1980, 185). Continuity, in this sense, is confirmed by way of an ethical relationship to others within a lived tradition, rather than through the promise of a transcendent outcome after death in which "'only' the body dies while the essence of the individual lives on" (Oppenheim 2006, 235).

Carse points to major postbiblical shifts in these views. With the destruction of the first Temple in Jerusalem in the sixth century BCE, and increasingly through the exile that followed, the notion of Israel being punished for its sins led to a link between sinfulness, suffering, and God's wrath. Though this link between sin and death was in place in implicit ways in the narrative of Adam and Eve, its role gained influence as historical suffering became a recurrent theme in Jewish political and religious life. One understanding of the major shifts in Jewish traditional thought points to catastrophe—the Temple's destruction, dispersion, and later the Crusades, the Inquisition, and the Holocaust—as turning points that brought about substantial change in belief and cultural outlook. Historical suffering led the Talmudic tradition to take "refuge," as Carse puts it, "in the theory of immortality" (Carse 1980, 202). Here a duality, or contradiction, arises in the tradition's response to death. Important modern Jewish philosophers such as Franz Rosenzweig and Emmanuel Levinas resist this development as an "inauthentic response to death" (Oppenheim 2006, 235), seeing in it a diminishment of the original ethical response to existence, and encouragement to feel "indifference to the issues of the world" alongside the belief that "God will restore what we want *somewhere else*" (Carse 1980, 202).

An influential source for Jewish notions of the afterlife is the Book of Daniel, whose ethos, though biblical, is dispersion culture, where the Babylonian exile and persecution under the King Antiochus Epiphanes provide the book's author with motivations for imagining what he refers to as the prospect of a messianic kingdom of heaven, "which shall rule over the whole earth" (Daniel 1993, 2:39). Daniel is a key Hebrew source for the notion of resurrection, as the writer acknowledges "those who sleep in the dust of the earth" of whom many will "awake, some to everlasting life, and some to shame and everlasting contempt" (Daniel 1993, 12:2). This passage raises themes and motifs that are reiterated in the Jewish New Year and Yom Kippur liturgies, where the notion of one being inscribed in a "Book of Life" is central, and where confession and self-acknowledgment are understood as necessary to guarantee that one will not be inscribed in the "Book of Death."

These themes run in enigmatic ways through centuries of Jewish cultural transformation. They help us understand contemporary views when set alongside ages-old customs related to Jewish ideas of a "good" or, as Jewish historical sources tend to put it, a "proper" death (Bar-Levav 2008, 397). A thoroughgoing picture takes shape by way of a number of the entries included in Gershon Hundert's 2008 *YIVO Encyclopedia of Jews in Eastern Europe* (2008), whose source material bridges Jewish life from Prague to the eastern limits of Russian Jewish settlement. A turning point can be recognized in mid-sixteenth-century Prague, where the first Jewish Burial Society was established, leading to an institutional trend that spread to virtually every Jewish community in Eastern Europe (Bar-Levav 2008, 397). Burial Society duties, which include cleaning the body, physical burial, and funeral arrangements, began at the "bedside of the dying," where, by the eighteenth century the family might be asked to leave while the Society's representatives said prayers. A person in the final stages of dying might take part in those prayers (398). Themes highlighted here include the tendency, into the twentieth century, for a person's final days and death to take place at home and the understanding of a "proper death" taking place "with intention, in a ceremonial context" (398). Ceremonial innovations in the seventeenth century are confirmed by the popularity—in Hebrew and Yiddish—of booklets of prayers to be read before the sick and dying (398). Jews also prepared an "ethical will" or moral testament," which mirrored the "charge" Jacob offered Joseph and prefigured the personal directives of contemporary times.[4] In these undertakings, care, as we might think of it in modern medical terms, is not at stake; rather, ritualization, a level of intimacy, and attentiveness to the dying person are paramount. Contemporary ethical or living wills, which are available free on numerous Web sites, focus on appointing a particular rabbi as a patient's agent, and may assert as well a particular denominational affiliation.

In the Eastern European context an institution called *hekdesh* (from the Hebrew root word *kadosh*, or holy) was under the management of a communal charitable organization called *bikur holim*, or society for helping the sick. Its purpose was in part focused on responding to the substantial rise in poverty, indigence, and a culture of begging in Eastern Europe following the 1648 Chmelnitsky massacres, which devastated Jewish communal order (Shternsis 2008, 136). But the *hekdesh* was in place in Western Europe as early as the thirteenth century in Germany, Italy, and Spain (Kottek 1999, 163). The *hekdesh* was, physically, "a neglected structure at the edge of a settlement," often in the vicinity of the cemetery, which housed "people with infectious illnesses, the homeless, and the itinerant poor" (Zalkin 2008, 307). In smaller communities, little medical care was provided, but the *hekdesh* had its own director or beadle who often lived in the same building with his family and the people he oversaw. Larger communities hired a doctor or surgeon whose duties included caring for the indigent.

The *hekdesh*, a long-standing independent Jewish version of hospice, is little known or talked about today. It appears—though hidden in the English translation—in the most commonly anthologized story by the Nobel laureate Isaac Bashevis Singer. "Gimpel the Fool" has a folkloric quality, especially in its most famous 1953 translation by Saul Bellow, and its action ends in a structure whose ambiguous mixture of poorhouse and cemetery outbuilding is suggestive of prewar Eastern European simplicity in things related to life and death:

> At the door of the hovel where I lie, there stands the plank on which the dead are taken away. The grave-digger Jew has his spade ready. The grave waits and the worms are hungry; the shrouds are prepared—I carry them in my beggar's sack. Another *shnorrer* is waiting to inherit my bed of straw. When the time comes I will go joyfully. Whatever may be there, it will be real,

without complication, without ridicule, without deception. (Singer 1990, 1488–89)

In the story's Yiddish original the "hovel" of Bellow's translation is in fact the *hekdesh*—"By the door of the *hekdesh* where I lie" is a direct translation of Gimpel's final words. Here we find a loss of clarity that is common in efforts to translate aspects of Jewish daily life into a mainstream context (Singer 1963, 17).

The Hospice Movement in Light of Jewish Ideals and Practice

The hospice movement founded by Cicely Saunders in the 1960s provides the background against which this volume examines each religious tradition's notions of end-of-life care and a good death. Coincidentally, Saunders's own progress, her personal life, and professional undertakings include a link between the movement's accomplishments and post–World War II Jewish identity. Biographical writing about Cicely Saunders, as well as her own autobiographical writings and letters, highlight the importance of David Tasma, a young Polish Jewish patient for whom she cared until his death in 1948. In Tasma, it seems that Saunders recognized what would come to be understood as the impact of "total pain." Shirley du Boulay's biography of Saunders characterizes Tasma as

> someone in real need, a need so great and so poignant that it overshadowed even the tragically sick and lonely patients she had already come across. He was separated from his own family, he was in great physical pain, he was desperately lonely . . . and he was dying after an unfulfilled life. (du Boulay 2007, 35–36)

Upon his death Tasma bequeathed £500 to Saunders's future work, with the wish that he "be a window" in the "home" she planned to build (du Boulay 2007, 36). David Clark describes this narrative as "a foundation myth for the hospice movement" (Clark 2001, 355).

Clark and du Boulay each recognize that Tasma's Jewishness influenced Saunders's sense of the religious character of the hospice movement, and that her personal relationship with him brought to the fore the need, in the treatment of the dying, for "a context of real concern for the individual person" (du Boulay 2007, 36). As a case study in the relationship of contemporary Jewish identity to mainstream Christian culture, the Tasma "foundation myth" raises peculiar challenges. Of note is the fact that exactly what Tasma's experience was of wartime Jewish history remains confused in the major sources such as du Boulay's biography and Clark's edited volume of Saunders's letters. Du Boulay recounts Tasma's personal history this way:

> He was a Polish Jew, an agnostic, who came from the Warsaw ghetto and had come over to England before the uprising. . . . His grandfather was a rabbi . . . he had spent the war in France. (Du Boulay 2007, 33)

Clark reiterates the "Warsaw ghetto" connection in his essay "Religion, Medicine, and Community in the Early Origins of St. Christopher's Hospice" (Clark 2001, 354). In a letter included in Clark's volume of Saunders's *Selected Letters*, dated February 3, 1987, Saunders tells a relative of Tasma who has written to her that Tasma "left Poland before the war and had been working in Paris. . . . What he told me about his family was that they had certainly lived in the Ghetto" (Clark 2005, 291). The confusing aspects of these reports arise from the use of the words Warsaw ghetto (or Ghetto), the mention in du Boulay of "the uprising" (whether the Jewish Ghetto Uprising in April 1943 or the Polish Underground Army Uprising that followed it in 1944), and then the acknowledgment in both du Boulay and Saunders's letter that Tasma was not in Warsaw during the war. Though Tasma's importance to Saunders is clear, as is his own commitment to a still-inchoate plan on Saunders's part, the man—as Jewish historical figure—at the core of the hospice movement's foundational myth remains obscure. What is apparent is that Tasma, a Polish Jewish emigrant to England, for whom a reliable biography is unavailable, finds himself portrayed in hospice literature as representative of the movement's ideals. Though Saunders decided early that her movement would not be evangelical and would proceed on the principle that "agnostics, atheists or non-thinkers" should be "helped to accept death in the way most suitable to *them* as individuals," the fuzziness surrounding Tasma's Jewish particulars sounds a warning that may help readers understand Jewish discomfort with social institutions whose foundations are Christian (Du Boulay 2007, 48). The misapprehension of who Tasma was seems to suggest a movement's inability to recognize a Jew for what he or she is. If it is true that a Polish-born Jew helped crystallize Saunders's approach, then particulars are of the essence. They motivate a careful consideration of the divide between a mainstream Christian context and the minority groups who may fail to adapt themselves to available institutions such as hospice care. A specific example may be of note here; that is, the energy with which Montreal Jews developed a Jewish General Hospital, in part because of the incompatibility of Jewish patients with hospitals run by the Catholic Church.

The Institutional Context

The availability and variety of hospice and palliative care with attention to Jewish ideals is in part based on the size of communities and the degree to which medical and social service infrastructures have adapted to these needs. Viewing these issues from Montreal sets a particular standard. Once the largest and most cohesive Jewish community in Canada, it is often cited as an example of Jewish institutional completeness (Weinfeld 2001, 39). This characteristic is reflected in the type of end-of-life care available to Jewish patients. The Montreal Jewish General Hospital has a substantial, well-resourced palliative care unit, where issues of *halachic* respect—whether in the area of kosher food or laws regarding a patient's final days—are considered. (The *kashrut* rules applied in the kitchen have made the hospital the first choice of Montreal's Muslim community, since their dietary system, *Halal,* resembles these rules.) The hospital's Director of Spiritual Services is Rabbi Raphael Afilalo, who coordinates with religious representatives from other traditions. In an interview, Afilalo cited the "wide range" of religious backgrounds represented in the hospital's patient population, with roughly 30 percent being Jewish and the same number citing Catholic faith. Rabbi Afilalo feels he has a good relationship with palliative care physicians, but says he is most commonly alerted to religious needs by the family of a dying patient and not by medical staff. Discussions with family members regarding pain relief and the possibility of removing a patient from life support are relayed to physicians. Yet Afilalo asserts the prohibition against stopping oxygen, food, or liquids as representing the ideal that one should never hasten death. An interesting avenue of adaptation in the hospital's Pastoral Services is reflected in the rabbi's ongoing discussions with the head of the city's Vaad Hair (Jewish Community Council), Rabbi Y. B. Weiss, on issues of end-of-life care. These discussions are motivated by the fact that Weiss has himself issued responsa related to these questions. Afilalo mentions, as well, his meetings with Wolfe Ber Lerner, the head of the *Belzer Chasidim* in the city, following the need to address that group's particular expectations regarding end-of-life treatment. Though Chasidic sects in Montreal, descending from Eastern European rabbinic dynasties, might have expectations like other Orthodox Jews, they maintain separate leadership, synagogues, education, and cultural life to the extent that commentators have called them "a people apart."

Pastoral Services at the Montreal Jewish General Hospital have created a pamphlet titled "A Guideline for Families of Dying Jewish Patients." This sweeping title suggests a broad address to end-of-life care—and in fact it does differentiate between Ashkenazi and Sephardi expectations—yet the pamphlet's goal is specific, and, one might argue, narrowly focused on expectations related to the actual time of dying. "It is critical," the pamphlet tells us, "that the dying person hears the following before and as his soul departs," then cites the introductory passage of the *Shema*, the central prayer of Jewish faith: "Hear, Israel, the Lord is our God, the Lord is One" (Jewish General Hospital 2009). The appropriate passages appear in Hebrew, in transliterated Hebrew, and in English and French translation. Some Orthodox Jews wish to say a final confessional prayer known as the *vidui*. Codified in the sixteenth century, the *vidui* acknowledges God's will in the patient's eventual cure or death and requests the expiation of sins. There is no role in the saying of the prayer for family members, and it requires, beyond its recitation, no grander ceremonial context.

Research on end-of-life care is undertaken at the Montreal Jewish General through its ties to McGill University medical school and its activities as a teaching hospital linked to the Montreal General Hospital, Mount Sinai, St. Mary's Hospital, and the palliative care unit at the Montreal Children's Hospital. Dr. Robin Cohen has been involved in research teams pursuing what she and her research partners quantify as the "quality of life . . . of palliative care patients with cancer" by asking "what was important" to them in the final stages of life (Cohen 2002, 48). In an interview she sketched a typical end-of-life scenario for a terminally ill patient making use of hospice care in Montreal. Though the recently completed West Island Hospice offers long-term care, Cohen says that hospice care in Montreal does not usually include such care. Rather, the average length of stay in a palliative care unit at the Montreal Jewish General is nine days. If a patient improves, he or she might be sent home or moved to a long-term care institution (this option, likely a nursing home, is in many cases an undesirable option). Many patients "come in [to the hospital's palliative care unit] to die," and may spend two or three days on a palliative care ward. Hospice care might be applied, as well, for patients who leave palliative care. Quebec neighborhood health clinics, or CLSCs (*Centre Local de Services Communautaires*) offer this in-house rather than providing home care, as government-sponsored hospice programs do in other Canadian provinces. The CLSC offerings, according to Cohen, vary widely from one part of the city to another and are unpredictable at best.

During the interview with Robin Cohen I was introduced to one of her researchers, Lisa Chan, whose focus is end-of-life care on the Montreal Jewish General's acute care ward. When asked which issues were most commonly raised by patients as end-of-life spiritual concerns, she cited aesthetic pleasures, notions of beauty, fears associated with dying, and the meaning of a patient's "life's work." She recognized, with some surprise, that issues related to the afterlife almost never came up. She thought this could be accounted for by the fact that she was viewed as a scientist, or a researcher directly related with social services. But her overall sense was of a fairly strong institutional disconnect between the demanding duties of acute care staff and possible patients' spiritual and religious needs. Since the Director of Pastoral Care and his associates from other religious traditions do not attend rounds, they do not develop a pattern of involvement and independent response. Rather, they visit if specifically called for by a patient. Cohen pointed, however, to the well-developed protocols associated with religious expectations in acute care, which have become the de facto checks and balances with relation to a patient's religious expectations regarding end-of-life care. Included among these is the Muslim prohibition against touching a dying patient's body. These protocols, increased physician and nurse attentiveness and knowledge, the contribution made by researchers such as Cohen and Chan, and artifacts like the Pastoral Service "Guideline for Families" all point to efforts to adapt religious expectations to end-of-life care. Part of this challenge, which was recognized by Chan in the course of her research, remained unaddressed: that is, the avenues for understanding both a patient's spiritual concerns (which might not be directly related to a religious tradition) alongside the ways in which Pastoral Services, volunteers, and researchers could better understand expectations with regard to religious heritage.

Studies focused on the treatment of dementia in Jewish and non-Jewish medical institutions have found differences that may derive from Jewish views of end-of-life care. Jewish ethical responses to the gravely ill—even those understood to have reached *goses*, to be actively dying—resist medical treatment "judged as futile, which can be withdrawn or withheld." Following from this, when there is no evidence of feeding being beneficial, there "would be no reason to artificially feed a dying patient" (Jotkowitz 2005, 883). Still, studies comparing practices in Israeli hospitals with both Jewish and non-Jewish institutions in Montreal and Canada found that the use of feeding tubes for patients in end-stage dementia was highest in Israel, lower in Jewish Canadian hospitals, but lowest by far in non-Jewish Canadian institutions. The authors of this study suggest that even with the understanding that "futile therapy is not to be offered to a patient in the actual process of dying (*goses*)," for Jews, "fluids and food are not considered 'disproportionate' therapies" as they might be "in Catholic terminology" (Clarfield 2006, 625).

Case Study: End of Life and Change in Jewish Communal Custom in Canada

Jewish life in Canada has undergone great change since its inception. The earliest immigrants were a well-assimilated merchant class who involved themselves with the colonial economy and administration. This group was swamped by a large wave of Eastern European immigration in the late nineteenth and early twentieth century. These immigrants, coming largely from Russian Poland and other parts of the Czarist empire, were largely Yiddish speaking, often working-class, with observant or left idealist tendencies that reflected the variety in pre-emigration Eastern European Jewish life. The early dominance of Montreal as a kind of *hoiptshtot*, or Jewish capital city, has since been overshadowed by the size and wealth of Toronto's community, as well as by the increased influence of wealthy and diverse communities in Calgary and Vancouver. This case study focuses on the end-of-life decisions made regarding a fifty-five-year-old Calgary-born woman I will call B. B's cultural and religious background follows the above template; her grandparents' home was observant, her own childhood home was not, and there existed, in her adult years, no relationship with any form of organized Jewish communal or religious life. Though affected by a childhood case of cerebral palsy, and at one time institutionalized for what doctors diagnosed as a manic-depressive disorder, B lived alone in a downtown Calgary apartment, which was not far from the house where her grandparents had raised her mother. B's complicated medical history included chain-smoking, long-term use of lithium, and in later years heavy reliance by her general practitioner on anxiety-reducing drugs. The effect of the latter was notable in her weight gain, which in the last years of her life doubled her size from one hundred pounds to nearly two hundred. B's health declined in the final two years of her life; she was admitted to acute care wards for respiratory illness; and, finally, rushed to a major Calgary hospital, unconscious, with what was diagnosed as a brain inflammation. In the intensive care unit, B entered a comatose state, the cause of which doctors could not understand but eventually attributed to a possible virus that had grossly inflamed portions of her brain. It was confirmed, after a number of days of careful attention, that the comatose state had become a persistent vegetative state. B's medical history, in particular her cerebral palsy, seemed indicative, but did not allow physicians to confirm either the source or any possible cure for her condition. Pastoral Services on the acute floor included a volunteer representative with a pamphlet informing families of availability of counseling, but no representatives of religious faiths in the city made contact with B's family.

A period of dialogue between family members and medical staff ensued. Some of the questions raised included: Was B aware of her surroundings? How catastrophic was the damage to her brain? What was the likelihood of her recovering consciousness? If she were to do this, what would her condition be? Doctors on the intensive care unit conveyed the extent of the damage, the unlikelihood of recovery, and the minimal state B would find herself in if she escaped the vegetative state. For a further opinion, the case documents were sent to a brain surgeon in the United States, who was most emphatic that B could not recover from the injury to her brain caused by the inflammation.

Near the end of these investigations the ICU staff began to convey the need to move B to a lower level of care, which would lead to a kind of warehousing of her during the course of the vegetative state. Discussions with doctors and nurses confirmed the lack of options for this as well as the prospects: long-term life support with no hope of recovery and the absence of attentive care like that offered on the ICU floor. Once all family members with involvement in B's life had been consulted, the decision was made to do three things: lower the input from the ventilator that B had been on since arriving at the ICU, continue feeding, and increase the dose of morphine to ensure pain relief. B's energy waned. Her breathing slowed and in a matter of days she died.

Nothing was done in this case that contravenes a wide range of Jewish ideals and law regarding end-of-life care. Even the common Orthodox injunction that nothing be done to hasten death while nothing be done to impede it was acknowledged. One of B's relatives insisted on staying in the room with her as she neared death and was there when she died. This ensured that the dying person not be left alone and mirrored the biblical story of Jacob gathering his sons to him, though B, catastrophically ill, could not symbolically place her feet on the floor and offer a "charge" to her family. One of the medical writers cited in this essay might recognize in B's death her encounter with aspects of what he refers to as Jacob's experience of "the first 'hospice' death in recorded history. When he became ill, there was no unnecessary medical intervention. Jacob was surrounded by his loved ones . . . following which he died peacefully" (Kinzbrunner 2004, 559). In the time that B was *goses*—actively dying— medical attendance ensured only that she was in no discomfort, and the family member, acting like the maidservant of Rabbi Hanasi, took the role of doorkeeper, preventing distractions or interruptions to the process of a natural death. Even though the "sages prohibited one from ever touching a *goses*," Orthodox responsa have acknowledged that this should not prevent routine procedures that allow for feeding and other basic needs (Kinzbrunner 2004, 564). Although the decisions regarding B's care were made without the involvement of any kind of religious advisor, they reflect a number of key Jewish attitudes toward the final stages of life. These include the urge to prevent unnecessary suffering through pain relief; the desire for a "natural" death, or, as Marc Angel writes, a "return, at least in some measure, to the old style of dying" (Angel 1986, 18). The fact that B, years before her death, had expressed the wish not to be "kept alive like a vegetable" informed the family discussions. The absence of a rabbi in the discussions is notable. The need for one was never raised, either by the family or the medical staff (who may not have been aware of B's cultural and religious background). B herself was in no way religious. And although the family included observant members, none of the people involved in the decisions associated with B's care were observant in the conventional sense. Ethics, respect for B's wishes, a regard for the hope that she might recover, and the need to be well-informed and to understand her condition were the crucial factors in play. Upon B's death, the prospect of an autopsy was raised to further understand the nature of the virus that had attacked her brain. But no guarantee was forthcoming as to how quickly this could be done, which risked contravention of the Jewish expectation that the dead be buried within twenty-four hours. The autopsy was not performed, and B was buried in a Calgary Jewish cemetery the day after her death.

Notes

1. The Talmud, a collection of rabbinical debates on matters of Jewish law, with both legalistic and narrative components, was created in ancient Palestine and Babylonia between 600 and 400 CE. It is based on what is understood to be an accumulation of oral law and lore gathered from 500 BCE to 200 BCE. It forms the basis of observant or orthodox Judaism and ranges over discussions of law detailed in the Bible, commentary on it, and further rabbinic discussion of philosophy, domestic relations, medicine, and stories regarding rabbinic figures. Talmudic discourse is characterized by dialogue, what one might refer to as a give and take over a biblical text or item of law. The Talmud codifies this formal debate. Responsa are the replies offered by leading scholars to questions regarding legalistic questions, which represent the ongoing debate over established questions.

2. The Reform movement appeared in nineteenth-century Germany and promoted a "liberal, rational, and universalist philosophy." It downplayed the use of Hebrew prayer as well as Zionism. In Canada, these antitraditional views have been tempered so that while Reform temples focus on interfaith dialogue and welcome mixed marriage couples, they have become "more ethnic, more open to Israel" (Weinfeld 2001, 297). The Conservative movement is a late-nineteenth-century American development, which aimed for a middle ground between Reform and Orthodoxy.

North American Judaism is further divided between Ashkenazi, or European-descended Jews, and Sephardim, who trace their ancestry to the Jews expelled from Spain and Portugal under the Inquisition. Their geographical connections are often to the West Indies, Israel, North Africa, and other parts of the Middle East. The Hebrew words refer to Germany and Spain, respectively.

3. A booklet produced by the American National Institute on Aging stumbles over some of these issues. Though the booklet aims to explain and promote hospice care, it does frame such care in a "nothing more can be done" framework noxious to some Orthodox Jews. Though the language is moderate, it could send an unappealing message: "At some point, curative medical treatment may no longer make sense—it might not help or may actually make the patient more uncomfortable. *Hospice* is designed for this situation. The patient beginning

hospice care understands that his or her illness is not responding to medical attempts to cure it or to slow the disease's progress. . . . In hospice, attempts to cure the person's illness are stopped" (24). The booklet does acknowledge, as do Jewish writers on hospice care, that "stopping treatment specifically aimed at curing an illness does not mean discontinuing all treatment"; and "[c]hoosing hospice does not have to be a permanent decision" (25). Notable in the booklet, is the tendency to raise spiritual questions without any direct address to major American religious traditions. Pull quotes throughout the booklet avoid source material from these traditions and quote instead from Leonardo da Vinci (31) and African and Tuscarora sayings (17, 62). Meant to offend no one, these choices miss an opportunity to include a discussion of Jewish, Christian, or Islamic observant views as they relate to end-of-life care.

4. The custom of ethical wills remains common, especially in families influenced by a prewar Eastern European outlook. My paternal great-grandfather, Yale Shapiro, whose Russian youth was capped by years spent in Calgary, wrote the following will in Yiddish in 1956, before his death in 1957. The translation is by his youngest daughter, mentioned in the will:

> My dearest children, dear sons-in-law, dear daughters-in-law, wonderful grandchildren and great grandchildren. I hope your life is filled with good health and much happiness. My dearest, I'm writing to you as a memory for later. No one lives forever. I want to tell you about my life in my later years. The good things and the bad things. The good things are that I'm 93 years old and still enjoy good health and a clear mind. All my children and their families are here from Russia, feel fine, making a good living and have wonderful children. Also my dear youngest daughter, Vera, and her family moved to Calgary and is with us all and are happy and making a fine living. This thank God is all good. The not so good is that I'm alone without my dear partner, your mother Leah, for 21 years and this is a very great loss. Also that my two wonderful daughters, Rivka and Ethel, have gone at such an early age. But you can't question God, as his judgment is always right and you have to accept it.
>
> Dearest children, I want to thank you all for helping to make my life more comfortable and making it possible for me to go to shul every day and do my volunteer work for the deceased, Israel and our shul. For all this I bless you and thank you and wish you much nachus from your children. I want to thank so much my good son Joe and Roske for trying his best to make my life easier by collecting from all the children and giving me a cheque every month enough to live on. I also want to thank my good daughter, Sorke, for helping me to make my old years more comfortable.

My dearest children, I'm asking all of you that before mine and your Mother's Yahrtzeit you should all give to Joe $5.00 to send to Rabbi Gourary in New York for the Yeshiva in Lod Israel. My dearest children, I wish that you all will live as always, in peace and harmony as a close family. Give to charity as much as you can as all this helps to be a better person. Be good Jews and a good mensh.

   I kiss you all and bless you all. . . .
   Your father, grandfather and great grandfather
   Yale Shapiro

References

Abramovitch, H. 1987. Death. In *Contemporary Jewish religious thought*, ed. A. A. Cohen and P. Mendes-Flohr, 131–35. New York: Free Press.

Afilalo, Rabbi R. 2009. Personal interview. Aug. 24.

Angel, M. 1986. Halacha and Hospice. *Journal of Halacha and Contemporary Society* XII (Autumn): 17–26.

Attaran, A., and M. Stanbrook, M. 2008. Ending life with grace and agreement. *Canadian Medical Association Journal* 178(9): 1115–16.

Bar-Levav, A. 2008. Death and the dead. In *The YIVO encyclopedia of Jews in Eastern Europe*, ed. Gershon David Hundert, 2 vols., 396–99. New Haven: Yale University Press.

Borowski, M. 2000. Hospice care. *Jewish Action* (Winter) n.p.

Carse, J. P. 1980. *Death and existence: A conceptual history of human mortality.* New York: John Wiley and Sons.

Clarfield, A. M. et al. 2006. Enteral feeding in end-stage dementia: A comparison of religious, ethnic, and national differences in Canada and Israel. *Journal of Gerontology* 61(A6): 621–27.

Clark, D. 2001. Religion, medicine, and community in the early origins of St. Christopher's Hospice. *Journal of Palliative Medicine* 4(3): 353–60.

———. 2005. *Cicely Saunders: Founder of the hospice movement. Selected letters 1959–1999.* New York: Oxford University Press.

Cohen, A. 1971. *The Soncino Chumash: The five books of Moses with Haphtaroth.* London: Soncino Press.

Cohen, R. 2009. Personal interview. Sept 25.

———. et al. 2002. What determines the quality of life of terminally ill cancer patients from their own perspective? *Journal of Palliative Care* 18(1): 48–58.

Daniel. 1993. *The HarperCollins Study Bible.* New York: HarperCollins, 1303–28.

Dorff, E. N. 1991. A Jewish approach to end-stage medical care. *Conservative Judaism* XLIII(3) (Spring): 3–51.

du Boulay, S. 2007. *Cicely Saunders: The founder of the modern hospice movement.* London: Society for Promoting Christian Knowledge.

Encyclopaedia Judaica. 2007. 2nd ed. Detroit: Keter.

Golbert, R. 2006. Judaism and death: Finding meaning in ritual. In *Death and religion in a changing world*, ed. K. Garces-Foley, 45–68. New York: M. E. Sharpe.

Hundert, G. D., ed. 2008. *The YIVO encyclopedia of Jews in Eastern Europe.* 2 vols. New Haven: Yale University Press.

Jewish General Hospital Pastoral Services. 2009. A guideline for families of dying Jewish patients. Montreal: Jewish General Hospital Pastoral Services.

Jotkowitz, A., et al. 2005. The care of patients with dementia: A modern Jewish ethical perspective. *Journal of the American Geriatrics Society* 53: 881–4.

Kashani, R. 2007. Death. In *Encyclopaedia Judaica*, 2nd ed., 510–13. Detroit: Keter.

Kinzbrunner, B. M. 2004. Jewish medical ethics and end-of-life care. *Journal of Palliative Medicine* 7(4): 558–73.

Kolsky, K. 2008. *End of life: Helping with comfort and care.* Bethesda: National Institute on Aging.

Kottek, S. 1999. The Jewish Hospice. In *Illness and health in the Jewish tradition*, ed. D. Freeman et al., 162–65. Philadelphia: Jewish Publication Society.

Kugelmass, J. 2006. Introduction. In *Key texts in American Jewish culture*, 3–21. New Brunswick: Rutgers University Press.

Mackler, A. L. 2003. *Introduction to Jewish and Catholic bioethics: A comparative analysis.* Washington, DC: Georgetown University Press.

Millen, R. L. 2007. Kaddish. In *Encyclopaedia Judaica*, 2nd ed., 695–98. Detroit: Keter.

Neufeld, J. 2008. Golubchuk case leaves ethical questions unanswered. Christianweek.org 22.9.

Oppenheim, M. 2006. *Jewish philosophy and psychoanalysis.* Oxford: Lexington Books.

Shternsis, A. 2008. Beggars and begging. In *The YIVO Encyclopedia of Jews in Eastern Europe*, ed. Gershon David Hundert, 2 vols., 136–38. New Haven: Yale University Press.

Singer, I. B. 1990. Gimpel the Fool. In *The Norton anthology of short fiction*, 4th ed., ed. R. V. Cassill, 1477–89. New York: W. W. Norton.

———. Gimpl Tam. 1963. In *Gimpl Tam un andere Dertseilungen*, 5–17. New York: Central Yiddish Culture Organization.

Solomon, S. 2008. End-of-life war outlives Golubchuk. *National Review of Medicine* 5(7). www.national reviewofmedicine.com/issue/2008/07/5.

Union for Reform Judaism. 1995. Compassionate and comfort care decisions at end of life. urj.org/Articles/index.cjm?id=7228.

Weinfeld, M. 2001. *Like everyone else . . . but different: The paradoxical success of Canadian Jews.* Toronto: McClelland and Stewart.

Zalkin, M. 2008. Charity. In *The YIVO encyclopedia of Jews in Eastern Europe,* ed. Gershon David Hundert, 2 vols., 306–09. New Haven: Yale University Press.

6

Dying Well in Christianity

Janet Soskice

The Christian movement, from the outset, has been characterized by diversity. Inspired by the life, death, and resurrection of Jesus of Nazareth, it offers a healing and redemptive pattern of living. It has been central in the founding of hospices, hostels, and care of the sick, the poor, and the disadvantaged. Evolving through many cultures and times, it finds expression in a wide variety of creedal, doctrinal, theological, artistic, and liturgical idioms.

In the Gospels, Jesus tells his disciples to "cure the sick, raise the dead, cleanse the lepers, cast out demons," and as they go, to "proclaim the good news, 'The kingdom of heaven has come near'" (Matt. 10:7–8; compare Luke 10:9). Caring for the sick, the outcast, the poor is not what one does to earn one's way into an afterlife but a sign that, however partially, the follower of Christ is already in some way sharing in the kingdom of God. In its biblical context, the Christian belief in the resurrection of the body is not to be uncoupled from hope for the coming of the Kingdom, and the exercise of justice and mercy in working for this great end. There are no absolutely universal and obligatory actions or rituals to be observed near or on the death of a Christian. There are, however, shared core beliefs which inform Christian understandings of a good death, to which I will return.

The Christian faith arose among Jews in first century Palestine who believed that Jesus of Nazareth was the promised Messiah of Israel. The writings and missionary voyages of St. Paul (d. 67 CE) promoted the new movement as one open to Jews and Gentiles alike. Consensus was reached over the first two centuries of the movement on the authority of certain central sacred writings: the four Gospels (Matthew, Mark, Luke, and John), the letters of St. Paul and some other authors. Along with these works of the "New" Testament, Christians retained a number of Jewish writings (called the "Old Testament" by Christians) as authoritative holy scriptures. Christianity's origins are thus Eastern and Semitic, and for many decades, possibly several centuries, these followers of Jesus were not differentiated and did not differentiate themselves from other Jews. Christians, however, believe that the Word, through which all things were made, "became flesh" (incarnate) in Christ Jesus, who through his death and resurrection brought salvation (healing restoration of union with God) to the world. The Nicene Creed, formulated in 325 CE and accepted by most Christian groups as constitutive of orthodoxy, confesses belief in God, in the saving work of Christ, and in the gift of the Spirit, and concludes with the proclamation that "we look for the resurrection of the dead and the life of the world to come."

In its first two centuries, the Christian movement quickly spread through the Greek-speaking lands of the eastern Mediterranean, across North Africa through Egypt and Libya to what is now Tunisia, and eastward across what is now Syria, Turkey, Iran, and Iraq. By 245 CE, a date when Northern Europeans were still painting themselves blue and kidnapping brides, there were already twenty-four Christian bishoprics in the Tigris-Euphrates valley. Hungary, by contrast, was not Christianized until around the year 1000.

This diversity needs mentioning because it is all too easy to have before our eyes a picture that tethers each of the "world" religions in one place, with Christianity in Europe and the European diaspora. But prior to the rise of Islam in the seventh century, most of North Africa, as well as the eastern lands spreading through what is now Turkey, Syria, and Iraq, were Christian. This ancient diversity of Christian life and practice continues today, for instance with the Copts in Egypt, the Syriac-speaking church of the East, the ancient Syro-Malabar Church of south India, and the Greek and Russian Orthodox communions. Each of these groups has its own practices and rituals to do with death and dying. Indeed, in an immigrant nation such as Canada, the same Catholic congregations might have worshippers from Nigeria, Mexico, Bavaria, and Sicily whose cultural religious practices surrounding death and dying differ considerably one from another.

The hospice movement as pioneered by Cicely Saunders (see ch. 1) was formed around her own Christian belief, although conceived from the outset for the benefit of all. The Christian churches continue to be active throughout the world with the care, both physical and spiritual, of the dying, as other chapters in this volume attest. In consequence, many specialist volumes have been written by theologians on the topic of death and dying. Busy clinicians will also benefit from conversations with chaplains, as well as the excellent reports (increasingly available online) produced under the aegis of the churches by groups of professionals including chaplains, hospice workers, bereavement counselors, nurses, and physicians.

A good example at the time of writing is *A Practical Guide to the Spiritual Care of the Dying Person: Consultation Draft* (Catholic Bishops' Conference of England and Wales 2010). I discuss this guide briefly here as a well-presented example of a Christian organization's attempt to educate health professionals on a range of matters related to spiritual care of the dying.

The above-mentioned guide was produced by the Catholic Bishops of England and Wales to assist health care staff "to provide good spiritual care at the end of life." The guidelines are based on the Liverpool Care Pathway, a framework incorporating the principles of the hospice movement. Explicit reference is made to "spiritual needs" (cf. Saunders's "spiritual pain"), and in keeping with hospice palliative care philosophy, the guidelines are devised for health workers and patients in general, regardless of religious belief or practice. A first section deals with "Providing Spiritual Care," the second with "Ethical Issues at the End of Life," the third, entitled "Respecting the Mystery," discusses shock and mourning, both of the bereaved and of the one who is dying, and the fourth, "Faith-Specific Needs," deals with the care of Catholic patients.

The first section is most relevant to our volume. Under the general heading of "Providing Spiritual Care," it discusses, among other things, the need to keep care personal and to watch out for signs of "spiritual distress." A list of indicators of "spiritual pain" is provided, which includes such indicators as fear of falling asleep and not waking, crying out to God, feeling lost, questioning the purpose of suffering, and asking for spiritual help. Rather than emphasizing the complexity of spiritual needs, the *Guide* suggests that many small things provided by nursing staff are of importance here—using the patient's name (keeping it personal), taking time, waiting for labored replies and behaving sympathetically to those with reduced capacity to communicate, ensuring proper privacy, and, where appropriate, providing physical touch. In one memorable phrase the *Guide* says, "Death is not so much a private affair as a social one. We share a common humanity if not always a common faith and warm human contact can help a patient who feels afraid as their life draws to a close" (Bishops' Conference 2010, 8). Personal or sentimental items and religious items such as prayer books or crosses may be important, especially when holding these brings solace and is, in its own way, a prayer for those otherwise too weak to pray.

The second section of the Bishops' Conference *Guide* considers ethical issues at the end of life (withdrawal of treatment, assisted nutrition and hydration, and so on). The third considers the "shock" of death to the patient and his or her family and friends. Emphasis here is put on being attentive to the "whole person" in the process of dying and on the importance of seeing death as part of life and not as simply medical failure. The fourth and final section is faith-specific, giving guidelines, again addressed to those of all faith or none, for "caring for the Catholic patient." In addition, Web site links are provided for information on caring for Hindu, Bahai, Jewish, Muslim, and Sikh patients.

Having pointed readers to the existence of concise and readily available resources for quick use, it remains for me as a Christian theologian to provide a framework for questions that arise when considering "good death in hospice care" from a Christian point of view. I hope to show something of the unity of Christian belief in God, the moral life, and expectations for life after death.

Understanding Christian Beliefs about Death and Dying

It is quite natural for anyone coming to a faith tradition that is new or little known to them to seize upon a few specialist religious terms— *karma, atonement, jihad, sin, resurrection*—and to seek clarification of each individually. No approach is likely to be more misleading. Not for nothing do social scientists speak of "belief systems," and Christianity, too, whatever else it may be, is a belief system where what is believed about God and creation affects what is believed about human pain and suffering, moral life, and final destiny. To begin, I will say something of *Christianity and the individual,* with reference to the teaching that each human being is made *in the image of God.* This will be followed by case study one. Building on this will be a discussion of those teachings, anchored in the Bible, that most inform Christian attitudes to sickness, death, and dying. Notable among these is the Christian belief in *the resurrection,* both of Jesus and of the faithful. I will draw threads together from the whole chapter with a second case study of an Anglican woman who died, aged, ninety-nine, in 2009, before some concluding comments.

Christianity and the Individual

Even among those who are committed Christians there can be no rigid template for a good death. We all come into life as roughly the same squalling bundle of possibilities, but by the time we take leave of it, most of us are marked by loves and losses, triumphs and defeats that will make each death, like the life that preceded it, entirely unique. If we consider a glade of beech trees in autumn we know that every leaf will fall, but how each falls will be the result of its previous season. Each tree has been subject to particular conditions of drought and inundation. Each leaf, while genetically identical to others on the same tree, has been formed in circumstances of sunshine and shade that, by definition, no other leaf can have shared. It will fade and dry into a certain shape, be marked with distinctive colors and, on falling, be caught by a particular wind, twisted in a particular updraft before settling to the earth. Its descent sums up a million contingencies, as does each human life and death.

This analogy highlights a distinctive aspect of Christian teaching—distinctive, that is, not from the teachings of its sister religions of Judaism or Islam, but certainly from some of the various philosophical "ways" current at the time of Christian origins—and this is Christianity's concern for the particular, and especially for the particular human being. In some belief systems the individual is subsumed in the destiny of the family or the cult. The Abrahamic faiths, with their emphasis on God as Creator of all, understand their god to be a God who cares about everything *in particular.*

This has implications for dying *well.* Human lives are not generic and nor are their endings. The template given for the human being in Jewish and Christian scriptures is that the human being "is in the image of God." This scarcely provides a restrictive delineation of human nature but rather, if anything, keeps it open to mystery—God is mystery, and the human being in God's image is a mystery.

The "Sanctity of Life" and the "Image of God"

The media and even the churches, when addressing the question of Christian teachings on life and death, usually bring in the notion of "the sanctity of life." As well as being ambiguous (are animals included? what about viruses?) this phrasing has, as far as I can see, no fixed Biblical root or deep presence in historical theology. Where reverence for human life is concerned, the directive teaching as found in the Bible would seem to be that the human being "is made in the image of God." I will return to the *imago dei*, but for the moment note that it has been the basis in Christian teaching regarding every human being, no matter how poor, burdened, or even dissolute, as entirely distinctive and worthy of reverence.

Christian Teachings on Sin, Sickness, and Death

The New Testament has a complex attitude to physical disability, illness, suffering, and death. These are not to be seen as punishment for sin. The decisive text for this historically has been the Gospel of John 9:2, where the disciples ask Jesus, "Rabbi, who sinned, this man or his parents, that he was born blind?" to which Jesus answers, "Neither this man nor his parents sinned; he was born blind so that God's works might be revealed in him" (John 9:2–3, NRSV).[1] On the other hand, death is an enemy, and one Paul believes Jesus Christ, in dying and being raised from the dead, has defeated (2 Tim.1:10). The Easter services in most Christian churches proclaim that, by his dying, Christ conquered death. The author of the letter known as Hebrews identifies death with the devil, arguing that Jesus shared our flesh and blood "so that through death he might destroy the one who has the power of death, that is, the devil, and free those who all their lives were held in slavery by the fear of death" (Heb. 2:14). Pain in the New Testament appears not to be the will of God but the work of the devil (although God mysteriously "allows" pain). A general picture may be discerned of a world that is disordered, out of line, and which suffers and groans awaiting its day of salvation. Individual suffering is not necessarily to be explained by individual wrongdoing but, as with the man born blind, our individual wrongdoings contribute to corporate disorder.

The ministry of Jesus was characterized by healings from sickness (Matt. 9:35), raising from the dead, and casting out of unclean spirits. According to the Gospel writers, his disciples were called to share this work (Matt. 10:1), even to the point of raising the dead.[2]

The marvel of these healings might seem to us to be their apparent violation of the laws of nature, but this is modern anachronism and not the point of the gospel writers. At the time of Jesus and Paul the general public had no difficulty believing in miraculous cures. The Gospels themselves suggest that people other than Jesus and his followers could heal and cast out demons. The significance of Jesus's healing miracles for the New Testament writers lies not in their outlandishness but in their perceived role as signs of the emergence of a new reign (or kingdom) of God, with Jesus as the anticipated Messiah. Thus, when, in Matthew's Gospel, the imprisoned John the Baptist sends his followers to ask Jesus "Are you the one who is to come, or are we to wait for another?" Jesus answers with direct reference to the Old Testament prophet, Isaiah: "Go and tell John what you hear and see: the blind receive their sight, the lame walk, the lepers are cleansed, the deaf hear, the dead are raised, and the poor have good news brought to them" (Matt. 11:2–5).[3] The disciples share in this healing ministry.

But healing is not only by prayer and miracle. The Parable of the Good Samaritan in Luke 10 was of decisive importance to the theologians of the early church. In this story a traveler is beaten up and left for dead on the road to Jericho. A priest and a Levite, both members of respected Jewish groups, passed the wounded man without wanting to be bothered by stopping. A member of a despised Samaritan community then came along, took compassion on the victim, bound his wounds, and made arrangements for him to be looked after at an inn at the Samaritan's own expense. In conclusion, Jesus asks his disciples, which one of these men was the neighbor to the fallen man. The story was important in early Christian teaching not least because it was understood to speak allegorically about Jesus himself: Jesus himself was seen to be the one who stopped to assist the man who had been beaten, robbed, and left half-dead on the road to Jericho. The oil and wine used by the Samaritan to dress the wounds anticipate the bread and wine of the Christian sacraments. Jesus was the "true Physician" whose gifts of bread and wine (his body and blood) were the true medicaments. Other medications, however, were equally important, and on a less allegorical level the Parable of the Good Samaritan was, and is, understood to suggest that care for the stranger should be blind to merit, kinship, or gain. Nor is there any question of the Samaritan requiring of the victim (presumably a Jew, since he was coming down from Jerusalem) any conversion or even thanks. This was the answer Jesus gave to the question "And who is my neighbor?" (Luke 10:29).

In many ways Christian admonitions care for the sick, suffering, and dying were simply continuations of Jewish ones: care for the widows and orphans, the stranger ("hospice" and "hospital" derive from the Latin for hospitality). Early Christians believed that Jesus would return, even within their lifetime, to inaugurate his new kingdom, and consequently felt an "end of times" urgency which informed their practice.

This was noted by others. The philosopher and convert Aristides, in an "apology" delivered on behalf of the Christians to the emperor in the first part of the second century, gives this summary of life among the Christians:

> [W]hen they see a stranger, they take him in to their homes and rejoice over him as a very brother; for they do not call them brethren after the flesh, but brethren after the spirit and in God. . . . And if there is among them any that is poor and needy, and if they have no spare food, they fast two or three days in order to supply to the needy their lack of food. They observe the precepts of their Messiah with much care, living justly and soberly as the Lord their God commanded them. (Aristides, trans. J. R. Harris 1913, 277)

The end of time was delayed, but care for the poor and sick continued. Guenter Risse, in his history of hospitals, *Mending Bodies, Saving Souls,* discusses at length the calamity that hit Edessa, in what is now eastern Turkey, in 499. Citing William Wright's nineteenth-century account of the story of Joshua the Stylite, Risse describes a desolate period in which droughts, agricultural failure, and plagues emptied the villages. Those who could walk fled to the cities where they begged and died in great numbers. The bishop, Eusebius, went personally to the emperor in Constantinople to appeal for emergency funds and supplies for these newcomers, who were to be found "wailing by night and day from the pangs of hunger, and their bodies wasted away . . . the whole city was full of them and they began to die in the porticoes and in the streets" (William Wright, cited in Risse 1999, 71). Joshua the Stylite, who chronicled the unfolding disaster, wrote of dead bodies of women and children in the streets, and that two priests "established an infirmary among the buildings attached to the Great Church of Edessa. Those who were very ill used to go in and lie down there; and many bodies were found in the infirmary in which they were buried" (Risse 1999, 74–75). Despite this and other measures from church and community leaders and Greek soldiers, many of those in the infirmaries "still 'died by a painful and melancholy death,' although surrounded by those devoted to their care" (73).

Incarnation and Resurrection

Christians believe that Jesus was not just a messenger of God or another prophet, but God himself, dwelling in humankind in the flesh (God "incarnate"). The doctrine of incarnation reconfigured Christian under-standing of the *imago dei*. As already noted, the Book of Genesis taught that the human being was made "in the image of God," but in the New Testament, St. Paul carries this teaching in a new direction by identify-ing Jesus as the true image, indeed "the image of the invisible God" (Col.1:15; see also 2 Cor. 4:4). All human beings, it is held, share this image, and (decisively for the developing Christian faith in matters of care for the poor or the sick) what is done for anyone in need is done for Christ. A central text here has been Matthew 25, sometimes called the Last Judgment. There is a long sequence of teaching on the kingdom of heaven in which Jesus says:

> Then the king will say to those at his right hand, "Come, you that are blessed by my Father, inherit the kingdom prepared for you from the foundation of the world; for I was hungry and you gave me food, I was thirsty and you gave me something to drink, I was a stranger and you welcomed me, I was naked and you gave me clothing, I was sick and you take care of me, I was in prison and you visited me." (Matt. 25:34–36)

Jesus clarifies for his puzzled audience that whatever service they do for the "least of his brethren" they do for him. This scripture has been foundational to the Christian conviction that one should see Christ in every person in need. The encounter of St. Francis with the lepers and the work of Mother Theresa of Calcutta are two memorable instances.

As those with even minimal acquaintance with Christianity will know, Jesus, understood by Christians to be the author of life, did not save himself from death. Indeed, he died a particularly painful and humiliating death, understood by his followers as an atoning death for the sin of the world. This tortured death is often represented in Christian art, sometimes to the consternation of modern viewers. One of the most shocking images of the death of Jesus is the Isenheim altarpiece (1512–16) of Matthias Grünewald. When the altarpiece wings are closed, the viewer is confronted with a savage portrayal of a lifeless Christ on the cross, his body not only wounded but gaunt, pallid, covered with sores. The distortion of the body, almost to the point of decomposition, is far in excess, we might think, of even the trauma a body would suffer in death by crucifixion. Yet we cannot "see" this painting without knowing that the altarpiece was painted for a hospice chapel. The order of monks to whom it belonged, the Antonites, was founded to care for the sick, especially by establishing hospices. At Isenheim, the community was famous for their work with those suffering from skin diseases and especially *ignis plaga,* or St. Anthony's Fire—ergotism. By the late sixteenth century the cause of this disorder was known to be poisoned rye, but at the time Grünewald executed his commission its cause was unknown. Victims had blackened limbs, gangrenous hands and feet, and suffered deforming muscular spasms (Haym 1989, 20–21). Before this altarpiece the ailing could map their own physical distress and disfigurement on that of the body of their crucified God—as could those who were caring for them. When the panels were opened they could see a gloriously risen Christ, his skin freed from sores.

Before the advent of modern medicine, hospice care offered little more than shelter, nourishment, kindness, and simple remedies.[4] The ill and the elderly would, for the most part, be looked after in their own homes, with physicians attending. The hospices catered for the indigent. They were also shelters for outcasts, victims of illnesses whose contagion or deforming symptoms terrified the general populace. In the hospice the afflicted would not only find what physical solace was available, but, as Christians, could be eased of "spiritual pain" by recalling that Jesus, too, had been, after the words of the Prophet Isaiah, "despised, and rejected of men; a man of sorrows, and acquainted with grief" and that "we hid as it were our faces from him; he was despised, and we esteemed him not." (Is. 53:3, King James Version).

Resurrection and Life after Death

Death is not the end in the Christian story. I have said as yet little about Christian belief in life after death or, more properly, the resurrection of the body. It should be said at the outset that individual Christians today vary widely as to how large this belief looms in their spiritual landscape— some find it of immense solace while others, equally devout, think relatively little about it or perhaps wonder if the belief is not incompatible with a modern scientific worldview. Many regard "what happens next" as a quiet horizon of hope—another aspect of the trust in God they experience in daily life but not necessarily highly theorized. When asked what is important in their life of faith, Christians speak of the love of God, their experience of Christian community, of healing and empowerment, of hope in adversity, the power of prayer—in short, being a Christian is felt as a source of blessing and new life in the here and now, which, God willing, will continue after death. Indeed, from the theological perspective, the Christian has already "died" in the waters of baptism and risen to new life in Christ, a life that does not end with death.

For the writers of the Gospels, St. Paul, and the theologians of the early church, the resurrection of Jesus from the dead was the essence of the "good news" and bound up with the promise that his followers, too, would be raised to eternal life. The Book of Acts describes the disciples, after the death of Jesus, as proclaiming the resurrection of the dead in Jesus (Acts 4:2). St. Paul makes the resurrection of Jesus central to his teaching and to Christian hope: "If Christ has not been raised," he writes in I Corinthians, "your faith is futile and you are still in your sins" (I Cor. 15:17). For Paul, belief that Jesus was the promised Messiah was inseparable from belief in his resurrection, and Christian hope for life after death inseparable from belief that Jesus was the Messiah.

Why was this so? It is not enough, as already mentioned, to say that the experience of a man rising from the dead was so unusual as to cause Jesus to be worshipped as God. And why was it that the followers of Jesus became so committed to the idea of life after death when Jews did not?[5] To begin to answer these questions we need to look to debates in Judaism at the time of the emergence of Christianity.

Discussion as to whether the dead would be raised seems to have arisen among Jews in the third and second centuries BCE. We know from the New Testament that the resurrection of the dead was a matter of dispute between the Pharisees and the Sadducees during the lifetime of Jesus, the Pharisees believing the dead would be raised, and the Sadducees not. This is the background to Mark 12 where Jesus is approached by some Sadducees:

> Teacher, Moses wrote for us that "if a man's brother dies, leaving a wife but no child, the man shall marry the widow and raise up children for his brother." There were seven brothers; the first married and, when he died, left no children; and the second married her and died, leaving no children; and the third likewise; none of the seven left children. Last of all the woman herself died. In the resurrection whose wife will she be? For the seven had married her. (Mark 12:19–23)

The Sadducees think they can catch Jesus out in unfaithfulness to the teaching of Moses for nowhere in the Torah (the books of the Bible that were held to have been written by Moses) does it say that the dead will be raised. They point out the logistical problems—will the dead marry or be married, what will they wear, and so on. Jesus's reply turns the tables and suggests that it is the Sadducees who have failed to understand Moses:

> Is not this the reason you are wrong, that you know neither the scriptures nor the power of God? For when they rise from the dead, they neither marry nor are given in marriage, but are like angels in heaven. And as for the dead being raised, have you not read in the book of Moses, in the story about the bush, how God said to him, "I am the God of Abraham, the God of Isaac, and the God of Jacob?" He is God not of the dead, but of the living; you are quite wrong. (Mark 12:24–27)

Jesus directs the Sadducees to Exodus 3, the encounter of Moses with God at the burning bush. There, after a request from Moses that

God give him a name, God replies "I AM WHO I AM" and then identifies himself with the name Jesus cites—"the God of Abraham, the God of Isaac, and the God of Jacob." The reasoning seems to be this: God identifies himself according to whose God he *is*, and this is "the God of Abraham, the God of Isaac, and the God of Jacob." These men therefore cannot be among the lost or dissolved but are among the living, even though by the time of Moses they had died. Since God is the God of the living, these men must be alive in a way we cannot conceive. Jesus does not abandon the teaching of Moses but seizes Moses for his side of the argument. It is worth noting that this passage from Exodus was also invoked by the rabbis, writing after Jesus but not thought to be indebted to him, in their defense of the resurrection of the dead (Levenson 2006, 28–29).

It appears that the previously little-considered question of the resurrection of the dead came to be a topic of debate among Jews as a result of the suffering and persecution they experienced in the centuries immediately before the common era. 2 Maccabees, a Jewish text written in the late second century BCE, tells the harrowing story of a mother arrested with her seven sons, whom the king attempts to force to eat pork. They declare that they would rather die than break the laws of their ancestors and, one by one, are tortured and slain in front of their mother. Before having his limbs cut off and being fried alive in a pan, the first son cites Moses, saying the Lord "will have compassion on his servants" (2 Mac. 7:6); the second, before dying in a similarly dreadful way, says that "the King of the universe will raise us up to an everlasting renewal of life, because we have died for his laws" (2 Mac. 7:9), and so on, each expressing belief in resurrection to life.

It is not a coincidence that the same period in which we see evidence of belief in the "raising of the dead" also saw developments in Jewish thought on creation, and particularly the consolidation of the belief in *creatio ex nihilo*. This teaching underscores that God freely creates everything, including time and space. We find in 2 Maccabees fairly clear insistence on the staples of *creatio ex nihilo*, in consort with growing interest in the possibility of resurrection. The mother of the seven martyred sons, for instance, expressly identifies the God who creates with the God can restore to new life. In 2 Mac. 7:28–29, she encourages her youngest son, "I beg you, my child, to look at the heaven and earth and see everything that is in them, and recognize that God did not make them out of things that existed. And in the same way the human race came into being. Do not fear this butcher, but prove worthy of your brothers. Accept death, so that in God's mercy I may get you back again along with your brothers." The connection is between a God who creates and a God who saves. Just as God made all that is in the first place, so God can raise from the dead.[6] The themes were not new—the Book of Psalms and Isaiah both have creation as a central theme and connect it with restoration and justice. The God who creates can save.[7]

It was this context of expectation into which Christianity was born. For the writers of the New Testament, and especially for Paul, belief in the resurrection of the dead is of a piece with expectation for a Messiah who was to bring justice to the poor and food for the hungry—the themes of the *Magnificat*, the song sung by Mary, mother of Jesus, in the opening chapter of the Gospel of Luke. Luke and the other gospel writers draw on Isaiah for "prophecies" of the one who restores sight to blind and makes the lame walk again. Jesus's miracles, including those in which he raises people from the dead show him as participating in the power of the Creator (Lazarus in John 11, Jairus's daughter in Luke 8). The Prologue to John's Gospel goes so far as to identify Jesus with the creative power of God as the Word, through whom all things were made.

Resurrection in the New Testament is thus not best seen as a private reward for a life lived well, but a sign of the even greater glory of the coming of the kingdom of God, a time of healing and justice when even the dead are not forgotten—thus St. Paul:

> For I am convinced that neither death, nor life, nor angels, nor rulers, nor things present, nor things to come, nor powers, nor height, nor depth, nor anything else in all creation, will be able to separate us from the love of God in Christ Jesus our Lord. (Rom. 8:38–39)

The collective "us" is important here, for Paul sees all the faithful as members of the one body of Christ, stones that go to build a living Temple to be the dwelling place of God. In Romans, Paul suggests that the redeeming of our bodies might be but a part of a restoration of creation—"We know that the whole creation has been groaning in labor pains until now: and not only the creation, but we ourselves, who have the first fruits of the Spirit, groan inwardly while we wait for adoption, the redemption of our bodies" (Rom. 8.22–23).

A Good Death: Case Study One

A good Christian death is not necessarily a physically painless one. Indeed, until very recently, and still in many parts of the world, it was not possible to afford much by way of pain relief to the dying, yet there are numerous stories of good deaths. Here is an account told to me recently by a friend.

Her husband was one of five brothers of a Catholic family. One became a monk but remained close to his brothers and to the nieces and nephews as they came along. My friend and her husband received word that the monk-brother, a vigorous man in his seventies, had had a slight stroke. The monastery physician was not worried but nonetheless thought he should go into hospital for a checkup. His family was told there was no need for concern, but one sister-in-law who, with her husband, lived a considerable distance away, felt uneasy. She was particularly close to her monastic brother-in-law who had helped her through some dark days. So she and her husband set out driving. En route, they received a message from the monastery that the hospital had detected a blood clot and feared it was serious. By the time they arrived, the monk was in a coma from which he was not likely to recover. His brother and sister-in-law stayed with him through the night, praying and singing religious songs. It happened that the following day was her birthday, and they prayed hard that the brother might last to that day—which he did, dying on his sister-in-law's birthday. None of the other siblings had been able to get to the bedside at short notice. As she concluded this story my friend, a university college principal, said of the deceased, "His guardian angel must have been working overtime to make him last to that birthday!"

There are a number of interesting facets to this story, and to why it was related to me as a good death. Although the death was unexpected, the monk died having led a good life and well loved. He himself very likely had no awareness his life was in danger, and no pain in dying. He was a man of prayer and close to a loving family and community. We might say that his death was "painless," both physically and spiritually, for him. But in telling the story my friend emphasized that it was a good death not mostly or even primarily because of its painlessness, but for those the dying man left behind. The "guardian angel" worked overtime on *their* behalf. They had time to be with him, to pray and recite prayers from the Catholic prayer book. They could be with him when he died and feel peace about what was at the same time a great wrench. His death was a time of spiritual growth, if not for him (but how can we know?) then certainly for his family and perhaps for those who cared for him in his final days. A good death does not concern only the one dying.

So this death has many of the marks of a good Christian death, but we could describe hundreds, thousands, and hundreds of thousands of others that are equally good, yet entirely different.

A Good Christian Death at Home: Case Study Two

How might these themes unfold in an individual Christian life? In persuading me to contribute to this project, Harold Coward reminded me that my husband and I had living with us my husband's ninety-eight-year-old aunt, Miss Effie Hunter; that hospice care was not just about what happened in patient hospices; and that our experience living with Effie might be important in the mix of our discussions. Effie was indeed raised in discussion at numerous times in our final project meeting and, in fact, died on its last day—aged ninety-nine years and seven months—and it is at the encouragement of the group and our editors that I include details of her life and last years.

Born in 1901, Effie was a lifelong and devoted member of the Anglican (Episcopal) Church. She never married (a boyfriend died in the war) and had a varied career driving ambulances during the war, as a social worker afterward (she knew Cicely Saunders at this time), and then as personal assistant to a bishop. As the only unmarried one of five brothers and sisters, it fell to Effie to help her mother nurse her father in his last years and then to look after her mother during the same process. In retirement she consecutively lived with (or had living with her) both of her sisters, whom she cared for during their last years. When the second sister died Effie, then aged ninety-one, moved to Cambridge to live with us. She had been very active up until this time, still driving at ninety, and in her first years would walk into the center of Cambridge on her own or take a bus to her church for services of worship. We had at this time young teenage children, cats, and a dog, and Effie fitted in well with this domestic mélange.

Having cared for others in their final years, Effie was insightful in thinking about her own. She kept active as long as she could, coursing the garden with a Zimmer frame when walking farther afield became impossible. With the onset of macular degeneration she began to memorize poetry so that she would have it "in her head" when she could no longer read. Regular attendance at a Friday communion service ("Eucharist") attended by a number of other elderly parishioners and followed by a simple lunch was the mainstay of her formal worship. Over the years, Effie became gradually weaker and more confined to her room. She was no longer able to get out to church, and the priest or his assistant came instead to our home where he said a brief version of the Eucharistic service and gave her communion. Sometimes other family members would share in this. During the Lord's Prayer, those present held hands together. For her private devotions she enjoyed having candles in her room and saying morning and evening prayer from her Anglican prayer book, circumstances permitting, with one of the family. Family members going on travels would return with crosses, icons, or blessed stones which she treasured as gifts, as she did photos of her extended family, living and dead.

When Effie was ninety-seven, we found her one morning slumped on the floor in her duvet. She was seriously weakened and could not move or say more than a few words at a time. Our family doctor came round and arranged for an X-ray, and also for teams of nurses to come in, morning and evening, to wash and care for Effie, who could no longer manage to use a commode. Her parish priest came by almost immediately for a service of anointing—this is now Christian practice, rather than what was called "last rites." It is a service of prayers, blessings, and anointing with blessed oil for the purpose of healing and strengthening, whether for recovery or for the passage into death. As was to happen, Effie lived a further eighteen months, without however recovering ability to move or to do anything for herself. The National Health Service provided a proper hospital bed with a self-inflating, on-the-move mattress to keep bed sores at bay, and this was put by a big bright window looking onto a garden. A routine set in with nurses, family (especially my husband and daughters), and student helpers from a local theological college who would come and give Effie lunch, read to her, and so on.

Because we knew Effie's pattern of religious life we were able to continue with what we knew she liked—candles, morning and evening prayer from her prayer book (regardless of the religious commitment or lack of it from the reader), the Lord's Prayer holding hands. The team from her church came regularly with communion, and the congregation also mentioned her in their regular cycle of prayer. We reminded Effie of the passing of the seasons as she saw them from her window, and of the seasons of the liturgical year—Christmas, Lent, Easter, Pentecost—all of which were resonant for her. Effie spoke very little but always with lucidity when she did speak. Long after she ceased speaking she was able to repeat the words of familiar prayers (the Lord's Prayer, the Benedictus, the Nunc Dimitis) when others were saying them with her. Our understanding was that Effie was mentally present to us, although very sleepy most of the time. Sometimes she seemed to take little in, other times a great deal. My husband, who as a painter had a studio in the home and was Effie's primary caregiver, read her most of the Old Testament (making illuminative use of a Jewish commentary as he went) and the New Testament twice in her last months, despite having hesitations about its contents himself. This was mixed in with other things we knew she enjoyed—twentieth-century history, memoirs, obituaries from the daily papers, and so on.

From former discussions I knew that Effie had a strong conviction in the life after death, but we rarely spoke about this—it was, rather, assumed. She was confident that God was with her in life and would be with her, in whatever manner that might be, after her death. It seemed evident to all who knew her that Effie was very happy to be alive but not at all afraid of dying. Having nursed so many people in their last months during her own active life she was the least demanding of patients in her own weakness.

Effie died in her own bed at home in November 2009. In her last weeks she experienced serious pain in being moved by the nurses, probably from a crumbling spine. Prior to that time she was on no medication, but the doctor now believed the level of pain Effie was experiencing was unacceptable and prescribed morphine. Effie died within weeks of beginning this new regime. The district nurse who came to wash Effie's body asked my husband and twenty-two-year-old daughter if they would like to help, which they did—appreciating the invitation to take part in a last physical courtesy to someone who had loved us all so much. At her funeral service we said the same words of the Nunc Dimitis (Luke 2:29) that she had been able to recite well into her final decline—"Lord, now lettest thou thy servant depart in peace, according to thy word. For mine eyes have seen thy salvation; which thou hast prepared before the face of all people; to be a light to lighten the Gentiles, and to be the glory of thy people Israel." It was the experience of the family and of all who looked after Effie that she brought blessing in her decline and her death, as she had in her life. Assisted by a remarkably helpful National

Health System, our general practitioners, the district nurses, and special care nurses, we were all able to share in this good death.

Some Final Remarks on Good Death in
Hospice Palliative Care from a Christian Perspective

What might all of this mean for "dying well in hospice care" from a Christian perspective? Christians, like Hindus, think of life as a journey in which death is not an aberration (see chapter 2 on Hinduism), but one part of the whole. According to Dr. Robert Twycross, a colleague of Cicely Saunders and pioneer of the hospice movement in Britain, the role of the hospice is not to "help people die," but to "live well while dying." The dying person should feel comfortable, safe, loved, and, where appropriate, assured of the love of God. The teaching for children is the same as for adults—death is part of life and, for the Christian, not the end of God's abiding love.

A good death in Christian as in Buddhist understandings (see chapter 3) is a peaceful death. Ideally, this means being at peace with family, neighbors, friends, and oneself. In order to facilitate this, Christian patients may chose to forgo pain medications in favor of clarity of mind in their last hours, and this desire should be respected. Similarly, a willingness to let go and to leave oneself in the hands of God should not be interpreted by clinicians as, in every instance, giving up on life.

It is worth stressing that many intelligent and highly educated Christians believe in life after death: belief in life after death may be *inconceivable* but it is not *incoherent*. A related parallel is this: it is impossible to answer the question "Why is there something rather than nothing?," but this is not an absurd question. It is a metaphysical (not a scientific) question, which believers answer by saying that they believe in a Creator. If, indeed, there is a God who creates all that is, including space and time, then the idea of resurrection is not an affront to reason, even while remaining a matter of faith.

Of inestimable importance to the Christian message, and a lesson it takes from Judaism, is attention to particularity. Each individual, whether Christian or not, believer or not, an AIDS sufferer or not, senile or not, is in the image of God, and must be respected as such. As with some other religious traditions, the loss of sight and speech is not understood as a failure to somehow be present (see chapter 2). No individual life may be judged to be worthless. This is not to say that extraordinary measures should not be taken to keep a dying person alive for as long as possible. Yet a dying person, however frail, silent, and physically or mentally disabled, may be "living and active" in ways invisible to us but apparent to God. The song of the elderly Zechariah speaks of being delivered by God to "serve him without fear, in holiness and righteousness before him all the days of our life" (Luke 1:73–75). The most extreme "passive" serving of God recorded in the New Testament is the death, or passion, of Christ on the cross.

Suffering and weakness are not the ideal—indeed, they are to be resisted. But it is a matter of Christian faith that all human life, no matter how weakened or debilitated, is still life in the praise and service of God.

Health practitioners do not need to be taught by a theologian about the importance of caring for the individual. However, the emphasis in the hospice movement on the particularity of each patient reveals the influence of its founder, Cicely Saunders. In our own day, preserving the importance and dignity of individuals in their decline is increasingly at threat in a performance-obsessed society. "God has no hands or feet but ours." From the Christian point of view, the "hands and feet" here are both those of those serving, and of those served.

Notes

1. It's interesting that it is Jesus's own disciples, and not the Pharisees or some other rival group, who are represented as presenting Jesus with this unsatisfactory either/or. This seems to show it was by no means a silly question.

2. According to the Book of Acts, a member of St. Paul's audience in Troas, seated on a windowsill during a long talk from the apostle, fell asleep and plunged three floors to his death. Paul, having bored him to death, then raised him to life (Acts 20:9–10).

3. Compare Is. 29:18–19; also the *Magnificat* of Luke 1.

4. For a good treatment of the origins and history of early Christian hospice care see Geunter B. Risse (1999), especially chapters 2–4. Risse points out that "Beginning in the eighteenth century . . . institutional crowding and cross-infections produced high institutional death rates, creating a long-lived negative image in which hospitals were categorized as 'gateways to death'" (5).

5. There is actually divided opinion among contemporary Jewish groups as to the question of life after death.

6. Islamic texts use the same argument.

7. This hope is in the Jewish prayer, the *Amidah*, which according to Rabbinic law is to be said three days each weekday and four times on Sabbath: "You are mighty forever, my Lord, You are the one who revives the dead, powerful to save (YOU make the wind blow and the rain fall.) . . . Faithful you are to revive the dead. Blessed are You, O Lord, who revive the dead" (Levenson 2006, 3).

References

Aristides. 1913. *The apology of Aristides*, Syriac text, trans. J. Rendel Harris. *Ante-Nicene fathers,* vol. X, 5th ed., ed. Allen Menzies. Edinburgh: T. and T. Clark.

Catholic Bishops' Conference of England and Wales. February 2010. A practical guide to the spiritual care of the dying person: Draft consultation. www.catholicchurch.org.uk/catholic_church/media_centre.

Haym, A. 1989. *The Isenheim altarpiece: God's medicine and the painter's vision.* Princeton: Princeton University Press.

Levenson, J. 2006. *Resurrection and the restoration of Israel: The ultimate victory of the good life.* New Haven: Yale University Press.

Risse, G. B. 1999. *Mending bodies, saving souls: A history of hospitals.* Oxford: Oxford University Press.

7

Chinese Religions and Hospice Care

Edwin C. Hui
Danny C. Leung

Introduction

Cicely Saunders's idea of "total pain" and her philosophy of hospice care have played an exceptional role in drawing health care professionals' attention to the psychospiritual aspect of illness as perceived by terminal patients. Research in medical anthropology and sociology has also suggested that apart from treating disease, the meaning of which is largely biomedical and scientifically measurable, health care professionals should also pay heed to various meanings of illness shaped by cultural norms, social values, and patients' "life-worlds" (Eisenberg 1977; Kleinman 1986, 43–50; Bates et al. 1993). In light of this, this chapter examines Chinese religious and cultural requirements for a good death, which might serve as reference material for hospice care providers working in multicultural communities.

Confucianism, Buddhism, and Daoism have been the most influential religious traditions in Mainland China, Hong Kong, and Taiwan. It is estimated that in China three hundred million people are religious believers and 66.1 percent (about two hundred million people) believe in Buddhism, Daoism, or goddesses of Chinese folk religions (Wu 2007). Ninety-three percent of Taiwanese are either Buddhists or Daoists (Index Mundi 2008). In Hong Kong, the Hong Kong Buddhist Association estimates that 70 percent of the Hong Kong population are believers of Buddhism or Daoism or both (Luk 2005, 40). Confucianism, as the axis of Chinese culture, has shaped the development of Buddhist and Daoist thought in China and is influential not only in Chinese communities but also in Japan and Korea. Today, it is widely accepted that a mixed system of Confucianism-Buddhism-Daoism represents Chinese culture.

In Confucianism, "man is a member of the triad of Heaven (*Tian*), Earth, and Man" (Hui 1999, 138). The nature of *Tian* is good, and humans inherit from it some of this good character. Through studying the teaching of the sages, fulfilling social responsibilities, and living out the virtues of *Tian,* a man can transcend himself to become a moral sage and shorten his distance from *Tian,* proceeding to the ideal of "Heaven and Man become One."

The nature of *Tian* is *ren* (commonly translated as benevolence, humanity, humaneness, and compassion). The central value of all social and moral practice in a Confucian society is to embody *ren,* and this is essential for the making of a sage. In Confucianism there are five key relationships in a society: the King/ruler-subject, father-son, husband-wife, elder-younger, and friend-friend. These relationships are in a hierarchical order: the lower ranks are supposed to be respectful, obedient, and loyal to the higher ranks; and for all these relationships Confucians provide the principles and guidance for engagement, behavior, and responsibility (Ho and Brotherson 2007, 4). For example, loyalty is the correct attitude in a ruler-subject relationship; filial piety is the correct attitude in a father-son relationship; and affection is the correct attitude in a husband-wife relationship. For each attitude, there are some behavioral rules. For instance, to have filial piety, one should respect, care, protect, glorify one's parents, be obedient to parents' commands, and worship deceased parents regularly (Woo 1999, 70). These rules, collectively known as *li,* would lead one to achieve *ren* and become a good person. The Confucians see a person as a "relational self," for whom social relationships, rather than rationality and individualism, provide the basis for moral judgment (Bowman and Hui 2008, 397). A good person is expected to fulfill social roles, respect the senior, and be ready to sacrifice for the family, country, and *Tian.* This is why obligations, rather than individual rights, are central to Chinese culture. Although today's young Chinese people are exposed to capitalism, individualism, and rights-based political culture and therefore become less submissive to authorities, when facing "big issues" in life, such as life and death or marriage, they are still happy to comply with tradition.

Pure Land Buddhism is the most influential Buddhist school in Mainland China, Hong Kong, and Taiwan. This school aspires to reaching

Pure Land, mainly through devotion to Amitabha Buddha and Guānshì yīn Bodhisattva. The theory of karma (see chapters 3 and 8) is also a moral guide for many Chinese people. It is commonly believed that the accumulation of good karma, which might lead to a good reincarnation (see chapter 3), is important for having a good death (Jin Yin 2006, 97).

Daoism can be divided into philosophical and religious Daoism, and both emphasize harmony with nature and nourishment of life and soul. *Dao* means "the way nature moves along and living beings grow and decline" (Kohn 2005, 9). While *Dao* is an abstract way, *Qi* is "the concrete aspect of the *Dao*, the material energy of the universe, the basic stuff of nature. . . . It is the basic material of all that exists. It animates life and furnishes functional power of events. *Qi* is the root of the human body; its quality and movement determine human health" (Kohn 2005, 11). *Yinyang* and the five elements are also central theoretical components in Daoism, and they form the foundation of traditional Chinese medicine (TCM), martial arts, and Chinese fortune-telling. In Chinese medicine, disease is due to imbalance of *yin* and *yang* with the five elements, each of which corresponds to one of the five major organs: wood-liver, fire-heart, earth-spleen, metal-lung, and water-kidney (Woo 1999, 70–71). To nourish life and soul, it is important to balance the *yin*, *yang*, and five elements within one's body and between one's body and the environment. To achieve this, meditation, herbal medicine, *taiqi*, and *qigong* are used. Like acupuncture, *qigong* has been increasingly recognized by Western medicine.

The Chinese Good Death

Confucianism-Buddhism-Daoism has an immense influence upon the Chinese conception of good death and hospice care. In a survey titled "What Is Good Death?" conducted by the Society for the Promotion of Hospice Care (Hong Kong) in 2004, it was found that a priority list of good death factors among 719 participants included (1) painless death, (2) things good for the bereaved, (3) things good for the deceased, and (4) traditional thoughts concerning preservation of body and funerals (SPHC 2004). It is notable that "things good for the bereaved" has priority over "things good for the deceased." This reflects the Confucian requirement of fulfilling one's social responsibilities before death. When a Chinese is going to die, he/she will hope that his/her death will not cause troubles to other family members, his/her family obligations are fulfilled, and he/she need not worry about family members' future living. These concerns are even more important than those about the patient's self. This is why items favorable to the bereaved are rated higher than those favorable to the deceased.

For dying patients, the family's "bedside company" is very important. In Wong and Chan's study, the bereaved subjects held that it was crucial for the nurses to inform the family in time about the deterioration so that they could take the last opportunity to see the patient:

> I would have liked the nurses to have informed us earlier . . . because we wanted to be with him when he was dying. We believe that he would have liked to see us one more time before he died. (Wong and Chan 2007, 2361)

If the family members were unable to see the patient, they would feel guilty, disappointed, and upset:

> I felt very depressed that I could not be with him as he passed away . . . as you know . . . being Chinese, it is very important to see him passing away . . . if the nurse could have told me two hours earlier, then that would have been much better. (Wong and Chan 2007, 2361)

In Confucianism, bedside company is a manifestation of filial piety and a sign of good death for a dying parent. The presence of children will give the parent a sense of completeness; and if the children have all married and the grandchildren are also brought to the bedside, the parent will think that she has completed her family duty—bringing up the children to adulthood and securing the flourishing of the family tree. In particular, the presence of sons, especially the eldest son, is very important. If the eldest son is missing at the dying moment, this will be seen as a bad death. For male dominance is part of the Confucian hierarchical family structure, according to which family members are categorized in terms of age, gender, and bloodline proximity (Chan et al. 1998, 793). Sons are supposed to be the heirs, in terms of bloodline, to their parents. Daughters are supposed to be "married away" and belong to their husbands' families. If a couple gives birth to a son, the husband's parents feel particularly delighted because this assures the continuation of their bloodline. When a parent has passed away, sons are supposed to be in charge of the funeral, and traditionally they are expected to take the parent's coffin to the grave, with other male relatives' assistance. This is also a way to fulfill filial piety. If no son is present in the funeral, this will be regarded as a very bad death. The Cantonese curse, "the last journey to the grave without a son," is one of the worst curses in Cantonese-speaking Chinese.

The following case illustrates the importance of "bedside company" by family members. On December 22, 2009, Mrs. Pang was hit by a car and was sent to a hospital in London. Having been seen by senior doctors, she was judged to have no chance of recovery and the physician in charge told her husband that in a very short time the patient must be withdrawn from life-sustaining treatment, due to "tight resources." Mr. Pang, who had emigrated from Hong Kong to England with his wife in 1995 and had served with the British Police and in the British Army, had three sons. Two of them were living in Hong Kong, and they had already taken the first flight to England when they heard of their mother's accident. Mr. Pang pleaded with the doctor to wait for the arrival of his sons so that they could have a chance to see their mother one last time while she was alive. The request was turned down, and the patient was finally withdrawn from ventilation thirty minutes later, under Mr. Pang's strong opposition. When the patient's sons arrived on December 24, they could only see their mother's corpse in the mortuary (Harding 2010; Ballinger 2010).

This incident aroused a controversy in the Hong Kong media. Many criticized the British doctors involved for their lack of cultural sensitivity about a Chinese good death. They should have understood that, for the Chinese, it was very important for the dying patient's sons to see the patient one last time. Even if the patient was in a coma, this bedside company is still significant, to allow the sons to express their filial piety. The sons will feel great regret if they cannot complete this step. In Hong Kong, cases such as Mrs. Pang's would be treated in a different way. First, only those with a certified brain stem death would be disconnected from ventilators, and the doctors would explain this to the patients' families and seek their consent. The families would also be given sufficient time to see the patient one last time. If a family tenaciously opposed the withdrawal, the case would then be handled by the hospital's ethics committee. If discrepancies were still unsolved at this level, the case would be passed to the court. Cases like Mrs. Pang's could happen again. In view of this, physicians working in multicultural communities are strongly advised to adopt Hong Kong practice as a reference in order to fulfill notions of a good death in hospice palliative care.

Patient Autonomy and the Chinese Family

In end-of-life care, health care service influenced by Confucian culture is significantly different from that based on individual autonomy and rights (Tong 1994; Bowman 1997; Woo 1999). In Confucian culture, physicians enjoy high social status, and social responsibility requires them to look after their patients as if they were parents looking after their own children, as is made evident in the Chinese saying, "Physicians have the heart of parents" (Hui 1999, 132). Since a physician is supposed to deliver paternalistic care to patients and respect the centrality of family, the physician would feel comfortable reporting his diagnosis to and discussing treatment plans with the patient's family members without the patient's consent, and would encourage the whole family to get involved in decision making (Tong 1994, 27). Moreover, since breaking bad news to an elderly patient is regarded as both disrespectful to the patient and likely to accelerate the patient's deterioration, some physicians are willing to cooperate with the patient's family to withhold bad news from the patient temporarily and disclose the truth step by step (Liu 2006, 191).

A survey conducted in 2004, concerning Chinese oncology clinicians' attitudes toward issues in end-of-life care, confirmed the notion of diminished patient autonomy in Chinese health care. When asked about their attitudes toward truth telling about diagnosis and terminal illness, "70% [of the clinicians] believed that few families wanted the patient to know the truth, with 51% reporting that most families asked clinicians to withhold the truth from patients." In deciding who should be informed about a cancer diagnosis or prognosis, 5 percent would tell only the patient; "52% would tell the patient's family only"; and "43% reported that they would tell both the patient and the family." Regarding treatment decision making, although 39 percent agreed that physicians should make decisions jointly with the patients, "only 9% reported this to be the case in their current working environment." Fifty-three percent said that, in most cases, the physician "makes treatment decisions after consulting with the patient." Another 26 percent reported that physicians are the sole decision makers (Wang et al. 2004, 127–28). These results are consistent with the findings in other end-of-life care studies (Li and Chou 1997; Feldman et al. 1999).

Secondly, for the Chinese, the family is the primary basis of social-cultural-political reality. Since Confucian personhood consists of social relationships, one defines oneself, and is defined by others, as a son, a husband, a parent, a servant (of an emperor), and a friend. Within a family, children are supposed to fulfill filial piety, and when a parent is sick, children's explicit concern for their parent's physical well-being manifests this. They are expected to provide around-the-clock care for the parent, and the parent feels no shame in being dependent on the children. Rather, the dependence is seen by the parent as something to which she or he is entitled. As a recipient of filial piety, the parent does not feel uncomfortable having the children as decision makers regarding her own medical care, and the children are keen to take up this responsibility. For fear of accelerating their parent's deterioration, the children are also comfortable withholding bad news from the parent (Hui 1999, 132).

Lastly, individual autonomy is also undermined by the idea of *Chengfu*, a Daoist concept explained in the famous Daoist treatise *The Scripture of the Great Peace*. *Cheng* means "to bear the consequences of the ancestors' deeds," and *fu* means "being responsible for descendants' fortune." According to this notion, on the one hand, one is supposed to be responsible for one's ancestors' good deeds/sins, and on the other hand, one is also the creator of later generations' good/bad fortune. In *Yijing*, an ancient Daoist treatise, it is said that "a family which accumulates good deeds will bring good fortune to its descendents, a family which accumulates bad deeds will bring misfortune to its descendents" (Yuan 2002, 171; my translation). Thus, everyone in a family is morally tied to other family members, and members in a family are collectively responsible for the family's fate (Yuan 2002, 172–73). In light of this, family decisions are more important and privileged than individual choices.

The following case illustrates the discrepancy between the Chinese end-of-life care and Western bioethics. A Chinese man, aged seventy-one, was admitted to a U.S. hospital due to left arm weakness and urinary incontinence. Computed tomography suggested that he had primary renal cell carcinoma with brain metastases. Further confirmation would require a biopsy of the kidney. The patient's family, however, refused this request, claiming that the biopsy would not make the patient live longer and would only cause further discomfort. Moreover, the family insisted on withholding the bad news, and asked the physician to tell the patient that he had pneumonia. The physician, feeling strongly that it was immoral to lie to the patient this way, declined this request. The ethics committee of the hospital was called on to examine the case. During the meeting, the family pleaded for the patient's discharge so that they could bring him back to China and let him die there. They emphasized that breaking bad news to the patient would only make him deteriorate faster and that it was important for Chinese people to die in their homeland. The ethics committee, on the other hand, disapproved of a physician's lying to a patient. They suggested that the physician should ask the patient if he preferred the disease information to be disclosed to himself or to his family and if the family could make decisions for him. When asked, the patient readily delegated all the tasks and rights to his family. He was then discharged without a biopsy and later died in his homeland (Lapine et al. 2001, 476).

As Lapine et al. commented, the ethics committee understood that withholding bad news from elderly patients was a norm for the Chinese. The committee's suggestion was an intelligent one; it prevented the physician from lying to the patient, respected both the patient's and his family's autonomy, and fulfilled the patient's cultural expectation to die in his homeland. Similar cases could happen frequently in countries with a Chinese population. Hence, if health care providers such as physicians feel it is unacceptable to withhold bad news from their elderly Chinese patients, they should be instructed to ask the following questions when a patient is sent to a hospital: (1) Whom should we talk to about your treatments and potential outcomes? (2) Whom do you want to know about your condition? (3) Whom do you want to make health care decisions for you? (Lapine, Cheng et al. 2001, 476–78). If the physicians really need to break bad news, their strategies should "resemble a process of slowly unfolding and carefully releasing information in relation to the patient's ability to receive it" (Bowman 1997, 131); words such as *die* or *incurable* should be avoided.

Family Involvement in Direct Patient Care

A patient's family members are not only gatekeepers concerning dissemination of disease information and treatment decision making; very often they are also primary treatment providers. In his qualitative study examining 411 sickness incidents reported by 724 family members in 115 Taiwanese families, Arthur Kleinman found that "93 percent of all sickness episodes were first treated in the family, and 73 percent of all sickness episodes received their *only* treatment from the family." In particular, "a smaller, if still very high, percentage of children (88 percent) were first treated at home than adults (98 percent) or the elderly (100 percent)," and in the sickness episodes in elderly, 86 percent only received family treatment. Common home remedies included (1) diet that could balance the "hot" and "cold" constituents of the body or easily digested foods; (2) special foods, such as "coconut milk to lower 'huo ch'i'; hot and sour soup for nasal congestion and cough; bird's nest for respiratory diseases; snake meat for eczema"; (3) "prescription and non-prescription medicines (both Chinese and Western) and herbs . . . used without consulting practitioners." The usual treatment pattern was that home remedies or medicines obtained at pharmacies would be tried first; only when they were found ineffective, patients and their family members would proceed to Western-style doctors and/or Chinese-style physicians (Kleinman 1980, 182–89). Even though Kleinman's observations are not drawn from end-of-life care or hospice patients, the lessons learned may have relevance to the field of hospice palliative care.

This strong commitment to caring for the patient is also evident in a qualitative study by Wong and Chan (2007). This study examined the experience of a bereaved family in Hong Kong in which the participants revealed strong desires to provide basic care to the patients:

> I would have liked the nurse to teach me how to take care of his oral hygiene . . . turn him in bed . . . do exercises etc. We would have liked to take care of him ourselves, but we did not know how to carry out basic care. We worried that we might hurt him. (2361)

Many of the participants believed that the meals provided by the hospital were not good enough. They preferred to cook for the patients themselves and therefore were eager to know what the patients could and could not eat:

> I hoped that the nursing staff would teach or suggest to me what I should cook for the patient. . . . I did not know what he was allowed or not allowed to eat. (Wong and Chan 2007, 2361)

Cooking soup for the sick is very common in Chinese culture, and in general it is a symbol of family life. There is a Cantonese saying "having no soup to drink," which is used to describe single people studying or working away from home. Soup cooking is regarded as a housewife's domestic service, and it is a sign of warmth and care. For Chinese people, the longer it takes to cook the soup, the better its quality and the stronger the care embedded in it (Chan 1998, 793). The Chinese notion of "long-boiling soup" refers to soup under slow boil for at least four to five hours. The long boiling can extract the essence of the ingredients and the soup will become very good nourishment. For the terminally ill, long-boiling soup represents a strong sense of family support and attention. Family members usually would not see this type of caregiving as a burden even if they were tired and sad (Wong and Chan 2007, 2363; Liu 2006, 186).

Today, many Chinese people uphold a mixed Chinese-Western medical belief system. They think that traditional Chinese medicine can fix the cause of disease (disharmony of yin and yang) and therefore is a thorough treatment, whereas Western medicine is more effective in alleviating symptoms. In addition, it is commonly believed that these two therapies are compatible. Many patients suffering from cancer, stroke, or dementia who are under Western medical treatment also take traditional Chinese medications.

In some cases, however, the therapeutic strategies of these two medicines might clash. The following case, presented by Bowman and Lee (1995), best illustrates this. Mr. L, a Chinese male, aged sixty-four, was admitted to a Toronto hospital. Mr. L was in coma upon admission and was diagnosed with vertebrosilar insufficiency related to possible arterial occlusion and dissecting aneurysm. After forty-six hours of intubation and ventilation, the physician in charge declared that Mr. L was in a persistent vegetative state and suggested a gradual withdrawal from the ventilator. Mrs. L, her daughter, and her son-in-law hesitated and preferred to wait for the eldest son, who was on his way from Hong Kong, to discuss the issue. After the eldest son arrived and discussed the whole issue with other family members, the family finally decided to try qigong, a traditional Chinese medical treatment. In view of the fact that the qigong treatment was noninvasive and that it was important to respect both the patient's and the family's wishes, the hospital permitted their request. After three days of qigong treatment, Mr. L started to open his eyes when his family talked to him. But he soon had a poor cough and gag reflex. The physician suggested a tracheostomy and feeding tube insertion. Since Mr. L had been showing improvement, the family asked for more time to see if the tracheostomy and feeding tube were really needed. After five days of *qigong* treatment, Mr. L was able to recognize people and express himself in whispers. His very first statement was that he was hungry. Having consulted with his family, the patient decided to receive a feeding tube treatment. The physician explained to Mr. L and his family the risk of not having the tracheostomy. But they still refused it, because they believed that opening a hole at the throat would affect the flow of *qi* and therefore make the *qigong* treatment futile. Thus, Mr. L continued to receive *qigong* therapy, but in the next three days he developed a high fever and mild respiratory distress with signs of pneumonia. He was then given antibiotics and oxygen therapy. But these treatments did not save him, and he was finally pronounced dead due to respiratory arrest secondary to pneumonia. The hospital requested an autopsy, but the family refused because, according to them, failure to keep the corpse intact and undisturbed was to disrespect the deceased (Bowman and Lee 1995, 338–39).

This case raises several important issues. First, it is common that families might propose the use of traditional Chinese medicine treatments during hospitalization. If the patient is competent and has not delegated autonomy to the family, then the patient is the one to choose treatment options. If the patient is incompetent, and if the treatment is noninvasive, it should be allowed out of respect for family autonomy. But health care providers should remind the family of possible side effects of the traditional Chinese medicine treatment, such as gastrointestinal bleeding (Liu 2006, 191). In any case, if an invasive traditional Chinese medicine treatment is proposed and if the physician anticipates any detrimental implications, based on the principle of nonmaleficence the physician should likely not allow the treatment and should provide a clear explanation to the family (Bowman and Lee 1995, 339).

Second, physicians might find it bizarre that in this case the patient's family would insist on trying *qigong* treatment even after medical futility had been declared. This is because the Chinese believe that there is an inherent positive value in living and they should fight till the last breath. According to Confucianism, humans, as members of the Heaven, Earth, Human triad, somehow inherit *ren* from *Tian*; and humans have a lifelong duty to grasp *ren* and to live it out through fulfilling one's social and familial responsibilities. Only when one has achieved this can the meaning of one's life be fully explored, and one can die without regret. As Confucius said, "He has not lived in vain who dies in the evening, having been told about the Way in the morning" (Confucius 1992, 4:8). Since there is no well-defined point as to when one can be said to have fully grasped the meaning of *ren* and to have completed all her responsibilities, one can always hesitate to give up living, worrying that there might be some unfinished social responsibilities (Hui 1999, 134). This is why the Chinese have the saying, "It is more preferable to hang on to life, even a 'bad life,' than to give oneself up to a good death." "To give oneself up to a good death" is seen as a way to escape the social responsibilities delegated by *Tian*. Even if life is painful and unbearable, the Chinese tend to endure it and fight till the last minute, and they see this tolerance as compliance to the arrangement of *Tian* (Hui 1999, 135).

Third, "the eldest son" in a Chinese family plays an important role, particularly in life-and-death issues. Health care providers should recognize this and help facilitate the presence of the eldest son at the bedside if at all possible (Bowman and Lee 1995, 339).

Fourth, for Chinese people, one of the factors of a good death is to have a well-preserved corpse. Autopsy somehow means a disrespect for the deceased and should be avoided. Some believers of Daoism hold that autopsy causes injuries to the spirit of the deceased (Bowman and Lee 1995, 340). Health care providers are advised to respect these beliefs in order to facilitate a good death.

Tolerance of Pain

Confucian and Daoist thought might also shape Chinese people's perception of suffering. Several studies have reported that cancer patients and their family members in China, when compared with those in the United States, displayed greater hesitancy in reporting pain and administering analgesics (Lin et al. 2000, 468–69; Chung et al. 1999, 200). Moreover, in a study of the quality of life of patients with terminal cancer receiving palliative home care, researchers noted that "it is remarkable that patients in palliative home care still suffered from a moderate level of pain despite the fact that a majority of them were treated with pain medication" (Yan and Cheng 2006, 265). Whereas these results are seemingly inconsistent with Arthur Kleinman's study of depression in China (Kleinman 1986), we agree with Kleinman that these complaints or non-complaints about pain have their cultural and ethnographic meanings which deserve further exploration.

Several reasons can explain the pain tolerance of Chinese cancer patients. First, due to doctors' highly paternalistic image in Chinese culture, patients, no matter how senior they are in their own circles, automatically put themselves in a junior or inferior position in a doctor-patient relationship. They worry that in chronic illnesses if they do not show any improvement they will be blamed by the doctors as "bad patients." Thus, it is sinful for them to have long-term pain, and being "bad patients" implies that they are failing to fulfill their social responsibilities in the doctor-patient relationship under the Confucian framework. Consequently, they choose to minimize their pain descriptions in front of their doctors.

Secondly, in Chinese culture, pain is seen as a pathway to achievement and its endurance is a virtue. This is evidential in Mencius's saying,

> When Heaven is about to confer a great office on any man, it first exercises his mind with suffering, and his sinews and bones with toil. It exposes his body to hunger, and subjects him to extreme poverty. It confounds his undertakings. By all these methods it stimulates his mind, hardens his nature, and supplies his incompetencies. (Mencius 6B:15)

Other Chinese sayings, such as "Only those who can endure the most bitter situations are the superior men" and "Endure humiliation and bear the heavy burden," are often used to encourage people to carry on with difficult missions. With all this, Chinese people are conditioned to tolerate pain.

Thirdly, many cancer patients are resistant to analgesics, partly because of a typical Chinese belief that taking too much Western medicine is not good for health, and partly because they believe heavy dosages of analgesics will put them into a trance and they will become "socially dead." Patients prefer to stay awake so that they can interact with their family members or go out with them. This reflects Chinese peoples' insistence on being socially alive as much as they can and the centrality of family.

The idea of *Chengfu* also helps to explain pain tolerance in Chinese culture. In a study of Chinese Australian patients' explanations of hereditary cancer, Eisenbruch et al. found that although all the informants explained the disease in terms of Western medical language, such as "faulty genes" and "mutations," "many also used underlying Chinese idioms; these idioms however were most notable when speaking of the senior family members' attributions" (Eisenbruch et al. 2004, 239). These participants held that their ancestors' sins would generate *baoying* (retribution) to be borne by descendents. As one of them said,

> Something the ancestors did that would cause her to suffer, e.g. did something bad, led a very bad life, did evil things to people, might have murdered people . . . they're not punished for what they did but their children and future children will suffer . . . will see their children suffer, will see their children or grand-children die . . . (Eisenbruch et al. 2004, 242)

If suffering is a kind of retribution, tolerating it can prevent further harm to oneself and others, "settling the ancestors' debt," so to speak.

Lastly, according to Daoist thought, disease is naturally accompanied by pain. Illness is described as *bingtong* (disease and pain). Daoists see birth, aging, disease, and death as a natural path of life and pain as a natural sensation for sick people. Hence, in chronic illnesses, pain does not have to be totally eradicated.

Experience of Hong Kong Buddhist Hospice Caregivers

According to Buddhism, one's last thought before death is very important; it determines which pathway one will reincarnate to, and the content of this last thought is often determined by three kinds of karma, namely, weighty karma (*garuka-kamma*), habitual karma (*cinnaka-* or *bahula-kamma*), and death-proximate karma (*maran-sanna-kamma*). Weighty karma refers to the extremely good or bad deeds one has done before death. At the moment of death, these extremely good or bad memories might occupy one's mind and become his/her last thought. Habitual karma refers to one's habits. If there are no extremely good or bad memories, one's habits might occupy his mind at the moment of death. For those who have no weighty karma and habitual karma, what appears in their mind at the dying moment could come by chance. This is death-proximate karma. For these kinds of people, Buddhism suggests that they should try to recall their past good deeds. This might help them to have a good rebirth (Jin Yin 2006, 97–99). This may explain why some Chinese hospice patients resist the use of sedatives in their dying moments.

Buddhism followers believe that if a patient, at the moment of death, can understand the Law of Buddha, determine to have a retreat at Pure Land after death, and promise to return in the future to help others, it is possible that this patient can really reach Pure Land after death. If the retreat is done well, it is possible that the patient can finally leave the six pathways, that is, deva, asura, human, animal, hungry ghost, and hell, and no longer suffer from reincarnation.

For terminally ill patients, making habitual recitation of the name of Amitabha Buddha with the hope that they will be reborn in Pure Land is important. This will help them purify their souls, reinforce their ambitions of reaching Pure Land after death, and help them refrain from thinking of the people they hate and past bitter experience. All this is to ensure that the patients will have a good last thought and a good reincarnation. If the patient is too weak to do the recitation or the family thinks that stronger mental power is needed to help the patient head toward Pure Land after death, they can invite a Help Chant Group, made up of devout Buddhists, to provide *zhunian*, a long and continuous chanting. Ideally speaking, the chanting should continue for eight hours after the medical certification of death. This is because during that period the patient's soul will be leaving his/her body slowly and will still be able to hear and be influenced by the chanting.

In Hong Kong, Buddhist hospice care is provided to cancer patients mainly by trained volunteers, through home and hospital visits. A volunteer who has been working in this area since the 1980s, initially at Nam Long Hospital and later in other hospitals after Nam Long was closed in 2003, said that volunteers at Nam Long usually worked in pairs, an experienced worker leading an amateur. They were interviewed and received one and one-half days of training before they started the visiting. After a visit, they were required to write a report summarizing the patient's progress. If they found something unusual, such as a patient's suicidal ideation, they were to inform the hospital immediately.

These volunteers would not attempt to impose their religious values on their patients. Their prime concern was to help the patient accept the disease, look after the patient's emotions and worries, and provide assistance in practical matters as much as they could. They found that if a patient accepted their situation without annoyance and agony, they would pass the "last period" more peacefully. This was not to ask them to give up, but to encourage them to "follow the course of nature" and make the best use of the rest of time they had. In a sense, this was opposite to the Confucian view of "fighting until the last breath." In fact, the volunteers had encountered such "Confucian" patients. Their observation was that if a patient had a strong will and tried to resist death, the patient might endure for longer but in the end would leave quite painfully. In contrast, if they had accepted the prognoses, they could use their time in meaningful ways and would have an easy death.

The volunteers would approach the patients as friends. Only if the patients were interested in Buddhist thoughts would they introduce Pure Land Buddhism to the patients, encourage them to recite the name of Amitabha Buddha, and do some reading on Buddhist thoughts, when the patients' physical condition allowed.

Reciting the name of Amitabha Buddha, according to the volunteers, could actually relieve pain. One of them recalled the following experience:

> Sometimes the patient's family members would do *zhunian* [bedside chanting] together with us. About two years ago, there was a patient whose wife was actually a Catholic. But since she respected her husband's religion, she was willing to do *zhunian* with us for him, together with her children and the patient's younger sister. The wife told us that before we went to the hospital to do *zhunian* for him, he felt very painful and needed to receive morphine injection once per hour. But since we started *zhunian*, from seven p.m. until ten p.m., continued by his family until he passed away at about one a.m., he needed no injection and he passed away peacefully. *Zhunian* could help him to have good and positive thoughts in his last moments. Even if he could not reach Pure Land after death, at least he would not reincarnate to the pathway of animals, or hungry ghosts, or the hell. (Interview with hospice volunteer, Oct. 2009)

When dealing with patients with dementia or Alzheimer's disease, hospice workers and family members are still advised to encourage patients to read some simple Buddhist texts if they are able. However, since these patients are forgetful and will lose the ability to read and comprehend, this approach is rarely effective, particularly in the later stages of the disease. Sometimes, if able, patients are encouraged to recite the name of Amitabha Buddha in order to help them relieve anguish or negative emotions, and foster in them a Buddhist-inclined mentality. At their last moments, *zhunian* is still done for them, upon their families' request. But their reception and comprehension of the religious message will not be the same as cognitively able patients. It still depends on other factors. For instance, if the patient has believed in Buddhism for many years, and they can still remember their religion at their last moments, the effect of *zhunian* might not be too weak. There is still hope that they can have a good reincarnation.

It has been widely agreed that in multicultural communities it is important for health care professionals to provide culturally competent care (McNamara et al. 1997; Schim et al. 2005). Hospice care providers in these communities are encouraged to contact local Buddhist organizations, to explore the possibility of Buddhist hospice care. When facing dying Buddhist patients in need of *zhunian*, health care professionals are advised to provide a quiet environment and some time (ideally up to seven hours) for the Buddhist caregivers and family members to complete the ritual. Moreover, since in multicultural communities language is often a barrier to quality palliative care, it is advisable for hospitals and hospices to employ a few multilingual interpreters or caregivers who can speak the languages of the targeted populations, and to include translations in printed materials (McNamara et al. 1997; Feser and Bernard 2003).

Concluding Remarks

Religiosity is an indispensable component in hospice palliative care. It answers one of the most important questions for the terminally ill—What happens after death?—and provides channels for self-transcendence. The Confucian idea of "Heaven and Man become One," the Buddhist idea of "breaking up with attachments," and the Daoist idea of "complying with the course of nature" are profound and positive insights for everyone to take death seriously. When Cicely Saunders proposed her philosophy of hospice care, her "spirituality" presupposed religiosity. Confucianism-Buddhism-Daoism, separately or jointly, provide a framework in which Saunders's concerns are attended to. Death is perceived by most as the ultimate break between one's self with the non-self. But if the distinction between self and the non-self is removed, as in the Confucian notion of "Heaven and Man become One," the Daoist notion of "harmony in nature," and the Buddhist notion of "elimination of ego," this "ultimate break" will disappear.

References

Ballinger, L. 2010. Did hospital pull plug on Mother Lai-Mai Pang-Cheung to save cash? *Mail Online, Case: A0113.* http://www.dailymail.co.uk/home/ index.html. (Accessed Feb. 2, 2010).

Bates, M. S., W. T. Edwards et al. 1993. Ethnocultural influences on variation in chronic pain perception. *Pain* 52: 101–12.

Bowman, K. W. 1997. *Chinese Canadian attitudes toward end of life decisions.* Ottawa: National Library of Canada.

———, and E. C. Hui. 2008. Chinese bioethics. In *The Cambridge textbook of bioethics*, ed. P. A. Singer and A. M. Viens. Cambridge; New York: Cambridge University Press.

———, and R. N. F. Lee. 1995. Cultural issues in critical care: A Chinese case study. *Annals of the Royal College of Physicians and Surgeons of Canada* 28(6): 338–40.

Chan, K., S. Zarina, C. L. Lam et al. 1998. Chinese patients with terminal cancer. In *Oxford textbook of palliative medicine*, ed. D. Doyle and G. Hanks et al. New York: Oxford University Press.

Chung, Tai-ki, P. French et al. 1999. Patient-related barriers to cancer pain management in a palliative care setting in Hong Kong. *Cancer Nursing* 22(3): 196–203.

Confucius. 1992. *Analects.* Trans. D. C. Lau. Hong Kong: The Chinese University Press.

Eisenberg, L. 1977. Disease and illness: Distinctions between professional and popular ideas of sickness. *Culture Medicine and Psychiatry* 1(1): 9–24.

Eisenbruch, M., S. S. Yeo et al. 2004. Optimizing clinical practice in cancer genetics with cultural competence: Lessons to be learned from ethnographic research with Chinese-Australians. *Social Science & Medicine* 59: 235–48.

Feldman, M. D., J. Zhang et al. 1999. Chinese and U.S. internists adhere to different ethical standards. *Journal of General Internal Medicine* 14: 469–73.

Feser, L., and C. B. Bernard. 2003. Enhancing cultural competence in palliative care: Perspective of an elderly Chinese community in Calgary. *Journal of Palliative Care* 19(2): 133–39.

Harding, E. 2010. Battersea woman's life support cut "without family's permission." *Guardian.co.hk, Case: A0113.* http://www.your localguardian. co.uk. (Accessed Feb. 1, 2010).

Ho, Sio-wa, and S. E. Brotherson, 2007. Cultural influences on parental bereavement in Chinese families. *Omega* 55(1): 1–25.

Hui, E. 1999. Chinese health care ethics. In *A cross-cultural dialogue on health care ethics*, ed. H. Coward and P. Ratanakul, 128–38. Waterloo, ON: Wilfrid Laurier University Press.

———. 1999. Confucian ethic of medical futility. *Philosophy and Medicine (Confucian Bioethics)* 61: 127–63.

Index Mundi. 2008. Taiwan demographics profile 2008. http://www.indexmundi. com/taiwan/demographics_profile.html. (Accessed Sept. 2009).

Jin Yin. 2006. Death from the Buddhist view: Knowing the unknown. In *Death, dying, and bereavement: A Hong Kong Chinese experience*, ed. Cecilia L. W. Chan and Amy Yin Man Chow. Hong Kong: Hong Kong University Press.

Kleinman, A. 1980. *Patients and healers in the context of culture: An exploration of the borderland between anthropology, medicine, and psychiatry.* Berkeley, Los Angeles, London: University of California Press.

———. 1986. Culture, the quality of life and cancer pain: Anthropological and cross-cultural perspectives. In *Assessment of quality of life and cancer treatment*, ed. V. Ventafridda et al., 43–50. Amsterdam: Elsevier.

———. 1986. *Social origins of distress and disease.* New Haven, London: Yale University Press.

Kohn, L. 2005. *Health and long life: The Chinese way.* Cambridge: Three Pines Press.

Lapine, A., R. W. Cheng et al. 2001. When cultures clash: Physician, patient, and family wishes in truth disclosure for dying patients. *Journal of Palliative Medicine* 4(4): 475–80.

Li, S., and J. L. Chou. 1997. Communication with the cancer patient in China. *Annals of New York Academy of Sciences* 809: 243–48.

Lin, C-c., P. Wang et al. 2000. Identifying attitudinal barriers to family management of cancer pain in palliative care in Taiwan. *Palliative Medicine* 14: 463–70.

Liu, F. C-f. 2006. Community palliative care in Hong Kong. In *Death, dying, and bereavement: A Hong Kong Chinese experience*, ed. Cecilia L. W. Chan, and Amy Yin Man Chow. Hong Kong: Hong Kong University Press.

Luk, B. H. K. 2005. Religion in Hong Kong history. In *Colonial Hong Kong and modern China: Interaction and reintegration*, ed. Lee Pui-tak. Hong Kong: Hong Kong University Press.

McNamara, B., K. Martin et al. 1997. Palliative care in a multi-cultural society: Perceptions of health care professionals. *Palliative Medicine* 11: 359–67.

Mencius. 1984. *Mencius.* Trans. D. C. Lau. Hong Kong: Chinese University Press.

Schim, S. M., A. Z. Doorenbos et al. 2005. Cultural competence among Ontario and Michigan healthcare providers. *Journal of Nursing Scholarship* 37(4): 354–60.

Society of the Promotion of Hospice Care. 2004. *What is good death?* http://www.hospicecare.org.hk/download/release/0402gooddeath.pdf. (Accessed Feb. 2010).

Tong, K. L. 1994. The Chinese palliative patient and family in North America: A cultural perspective. *Journal of Palliative Care* 10(1): 26–28.

Wang, X. S., J. D. Li et al. 2004. End-of-life care in urban areas of China: A survey of 60 oncology clinicians. *Journal of Pain and Symptom Management* 27(2): 125–32.

Wong, M-s., and S. W-c. Chan. 2007. The experiences of Chinese family members of terminally ill patients: A qualitative study. *Journal of Clinical Nursing* 16(12): 2357–64.

Woo K. Y. 1999. Care for Chinese palliative patients. *Journal of Palliative Care* 15(4): 70–74.

Wu, Jiao. 2007 (Feb. 7). Religious believers trice the estimate. *China Daily*.

Yan, S., and K. F. Cheng, 2006. Quality of life of patients with terminal cancer receiving palliative home care. *Journal of Palliative Care* 22(4): 261–66.

Yuan, G-y. 2002. 《太平經》承負報應思想探析 (A research for the theory of Chengfu of *Tai Ping Classic*). 成大宗教與文化學報 *Journal of Religion and Culture* (2): 167–209. Taiwan: National Cheng Kung University.

Part II

Case Studies

8

Buddhist Hospice Care in Thailand

Robert Florida
Pinit Ratanakul

Thailand is a rapidly urbanizing and industrializing country with a population of around 65 million people, of which 94 percent are Buddhist. The health care system is a combination of state-supported and private institutions that offer a high standard of Western-style biomedical services, at least in the urban centers. Full medical services are less available in rural and remote communities, and patients there may have to travel relatively long distances, sometimes in difficult circumstances, to receive treatment at a major hospital. There are also numerous small government clinics throughout the rural parts of Thailand. Since 2002, the vast majority of Thai citizens have been covered under the 30 baht universal health insurance scheme, a government plan that limits the cost to the patient for a hospital visit or admission at 30 baht (IOELC n.d., 6) that is, about one dollar Canadian. Biomedical therapies are supplemented by traditional healing practices involving highly developed and effective herbal and massage therapies, some of which have been tested scientifically and integrated into the official system.

The Thai people are well steeped in Buddhist ideas and practices on many levels so that most notions of health and illness are shaped by Buddhist thought. In this holistic understanding of the world, all human and nonhuman phenomena are connected in an interdependent web of causality. Accordingly, health comes from being in harmony with oneself, one's social network, and the natural environment. Disease or illness arise when the harmony is disrupted. Physical symptoms of illness are expressions of disharmony and may be the result of one's own actions (*kamma* in Pali and *karma* in Sanskrit; see also in this volume chapter 2 on Hinduism and chapter 3 on Buddhism). *Kamma* is intentional action, whether mental, verbal, or physical, and also its result or fruit. As *kamma* may be good or bad, so the result or fruit may be good or bad. Actions that are performed in accordance with morality will produce good effects in this life and the lives hereafter. In the view of the Buddhists there are physical, mental, and *kammic* causes of health and disease. The latter are related to the consequences of one's own past actions in this life or the earlier ones.

The working of *kamma* is very complex, and only the Buddha can fully comprehend it. However, it is certain that every human being will reap what he or she has sown. We are the result of what we were, and what we will be is the result of what we are. This is not fatalistic, as each person has the power to change for the better in the present state. Part of *kammic* cause and effect is social, and some modern Buddhists advocate social action to help create conditions whereby harmony and health for all may be enhanced. The Buddha taught how individuals, human relations, and kingdoms should be governed in order to advance progress on the Eightfold Path. One traditional summary of his teaching is "cease to do evil, learn to do good, and purify your own heart." When individuals and societies follow this rule, then health and harmony thrive.

As mentioned earlier, illness comes when there is disharmony. A particular problem may be the result of some sort of disharmony with the physical environment. The problem can be tackled by searching for the physical cause and treating it with the proper medicine or physical therapy. In traditional Thai medicine there is highly developed knowledge of herbal cures, massage, and bone-setting techniques, all of which work very well for many ailments. Physical problems may also respond to bio-medical treatment. Since Buddhist principles call for the use of skillful means to alleviate all suffering out of the motivation of loving kindness and compassion for all beings, Thais will use both traditional and modern medical treatments.

The problem of mental disease arising from internal disharmony may be alleviated by practicing meditation. Socially driven illness can be tackled by social initiatives such as public health improvements, encouragement of better agricultural and environmental practices, and by welfare initiatives motivated by such Buddhist virtues as giving and doing no harm. If there is disharmony with the gods, local spirits, or ghosts, illness may result, and there are magical and ritual ways to try to restore the harmony. Illness that has arisen as a result of bad *kamma* may not improve until the effects of that *kamma* have exhausted themselves, but may respond to meritorious actions undertaken now. In any case, since the precise *kammic* causes are very difficult to know, it is better to use all curative methods to alleviate one's own and others' suffering.

One of the key teachings of the Buddha is that all life is marked by old age, sickness, and death. Everything that exists, most explicitly human beings, is a fragile and transient result of causes and conditions. Death is simply the natural fate of any being that is born and lives. The human body should not be clung to or valued too highly as it will inevitably decline and decay. In fact, there is a series of traditional Buddhist meditations on body parts and decomposing corpses that is meant to help us realize that our bodies and ourselves are impermanent and that death is to be confronted directly and accepted as part of the natural process. These are popular themes in Thai Buddhist preaching and in religious posters. Occasionally one finds a human skeleton or skull mounted in a prominent place in Thai temples, donated by a pious lay person as an aid to meditation on the temporary and unsatisfactory nature of the body. Students from young children to university age are taken to hospices to witness the reality of old age, sickness, and the dying process. As a result, there is generally a matter-of-fact acceptance in Thailand of the process of death, dying, and dead bodies that may be unsettling to people from places where thoughts and images of death are kept in the background and where experiencing its reality is avoided.

The Palliative Care System in Thailand

Traditionally, one dies at home in Thailand under the care of the extended family and a network of neighbors and friends. Today this is still the most common model, but it is under pressure for several reasons. With the migration of so many to the cities, the extended family network has been weakened in the countryside. Modern, urban homes tend to be very small and unsuited for the care of the sick. Urban lifestyles make home care difficult, and there is very little support in the public health system for palliative care at home (IOELC n.d., 6). And, of course, HIV and AIDS have had a considerable impact on the health system, greatly increasing the number of dying patients. The United Nations estimated that in 2007 in Thailand some 25,000 AIDS patients died, out of 546,000 diagnosed with AIDS. Their estimate for the total number of HIV infections in the country for that year was 1,100,000. Altogether, some 559,000 have died in the epidemic (UNAIDS 2008, 17).

Although palliative care is part of the 30 baht national health insurance plan, it has not been well funded, partly because of financial problems starting with the Asian financial crisis of the late 1990s (IOELC n.d., 6). Nonetheless, there has been modest success in establishing palliative care units in publicly funded and private hospitals, and there are a number of independent hospices sponsored by NGOs, care facilities for the elderly, Buddhist monasteries, and Christian charities. Many Thai universities and teaching hospitals have begun to include units on palliative care in the training of nurses and physicians since the 1990s, and in the same period, small professional organizations concerned with terminal care have been formed, some affiliated with Asian regional networks. These developments—still relatively small and new—were instigated in large part by local medical workers returning from study or employment in the West, where formal palliative care has been established for some time.

Toward a Good Death in Buddhist Thailand

For Thai Buddhists good death refers to peaceful death that leads to rebirth in the higher realms in the life cycle (*samsara*) or no rebirth at all (enlightenment). Such peaceful death is achieved when the mind of the dying is calm and clear, without defilements such as fear, anger, and anxiety. Most Thai Buddhists love life and prefer to be reborn as beings in heavenly realms, or as humans with least imperfections. To that end, they strive to purify the mind, making it free from greed, anger, and delusion, the roots of evil and rebirth in the more painful realms. Good death does not just happen to anyone, as it is the result of long and arduous efforts of preparation through mind training. Though such efforts are necessary to ensure good death, the nature of the last conscious state is of utmost importance, for it contributes significantly to the quality of the ensuing rebirth. If it is wholesome, this will produce good rebirth, or the opposite if it is unwholesome. The quality of this last consciousness depends on the nature of the action one does, or recollects, immediately before the dying moment. This action is known as a death-proximate *kamma* or technically referred to as "reproductive" *kamma*. The goal of spiritual care for dying patients, therefore, is to help the patient to conceive a wholesome thought at the moment of death. The Buddhist way of hospice care includes: (1) giving love and sympathy in thought, word, and deed; (2) helping to accept death as natural; (3) making the mind focus on the Triple Gems, the Buddha, the *dhamma* (teachings), and the *sangha* (the Order), and on the good deeds done; (4) freeing the mind from fear, anger, and anxiety; (5) helping to let go of all; and (6) setting a peaceful environment. All these underline hospice care in Thailand, which is discussed below.

Hospice Care at Hospitals

Compassionate Hospice Nurses

In state-run hospitals in Thailand, there are no exclusive wards for terminal patients. The dying are usually scattered in different wards alongside other patients and especially in ICU. With limited resources of funds, medical personnel, and facilities, doctors and nurses try to give the best care they can to them. For example, a practicing Buddhist nurse from Wachirapayabal hospital, sympathetic to their needs, comforts and encourages patients in their last moment to take refuge in the Buddha to gain inspiration, get rid of fears and other mental disturbances, and ensure good rebirth. Similarly, another nurse at a different hospital helps terminal patients to get rid of feelings of guilt and anxiety for unfulfilled plans. For example, she helped a husband who had been unfaithful and who felt guilty about having minor wives, to meet his angry wife and be forgiven. On that occasion he also forgave her for whatever wrongs she might have done to him. Both parted from each other in peace. By forgiving him the wife felt great relief and could live more lightly and happily without having to carry around the weight of her resentment. The dying husband, now free from regrets and remorse, died peacefully. The religious significance of forgiving is its power to sever the *kammic* knot that ties the doer to the person who suffered from the wrongs he did. The act of forgiving nullifies the *kammic* consequences the doer of the unskillful act has to bear in the next life as the forgiver seeks no revenge. Therefore, it is a custom for Thai Buddhists to give an opportunity to the dying and the relatives to forgive or let go of whatever wrong they might have done to one another, understanding that all of us still have our faults and weaknesses.

In another case, the nurse helped a dying patient to rid himself of anxiety for his unfulfilled plan to build a pavilion in a temple in Bangkok. The nurse arranged for his wife to come and inform him that she and her relatives would take care of completing the construction. The pavilion would bear his name, and a special ritual would be made to transfer the merit to him. The patient felt relieved and joyful and died peacefully after a few days.

Such skilful hospice care at state-run hospitals in Thailand depends upon individual nurses and is limited because there are not many nursing students who want to specialize in palliative care. When interviewed, nurse Angsana of a metropolitan hospital confided, "I had seen my mother die in agony, and I felt depressed that I could not do anything to help her. After that I began studying Buddhism and decided to use the knowledge gained to help terminal patients to die a good death." Compassion and sensitivity to the sufferings of others then are the main motives for entering the nursing profession, particularly for palliative care.

Three Factors Obstructing Good Death

A shortage of nurses interested in hospice palliative care is one factor that prevents a good death for many terminal patients in state-run hospitals. Second is the desire of the doctors and relatives to sustain or to prolong the patients' lives as much as possible by all means, even when death is imminent. This effort to keep the patients alive makes it difficult for them to die in a peaceful environment. They are usually hooked up to gadgets and wires and sustained by a machine. They usually die alone in a manner and in a place where they do not wish to end their lives. The situation will be better when doctors and relatives gracefully accept the imminent death and turn their full attention to the compassionate care of the dying. This may happen when the concepts of "living will" and "patients' right to die" are socially and legally accepted in Thai society. Thirdly, the patients are kept as free of pain as possible, so that they may die comfortably. As Cicely Saunders so clearly demonstrated, the use of analgesics or sedatives can keep the dying patients in a state of painlessness. However, use of these drugs can impair the faculties affecting their consciousness, and this makes it impossible for the patients to fill their minds with the wholesome thought that is necessary for good rebirth. There is then a tension between the Buddhist understanding of death and dying and the hospice palliative care model of drug use to keep dying patients free of severe unbearable pain. The challenge for the hospice palliative care team is how to use drugs to maintain the pain of the patients at the bearable level that does not impair or cloud their consciousness. For those patients who are meditation masters themselves and whose meditative mind is always one-pointed and tranquil, such use of drugs is not thought to be necessary. But to have this kind of mind requires a long and arduous effort of preparation over a lifetime and only very few succeed. For average patients the question of withdrawing pain killing drugs is a serious one. In some cases, the hospice palliative care team has to use drugs that have the double effects of relieving the patients of severe pain while dampening their consciousness. But these patients do not consider such impairment detrimental as their good deeds during their lifetime will be reasonably sufficient to ensure good rebirth.

A Supporting Factor for Good Death

Some of the state hospitals in Bangkok have pediatric wards to look after children with terminal cancer. Among them, Chulalongkorn Red Cross Hospital may be cited as a model. Here the hospice care team consists of doctors, nurses, psychologists, and social workers who provide pain management, psychological, and spiritual care to these children. Nearly all of them come from low-income families that cannot afford to take care of them at home. A remarkable feature in their treatment is the "Wishing Well" project initiated by Dr. Isarang Nuchpraysura to help children suffering from life-threatening diseases such as cancer and HIV to fulfill their special wishes. Dr. Isurang said, "All the children here will not live long though they will not die so soon. I want to help them to have their wishes fulfilled. To this end I usually listen attentively to what they have to say about these wishes. In some cases I ask them to write down their wishes. Then I try to find ways of meeting their wishes." Since its inception in 2004 the project has helped forty children to fulfill their special wishes. One boy, for example, wanted to see a panda before his death. Being aware of this, the doctor raised funds to fly him to a zoo in the northern province of Chiang Mai where a panda is kept. The boy spent almost the whole morning at the zoo with the panda. He came back with a happy face resulting from his wish fulfilled. He died two weeks later.

Some children want to go to the seaside with their families. Some want to return home to be with their parents and friends while some want to go to make merit at a certain temple. The doctor usually advises parents of these children to listen and be aware of the wishes of their children as well as help these wishes to be fulfilled so that the children may die in peace whether at home or in the hospital. Therefore, helping children to actualize their dreams, something they desperately wish for, in their last days is an important supporting factor for their good death. This involves love and compassion on the part of hospice teams and parents.

Hospice Care at Home

Sense of Gratitude

Hospice care at home among familiar surroundings with family members, friends, and relatives is more congenial for a good death. Some hospitals, such as Wachirapayabal and Chulalongkorn, have home care programs in which nurses go to visit terminal patients at home to teach the family members how to care for them, for example by administering oxygen and treating bed sores. Home visits are made based on the type and severity of illness and vary from weekly to monthly. Taking care of terminal patients at home poses problems for family members, as one sick person affects all in the family. In one family a daughter had to give up her job at a bank in order to take care of her mother suffering from cancer in the terminal stage. In spite of this inconvenience she was willing to provide the care herself out of a sense of gratitude. When interviewed, the daughter said,

> My mother was very good to all of us. She devoted her whole life to take care of us. After the death of my father who was the sole supporter of our family, it was very hard for her. I and my sister are very happy to have a chance to take care of her. Of course, this is not a burden but an opportunity for us to show gratitude to our mother. I gave up my work at the bank because the work prevents me from attending to the needs of my suffering mother. I have saved enough money and can use it all for her. We can have mother only once in our lives. If I lose her I cannot get her back again. But lost money can be regained.

For her, as for all Buddhists, looking after parents, especially when they are old and sick, is considered as a blessing in life. This sense of gratitude rests on the reciprocity of obligations among family members. It arises from the awareness on the part of the children that they owe some debt to their parents who gave them life, raised, and helped them along their way of life. It does not specifically convey to the children how to repay their parents, but it makes them cognizant about doing in return something good for the parents, even should it lead to self-sacrifice by the children. All these are done with willingness and great pleasure.

Perhaps the greatest challenge to this value of gratitude has to do with caring for parents suffering from Alzheimer's disease stretched over many years. This creates serious problems for a small modern family as the husband is the income earner and the wife has to take care of children. In many cases, the children have to send the ailing parents to hospitals or charity homes as they have neither time nor resources to provide the continuing care needed, and they often feel guilty about it. But there are also many cases where aging patients are kept at home in spite of the great burden the children have to bear. One daughter who has been caring for her suffering father for seven years said,

At the beginning it was very difficult for me due to the adverse change of my father's personality and behavior. I had to quarrel with him most of the time as he was not willing to make any adjustment to the situation. This put a great stress and strain on me. Later I knew from the doctor that my father is suffering from the second-stage Alzheimer's disease, and learnt about its nature. Then I realize that I, instead of him, should be the one to make all necessary adjustments. By making such adjustment on my part I found that he and I are much happier together.

In this case, the care provided is similar to hospice care already discussed before. It covers physical, psychological, and social well-being as well as spiritual care. The psychological and social well-being comes mostly through arranging visits to relatives, friends, and places. Through spiritual care the patient receives love and sympathy and need not feel neglected. The patient is always treated with love and dignity as the father, though he may not be aware of it. All of this lifts his spirit and makes his life tolerable and cheerful in his last days. When asked whether caring for her father is a burden, the daughter replied, "My father had been good to me since my very young days, and he was always loving. When I learnt about the nature of his disease I feel very sorry for him and sad to see how he deteriorates day by day. Taking care of him is no more a burden. It gives me opportunity to repay my gratitude to him." This approach to an aging and suffering patient is typically Buddhist. It teaches us to be optimistic and flexible in our relationship with terminal patients. Taking care of them is our *kamma*, but it is a good *kamma*. It gives us the opportunity to do good and gain merit for the future rebirth. Love and sympathy are manifestations of the human spirit which will enable us to survive through all difficulties.

It is also gratifying to know that there is a supportive social network in the form of an association of those who care for patients with Alzheimer's disease. They have a regular monthly meeting to which nearly all caregivers of these patients come. They then have a chance to talk, share, and learn from one another how to provide the best care for the patients and how to tackle everyday problems. This helps to relieve them of the strain and stress. Sometimes monks are invited to join them in their meetings to encourage them and to make them realize the religious importance of their altruistic work.

Spiritual Care

At home, the patient has more opportunity to have spiritual needs met, for instance, to accumulate merit by offering food to the monks almost daily, with the help of the family, by listening to tape-recorded chants, and, sometimes, to get the teaching and blessings from the monks invited by the daughter or son to visit. The visit and presence of the monks usually makes the patient happy and feel closer to Buddhism. It enables the patient to learn to adopt the Buddhist attitude toward death and dying, and to apply the teaching to enrich the patient's life till the last moment, getting rid of mental defilements such as anxiety and lust for life. Luang Phor Charan, a meditation master, said that whenever he visits terminal patients at home, he teaches them to accept the impermanence, suffering, and nonsubstantiality of existence, and to let go of attachment to everything including one's body and all that one has. He also teaches the patients to practice mindfulness of breathing to calm the mind and endure pain. Besides, he said,

> Sometimes I chant to make the patient feel joy by the rhythm of the chant even though the meaning of Pali words may not

be understood. There was a case when a dying patient looked unhappy. I encouraged him to take refuge in the Triple Gems, the Buddha, the *dhamma* [the Teaching], and the *sangha* [the Order], and reminded him of the good deeds he had done both for Buddhism and society. It made him look happy and joyful. Once, I visited a dying patient who looked miserable. I put my hand on his head for twenty minutes and radiated loving-kindness to him. Suddenly he looked at me, smiled and then passed away. There was also a case when the patient told me that he saw fire in front of him. I knew that it was due to the effects of his past defilements. It was not a good sign in his impending death. I then asked the relatives to find something for the patient to make an offering to me as this will change the vision of fire he was seeing. I knew this patient, as he was a monk at my temple for two years. After receiving the offering from him I blessed him and asked him what he was seeing. He said he was seeing the image of the Buddha in our temple. That was a very good sign which showed that his mind had become free from defilements at that moment. He died a few hours later and I am sure it was a good death leading him to be reborn next in a heavenly realm.

All of these approaches are typical of the practice of Buddhist monks to help terminal patients to die a good death. According to Buddhism, a dying person usually sees a mental image at the last moment before death, which indicates his or her previous *kamma* and thus future destiny. For example, the mental object of fire indicates the hell realms, a forest the animal realm, and a human body the human realm. Owing to the significance of death-proximate *kamma* in determining the subsequent rebirth, the custom prevailing in modern Thailand and other Buddhist countries is to encourage the dying person to take refuge in the Triple Gems, reminding him of his good deeds and helping him make merit on his deathbed. However, this does not mean that the bad *kamma* done in one's lifetime is offset by that good *kamma* in the last moments of life. Rather, it implies that the good *kamma* before death, however small it may be, will yield the first immediate *kammic* results and be followed by other *kammic* consequences. It is like a cow, nearest to the exit, who, even though small and frail, will get out first when the gate is opened, and will then be followed by other cows.

Radiation of loving-kindness and chanting are also used by Thai monks to help patients die in peace. Radiation involves direct transmission of the healing power of loving-kindness generated by the meditative mind of the monk to the disturbed mind of the dying. It may be done by touching or just sitting close to the patient. Chanting done in Pali by the monks is also very comforting to the dying. Some chants are believed to have curative powers. The patient who understands the meaning of the chanting will be joyful and appreciative of the truth of the *dhamma* and the Buddha's limitless compassion embodied in the verses chanted. Even without understanding the Pali words, listening to the vibration of the chanting sounds will soothe the mind and calm it. Some Buddhists, while listening to the chanting, visualize the Buddha standing before them and blessing them with the healing *dhamma* flowing from his mouth into their entire bodies to reduce suffering and to ward off illness. Listening to this chanting and mentally seeing the Buddha are also regarded as meritorious deeds that will yield good *kammic* result in the future.

Informal Hospice Care at Buddhist Temples

Wat Doi Gueng and Preparation for Good Death

As we can see in the previous discussion, palliative care at hospitals is rather inadequate, and what is provided at home also has problems, though it has its own benefits. In spite of their deteriorating health condition, terminal patients continue to have hope that they can be cured of their deadly diseases. They seek healing both in Buddhism and modern medicine. Many of them supplement the medical treatment with the practice of meditation at temples. Out of compassion, monks open the doors of their temples (or *wat* in Thai) to them and take care of them without charge during their stay there. Among these temples, Wat Doi Gueng in Mae Hongsorn Province in Northern Thailand may be cited as an example of informal hospice care. This care primarily consists, on the part of the patients, of daily chanting, learning the *dhamma*, and practicing morality and meditation to prepare themselves for the inevitable death in the last days of their life. By chanting they are taking refuge in the Triple Gems. For meditation they practice both mindfulness of breathing to calm the agitated mind and loving-kindness meditation to cultivate love and compassion in place of negative emotions such as ill-will or resentment. Learning the *dhamma* enables them to gain insights into the reality of life and death. Practicing morality and meditation helps purify their conduct and the mind. In addition, they are encouraged to practice generosity to make them happier and healthier. This involves giving time, wealth, knowledge, and love to benefit others. The religious significance of generous giving is to reduce egoism on the part of the giver, which has good *kammic* effects now and on rebirth.

Meditation and Pain Control

The abbot teaches dying patients about the impermanent nature of the body to make them aware that the body is not essentially oneself, as one cannot control it. The body is subject to decline and decay. It is impossible for the body to be free from illness at all times. Though the mind and the body are interdependent, the mind, to some extent, can detach itself from the body. When the body is sick the mind need not be sick also. One may have a healthy mind in a sick body. Therefore, one must not be preoccupied with the sick body but should be more concerned with the quality of the mind. For pain control, the abbot advises them to practice mindfulness meditation focusing on the feeling of pain. It is to make them conscious of the feeling of pain as it really is, without being stuck in it. Pain belongs to the body, which itself is not oneself. A person may have pain or feel painful, but that person is not to be identified with pain or the painful feeling. The more the mind is concentrated on pain the less painful one will feel. When the mind achieves one-pointedness, known as *samadhi,* pain will be no more. All terminal patients learn the teaching and practice of mindfulness meditation earnestly as it is their only chance. With regard to the use of this Buddhist method for pain control, one terminal patient said, "By realizing that I am not cancer I feel better. When I am not preoccupied with the sick body I feel happier and have more time for mind training to prepare myself to face death with confidence and courage. I like to meditate on pain to reduce its severity and to escape it in *samadhi.* I am taking less quantity of prescribed painkilling drugs, and hope to stop using them altogether soon." The power of meditation goes back to the time of the Buddha when he and his disciples used meditation to reach the painless level. Since that time, the same method, known as *dhamma* therapy, has been used by Buddhist monks to deal with illness and suffering. Among them are well-known meditation masters such as Luang Phu Mun and his disciple Luang Ta Maha Bua of the forest hermitage in Northern Thailand.

The gist of *dhamma* therapy is the development of mindfulness. When one has mindfulness the mind distances itself from the suffering body and acts as a mere spectator. Thus, the mind is not bound up with the pain of the body. Though the pain is still there it cannot affect the mind, as the latter does not allow itself to be tormented by it. This is like someone looking at the burning fire from a distance without being affected by the heat as he is not jumping into the flame. *Dhamma* therapy is possible only if one does not cling to the "I and Mine." Such clinging results in the wrong belief that "I am the suffering body and am the pain itself." When this clinging is too strong the mind cannot detach itself from the body's pain. Only mindfulness can make us detach from such clinging and its negative consequences, and help the mind to reach the stage of one-pointedness in which tranquility and joy arise naturally.

There are many temples like Wat Doi Gueng that give care for cancer patients. The facilities they provide are not as good as at the hospitals or home. It is the warmth, generosity, and the profound knowledge of Buddhism that the monks have that attract the patients to go to the temple. Some stay for a few days, a week, or a month or more, according to their need.

Wat Phrabat Nampu and the Dhammarak Foundation

Many terminal patients are AIDS sufferers. At the beginning of the outbreak of AIDS, there was no place for them to stay at hospitals and they were often rejected by their own families. Though people at present understand more about this deadly disease there is still stigma attached to it. Hospitals and some families are beginning to accept and care for them. But the patients themselves are reluctant to admit the nature of their disease for fear of discrimination. Wat Phrabat Nampu in Lopburi province is a place AIDS sufferers feel safe going to. There they are always accepted and cared for without charge. Out of compassion, the abbot Prakru Udompaschadhorn established the Dhammarak Foundation in 1992 with initial funds donated by the Queen Mother. He said, "My job is to help AIDS patients die peacefully and in as little pain as possible. Some people say my work is futile, because the patients are going to die anyway. My answer is, we are all going to die one day. Surely we should be providing these people with kindness and mercy. If we turn our backs on them, how can we call ourselves human?"

Most of the support for Abbot Prakru's work comes from NGOs and other agencies. Their donations have funded extensive building projects in two large complexes. In addition to the temple for monks to live in, there is a hospice building for patients, pavilions for instruction, administrative buildings, museums that are used to teach about impermanence of the body, and residences for mobile patients. When possible, families live together with their children. A health team consisting of the abbot himself as well as doctors and nurses from different hospitals, both in Thailand and abroad, look after the sufferers according to the severity of their condition. There are three categories of patients: those who are bedridden and cannot help themselves at all; those who can move about and help themselves to some extent; and those who are quite able to work for the temple. They are lodged in three different buildings. The Dhammarak Foundation is by far the largest hospice operation in Thailand.

Mental, Social, and Spiritual Needs

In 2009, there are 215 AIDS patients and four hundred beds in the temple ward. Hospice care at this temple is more comprehensive than the temples mentioned previously. Here, care includes also meeting mental and social needs of patients as most are rejected by society and even by their families. Accordingly, they are so depressed that they need to be encouraged to have a positive attitude toward themselves and to regain confidence as moral people. They are taught the law of *kamma*. Regarding this, some may think it is not appropriate for them as it may make them fatalistic. On the contrary, from the abbot's teaching they realize that this law is not ironclad, but permits them to take care of their present lives. Even in the last moment they still have chance to shape their future. Whether they have a good death or not is up to them. The teaching therefore enables them to overcome resentment against those who reject them. They are also taught to practice loving-kindness meditation to replace the negative with positive feelings and to radiate compassion toward hostile people. Radiating to oneself is to forgive oneself for the wrong one did in the past so that one need not brood over it with remorse. The practice of such meditation makes patients calm and joyful and enables them to participate in various activities organized by the abbot. When asked about his reaction to the law of *kamma* one patient said, "The teaching helps me accept AIDS with tranquility, without negative and depressing mental states. Through the understanding of the law of *kamma*, as explained by Luang Phor, I know better how to live, and skillfully use the condition of my body and mind to ensure good rebirth."

One of the important activities, which other temples do not organize, is the formation of support groups as a social force by which the AIDS sufferers themselves help one another and are encouraged to join in different activities such as exercise, temple work, and raising herbal medicinal plants. Those who have come earlier share their experience with the newcomers, encouraging and comforting them. They also have the opportunity to use their talents, such as in cooking or music, for self-fulfillment and community benefit. These activities also promote self-esteem and make patients feel at home. One patient admits, "This is my second home. Everyone including the caregivers have been good to me, and no one here looks down on me, unlike those outside the temple. When I first came I could barely walk, but one sufferer in a worse condition than me encouraged me to improve my health. Now I am walking better." In addition to the benefit from the support group, individual patients also gain from the teaching of the abbot. One female patient expressed, "I am no longer afraid of death as Luang Phor taught that all human beings have to grow old, get sick, and face death. Even the Buddha himself could not avoid this condition. I want to do good by helping others, to gain merit and have a good rebirth. Every day I am doing temple work as much as I can to show my gratitude to Luang Phor." All patients are taught to practice meditation on death, to remind themselves of the inevitability of death and to make an effort to live each moment as a meaningful and fulfilling life.

With regard to bedridden patients, the abbot gives them spiritual care by radiating his compassion, by holding their hands, and by performing rituals for them, for example, by putting flowers in their hands as an offering to the abbot. This helps them to calm the mind and to gain merit. The physical needs of the patients, such as bathing and having their beds cleaned, are also taken care of daily. After their death other AIDS sufferers join the rituals, and merits are transferred to the dead.

Outreach Programs

The temple also has outreach programs to promote community participation in hospice care and to counter fears about the deadly disease. To this end the abbot and his team visit the villages and the schools to build relations between them and AIDS sufferers. Over time, these relationships have become stronger, with increasing numbers of villagers and school children coming to give assistance as needed. The abbot, volunteers, and some of the AIDS sufferers occasionally go to villages and schools to talk about the nature and causes of the disease, the kind of suffering it brings, and the effective ways to prevent it. This is in accordance with the abbot's desire to promote better understanding about AIDS among the public and to dispel prejudice. It is also a preventive measure to control the spread of this pandemic. There is also a large, well-equipped modern theater where groups of visitors are educated and entertained by performances put on by patients, some of whom were professional entertainers before becoming ill.

The outreach programs include a home care project for sufferers. The project was initiated a few years ago with assistance from the Ministry of Public Health and some NGOs to provide them with a supportive community. In implementing it the abbot had persuaded people in different villages to take care of AIDS patients in their own localities without bringing them to the temple. It may take some time for the project to be effective, as most people are poor and still are scared of the deadly disease. The abbot's work is beginning to be known worldwide, and with assistance from the AIDS Healthcare Foundation, the temple has become a major AIDS treatment center providing lifesaving care to a low-income population.

Care at Wat Phrabat Nampu for Children of AIDS Sufferers

Wat Phrabat Nampu also cares for a large number of AIDS orphans and children of adult patients. Some of the children are infected themselves. To educate all these children, most of whom have no family resources to support them, a secondary school was established in 1999 about eighty kilometers from the main temple compound. It was followed in 2001 by a kindergarten and primary school. Expenses for these schools are met by the temple in cooperation with the Ministry of Education. The children study at the same school with children of the villagers. The orphans stay at the temple in a family atmosphere and learn to be as self-sufficient as possible. Birthday parties and other activities are held regularly to make them feel at home. Kitchen facilities are provided and AIDS patients cook for them. During summer vacation the abbot ordains the children to be novices to learn the *dhamma* and to practice meditation.

Love and compassion make a difference in the lives of these children and other AIDS sufferers by giving meaning to their last days and allowing them to be of service to others. They are taught basic breathing meditation which is very successful in calming the mind and reducing pain. What has been discussed so far clearly shows that AIDS sufferers can die in peace at Buddhist temples. Hospice care is possible at these temples even when resources are limited. We have to recognize and admire the crucial and exemplary service of the abbot, who has significantly contributed to the changed attitude and behavior of the Thai public toward AIDS. Similar work of other temples such as that of Wat Thepmongkol in Amnat Charoen, a district of Issan in Northeast Thailand, is also worth mentioning.

Wat Thepmongkol and Quality Development of Life Center

Wat Thepmongkol is a fine example of a monastery that has seriously undertaken to put Buddhist principles into practice in the community. Its basic philosophy is captured in the saying, "To grow plants, you must prepare the soil; when you want to eat you must have food; to develop better work, you must develop a better man; to develop a man, you must train his mind first." The development projects are under the direction of Luang Phor, Thawin Sunyathat, a disciple of Buddhadassa. The abbot of Wat Thepmongkol is Phra Khru Monkol Worawat. Our information was gathered primarily by the monk Phra Narong, who was a very active worker in the wat's social outreach programs. He is forty-seven years old and a doctoral candidate at Mahidol University, in the College of Religious Studies. He has been a monk or novice since he was a young boy.

The Quality Development of Life Center has a number of programs where monks and laymen work together to take care of the elderly, rehabilitate released prisoners, and care for dying patients and HIV/AIDS patients. In general these programs attempt to involve all levels of the community members, along with local politicians, respected local community leaders, businessmen and women, school teachers, nurses, doctors, HIV sufferers, and ex-addicts. The basic idea is to apply the principles and practices of Buddhism to help individuals rebuild broken lives and

to renew the community. Buddhist meditation is an important part of
the program as well. Economic self-sufficiency is an important part of
such success. Clients are given jobs around the monastery, taught basic
skills, and encouraged to grow as much of their own food as practicable
following one of the king's agricultural initiatives.

There are no hospice beds under the monastery's supervision, but
there are active programs to help patients die at home as well. These are
very useful, as the hospitals in the area, as is typical in Thailand, have
little to offer in the way of home care. All the staff members who work
with AIDS patients are themselves in remission from the disease. They
make home visits and set up plans to enable the family to take good care
of patients. In order to raise morale and impart information about how
to deal with the disease, they run a "morale camp" for AIDS sufferers,
where medical people teach about the nature of the disease, how to treat
it, and how to avoid secondary infections. In addition, there are discussion groups and individual counseling sessions, with monks listening in
at many of the meetings. Participants share their experiences, problems,
ideas, feelings, and daily activities and encourage one another. Patients
are taught Buddhist meditation, which is found to be very helpful for
maintaining calm as one's disease progresses.

The Center and Child Sufferers of AIDS

Children with HIV are of special interest to the Quality Development
of Life Center, which offers an Alternative Care program where young
patients are taught about the disease and offered emotional support. The
children are also taught meditation techniques, which they enjoy. There
is also an art camp for kids. For those who are not infected, there is a
"morale camp" where they are taught about the disease and encouraged
to follow Buddhist moral guidance as a preventive measure. The Center
runs an educational program for novice monks about HIV/AIDS, both to
prevent their getting infected and so they will not stigmatize the afflicted.
The monastery, which aspires to be a "green temple," grows medicinal
herbs to help the patients and plants flowers to make the place cheerful and pleasing to be in. As part of the emphasis on self-sufficiency,
patients in remission and patients' families are encouraged to grow herbs
and flowers for income as well. Families are supported as they care for
dying patients at home, and when necessary, patients are moved to the

district hospital for extra care and when pain becomes too severe. The wat and local medical services are in close contact and cooperate in care plans for their clients.

Monks play an important part helping patients achieve a good death, and the Buddhist teachings, rituals, and meditation methods they use are very similar to those presented earlier in this chapter. Phra Narong said, "Children and adults receive the same message and help, as adapted to their different capacities. I use mindfulness meditation by focusing on breathing. It helps them understand what is going on in the mind every minute. This builds confidence. The idea is to die with a calm mind, without anger, with no grasping." Most of the monks' visiting is done at patients' homes, but when necessary, they offer their help in hospital as well.

Monk Network on AIDS

Phra Narong's account of how patients can achieve a good, Buddhist death in rural Isaan shows the great value of monks organizing to apply Buddhist principles to the very real problem of providing palliative care in a system where it is not well funded or supported by government services. Wat Thepmongkol is affiliated with the Monk Network on AIDS in Thailand (MNAT), a grouping of some thirty wats, which has only been going on for three years. Currently, there are five member temples in Isaan. Unfortunately, mention of the work of Wat Thepmongkol, the MNAT, and the palliative section of the local hospital was overlooked in the 2007 International Observatory survey of palliative care in Thailand (IOELC n.d.). The idea of MNAT is to develop teamwork and linkages with several groups to improve care for HIV patients and to promote prevention. The groups include MNAT, hospitals, AIDS Net (an organization in Isaan that brings together families affected by HIV/AIDS for mutual aid), and community groupings of elders, politicians, housewives, youth, etc.

Concluding Remarks

From the cases we have discussed, it is clear that in Buddhist understanding, death is not the end of life but the beginning of a new life in the endless life cycle of births and rebirths. For Thai Buddhists, apart from the physical and mental contributing factors, disease is the sum of one's unmeritious deeds in this and earlier lives. Good death does not mean painless or sudden death. Rather, it means dying with wholesome consciousness on the part of the patient. This is the aim of hospice care in Thailand whether in hospitals, at homes, or in temples. The hospice team is willing to let the dying prepare in full consciousness for imminent death. But in some cases the team has to use medication to reduce the patient's pain even if it makes the consciousness clouded. Cicely Saunders's fundamental principles of "pain control, a family or community environment, and an engagement with the dying person's most deeply rooted spirituality" (see chapter 1 of this volume) are relevant, but they are implemented with a particular Thai slant.

As more people die at hospitals, there is now a need for the hospitals to add hospice care units and to staff them with specially trained health care personnel. Some hospitals such as Chulalongkorn Red Cross Hospital are already moving in this direction. Hospitals must also try to recruit volunteers, including Buddhist monks, relatives, and concerned people, to meet the shortage of personnel in caring for terminal patients. The Red Cross Hospital successfully initiated such a program about three years ago. It has quite a number of volunteers to keep the patients company and give comfort and spiritual care using *dhamma* books and tapes or by putting Buddha images or pictures of well-respected monks in places where they can be seen easily. This does not mean that Buddhists are idol worshippers. The image of the Buddha is used as an object of concentration to gain peace of mind and as a visual aid that helps one to recall the Buddha's teaching and to remember his great qualities.

For hospice care at home, as mentioned earlier, there are some outreach programs to help families with their care for the dying and for those with Alzheimer's disease. These programs also need to give attention to the other members of the family who are affected by the all-absorbing care they are giving to the patients. It is hoped that more hospitals in the near future will take measures to help them. When this is done it will make hospice care in Thailand become really what it should be. At present, the family members themselves have to bear the strains and stresses nearly always without any professional help. Only monks, on their occasional visits, advise them to use *dhamma* and practices of meditation to relieve them of their distress.

In Thai society, Buddhist monks always play crucial roles in the life of the community. At present their role is expanded to include social work. Those who are in need always get help from the monks. The role of the monks in hospice care should be strengthened and their hospice-like temples need to be assisted both by the state and the Ecclesiastical Council, as well as by relevant agencies, to enable these temples to provide more efficient and accessible services to the wider public. The monks have successfully demonstrated that the practice of *dhamma* and meditation provide physical and mental healing. Mindfulness meditation has the power to relieve pain and make the mind calm and peaceful. Similarly, meditation on loving-kindness is an effective means against all forms of anger, hatred, and ill-will, which are the unwholesome mental states that lead to suffering. The two kinds of meditation therefore should be integrated in hospice care as part of pain management as well as psychological and spiritual care. These are important both for the patients and the caregivers. The *dhamma* is a precious jewel given to humanity by the Buddha. It will be a pity if we do not realize its value and make utmost use of it.

References

Bennett, E. 2001. *The severed heart: Death and dying among the Isaan of rural northeast Thailand*. University of Melbourne: Dissertation, Faculty of Medicine, Dentistry and Health Sciences.

Coward, H., and P. Ratanakul, eds. 1999. *A cross-cultural dialogue on health care ethics*. Waterloo, ON: Wilfred Laurier University Press.

Engstrom, D., and T. Kubotani. 2005. The roles of Buddhist temples in the treatment of HIV/AIDS in Thailand. *Journal of Sociology and Social Welfare* (Dec.). http://findarticles.com/p/articles/mi_m0CYZ/is_4_32/ai_n16418558/pg_6/?tag=content;col1. (Accessed July 14, 2009).

Florida, R. 1999. Abortion in Buddhist Thailand. In *Buddhism and abortion*, ed. D. Keown. London: MacMillan.

———. 1994. Buddhism and the four principles. In *Principles of health care ethics*, ed. R. Gillon. London: J. Wiley.

International Observatory on End of Life Care (cited as IOELC). n.d. Thailand country report. http://www.eolc-observatory.net/global_analysis/thailand.htm. (Accessed July 3, 2009).

Nyanaponika. 1997. *Buddhist dictionary*. Kandy, Sri Lanka: Buddhist Publication Society.

Ratanakul, P. 2008. Health, disease, and healing: The Buddhist contribution. *Dharma World* 35 (Oct.–Dec.): 30–36.

———. 2003. Bioethics and AIDS in Thailand: A Buddhist perspective. In *Asian bioethics in the 21ˢᵗ century*, ed., Eubios Ethics Institute, section 9.6, not paginated. http://www.eubios.info/ABC4/abc4299.htm#top. (Accessed July 14, 2009).

———. 2004a. Buddhism, health, and disease. *Eubios Journal of Asian Bioethics* 14(5): 162–64. http://www.eubios.info/ejaib145.htm. (Accessed July 2, 2009).

———. 2004b. The Buddhist concept of life, suffering, and death and related bioethical issues. *Eubios Journal of Asian Bioethics* 14(4): 141–46. http://www.eubios.info/EJ144/ej144f.htm. (Accessed Aug. 26, 2009).

UNAIDS. 2008. *UNGASS country progress report: Thailand reporting period January 2006-December 2007.* http://data.unaids.org/pub/Report/2008/thailand_2008_country_progress_report_en.pdf. (Accessed Aug. 27, 2009).

———. 2009. *Thailand.* http://www.unaids.org/en/CountryResponses/Countries/thailand.asp. Accessed Aug. 27, 2009).

9

The Ugandan Way of Living and Dying

Michael L. Hadley
Godfrey Agupio

Religion permeates the social and cultural fabric of Uganda. Belief systems find expression everywhere in a rich variety of religious practices and liturgies. Christian churches—from Roman Catholic to Pentecostal and other charismatics—fill to overflowing on Sundays. With major places of worship in prominent and dominating locations in the capital city of Kampala, Roman Catholic, Anglican, Bah'ai, Hindu, and Muslim congregations nourish communal life. The life of faith is overt, vital, and existential. A striking feature of religious life in Uganda is the fact of its omnipresent expression in the public arena. Even the world of commerce bears witness to living faith traditions: "Ave Maria Hair Salon," "Hail Mary Take-Away," "Holy Trinity Secretaries," "Jesus is Alive Family Shop," "God"s Grace Internet," "Glory be to God Gift Shop," "God"s Mercy Taxi," and "Back to God Medical Centre." Garish signage on the windshields of smoke-belching *matatus*—jalopy buses hogging the overcrowded, chaotic highroads and rutted byways—proclaims the omnipresence of God: "Allah is Great," "Jesus Lives," "The Holy Spirit Calls." All this outward evidence in the pulsing hustle and bustle of crowded markets and taxi parks underscores a cacophony of interwoven narratives. They are narratives of a spiritual journey undertaken in the hand of Providence, a path from birth through travail and ultimately to death. In terms of African mythology, these are about "people on the underground journey to God-realization; people of immeasurable radiance; people of infinite compassion" (Ford 1999, 9). In this light the nation's motto "For God and my country" enunciates a palpable set of moral priorities.[1]

While Uganda has no official state religion, its religious traditions since the arrival of Muslim traders and Christian missionaries in the 1860s are predominantly tripartite: indigenous religions, Islam, and Christianity. Statistically (census 2002), the ratio stands at 80 percent Christian and 10 percent Muslim. The predominant branches of Christianity are Roman Catholic (41.9%) and Church of Uganda, that is, Anglican (35.9%). Yet, the Pentecostal/Evangelical churches are growing rapidly. Significantly, it is "the rise of Pentecostalism that is giving Christianity its high profile today" (Gifford 1999, 99). Indeed, Pentecostal congregations, in all their manifold variety, actually shape and project the identity of Uganda as a Christian country. They draw their increase not so much through new conversions as through what is regarded as a "hemorrhaging" of nominal members from mainline churches. The appeal of the Pentecostals for a largely impoverished population lies in the churches' emotional energy and exuberance, in their intensity and seriousness of purpose, and in their emotive assurance of self-actualization and ultimate purpose. They even offer hope for material success. Television stations carry round-the-clock programs of evangelization, often in crassly capitalist terms. While all churches have the potential to uplift their people, "in fact it is the intensity of the born-again experience which has proved it can take people on to another plane" (Gifford 1999, 115). Importantly, Pentecostalism in its various forms is as much a cultural phenomenon as a theological one.

Concurrent with these faith traditions—some would say as an undercurrent to them—are the indigenous African religions. Some indigenous thinkers regard the revealed Europeanized religions as "imports." They hold that "with relevant adjustments to changing situations and circumstances in Africa, the traditional [indigenous and religious] ethic should be recaptured and used as a basis for moral reasoning and decision-making" (Kasenene 1998, iii; Ani 2000). Significantly, these religions stand in syncretic relationship with the major traditions. An extreme example of this is the Holy Spirit Movement in which the supposedly Christian spirit Lakwena possessed an obscure woman and inspired her to lead an army. Ultimately defeated by the National Resistance Army of current president Yoweri Museveni (Behrend 1999), she was exiled to Kenya. As some believe, the spirit Lakwena then left her now-discredited "Ugandan St. Joan" and took possession of Joseph Kony. Now "spirit possessed," the notorious leader of the Lord's Resistance Army in the Gulu district of northwest Uganda has been savaging the populace for decades (Museveni 1997, 211–14). As *The Guardian* reported on November 11, 2009, Kony's dying mother earnestly believed her son to be possessed by "evil spirits" and begged him to make peace. But having heard "God's word," he still remains firm. Other indigenous traditions are less severe.

Ugandan writer John Ssemuwanga poignantly captures these overlapping magisteria in his poem "Dual Piety." Here the poetic narrator ponders his experience of being a committed worshipper caught between two equally compelling spiritual cultures. "It is Sunday morning—and the bells seem to toll / The ebb of ancestral piety, / Piety dimmed by Christian chime / And tarnished by rituals ministered by infallible arrivals" from abroad. For him the Christian church has spoken convincingly and persuasively with all the authority of doctrine, ritual, scripture, and sacrament. The truth it preaches is palpably real, experientially authentic. He earnestly believes in and trusts the Lord his God. As he writes, "And my servile soul harks to the angelic melody / and murmurs the words of the third commandment." That line in the poem forms the crux of the dramatic dilemma. The poet has no need to add a footnote to explain his allusion to the Ten Commandments from the Book of Exodus. The words "You shall not take the name of the Lord your God in vain" would have leapt immediately to the mind of his biblically grounded fellow-Ugandans. But *which* God or god, the poet tacitly implies, shall one *not* take in vain? As his deeply meditated poem continues, "Thus my confused self floats between the two temples / and reveres the God of gods / And communes with the god of yore." He finds himself in a binding covenant relationship with two distinct traditions. The final haunting verse leaves him suspended between two life-determining realities, with hints of a resolution toward his aboriginal roots: "And in dual piety I cry out to God / To water the plains / and the gods whisper: / It will rain."

If Ugandans can be caught in spiritual dilemmas such as Ssemuwanga portrayed, they can also be caught in unique ethical dilemmas when confronting medical decisions. One of many scenarios illustrates not only the family dynamics involved in medical decisions, but also the potential conflict between modern medicine and traditional healing. The ethical dilemma the scenario illustrates involves a pregnant woman in Uganda's typically patriarchal and patrilineal society. Here, tribal practices find support in selective interpretations of biblical sources that endorse male dominance. Conditioned by cultural practice and a narrowly interpreted biblical tradition, the patient in this scenario feels obliged to accept her husband's moral authority. (While Ugandan legislation and educational programs are gradually empowering women and restoring the imbalanced—and unjust—gender roles, the patriarchal system remains firmly entrenched [Tuyizere 2007, 362–427].) The patient is admitted to hospital with swollen legs and hands, severe headaches, and vomiting. She is diagnosed with preeclampsia, or pregnancy-induced hypertension. This is a rapidly progressing condition that threatens the life of both mother and fetus; it has no known cure apart from termination of pregnancy. Her doctor correctly orders complete bed rest and hospital care. Fearing that her husband would marry another wife if he found out about her illness—polygamy is not uncommon in Uganda—she begs the doctor not to reveal her condition. When the husband arrives, the doctor refuses to betray patient confidentiality. Three days later the husband returns with a number of relatives to take her home. A traditional healer, they argue, would heal her faster. The doctor tries in vain to persuade his patient not to follow her husband's dictates, but she leaves against his best medical advice. Two weeks later family members return her to hospital suffering from full-blown eclampsia—in a coma and suffering convulsions. She dies three hours later (Kasenene 1998). Adapted and reshaped as above, this story formed the basis of a case study in a course designed to train Ugandan health care workers in ethical decision making (Hadley 2008, 31–34). It was a foil for exploring such issues as patient autonomy and consent, confidentiality, substitute decision making, and nonmaleficence. Nursing staff at Kampala's Mulago Hospital found it representative of the type of conflictual case they meet on a daily basis. Significantly, nothing indicates that this was a good death by any measure.

For traditional medicine, "healing" and "salvation" share a common conceptual root, for the practice of traditional healers is embedded in traditional principles found in African religions. One primary concept is the vital-force or life-force principle. In this paradigm supreme happiness is the ultimate goal. This principle is understood as a hierarchical, mystical power that creates personal meaning and happiness (Kasenene 1998, 25–38). The vital force is deemed to derive from God, and is transmitted through ancestors and "spirit-filled" people such as medicine men. The force can be enhanced by ritual and prayer—or diminished by illness, evil powers, or "witchcraft." Hence, whatever increases life or energy is a force for good; whatever decreases it is intrinsically bad.

The demands for health care and palliative care in this complex cultural setting are enormous. Uganda has a population of roughly thirty-one million (2007), most of whom live in rural areas. It is estimated that 51 percent have no contact with a health worker. With a patient to physician ratio of 24,000:1, that is scarcely surprising. Moreover, many patients "cannot even afford to reach a health worker, or delay going because they are consulting traditional healers and reach hospital too late for curative treatment" (Hospice Africa 2008, 2). Significantly, some 48 percent of the population is beneath the age of fifteen years. The ravages of HIV/AIDS have created the phenomenon of child-headed families. These eke out a meager existence by foraging, and live without education or any adult assistance. One child in every five is an orphan. According to the AIDS Control Programme managed by Uganda's Ministry of Health, Uganda has the highest proportion of AIDS orphans in the world. Since the beginning of the AIDS epidemic more than a million Ugandans have died of the infection, while over a million more continue to live with the disease. Statistics on mortality remain incomplete despite attempts at reporting by "verbal autopsy" (Kamali 1996). Most of the deaths occur at home, as indeed does most of the very limited palliative care. Though the infection trend is declining, the numbers of new cases annually (some 90,000) are still alarming. Nearly 80 percent of those infected are between the ages of fifteen and forty-five. Adolescent girls between the ages of fifteen and nineteen are four to six times more vulnerable than their male counterparts. Meanwhile, life expectancy in Uganda has been slowly increasing: from forty-three years in 2000, to fifty-two years in 2008.

Set in the complex interrelationships of an overtly religious culture and a socioeconomically disadvantaged populace, Hospice Africa Uganda aims at offering palliative care that is both affordable and culturally appropriate. Through a variety of promotional literature and brochures it acknowledges a guiding principle: "Caring is an essential part of God's plan for the world [and] caring and being cared for are two sides of the human condition that can make us truly human." Material designed for public education outlines the religious component further:

> Modern day Hospice, as were the Hospices of the past, is strongly linked with Christian religions. . . . The Hospice team prays together and seeks that we continue God's healing work on earth. Islam and other religions pray with us and we with them. . . . Hospice supports patients and families in their own religious beliefs unless special needs are identified. Our aim is reaching peace with God through their own beliefs, before the

end of life. Praying with patients is . . . a natural part of communication in African culture. (Hospice Africa 2008, 5)

Founded in September 1993, and financially dependent on donors,
Hospice Uganda is a registered nongovernment organization (NGO)
situated in Makindye, a district in the capital city Kampala. Though
Hospice Uganda was the third in sub-Saharan Africa (excluding South
Africa, which commenced in 1980) to commence palliative care, it was
specifically designed as the model for Hospice Africa, which has the
vision to support palliative care for all African countries. The first to
introduce Hospice was Zimbabwe (1977), and the second Kenya (1990).
Hospice Uganda endorses the founding principles of Cicely Saunders,
and embraces her conviction that the medical and spiritual dimensions of
each case are inextricably linked. In effect, Hospice Uganda has adopted
the key principles of the founding document *Aim and Basis* as enunciated
in chapter 1 (Wright and Clark) of this volume. In doing so, they have
created a "community of care" as she had envisioned it.

In January 1998, Hospice Uganda opened its first satellite unit,
Mobile Hospice Mbarara, in the university town of Mbarara, some 283
km to the southwest. In June 1998 it established its second satellite, Little
Hospice Hoima, some 200 km to the northwest. Given the often difficult
road conditions, these distances can be a considerable challenge. Hospice
Uganda looks after cancer and/or HIV/AIDS patients, and estimates
that 50 percent of its cancer patients also have AIDS. Using modern
methods to control pain and symptoms, it focuses on home care, as well
as day care and clinics at Hospice. Outreach and roadside clinics have
been introduced through Mobile Hospice Mbarara and are being taken
up by other African countries. Encouraged by the Ministry of Health,
it reaches out to the poorest among the dying. While most patients are
referred to Hospice either by hospitals or by trained health workers, a
system of community volunteers reaches out to needy people in villages.
Others come for care on their own initiative. While Hospice accepts day
visits, it does not have facilities for live-in patients. In any event, most
patients prefer to die at home close to their ancestors, where they will
be buried. In the words of the poem "Take Me Back Home" by Abago
Mary Nyar' Obote, "There where my heart is / There where my home
is / There where my grave shall be." Besides, the cost of transporting a
body is exorbitant, and many families simply cannot afford it.

To date, Hospice has cared for 8,039 patients in Kampala alone, and currently has 358 in its program. The Mobile Hospice Mbarara has had 4,541 patients referred to it, and currently has 539 in the program; Little Hospice Hoima has looked after 1,492 patients, and presently has 200 in the program. As part of its objectives, Hospice runs education and training programs—including a spiritual carers' course—not only in Kampala, but in the neighboring and up-country districts. These courses target undergraduate and postgraduate health professionals in universities and health institutions as well as at Hospice. Other groups include allied professionals, health workers and non-health workers, traditional healers, community volunteers, spiritual caregivers, as well as students at other higher health institutions of learning. Hence, to date it has trained a total of 6,512 people—2,197 medical students (since 1993), 74 health tutors, 2,122 health professionals and 1,920 non-health professionals. Of these, 598 are community volunteers.

Spiritual discipline forms the basis of the multidisciplinary Hospice team. It begins work each day with a short hymn, reading, and prayer, with announcements on the work of the day and introduction of visitors. Then follows professional work and consultation. The clinical team of specialist palliative care nurses and others receive spiritual training during the clinical palliative care training course. An annual one-day retreat focusing on a spiritually enriching theme fosters reflection on how to "apply God" to Hospice ministry. The theme of the 2009 retreat, "How big is your God?" was a typical example of strategic planning that identified spiritual plans of action. Case sheets bring out spiritual issues that act as a guide to the team during patients' assessments and care. All this is done to enable staff to reflect on how their own personal lives impact upon palliative care. Staff members' self-knowledge links directly to the principles and practice of holistic assessment of patients and their needs. Here staff follows closely the principles and practice of their model, Cicely Saunders.

Spiritual evaluation—as distinct from clinical evaluation—is a formal part of the holistic approach. This is where patients are identified according to their individual spiritual problems, and then managed accordingly. But it may be difficult to diagnose spiritual pain or distress, if only because some of the signs of spiritual distress may be similar to those of psychological distress. Patients can become isolated, angry, hopeless, withdrawn, numb, and helpless, and these emotions can overshadow spiritual pain. Caregivers enquire about their current faith, beliefs, and their relationship with their God. They also establish how these patients relate to their family members, the larger community, and deal with any regrets or guilt that haunts them. Hospice workers help patients identify their fears about death and dying, how they would like Hospice to support them through their journey, and their principal distresses about the well-being of family members they are leaving behind.

Culture and belief systems impact upon patient care in often troubling ways. For example, some patients and their familial carers in Hospice associate illness—especially terminal illness—with what they call "witchcraft," or the work of "night dancers." Unlike herbalists, practitioners of "witchcraft"—whom the national press disparagingly calls "witch doctors"—are known to practice child sacrifice and to harvest body parts as antidotes for illness. (Police reported twenty-eight cases of child sacrifice in 2009, an increase over 2008). As the *Daily Monitor* explained on November 23, 2009, people resort to "witchcraft" "because they believe it works." The belief is not restricted to peasants or the uneducated. For surely, even more educated believers argue, "because God exists, the Devil must exist too." They therefore attribute their suffering to "evil influences," or to a member of the community having caused the illness by casting a spell. Indeed, while most systems of culture and belief can support the palliative process, others such as this frustrate it. Caregivers then face the challenge of combating an aberrant belief system with the hard data of disease control. Others blame their illness on their failure to fulfill the demands of the ancestral spirits. Indeed, prior to entering Hospice some patients have been ill-prepared by their faith community for the palliative process. Persuaded that God alone effects cures, they refuse their medication—including antiretrovirals (ARVs). Hospice counters this with the argument that God does indeed heal, but *through* health care providers, who are the agents through whom the dying patient can see God working His purpose. Patients are encouraged to continue praying—but to take the prescribed drugs as well. Hospice trains spiritual leaders on this very point of doctrine. Some denominations, sects, and churches promise miraculous healing for incurable illnesses such as HIV/AIDS and cancer, even when the patients are quite obviously dying. Some even coerce the dying to convert as a guarantee of salvation. Patients are frequently caught in a vortex of conflicting social, cultural, and tribal interests. All of these are vitiated by lack of resources and education, and poverty. Interwoven by patriarchal, authoritarian, and often punitive networks of relationships, they sometimes find themselves a "plaything of the gods."

In the initial stages of palliative care, patients are often poor judges of their spiritual needs. Fears and psychological pain trigger existential questions. Some patients have not yet come to terms with their terminal illness, and rail against the "injustice" of their affliction. They may find themselves wrangling with God, who they feel is punishing them. Sometimes patients wish to receive the Holy Sacraments from their churches, but worry that past sins make them unworthy; wanting forgiveness but fearing that God will withhold it, they become restless and experience an aggravated level of physical pain and other symptoms. Then there are those who vacillate in their search for meaning, sometimes drifting from faith to faith in their search for healing. Patients can be troubled by uncertainty as to what will happen after death, and experience self-blame for having no personal relationship with God, or for not adhering to any faith. Yet others reject the consolations of faith altogether, thus making it difficult for caregivers to control their pain and give them spiritual satisfaction. On the other hand, many patients may go to church and pray with others, believing that their religious satisfaction comes through institutionalized structures. Others carry out these formalities, but without understanding the meaning of what they are doing.

Reflecting Saunders's own ever-broadening personal sense of spirituality, Hospice caregivers help patients of all faiths in these last stages of life to find meaning. The team is trained to help patients in their religious understandings, especially praying with them if they wish, helping them to identify spiritual leaders of their choice, and explaining some of the spiritual dilemmas. At the same time, caregivers remain sensitive to those spiritual issues they themselves cannot handle. Some patients, for example, need particular spiritual leaders or caregivers to offer prayers or spiritual support. Hospice then seeks the assistance of such specialists. Muslims have recognized that Hospice ministers to all faiths, and have accepted prayer partners who were not themselves Muslims. They recognized, for example, that Christian caregivers were committed solely to their holistic care, not to convert them. Hospice is there to care, guide, and support them toward their religious well-being, and a peaceful death in their own beliefs.

Hospice Uganda has developed its own understanding of a good death, namely, peace with one's God and one's community. By the time patients come into the Hospice program, they are already experiencing overwhelming pain and distressing symptoms, which risk making them lose hope and meaning for life. Hence, Hospice practice helps them experience a good and peaceful death by encouraging both them and their carers to see meaning in their "journey," to recognize their achievements and share them with their family. Helping them to recognize that they have lived a meaningful and purposeful life nurtures a peaceful death. It helps overshadow the final, sorrowful moments at the end of life. Experience has shown that when physical, psychological, social, and spiritual pains are well controlled, patients die peacefully. In most cases, as well, their understanding of death is deeply affected by cultural or social issues. As Hospice caregivers address some of these issues, they see patients remaining in control, making decisions that let them cope with their situation.

Religious rituals play a fundamental role in the holistic approach. These may include having ministers of religion offer the sacraments or perform the last rites. The rite of extreme unction, or anointing, quietens those patients who all their life have seen in it—at its most simplistic level—a guarantee that they are going to heaven. Unmarried patients who had been living with their partner "in sin"—and now need to experience resolution and closure—welcome the opportunity for religious marriage. Whatever the underlying beliefs, most still have to carry out rituals to the ancestors before death and may ask to return to their ancestral home for this very reason. They need to undertake ritual cleansing or healing according to indigenous practice, for their own and/or their families' sake.

The range of cases is so broad that few cases are fully representative. Yet one not unusual case concerned an elderly patient at one of the isolated upcountry sites. She had been an abrasive and difficult patient during previous visits, and the team knew the challenges it faced. But on this visit she realized the problems she had been causing the caregivers. Her first words of greeting when the team arrived were, "Please forgive me; I know I have given you a lot of trouble." Her expressed desire to "make things right" opened the way to spiritual discussion for which the Hospice caregivers had been trained. Asked whether she would like team members to pray with her, or whether she would like to choose a prayer leader, she chose the medical doctor. Both to her and the team, it was natural and comforting that the physician should conduct prayer. In short, the team respected her wishes, shared her suffering, upheld her in prayer, and committed themselves to her until her final breath. The message of thanks for her physician—which her relatives later found—also left her relatives at peace. Thus, the religious context of Hospice opened doors that led to a good death.

Being supportive to patients, allowing them to recount their life's achievements, or listening to their reflections on life also contributes to a peaceful death. Another case concerned a patient who earlier in life had lost an arm and a leg. He had given up on life, and expressed his hopelessness to the team: "Okay, I'm dying, I am useless now. . . . I am reduced to nothing. But in life I *have* achieved something." The team's holistic approach quickly picked up his words, noting his deep need to find positive dimensions in his life that would afford him peace. A family album shared with the team proved a key to his gaining control in his final days: pictures of his wedding, his beautiful children, and family events. All this led to storytelling and happy memories relived. According to the way in which the team interpreted this case, even patients who have been severely handicapped by terminal illness have been helped by God to achieve much in life. That knowledge of God's participation in their lives has enabled a patient to experience a peaceful, and therefore "good," death. Similar cases—such as that of a dying mother of a two-year-old child—led to similar conclusions: a fully supportive partner and family whose reassuring and prayerful love and commitment the patient continues to experience lead to a peaceful end.

The regular and consistent holistic care and support offered by Hospice Uganda nurtures healing. This impacts not only on patients, but on their family, neighbors, and friends. Patients and their family constantly express appreciation for the readiness of Hospice to visit whenever needed and encourage others to visit as well. They appreciate especially the willingness of Hospice teams to bring a minister of religion if requested so that they can die in peace. According to team members, if pain and symptoms are controlled, and if patients have their illness explained to them carefully and honestly—and accept it—closure follows. They can be guided in putting their life in order, even writing their own will. They feel both forgiving and forgiven, and find peace.

Significantly, women and children play a huge role in providing palliative care in Uganda. Most terminal care patients depend on them. This is particularly pronounced among child-headed families where the scourge of HIV/AIDS has killed the parents. In most cases, families intend to give good care, but because they are ill-informed, their actions may sometimes upset the patient. Often they will compromise patient care by working at cross-purposes. For example, they might start preaching to the patient about God, or order her to do things against her will such as to pray, or to go to church. This is particularly upsetting when they themselves are neither exemplary nor practical. Such destructive relationships between the patient and the caregiver angers the patient and leads to a harsh death. Nothing is more conducive to a "bad" death than broken relationships. And nothing—neither pain control nor money—can compensate for such loss. In such circumstances, the Hospice team aims to bring peace and harmony to all concerned.

Men are less motivated to become caregivers and therefore need encouraging by the Hospice team. Whereas women will invariably be supportive of their men, even after a "bad" relationship, men will not readily step in even after a "good" one. This reticence causes the women considerable mental and spiritual pain, especially at a time when they are dying. It is at such times that they need their husband's support; they need to converse with him about the children, and deal with unresolved issues such as an unfulfilled marriage. Left to reflect on the bitter relationship they have experienced throughout their lives, they feel particularly abandoned at the time of death. The resultant spiritual and social distress offers a challenge to patients and caregivers alike.

The northwestern area of Uganda constitutes a special region with its own unique challenges. Terrorized by the rebel Lord's Resistance Army for more than twenty years, and torn by civil war, they have witnessed years of horror: abductions, murder, rape, hard labor, child enslavement, and other forms of human rights violations. Their spiritual needs are great. Confined to refugee camps, they no longer have access to the churches and spiritual leaders who once nourished them. Nor do they have the pastors to teach their surviving children. The horrors they have experienced cast their faith into doubt. This is not the intellectual doubt of academic debate, but an existential doubt about the very nature (and even the existence) of a loving God. The questions remain throughout palliative care. Thus, they observe: "It's me who has gone through all this, been displaced, been raped and infected with HIV/AIDS, been forced to kill, [and suffer] the numerous social problems." In such cases the Hospice team members become pastors. The patients' questions are probing: "You are telling us about God, but is God *really* there to see all this suffering?" "And why does he not *do* something?" The horror deepens at the thought of a miserable death in a refugee camp, and of parentless children living in the streets. At times like this, proper spiritual assessment and staging proves critical. Yet, despite increased pastoral care, overwork frequently causes the Hospice team to emphasize physical suffering over spiritual suffering. In cases such as these, caregiver pain, as Cicely Saunders articulated it, is profound. And caregiver burnout is always on the horizon.

Throughout Uganda, grief management is part of holistic care. If patients have experienced a good death, then the surviving family members will be at peace. Of course, they continue to grieve, but they cope with bereavement more quickly and easily than those whose relatives have suffered through to the end without pastoral care. Remembering that the majority of people are dying at a much younger age than in the developed countries, and that Ugandans have experienced death and bereavement in their families since childhood, traditional mourning and support from their community is much more successful than in the developed world. There is a fixed period for mourning and closure of mourning. Families have to return to heavy duties at home and in the farm or at work. In economic circumstances where school fees have to be paid and there are no washing machines, dishwashers, or fast-food outlets, the work has to go on and does support the bereaved. For families, closure means the opportunity for forgiveness, for the expression of love, and words of farewell. The Hospice team keeps in touch with the family for as long as a year after the patient's death, a much shorter period than in the developed world.

Case Study One: The Dying Child

Children are among the most disadvantaged citizens of Uganda, even though their rights are nationally protected by Article 34 of the Constitution. A variety of socioeconomic factors contribute to their marginalization—widespread poverty, disease, and lack of education among them. Some areas of the country are simply not child-friendly. Many young children, as we have seen, have themselves had to assume responsibilities for younger siblings due to the ravages of HIV/AIDS. This situation stands in marked contrast to the "Western" realities of children and child care. Yet even in the West, as chapter 12 of this volume points out, pediatric palliative care is a relatively new field. All the more striking, therefore, that the practice of pediatric palliative care in Uganda is a major component of Hospice.

Child-patients benefit from all the models of Hospice care, though these models are modified to suit their age. When dying children see their friends die, all sorts of questions assail them. Some will ask team members, "I saw my friend coughing like I am doing now—and then died. Am I going to die like my friend?" This and other issues are met with truth and compassion according to their age and level of understanding. By attending to the physical needs of children, Hospice supports their psychological, emotional, and spiritual treatment. Hospice treats their pain and other symptoms, provides recreational materials of their choice, and brings them together to interact with friends. It sees to their social and nutritional support. The main Hospice facility in Makindye offers day care and a play area containing games, videos, and balls. At the National Teaching Hospital—where Hospice has a presence in the children's cancer ward—they have built a playroom and classroom for children undergoing chemotherapy. Where possible, Hospice involves their parents and other carers as well. In such moments, children are visibly happy, even though some of them die within hours or days. They express their happiness, and openly tell you they wish they could stay in this room forever. Those who are too ill to sit or join the rest of the team are attended to in their beds. The team goes straight to their bedside, sits and talks to them, finding out their concern—either through them personally or through their carers. Initially, one sees misery and distress in their faces, but the team communicates clearly, draws them out, and provides care and support. In time, the initial terrible distress shifts to a state of comfortable joy.

Such was the case of a twelve-year-old Catholic girl from Mbale, a rural upcountry district, who was now living in a suburb of Kampala. Stigmatized by being born out of wedlock, she was her mother's only child. Now, it is a Ugandan tradition that a child belongs to the father, not to the mother. Often, the child is taken to a stepmother or other member of the father's family to be brought up. Under such circumstances the child is a "second-class" member of the household. She is disadvantaged in many ways, and is sometimes made to perform menial tasks not required of the siblings. In this case, the young patient was taken to live with an uncle. But when her illness worsened, she was taken to her paternal aunt, who received a month's leave from employment to take care of her. Born a Catholic, and living as such, the young patient liked praying and was always happy when taken to her church for prayers. Sometimes the priest from her church would come to pray with her in her home. She was visibly comforted by her priest's visit. Sometimes she was taken to pray in church.

According to her mother, the girl had been well until November 2007 when she developed pain in the left-lower abdomen, followed by abdominal distension. Taken first to Mbale Hospital in her home region for initial medication, she was later referred for further management to Mulago Hospital some 200 km distant in Kampala, the national referral hospital. A needle biopsy revealed Burkett's lymphoma, a very common cancer in Ugandan children. By March 2008 she had completed six cycles of chemotherapy.

The Hospice team assessed her holistically when she was referred to them on May 19, 2008, for management of pain and symptoms. Physical examination by the Hospice team confirmed her illness and showed a range of distressing symptoms: quadriplegia (flaccid arms and legs that were weak and painful), fear of moving her head and neck, high pulse rate, paroxysmal breathing, constipation, and acidic fluids in the abdomen. The team therefore concluded that her cancer was metastasizing to the cervical spine. After the assessment, the team came up with a problem list and managed each of the manageable problems accordingly.

She subsequently improved to the point where she could sit up and stand on her own. All this time Hospice controlled her pain and symptoms. During the team's visit to her aunt's home, they asked her to pray with them. The way she "spoke to God" and "prayed for all who were caring for her," inspired the team. Surely, they thought, she is "a special child of God." In light of her piety the Hospice team encouraged her aunt to take her to church whenever the girl wished. But as her aunt's employment leave was ending, she called on the child's mother—with the support of Hospice—to assume her child's welfare.

Hospice enrolled the child in its day care program, where she spent time playing with other children as much as she could. Yet she began worrying about whether she would ever be able to return to school. Hospice avoided raising false hopes. Instead, the team encouraged her mother to take her to visit her friends at school, and ask her classmates to write her letters to comfort her and show they had not forgotten her. Constantly reassuring her, the Hospice team explained their uncertainty about the possibility of her ever going back to school. This she eventually understood. Each time they visited her in her home, they made her happy by bringing books or Bible verses to read. The day care teacher taught her more prayers, and also involved her in other activities with friends. This type of holistic therapy controlled her pain further—to the point of discontinuing her morphine. On completion of chemotherapy, her appetite improved, and she began putting on weight. However, in December 2008—six months after her first referral—her condition deteriorated. Her tumour now relapsed for the third time.

The Hospice team could not justify the third line of chemotherapy. Under the circumstances, it was simply not the right thing to do. So the team kept praying with her, counseling her, helping her mother and other relatives to interact with her as they had done before. Gradually, the team brought home to the family that the young girl was no longer just seriously ill, but actually dying. This caused the child yet another move "across town," from her aunt's home in the borough of Kajjansi to that of her mother in Ntinda. They received help and support from people in the neighbourhood who could take care of the child whenever the mother was away working. Their involvement developed naturally. Sometimes they brought the priest to pray for her. Hospice counselled all the relatives involved, telling them what they could anticipate. But the team members also explained that they could not estimate precisely when the child would die. They could, however, assure them that her death would not be painful. Having controlled the pain as much as possible, they continued helping her fulfil her spiritual needs. Hospice remained with her and the family throughout the final days. As the end approached, her mother and other relatives grieved.

She passed away on January 6, 2009, nine months after her suffering had begun. But her death was peaceful, if not happy, for her pain had been controlled. Indeed, her wish had been fulfilled: people had kept on praying for and with her in her presence—especially her own Catholic priest. Even the team members who had given her palliative care had been praying with her, counseling her, and comforting her. At her passing, all were convinced they had really done all that they could, both in hospital and in the home, and that their little patient had died with peace and dignity. Pondering all the pain and suffering her daughter had endured, the mother confided: "At least my daughter died peacefully, and she really needed to rest [after] all the treatment." The team counselled her on how to cope with the loss of her daughter, "who was now at peace, wherever she was." The Hospice team encouraged the mother to continue praying, and prayed with her as well.

This was a good death. The child's physical pain had been well controlled; her spiritual needs addressed both through prayer and reflection, and through the constant pastoral ministrations of family and priest. The parents, though separated, had both been very supportive, and the mother had accepted her maternal responsibility to care for the child both in the hospital and at home. Family and relatives had kept on visiting her and supporting her during her final days. The principal challenge had been for both the patient and her nonprofessional carers to accept both the diagnosis and the prognosis. In the end, they gratefully accepted and appreciated that the best had been done and that this death was inevitable. As for the child herself, at no point did this illness cause her to drift from her faith. On the contrary, it strengthened her faith in God. She always lived in hope because—though but a child—she remained convinced that God was with her.

Case Study Two

This case concerns the sudden death of a Muslim patient whom a Hospice team member had been visiting. The patient was a fifty-three-year-old female with serious bipolar affective disorder and advanced breast cancer. Of her five children, four had died of HIV/AIDS in adulthood. At the time, she was living with her only remaining sibling, a widow whose husband had died of HIV/AIDS. As her sister went out to work, the patient was always left alone. Sometimes she undressed herself and wandered away from home totally naked. She could not be relied upon to take her medicine, except when she was experiencing a severe attack. When she had no money, she missed her appointments at the mental hospital. Knowing that her condition could worsen at any time, she was nonetheless at peace with her God. Yet her thoughts turned to the sibling who was caring for her, a woman who herself was HIV positive and on antiretrovirals (ARVs). Realizing that she was totally dependent on her sister, the patient became distressed. Fully mindful of the sacrifices her sister had been making for her, she frequently expressed the wish to release her sister from her burdensome responsibilities by being the first of them to die. She always asked to pray with the Hospice team at the end of each visit.

The Hospice team intervened by enrolling her in a program for total psychiatric care (physical, social, psychological, and spiritual). Hospice saw to her creature comforts and that she had physiotherapy, food, transport money for regular treatment at the mental health clinic, basic needs support, and bedding. Hospice engaged a community volunteer with whom it had worked. This volunteer followed up regularly with care and support, and to administer medications. Family meetings were held, and a sister agreed to hire a nurse to change her dressings thrice a week and to engage a relative from the village to assist in personal care. The Hospice team withdrew long-unused drugs. Suddenly, one day, she collapsed and died—alone.

The suddenness of her death caused the family considerable grief and pain at first, as they themselves had not had time to prepare for what was clearly imminent. Nor had they been able to nurse her in hospital. Yet as the family reflected on her passing, comfort came. She had gone "to dig"—tend her vegetable garden, in local parlance. She had then prepared her dinner, taken a shower, gotten her prayer mat, and prayed what the family now knew had been her final prayer. She sat down to dinner, suddenly collapsed, and died. This struck the family as the fitting end of a life of dedicated work and prayer. Indeed, they saw her death as a special blessing. Not only did few people get such an opportunity to die in this manner, they reflected, but she had died after performing her religious rituals on the first Friday of Ramadan. (According to Muslim tradition, this is the sacred month during which the Holy Qur'an was revealed). To the family, this was a good death that gave them strength. Dying on a Friday in Ramadan was particularly holy and blessed. Some wished that they, too, could die in this way. As the family informed the team: "You could tell we were grieving, but when we thought about all those events surrounding her death, this is how any Muslim would wish to die; on a Friday, in Ramadan, after saying her prayer, facing Mecca, so we are greatly comforted."

Typically, when people have fulfilled their religious obligations and rituals, they experience a good death and leave their relatives less distressed. Patients who fully accept their illness and are at peace with their God will even comfort their family members. "Don't worry," they say, "I am going to meet my Creator and you will meet me one day in heaven because I have lived my life." These relatives reflect on the experience, saying: "Oh, she was at peace with God," and this leaves them with wholesome memories. Usually, the Hospice team has not been present at a patient's death, because most of their patients die in their own homes and sometimes in the hospital. But the Hospice team continues to minister to the family. Hospice caregivers encourage them to mourn and to talk about the death. If requested, the team carries out the last offices, offering emotional support and praying with them while guarding against even the slightest hint of evangelizing.

The work of Hospice Africa Uganda is deeply embedded in diverse expressions of religious traditions and culture. Indeed, the Hospice ethos regards the act of caring as an essential part of God's plan for humanity and the world. Particularly important is the insight that Hospice care marks the final phase of a person's spiritual growth. In this light, palliative care emerges as part of a "journey." The metaphor is rooted in the

"African way" of envisaging the sequence of birth-life-maturity-death. Of course, many mainstream "imported" traditions embrace the notion as well, and make it possible for caregivers of different religious traditions and practices to work and pray comfortably and confidently together. As Hospice Uganda has found, praying with patients is a natural way of communicating in African culture.

Significantly, the spiritual discipline fostered among Hospice staff is central to their ability to remain open to patients of *all* traditions, as well as to those few who claim none. But given the view that dying is the most profound rite of passage on life's journey, all patients are nurtured toward actualizing their potential self-realization, and transcendence. "Every patient needs spiritual care," according to the tenets of Hospice's Spiritual Carers Course.

Spirituality is generally listed as the final link in Cicely Saunders's triadic set of key principles: pain control, family involvement, and spirituality. In practical and clinical terms, the first of these—pain control—is paramount. In effect, however, this sequence is not necessarily linear or in chronological order. Ugandan experience suggests that these dynamic principles create their own interacting synergies, and express themselves as nonlinear feedback loops. These progressive-regressive feedback "loops," in turn, contain "event markers" such as pain and sedation, growth and relapse, and confusion and clarity. Patients frequently vacillate among these various psychosomatic states until their "spirit" coalesces, and the struggle to hold onto life merges into a "good" death. It is in the context of such synergies that the holistic approach fostered by Hospice Uganda finds both its challenge and its success. The foundational touchstone is spiritual growth. This principle has been found to be of pivotal significance when addressing the issue of what Cicely Saunders termed "total pain," that amalgam of critical components ranging from physical pain, through psychosocial pain, and spiritual suffering. In the holistic approach of Hospice Uganda, the principle of spiritual growth is as much a function of meditations on the perennial philosophy, as it is of the formative practices of institutionalized religion.

Notes

1. We acknowledge the advice of the team of Hospice Uganda, Dr. Jack Jagwe, Dr. Jennifer Ssengooba, Nina Sharita, Martin Othieno, and especially that of the founding director Dr. Anne Merriman.

References

Ani, M. 1994, 2000. *Yurugu: An African-centered critique of European cultural thought and behaviour.* Eritrea: Africa World Press, Inc.

Behrend, H. 1999. *Alice Lakwena and the Holy Spirits: War in northern Uganda 1985–97.* Kampala: Fountain Publishers.

Ford, C. W. 1999. *The hero with an African face: Mythic wisdom of traditional Africa.* New York and Toronto: Bantam Books.

Gifford, P. 1999. *African Christianity: Its public role in Uganda and other African countries.* Kampala: Fountain Publishers.

Gwyther, L., A. Merriman, L. M. Sebuyira et al., eds. 2006. *A clinical guide to supportive and palliative care for HIV/AIDS in Sub-Saharan Africa.* www.fhssa.org.

Hadley, M. L., and A. Hadley. 2008. *Christian ethics.* Victoria: ICMI.

Hospice Africa (Uganda). 2007. Ethos and spirit of hospices in Africa. www.hospiceafrica.or.ug.

———. 2008. *Information. June 2008.* Kampala: Hospice.

Kamali, A., and H-U. Wagner et al. 1996. Verbal autopsy as a tool for diagnosing HIV-related adult deaths in rural Uganda. *International Journal of Epidemiology* 25(3): 679–84.

Kasenene, P. 1998. *Religious ethics in Africa.* Kampala: Fountain Publishers.

Museveni, Y. K. 1997. *Sowing the mustard seed: The struggle for freedom and democracy in Uganda.* Oxford: Macmillan Education.

Tuyizere, A. P. 2007. *Gender and development: The role of religion and culture.* Kampala: Fountain Publishers.

Waliggo, J. M., et al. 2006. Spiritual and cultural care. In *A clinical guide to supportive and palliative care for HIV/AIDS in Sub-Saharan Africa,* ed. L. Gwyther et al., 233–48. Adapted from Christina M. Puchalski, MD, and Rev. Carlos Sandoval, MD, Spiritual care, and Rev. Carlos Sandoval, MD, Culture and care. In *A clinical guide to supportive and palliative care for HIV/AIDS, 2003 edition,* ed. J. F. O'Neill, P. A. Selwyn, and H. Schietinger.

10

Punjabi Extended Family Hospice Care

Kamala Elizabeth Nayar

This chapter concerns a single case study of the "upstream" (earlier in the dying process) palliative care provided to an elderly woman—Durga Devi Marwah (ca. 1911–1999)—at her home when she was experiencing a gradual decline in health, moving toward death. The case study has been developed employing Cicely Saunders's perspective centering on three critical principles for hospice care: pain control, family/community environment, and engagement with the dying person's spirituality (see chapter 1 of this volume). Diagnosed with multiple chronic aging-related illnesses, Durga Devi received hospice care from her doctor and extended family. While her spirituality was embedded in Hinduism, the family context of her care was also rooted in traditional Punjabi culture.

"Punjabi" refers to the people originally from the geographical region of the Punjab in present-day India and Pakistan, living either in their homeland or the diaspora. Although they may be followers of one of several religions—most often Hinduism, Sikhism, or Islam—Punjabis share a common ethnicity and language. Regardless of the religious background of a Punjabi, much of the region's culture has been shaped by its folk traditions and by pan-Indian socioreligious law books such as the *Manusmrti*. While these lawbooks are sanctified by the Hindu religion, they have formed the mores characteristic of traditional Indian society even as regional and religious differences have also played an integral role in the development of the various Indian communities. For instance, a Punjabi Hindu shares more in common with a Punjabi Sikh than a Punjabi Hindu would with a Tamilian Hindu.

Situated in the cultural context of a Punjabi home, this case study involves a woman who was born into a Hindu family. Along with her neo-Vedanta philosophical perspective that all religions are but different paths toward understanding God, she was immersed in a Hindu devotional ethos that also embraced much of Sikhism, an aspect typical of her era and her homeland region of western Punjab. Her religious worldview encompassed Sikhism; not only because her maternal grandmother read Sikh scripture in Gurmukhi and she herself in her married state carried a Sikh name, but also because she periodically engaged in Sikh religious practices. In fact, the memorial service after her death was held in the neighborhood Sikh temple (*gurdwara*), during which passages from the Sikh scripture were recited. From the perspective of the philosophical understanding of suffering and the cycle of rebirth (*sansar*) there would seem to be little difference in the home care that would be traditionally provided by a Hindu or Sikh family of Punjabi background. Notwithstanding that, it is important to emphasize here that although the Sikh tradition bears some resemblance to Hinduism, it has developed its own unique set of beliefs and practices, which mark it as distinct (Nayar 2004, 121).[1]

Objectives

This representative case study of Punjabi extended family hospice care aims to shed light on two important areas: (1) the Hindu/Sikh philosophical understanding of pain; and (2) the Punjabi cultural understanding of how the aging and the dying ought to be cared for. In doing so, the first part of the chapter offers a brief biography of Durga Devi, including her family history and religious and cultural orientation; it also highlights the critical events that may have had a significant influence on the way she saw the world and experienced life, especially as she approached her death.

Based on the personal experiences of Durga Devi and her family members, the second part of the chapter focuses more specifically on the palliative care experience at her New Delhi home during the last ten years of her life. It offers Durga Devi's personal gleanings from the Hindu/Sikh philosophical understanding of pain; as well, it provides insights into the traditional and changing role of the Punjabi family with respect to caring for its dying members. The case study makes evident that, while the traditional Punjabi orientation has been to care for one's dying family members at home, the family structure is experiencing the impact of the forces of modernity and globalization. In respect of intergenerational relationships, the study also raises some pertinent sociocultural issues surrounding palliative home care.

Methodology

The research methodology employed here consists of two components: textual analysis of traditional religious beliefs and cultural mores, and case study fieldwork. The first component relies on analysis of the teachings of Hinduism (*Bhagavadgita*) and Sikhism (*Guru Granth Sahib*) concerning suffering and of *Manusmrti* for understanding the societal norms regarding family in order to establish "external validity" for the religious and cultural generalizations that emerge about "good" end-of-life care in a Punjabi home.

The second component comprises an analysis of four main types of data collected for the case study: (1) short biographies of Durga Devi published in the prefaces of two books authored by her eldest son; (2) transcriptive data from two interviews conducted as family oral archives, including an audiotaped interview with Durga Devi by her eldest son Baldev Raj in 1989 and an audiotaped interview with Baldev Raj in 2004 about the family's experience of the partition of India in 1947 and its aftermath; (3) participant observation by the present author (her granddaughter) who periodically stayed with Durga Devi at her New Delhi home during the last ten years of her life, in 1989, 1990, 1992, 1995, and 1997. The present author was, as a result, able to gain intimate access to the case because she actually lived in the situation. However, since she was not responsible for Durga Devi's care, she was able to examine a "real-life situation" (Yin 2003, 2) with some distance from the case. The fourth type of data (4) derives from eight semi-structured interviews conducted with various family members (five children, two daughters-in-law, and eldest grandchild) about Durga Devi's life and, more specifically, the last ten years of her life until her death in 1999. Using open-ended questions, four interviews were conducted in Hindi and four in English.

The multiple sources of evidence establish the "construct validity" of the single case study; the triangulation method was applied to the various sources of data gathered in order to determine reliability and validity of the themes (Yin 2003) relating to family home care. After the case study was written, it was shared with those family members with good proficiency in English in order to assure reliability and to account for potential investigator bias.

The Life of Durga Devi Marwah (ca. 1911–1999)

Durga Devi was born in a windowless cowshed inside a big mud house in a village named Saro Chak, situated in the Gujrat district of the Punjab in present-day Pakistan. Though born into a Hindu *khatri* (warrior caste) farming family of ten children, Durga Devi's village was almost entirely Muslim. Durga Devi never saw the inside of a school—because there was none in her village—nor did she ever learn how to read or write in any language. She typically acquired the skills necessary for married life through guidance and training by elders as part of growing up in a large family.

At the age of nineteen, she was married to Jamna Das Nayar, a *khatri* Hindu originally from the village of Kunjah, some twenty-five miles away from Saro Chak. At the time of the marriage, she was given the Sikh name—Jaswant Kaur—chosen for her at the wedding ceremony, when the presiding scripture was randomly opened and *j* was the first letter of the page. Marriage for Durga Devi also meant direct transplantation from the village of Saro Chak to the relatively modern city of Lahore (then referred to as "the Paris of India"). Soon after arriving in Lahore, she became pregnant with her first child. Three months into her pregnancy, she participated—in contrast to her village upbringing—in public protests against the hanging of Bhagat Singh, a revolutionary nationalist, by the British colonial authorities.

Following Indian custom, the birth of her first child occurred at her natal home in the exact place where she had been born. The birth of a son was undeniably an auspicious (*shubha*) occasion in her life. She is also said to have given birth two years later to a daughter (Darshana), who died at an early age. Durga Devi never spoke of the girl; her eldest child Baldev Raj—who was very young at the time—only remembers Darshana as "sickly." A family member was later forbidden to name her daughter Darshana for the reason that it would be inauspicious (*ashubha*) to use the name of someone struck by great misfortune.

Around 1934, Durga Devi and her family moved to Rawalpindi, where they lived in the railway hospital compound situated in the prestigious cantonment area known as Westridge. The 1930s in Rawalpindi were perhaps the best years in Durga Devi's life, during which she brought up her by then four children in a modest yet comfortable home (Nayar 1983, ix). With World War II, India was hit by inflation, impacting many, including Durga Devi's family. In trying to make ends meet, her husband secretly pawned off her jewelry, a woman's ultimate security. Subsequently, because of a housing shortage in the railways, the family had to move out of the railway hospital compound to a rented apartment. During this time, Durga Devi was forced into hospitalization in the course of a miscarriage. She had resisted going to the hospital because she believed that "people don't return from there." This has been a common sentiment among many Indians, especially from the rural areas; people mostly went to the hospital when someone was critically ill, in part because of the high cost. Thereafter, she successively gave birth to two sons, both of whom died of diphtheria at the age of two and one-half.

At the time India gained its independence from the British in 1947, Durga Devi's family was struck with the trauma of political dispersal. The partition of India and the creation of Pakistan forced her family to flee to India. Her husband, nonetheless, remained behind out of his "great sense of duty to job" (at least that was what the children were made to believe at the time; however, many years later Durga Devi admitted that he actually had no choice in the matter). When her husband bade the rest of the family farewell as the train pulled out of the Rawalpindi railway station at nightfall on August 25, 1947, Durga Devi had no idea of the frightful future that lay ahead for her and her family.

She, then nine months pregnant, along with her two sons (aged fifteen and nine) and two daughters (aged eleven and seven), were all—except Baldev Raj, who was in the men's compartment—huddled in a small separate women's compartment. There were bloody mob attacks on the way, but fortunately the military accompanying the train were able to foil them. After a prolonged journey, when the train crossed over the Sutlej River into India on the morning of August 27, shouts of joy and relief ruptured the eerie silence. Passengers, who were crouched in terror until then, burst into shouting "Long Live Mother India" (*Bharat Mata ki Jai*), "Long Live India" (*Hindustan Zindabad*), and "Hail India" (*Jai Hind*) (Nayar 2009, xiii).

When the train reached Bhatinda railway station, Durga Devi suddenly warned that she could no longer hold the baby. The family quickly got off the train and she was rushed to the one-nurse railway clinic, where she gave birth to a baby boy—a true "midnight's child" (Nayar 2009, xiii). After about twenty days in Bhatinda, Durga Devi and the children hurried to Delhi by another train to find out the whereabouts of her husband. Stranded at the Delhi railway station, the question they faced was "Where to go?" (Nayar 1983, ix). Durga Devi, with her five children—one only twenty days old in her arms—and with her husband's whereabouts unknown, nevertheless *defiantly* made her decision: "We will not go to any refugee camp" (Nayar 1983, ix).

The family ended up in Ghaziabad, some thirteen miles away from Delhi. After some struggle over several weeks to find a place to stay, Durga Devi and the five children occupied a deserted one-room windowless hut at II-F6/596 in Bhoor Mohalla, immediately on the other side of the Ghaziabad railway station. The hut was about six feet by eight feet, and had neither electricity nor water, which had to be brought in from a public tap near the railway station (Nayar 2009, xiii).

By the end of November, after a two-month (ordinarily twenty-four-hour) tortuous journey by railway and truck, Durga Devi's husband finally found them in Ghaziabad. But by the time of his arrival he was already a broken man. And, after about a three-month illness, he died at the age of forty-two on February 23, 1948, at the Delhi railway hospital. He left behind Durga Devi, an illiterate widow at the age of thirty-six, in a completely unfamiliar environment with now five children to bring up without any resources. On the demise of her husband, she was now under the care of her eldest son, aged only sixteen. Relatives came to Ghaziabad to offer their condolences, during which the women collectively performed the mourning ritual of beating their chests.

Politics and fate had certainly conspired to alter the life of Durga Devi so suddenly and so drastically: her life had gone from relative economic security and stability to radical insecurity. Now she not only had to raise her children singlehandedly, but also had to undertake the humiliating job of illegally carrying bundles of cloth and bags of wheat and rice on her head across state borders to earn money in order to survive. Baldev Raj remembers how Durga Devi taught him about self-reliance:

> Mother taught me two lessons in self-reliance: one, she cheerfully undertook hard labour jobs herself to provide for the family and,

two, by declaring one morning: "Son, this family cannot go on like this; you must leave the house and not return until you have found a job." (Nayar 1983, ix)

Baldev Raj eventually found a job with the railway. Since he found it difficult to commute daily, he rented some space in Delhi and then would only return to Ghaziabad for the weekends. Durga Devi found this hard, not only in terms of managing the children, but also because she was plagued with fear about the survival of her youngest child, since her previous two children had died early in life.

After Baldev Raj had found a better job as a stenographer at the American Embassy (1951), the family rented a house at Z-123 New Rajinder Nagar in New Delhi, consisting of two rooms, a kitchen, a bathroom, and a brick patio (1954). This improved not only the family's standard of living but also its social status. Her eldest daughter was married through prearrangement (1957). Baldev Raj also bought a lot, without viewing it, before venturing off to the United States for graduate work at the University of Chicago. Durga Devi, however, felt that her son, having already received high school education, needed no further education, least of all abroad. Indeed, it was frightful and unimaginable for her to have her male "guardian" so far away in some distant land. Perhaps Durga Devi's frequent references to Baldev Raj as "Ram"—the Hindu god exemplar of the ideal son and ruler who was sent into exile in the forest for fourteen years—was as much about his going into "exile" as it was about his fulfilling his duty of taking care of his widowed mother.

Baldev Raj returned to New Delhi (1961). Durga Devi wanted him to build a house on the lot that he had bought and also pay for her second daughter's marriage. However, because he was only able to afford one of her two requests, Durga Devi made the decision to build the house, with the understanding that her daughter would eventually marry. The new house was completed—in Durga Devi's name—at X-123 Rajouri Gardens Extension, New Delhi. Her youngest son remembers the importance of X-123 to Durga Devi:

X-123 was the biggest joy for her [since living in Rawalpindi]. After losing everything, it was a real joy for her to have a home, something of her own. You could see this in how she really cared for the house. It was her [new-found] security.

Though Baldev Raj returned to America to settle and raise a family, he continued to support her economically. Durga Devi's second daughter was eventually married through prearrangement (1964). And, soon enough, her youngest son—then twenty years old—also migrated to Canada (1968). Durga Devi refused to migrate to Canada; this decision was, in part, due to her second son's divorce—"Who would take care of him?" she would say. More importantly, she frequently stated that she would not want to live in a "sealed" house in a society where she did not know the people, the customs, or the language. She had heard from a couple of her friends who had gone to Canada that there is an "abundance of everything, but it is like a first class jail."

Durga Devi's second son eventually remarried (1981) and had a family of one son and two daughters. Interestingly, she seemingly began to move a little away from her widowhood customs by wearing bangles and colored clothing. Perhaps she felt that even though a widow from such a young age, her life was nonetheless complete; she had successfully raised her family and had grandchildren, not to mention that she had a grandson to carry the family name. Despite the tension that often typically occurs between mother-in-law and daughter-in-law in Indian society, she lived with her second son's family in her New Delhi home until she died on December 5, 1999, at the age of about eighty-eight.

Though Durga Devi was raised in a village typical of traditional Punjab, it is important to note that her life situation at the time of marriage and thereafter exposed her to the forces of modernity and globalization. These forces have had an impact on the family structure and the traditional practice of caring for the dying, which is made evident in the following case study. Below, Durga Devi is referred to as Dadiji, the honorific and affectionate term used for "paternal grandmother," because this was in fact the way she was called from the time of her first grandchild's birth (1963). The names of her eldest son Baldev Raj and granddaughter Kamala are used; all other family members have been given pseudonyms.

Case Study: Dadiji's Home Palliative Experience (1989–1999)

In the fall of 1988, at the age of seventy-seven, Dadiji came down with "fever" (*bukhaar*), which was eventually diagnosed as malaria. During the course of the illness, she suffered from a lot of fatigue, bodily pains, and vomiting. She had become very weak and found it difficult to keep food in her stomach. She likewise found it challenging to take the medicines.

The malaria devastated her health; it was a tipping point and she never regained her health back to how she had been prior to that illness. It was from this time on that Dadiji started to experience a gradual decline in her health.

Besides having the typical aging-related illnesses of high blood pressure, diabetes, asthma, and arthritis, she also developed cataracts. The doctor was reluctant to perform eye surgery because of her diabetes. She complained of a lot of burning in her eyes, which was exacerbated by light. She, therefore, preferred staying in a darkened room. On one of his visits to India, her eldest son Baldev Raj even interviewed Dadiji about the family story of partition on audiotape in the dark. It is perhaps the *only* time that she actually spoke of partition with Baldev Raj. In fact, Dadiji's conversations with her sons were otherwise primarily about what the household needed, and what could be done to meet those needs.

Though Baldev Raj had initially provided her with financial support, her youngest son Sanjay, who was living by now in Toronto, took on the responsibility from 1970 onward. He sent Rs2000 every month to cover her food and clothing costs. If Dadiji needed medical care, he would then send extra money for doctor's fees and medications, which was necessary several times a year. Also, Baldev Raj and Sanjay would customarily give Dadiji extra money whenever they visited her from Canada.

Dadiji's second son Rajiv, who permanently resided with her, was her main caretaker. He took care of her medical needs by taking her to the local doctor or hospital when necessary and by administering her medications on a daily basis. Although she remained mobile and able to attend to her basic daily hygiene, Dadiji stopped cooking and performing other household duties. Indeed, she was no longer an active participant in the household. As a consequence, Rajiv washed her clothes every Sunday. Likewise, her youngest daughter (Reeta)—a registered nurse—would come to the house every ten to fifteen days to wash and comb her hair.

Even though she was somewhat dependent, she had a great sense of dignity. Whether sitting up or lying on the bed, she would give directions to others, especially her grandchildren. She also felt respected when they served her meals and brought her water. When she was in the mood, Dadiji would praise Rajiv for his selfless service (*seva*) and speak of how he served her food before offering it to his own children. As the grandchildren got older, they too served her daily.

Her appetite was fair. She always had had stomach trouble, with acid reflux and an ulcer over the years. Furthermore, she did not want to wear her dentures anymore because of pain in the gums even as she refused to get new ones fitted. She nevertheless managed to eat her mild vegetarian meals, *unwillingly* prepared by Neena, her daughter-in-law. She would sit up on her bed to eat. For breakfast, she would eat unleavened bread (*roti*) and a small portion of lentils (*dal*); for lunch, she would eat one *roti* and a small amount of *dal* or vegetables; and for dinner, she would eat one *roti* and a small portion of *dal*. She would eat vegetables, depending on whether or not they were gas producing. Rajiv would daily heat milk early in the morning for her, as well as make her tea, which he served with biscuits, upon his return from work in the evening.

During the hot season, she would lie on a cot outside at an angle within the house compound where she could feel a cool breeze from the cross-ventilation. In the winter season, she would lie on the front patio under the sun for warmth. She enjoyed the company of her grandchildren, though their loud playing would often aggravate her. She would become irritable with the noise (*shor*) children typically make. She was neverthe-less quick to discipline them from the bed. Sometimes, she would ask someone to shut the door for some peace. The noise would leave her with a jarring headache. It was common to see her with a small piece of cloth wrapped around her forehead for some relief. It was truly a double-edged situation, because she felt lonely when the kids were at school, for then there was no sound of activity (*raunuk*).

In the fall of 1989, one of her granddaughters, Kamala—a regis-tered nurse—came from Canada to visit her for four months in order to help with her care. Ironically, Dadiji was not the least bit interested in Kamala's nursing advice or care. For Dadiji, medical care was the responsibility of her son and doctor; Rajiv was in charge of giving her medicines that the doctor prescribed. Dadiji simply wanted the presence of Kamala. When she felt up to it, she liked to talk. At times, she spoke about current events in the family like the latest marriages. At other times, she liked to reminisce about her past, including her joyful youth and the hardships she endured with the death of her husband. She also spoke at great length about the stressful time when Baldev Raj ventured off to the United States for four years.

When she was not preoccupied with her physical pain, Dadiji acted as if she was "ruling from the bed," giving a lot of directions and advice from the bed. She did not appear to feel as though she was putting any burden on others. Indeed, she had served her family and sacrificed for its members, especially Rajiv. Now it was her turn to be looked after. Conversely, Neena, who permanently resided with her, always saw her as a heavy burden. That is, she felt "stuck" in the house because the family could not go anywhere. Neena also compared herself to the other two daughters-in-law, who permanently resided in Canada, and therefore were free from responsibility of caring for their mother-in-law.

Dadiji became more bedridden (1991). She left the house only when she had to go for medical appointments or to the hospital. Her walk became unsteady; she had to support herself against the wall when walking to the bathroom. Even so, she now started to urinate and defecate in the bathroom since it was closer to her room than to walk to the toilet. Not only was that humiliating for her, but it also meant Rajiv had to routinely do the unpleasant job of cleaning the bathroom. She became very anxious over her declining independence. She would talk about her earlier life events when she had worked hard in order to survive.

One day, Neena phoned Reeta at her home, saying that "Dadiji has gone 'mad' (pagal)." Reeta then went over to the house to see what the matter was. According to her, Dadiji was experiencing much emotional distress related to her loss of independence. It was really hard for Dadiji not to be able to move around and care for herself. Reeta, along with one of Dadiji's old friends, discussed her new life situation and reassured her. This provided her some solace and the symptoms soon subsided. She was also scared of dying; and perhaps even more scared of dying alone.

Rajiv had to eventually hire someone to wash Dadiji's clothes and clean the house (1992). While Rajiv had readily assisted his mother with her care, it was now becoming too difficult for him to do so since he himself was getting older (fifty-four years) and suffered from high blood pressure even as he was responsible for raising his own three young children. And, Neena refused to serve her. Reeta came on a more frequent basis now, about once a week, to bathe her. Bathing was not only important in terms of hygiene but it also meant that Dadiji could pray.

When she was well, she went to local Hindu and Sikh temples on a regular basis. Even with the many hardships that she had endured, Dadiji never lost her devotion to Lord Ram. She now missed not being able to go to the temple. She had a small shrine in her kitchen and several icons and a picture of Guru Nanak in her bedroom. She also kept a vessel of Ganges water at her bedside. Usually, Rajiv or a visiting relative would go on Tuesdays (the day to worship Hanuman, the loyal devotee of Ram) to the neighborhood temple in order to bring the food offering (prasada) back home to her. This meant a lot to her. She was illiterate but, when praying, she would successively put her finger on the word Ram, which was continuously repeated in a long stream of lines in her prayer book. *Ram* was the one word she recognized. Even when she was sick at home but felt up to it, Dadiji would recite the *Hanuman Chalisa*.

She would visit her doctor when something was wrong, such as developing symptoms related to poorly regulated blood sugar and high blood pressure. She was lucid yet physically deteriorating. Massages to her legs, most often given by the younger grandchildren, provided some relief. When she was in the mood—and family members were around— she would like to talk. She would complain how she had pain "here and there" on her body. While discussing her physical pain, she would say, "I have suffered a lot" (*bahut bahut dukh paya*), and then speak of the pain of having lost her husband and her struggles thereafter. She spoke about how life goes on in the world, there is suffering (*dukh*) and joy (*sukh*), and how she had faced a lot of misfortune. She spoke, primarily to the female members of her family, of her life pain. In the midst of her discourse, she would fold her hands in prayer form (*anjali*) and raise them, reciting *Ram Ram*.

On several occasions she would speak of her two sons who had died at the age of two and one-half. She was plagued by "her mistake" for having renamed the second of them Inderjit after the first son who died—a very unusual act given Punjabi folk beliefs of spirit possession. When the second son named Inderjit was born, she thought it was the first Inderjit reincarnating. Talking about these deaths brought upon her great anxiety (*ghabrahat*). So she would have to stop. It was important not to encourage negative thoughts.

Dadiji's appetite and diet were deteriorating. She needed more help with her hygiene. Since there was tension between Dadiji and Neena, she preferred Reeta to bathe her. So, Reeta now came two or three times a week in order to bathe her and wash her hair (1994). Most individuals wish to face their impending death with the hope of a better rebirth, and therefore want to have scripture read to them for spiritual uplift. Reeta and her eldest daughter Geeta did this for her after she had been bathed.

During Baldev Raj's or Sanjay's visits from Canada, family life seemed to function smoothly, until the night before they would be departing back for Canada. There would be tension at that time during which Rajiv and Neena complained of Dadiji being "demanding," while she complained of them "not treating her well." It was hard for Rajiv to care for Dadiji day after day, as well as it was hard to know exactly what he was going through, especially since he never talked much. However, Rajiv and Neena would ask, "Why do we have to take care of her? It is such a responsibility!" In actuality, there was fear over the ownership of the house once Dadiji died. Attempts were made to help the situation, but it was all in vain. The house was in Dadiji's name, and she had willed it equally to all three sons: "Would those residing in Canada try to get their share?" was an underlying fear. In spite of these tensions, Dadiji spoke lovingly of one of her grandchildren, who resided with her, as one who loyally served her. This meant a lot to Dadiji.

In 1995, Dadiji had to be treated at the local hospital. She had confidence in her doctor, who, while trained in allopathic medicine, also simultaneously reverted back to traditional folk beliefs about illness and healing (relating physical symptoms to types of food ingested or the weather). Baldev Raj did not trust her doctor and felt that she should receive better medical care. He tried to arrange for her to be seen by a more "Westernized" allopathic doctor in New Delhi. It was, however, difficult for him to impose the inconvenience of a long commute for medical visits. In the end, the responsibility remained with Rajiv.

Baldev Raj and his wife also tried to take her to Canada, but she adamantly refused; they reconciled themselves to the existing situation, saying, "Ultimately you cannot force someone." Even though relations were very strained with Neena, Dadiji wanted to remain and die in her home. She liked the dropping in of family members or friends, which occurred on occasion. She would initially perk up upon the visit of family or friends, but then, once the visitors left, she complained of feeling fatigued with a headache. Even the occasional visits decreased over the ten years since the people belonging to her generation were becoming less mobile or had died.

Her talk of physical pain often would then slide into her telling of the pain in her life, especially in regard to her having become a widow with five children after the partition. Her physical pain was lumped together with her general understanding of *dukh*. Dadiji talked a lot about her comfortable life in Rawalpindi, when there was a lot of *sukh*, but then after her husband's death there was a lot of *dukh*. She had to put a lot of effort into surviving and had to work hard bringing up the kids. One day while Kamala was reading at her bedside, Dadiji began complaining about the pain in her legs. While having her legs massaged, she then started to talk about the partition and its aftermath, especially in respect of becoming a widow: "Lots of pain. Lots of pain. We were living in Ghaziabad. I would go into the room and cry. I cried. I cried so much. We lost our home. My husband died. [With] five children, what was I going to do? What was going to happen to us?" Dadiji then turned as if she had to tell Kamala a big secret: "You know, I *hid* in the room to cry. I did not want to scare the children."

Dadiji spent many hours lying in bed just staring at the wall quietly or reciting *Ram, Ram*. Although very vocal about her life pain, Dadiji spoke of her past in a matter-of-fact way. There were also things that were joyful for her, like the survival of her family and the education of her grandchildren. She would over and over again speak of how it is good her daughters and granddaughters know—unlike her—how to read and write.

Dadiji loved to have her grandchildren around. She also liked hearing them recall her active life in the past. She regretted that she could no longer cook for them, but then would light up as soon as a grandchild would speak about how she at one time had cooked their favorite dishes. Dadiji could never admit to enjoying something. She savored sweets although it was not healthy for her, given her diabetes. During the visit of her eldest granddaughter, Dadiji was offered milk-based sweets (*burfi*) brought from the market. She would agree to eating only a tiny bit of *burfi*, but would then actually take a huge piece and eat it on the sly.

By now, she was not getting out of bed at all. The doctor on occasion would come to the house. Her diet deteriorated from fair to poor: she ate only a little *dal* and one to two *rotis* per day besides tea and biscuits daily. She rarely had moments when she was not lucid. However, there was one incident when she was bewildered and shouted out *bebe* (a Punjabi term for grandmother but used by her and her siblings for their mother), calling out for her mother. Another time, there was an incident of incontinence in the bed (1998). She was then taken off a medication because of its side effects.

Death was not something Dadiji talked about, except in an impersonal philosophical manner. "One day we have to go" (*ek din jaana hai*), she would say. She never spoke of her actual impending death, for that would have been unsettling and inauspicious. However, on occasion Dadiji would raise her hands in prayer form and say "When it is my time, God will take me," with the understanding that there is a set time for death. Dadiji had lived a long life, worked hard but was now unable to work, and was in a sense waiting for her time to come.

The same routine—day in and day out—of feeding and bathing her in her room and the cleaning of her wastes made each day merge with the other. Nothing dramatic occurred, nor was there a major turn of events. Dadiji died on December 5, 1999, at 3 o'clock a.m. on her cot in her home.

An "Auspicious" Punjabi Death

Though death is regarded as inauspicious (i.e., a child's death is regarded as an extremely ill-fated interruption), it is the custom to celebrate the death of elderly persons. Certainly, Durga Devi had lived a long and full life, and she had been able to see her grandchildren and great-grandchildren. The time of day she died was also auspicious, since it occurred right after a neighborhood prayer procession (*nagar-kirtan*) the night before. However, Durga Devi did not die lying on the floor, which caused great distress to her second son; according to popular Punjabi folklore, the act of dying on the floor prevents any chance of the body becoming possessed by evil spirits (*bhut*) that may be under the bed. Fortunately, rituals exist to correct this: after taking her ashes to Hardwar (a pilgrimage center where all Nayars from western Punjab consign the ashes of their deceased members in the Ganges River), her second son made a special pilgrimage to Kurukshetra, the sacred place associated with the *Mahabharata*.

As one of Durga Devi's granddaughters—who is less given to ritual practices—I felt differently about the matter. My grandmother physically died on the one possession that the family had recovered by chance after the dispersal at the time of the partition: One day, my father was returning home from his job in Delhi, when he spotted a cot through the window while waiting for his train to pull out at the Delhi railway station. The cot looked like the one the family had owned back in Rawalpindi. He quickly got off the train and examined the cot. It was the family cot, albeit with one broken leg. Finding the cot brought the family an odd sense of wonder in actually recovering something from the past. It was that cot that my grandmother slept on for the remaining fifty-two years of her life.

Good Family Hospice Care

Contrary to Saunders's Christian perspective on the redemptive nature of suffering (see chapter 1), the Hindu/Sikh perspective encompasses insight into the reality of *such-dukh* that goes with birth and death. According to

Hindu/Sikh philosophy, birth and death go together. Similarly, joy and suffering go together. Even during the difficult times in life—including the decline in one's physical health—one has to accept suffering as part of the "life package" (see chapter 2 on Hinduism). Despite that, there are features that would qualify Durga Devi's family hospice care as "good": (1) she had been able to practice her religion with the help of others; (2) she was primarily cared for by one of her sons, albeit not her eldest; (3) she had other family members involved with providing her care and company; and (4) she was taken care of at her own home.

There is a popular Punjabi saying: "One comes into the world naked and one leaves the world naked" (*nangey aana, nangey jaana*). Before that departure, Punjabis—given the choice—prefer to spend the last few days of their lives at home amid their family and surrounded by a lifetime of memories (Gupta unpublished). As the group that is the most important to all social organization, the extended family provides economic and emotional security. The house itself is traditionally ancestral property, linking the individual to the past; the presence of family members—especially the grandchildren—is the link to the future.

X-123 can be seen as a metaphor of what a home meant to Durga Devi. Even though she had been dispersed from her homeland, X-123 re-created for her the economic and emotional security that one associates with home. For a traditional woman such as Durga Devi, it would have been traumatic for her to be placed in an institutional health care facility in order to die, even as it would have been humiliating to move into her daughter's home for much better care than her daughter-in-law was willing to provide.

Sociocultural Issues in Providing Palliative Care in a Punjabi Home

Punjabi families tend to be large, with strong ties, which can result in better palliative home care in a resource-constrained environment even as they may bring families closer in a familiar setting. In the last decade, there has been some attention given—through organizations like Can-Support—to assisting families to provide palliative home care in large cities such as New Delhi, even as India does not have a universal or comprehensive health care system (Gupta 2004, 37–38). Meanwhile, the traditional Punjabi extended family is viewed as an asset by health authorities in Western countries that have universal health care systems, such as Canada, where providing home-based palliative care is encouraged as part of an effort to curtail health care costs. Regardless, there are pertinent issues that emerge in respect of palliative home care, especially as Punjabi families encounter the forces of modernity and globalization, both in India and the diaspora.

First, there is a tendency to view the "traditional" Punjabi extended family as static, when, in fact, the family structure and role are undergoing change. The Punjabi family, which at one time existed as a single interdependent economic unit with a strong collective orientation, is now in the process of change. Economic and social mobility in the modern era has made for a change in the household structure by way of the household shrinking to a "modified" extended family or even "nuclear" size family (Nayar 2004), where many family members have migrated away from their natal home, either to another place in India or abroad.

Second, there is the issue of the patriarchal and authoritative system in which the eldest male family member has been the decision maker. Since pension and public health care systems were absent in traditional Punjab, it was the eldest son who would become the "guardian" of aging and ailing parents and the one to make health care decisions. The care for ill family members, on the contrary, was the responsibility of the wife or mother. The imperative value of duty and respect may, however, become a heavy burden. Besides, while the "burden" of providing the physical and emotional care fell most often on the female family members, they were not the ones with decision-making power nor were they often the ones to speak with the doctors even though as caregivers they would have had greater insight into the patient's physical and psychosocial needs. And, those who actually carry the "burden" of providing care may need community support but may not be familiar with the system of community health. Although older generations may accept the earlier authoritative structure, younger generations are likely to find it problematic. Moreover, as more women enter the paid workforce, female family members may be less available in the household to provide palliative care.

The third issue concerns the reluctance of caregivers to reveal the diagnosis and treatment to the patient. There are also the matter of lack of privacy and confidentiality in the traditional cultural orientation toward the family. In fact, doctors often collude with families, whereby the patient is not actively involved with the decisions on care. It is generally not the practice for a physician to inform a patient of the prognosis. The family may wish to discuss the prognosis or impending death of a patient with a physician. It is, however, unlikely that the family would disclose the information to the patient since it is considered improper to upset the critically ill or dying patient. Conversely, Punjabi elders may openly talk about their impending death with relatives within the impersonal philosophical context of the stages in life and the cycle of rebirth (Nayar and Sandhu 2006). However, now the younger or more "Westernized" generation may want a more direct approach toward the individual.

Fourth, physical pain is lumped together with a general understanding of *dukh*. It is, therefore, crucial to address all components of pain (Clark 1999), even as traditional means (such as massage)—along with allopathic medicine—are used to alleviate pain. Alternative practitioners or healers may recommend traditional treatments along with miracle cures. While the older generations may have found solace in turning to traditional healers, the younger generation may feel disdain toward the practice of "selling hope" and taking advantage of peoples' vulnerabilities. Moreover, patients may be disappointed with the seeming lack of support for their (non)allopathic treatment of choice from their community members.

The fifth issue relates to secrecy occasioned by the stigma attached to cancer, AIDS, or impending death. Family or community members may fear rejection, especially when there are younger family members, who may consequently have trouble getting married should the situation become publicly known. The patient may experience social isolation due to the family practice of honor or on account of ignorance about an illness. The younger generation, since it may have a stronger self-orientation, may have less concern about maintaining family honor. On a practical level, the handling of body fluids is deemed as polluting in India, but this aspect can often be mitigated with education.

The sixth issue pertains to lack of empathy, even disregard, for the patient since the topic of death is regarded as inauspicious. Indian caregivers, whether working in India or for ethnic-specific NGOs in the diaspora, may, therefore, not be trained adequately to disclose "bad" news to patients and their families.

Summary

This case study of the palliative home care experience of a Punjabi highlights the particular Hindu/Sikh philosophical understanding of pain as the agglomeration of the physical, emotional, and spiritual dimensions, and the home as the primary locus for hospice care for the aging and dying. While the traditional practice has been to care for dying family members within the home, the Punjabi family today confronts many challenges as it comes to terms with modernity and globalization besides the forces of geopolitics (partition). In addition, the case study articulates some pertinent sociocultural issues in the context of intergenerational relationships—whether in India or in the diaspora. Though Durga Devi received palliative care in her home, varying from indifferent to very helpful, her Punjabi family was under considerable strain since two central family members had moved away from their home to Canada. Moreover, the younger generation seems to be moving away from traditional perspectives on the family and health and illness.

Notes

1. Irrespective of a Sikh's stage in life (*Guru Granth Sahib*, 74–78, 137–38), the spiritual goal is liberation from *sansar*, when there is a break from the dualistic mode of thinking and individual consciousness is absorbed in the cosmic resonance of *EkOankar* (*Guru Granth Sahib*, 938–46). For an overview of the Sikh tradition, see Gurinder Mann, *Sikhism* (NJ: Prentice-Hall, 2004).

References

Bhagavadgita. 1996. Trans. William Johnson. Oxford: Oxford University Press.

Clark, D. 1999. "Total pain," disciplinary power and the body in the work of Cicely Saunders, 1958–1967. *Social Science & Medicine*, 49: 727–36.

Gupta, H. K. 2004. A journey from cancer to "CanSupport." *Indian Journal of Palliative Care* 10(1): 32–38.

———."CanSupport: Pioneering home-based care in a resource constraint setting," unpublished paper.

Manusmrti. 1979. Trans. M. N. Dutt. Varanasi: Chowkhamba Press.

Nayar, B. R. 2009. *The myth of the shrinking state: Globalization and the state in India*. New Delhi: Oxford University Press.

———. 1983. *India's quest for technological independence*. Delhi: Lancers Publishers.

Nayar, K. E. 2004. *The Sikh diaspora in Vancouver: Three generations amid tradition, modernity and multiculturalism*. Toronto: University of Toronto Press.

———, and J. S. Sandhu. 2006. Intergeneration communication in immigrant Punjabi families: Implications for helping professionals. *International Journal for the Advancement of Counseling* 28(2): 139–52.

Sri Guru Granth Sahib (Sri Damdami Bir). Amritsar: Sri Gurmat Press. (Original work published in 1706).

Yin, R. K. 2003. *Case study research: Design and methods.* Thousand Oaks, CA: Sage.

11

Seeking Physical, Cultural, Ethical, and Spiritual "Safe Space" for a Good Death

The Experience of Indigenous Peoples in Accessing Hospice Care

Joseph M. Kaufert
Rhonda Wiebe
Margaret Lavallee
Patricia A. Kaufert

Death comes to us in many ways.
It is in a broken flower,
in a carrot we eat,
or in a small child.
Death is ugly and beautiful.
It is useful and wasting.
It is tragic and happy.
It is in everything and
it is everything.

—Chief Dan George, 1982

Introduction

Access to hospice care and palliative treatment has increased rapidly over the past three decades, but not for everyone. A 2000 Senate subcommittee report on quality end-of-life care in Canada, for example, estimated that approximately 15 percent of Canadians who require hospice palliative care services have access to these services (Senate Committee on Social Affairs, Science and Technology 2000). Although there are few statistics, Indigenous peoples[1] are generally recognized as being one of the groups underrepresented among patients receiving palliative care (Menec et al. 2004), despite the fact that they constitute up to 60 percent of the patient population in some wards of Canadian hospitals (Gao 2008). This chapter will explore some of the factors that may act as barriers to palliative care, but its primary focus is the three key principles of the good death as originally defined by Dame Cicely Saunders, namely, pain control, a family or community environment, and a deeply rooted spirituality (du Boulay 2007). We are interested in how well these three principles are honored in the care available to Indigenous patients, but also in how they are interpreted and understood by providers of palliative care within Indigenous communities.[2]

This chapter will also contrast the "good" death and "safe place for dying" with a "bad" death and a place of dying that is both physically and spiritually dangerous. We cannot follow the example of some of the other chapters in this book regarding teachings on death and care of the dying in Hindu, Buddhist, Jewish, Christian, Sikh, and Islamic religions. This is partly because cultural beliefs and traditions vary widely among the Ojibwa, Cree, Dene, and Sioux, the linguistic groups that make up the First Nations of Manitoba. These differences are compounded by the influence that Christian churches of various denominations have had on many of these communities. Most importantly, we have honored the elder on our team and taken her advice not to attempt to summarize cultural and religious values or describe complex oral traditions and ceremonial practices, but simply to accept narratives describing death, dying, and spirituality.

Methods

The background to this chapter is formed by two studies. Over the past four years, and as part of the Vulnerable Persons New Emerging Teams (VP NET) project, more than sixty interviews were completed with key informants, including patients, family members, and palliative care providers (physicians, nurses, and hospice program directors). Approximately one-third of the key informants had experience in Aboriginal health and care provision. The range of their experience extended from working in hospitals as providers of spiritual care, interpreters, visitors to family members, or being themselves a patient. Discussions from these interviews ranged widely but focused on the pragmatic obstacles to access for Indigenous people within the current system of palliative care, and how best to reduce the number of Indigenous patients dying in hospital without the comfort of family or appropriate spiritual care. The second study was completed in 2004 and co-authored by one of the authors of this chapter, Rhonda Wiebe (Steinstra and Wiebe 2004). This study documented the impact of poor housing conditions and lack of access to hospice care among people dying in the inner city. Out of the twenty-four people from the core area of Winnipeg involved in this study, thirteen self-identified as being of Indigenous descent.

This chapter draws on both these studies, but our core material is taken from eight additional interviews with elders and traditional healers, interpreters, nurses, and specialists in palliative care. These informants helped us to explore the meanings of a "good" and a "bad" death in greater depth. They also provided us with twenty case descriptions of the experiences of individuals who were dying, with detailed information on their care and the barriers to care that they faced. For reasons of confidentiality and to avoid recognition of any single individual, we developed two composite case studies that integrate details from several interviews so that no actual individual can be identified. We have given a fictional name to each case study.

Approaches to caregiving that respect spiritual, cultural, and ethical values are integral in defining a good death. Most importantly, our consultations with traditional spiritual practitioners as well as elders from Christian traditions in Indigenous communities revealed that "hospice" is as much the act of gathering people to be present as it is an actual physical location. A good death, in that context, is a spiritual journey of "coming home" to one's origins and one's people. This means that the care environment of a dying patient allows safe physical and emotional space for extended family involvement and ceremonial practices. We have developed the following example using a composite of cases describing the experience of older patients who were deeply engaged in traditional spiritual practices and interaction with healers. These individuals were able to experience end-of-life care within the context of their families, their Indigenous community, and their traditional spiritual practices.

A Good Death

Mrs. M had lived much of her life in a remote First Nations community only accessible by air and winter roads, but had moved to the city a number of years ago to live with members of her extended family. However, she returned to her First Nations community several times yearly to participate in ceremonies, including the sun dance. She was also active in cultural programs in the city, taking part in sweat lodge ceremonies and joining a network of elders who practiced traditional healing.

After complaining of symptoms at a walk-in clinic, Mrs. M was referred to the cancer treatment center for specialized diagnostic tests. An appointment was made for her to see an oncologist who would explain the results of the tests to her. At their first meeting, the oncologist went through the tests and began to tell her she had pancreatic cancer, before he realized that she spoke Ojibwa and had only limited proficiency in English.

Another appointment was made, but this time it included an Ojibwa-speaking medical interpreter. The oncologist repeated his explanations of the diagnostic tests, although he was asked by the interpreter to pause after each statement so that the interpreter could translate it and make sure it was understood by Mrs. M. The oncologist explained how the cancer had spread to other organs and that most people with this condition usually lived no more than six to eight months. At this point, Mrs. M. started speaking in Ojibwa to the interpreter, who explained the interview could not continue until she returned the next day bringing family members with her to hear what the oncologist had to say.

The oncologist asked the interpreter to explain Mrs. M's reaction. The interpreter told him that the explicit discussion of the nature of her illness, her prognosis, and references to impending death, coupled with the offer of palliative care, had been culturally inappropriate. According to traditional beliefs, the communication of "bad news" could impede a good death or hasten the process of dying. The interpreter said that for many elders, "bad news" should be given indirectly, little by little, and only when family members were there and able to give support. The interpreter suggested that when he next met with Mrs. M and her family, the oncologist should involve them in a less direct discussion, while also trying to determine what she understood about her illness, its prognosis, and her palliative care options.

The following day, the oncologist welcomed the family, stating that their support was vital in helping the care team to develop compassionate, community-based care options for Mrs. M. Using the interpreter, the oncologist asked Mrs. M what she understood about her own illness and her care. Mrs. M avoided using the Ojibwa word that denoted cancer, but she replied that she knew that this was the end of her life journey and that she understood that the medical team could help control her pain but not cure her illness.

Mrs. M then told the oncologist that she wanted him to be truthful about her prognosis, so that she could make her own decisions about her care. The oncologist responded by asking, "What should we as care providers know about your life and your family that would help us to give you the best care?" Her answer was that she was deeply involved in traditional Ojibwa spiritual healing practices and wished to "go home" to participate in ceremonies and die in her community.

The next two hours were spent in discussion with the family, the oncologist, the interpreter, and Mrs. M about palliative and community care options. The family included individuals with a range of spiritual beliefs, including some who followed traditional practices and others who belonged to Christian churches; however, everyone agreed that Mrs. M should make the final decisions about her medical and spiritual care or "leave choices to the creator."

The oncologist referred her to palliative care, and the following week Mrs. M and her daughter met with the physician who directed the palliative care program and a social worker who coordinated community care placements. The palliative care physician advised that the best way to provide personal care and pain control would be for Mrs. M to remain in the city to receive palliative home care and be admitted to an inpatient palliative care unit when more complex care was required. Her answer was that a good death for her involved returning to her home and dying with her family present. Mrs. M also wanted to be in her community so as to participate in traditional ceremonies and healing practices.

Her daughter asked if Mrs. M could get appropriate pain management and personal care services in her home community. In response, the palliative care physician offered to contact the nurse practitioners and family physicians in her community to discuss pain control and home care options. He also discussed "tool kits" developed by the palliative care program for use in remote locations to administer pain control and antinausea medication noninvasively in the home.

A week before Mrs. M went home, the palliative care physician arranged for a teleconference between Mrs. M and her daughter, the palliative care team, and the caregivers in her community. He also asked her to sign an advance directive. She refused on the grounds that to do so was incompatible with her traditional beliefs, but said that she would involve her family in these decisions when the time came. Her intention was to ask elders and practitioners of traditional medicine in her community to help guide her spiritual journey.

Mrs. M was able to fly home to her community accompanied by her daughter. One month later she participated in and led a traditional ceremony, assisted by family members and medicine people in her First Nation. This support reflected the continuous connection between Mrs. M. and her community with the spirit world. The acknowledgment of her impending death was an integral feature of community life.

One month after the ceremony, Mrs. M died surrounded by her family and members of her community. Everyone agreed that no medical autopsy be performed and that Mrs. M's burial be conducted according to the traditional practice; Ojibwa spiritual practitioners were present and performed ceremonies to assist her passage. They smudged the space where she had received final care, burning sage and sweet grass. Following her death, her family and community celebrated Mrs. M's life through wake-keeping. Members of her family from Christian churches also participated in a memorial service.

What Is a Good Death?

Maintaining Respect for the Individual and Inclusion of Family in End-of-Life Decision Making

The support Mrs. M needed for a good death involved both family participation and professional support to provide her with adequate palliative and home care. This required coordination between palliative care and community-based health care providers and members of her kinship network. Her environment was a safe and caring physical, social, and spiritual space, which enabled the extended family to meet and allowed Mrs. M to participate in healing and life passage ceremonies.

Mrs. M's initial reaction to the oncologist's attempt to discuss her diagnosis and options for end-of-life care reflects the conflict of cultural and personal values that can occur when direct communication of information about impending death is imposed on Indigenous elders. Mrs. M and the Ojibwa interpreter emphasized the need to communicate bad news more gradually and to do so in situations where the person has maximum family support. Palliative and spiritual care providers should consider communication strategies that "offer truth" (Ellerby et al. 2000) rather than imposing information. This mode of conveying information is similar to the tradition of Jewish ethics elaborated by Freedman (Freedman 1993). The concept of "offering truth" could be achieved if, in conversation with patients, physicians take the time to determine how much patients know about their own illness and how much they "want" to know. Mrs. M's palliative care physician asked what questions she would like him to answer to facilitate her own end-of-life care planning. In later meetings with Mrs. M and her family, the physician "offered truth." The physician's acceptance and facilitation of Mrs. M's decision to die at home also reflects the strong cultural value placed on noninterference observed by Aboriginal ethics scholars. The Mohawk psychiatrist Clare Brant concluded that Aboriginal values defining ethical decision making should emphasize noninterference rather than formal autonomy rights protected by biomedical consent forms and advance directives (Brant 1990). Brant's framework for incorporating Indigenous ethical principles emphasizes that traditional values are best recognized when caregivers provide information to patients from traditional backgrounds in a way that avoids imposing truth in situations where patients and families are most vulnerable (Brant 1990).

The other dimension of Indigenous approaches to ethical practice in facilitating good death is seen in the communication that recognizes the interests of the patient as an individual and the family as a collective unit of individual members. The interpreter facilitated communication with Mrs. M, the palliative physician, and family members, thereby balancing her individual interests with the interests of family members practicing different spiritual traditions (Ellerby et al. 2000).

An experienced Ojibwa interpreter described a situation in which she facilitated a family sharing circle of an elder and her family members. They reviewed and celebrated the elder's life experience and family involvement and then were led in a smudge and prayer by a traditional healer:

It's more comforting for them . . . when you speak in the language and so we sat around and discussed her situation, what
she'd been through in her life and . . . the things she had done,
and spoke with the family in a circle at the [hospital], where
we had a room there, and gave each individual a chance to talk
about her and her life and what they saw and what she was going
through. And it was the two older sisters that spoke, and . . . they
smudged and prayed together and then brought in a traditional
man to come and say prayers.

In the case study of Mrs. M, she and the interpreter mediated
between the values of traditional and church-affiliated family members.
These differences were manifested when the palliative care physician
asked questions regarding when and if life-sustaining treatments should
be discontinued. Ultimately, Mrs. M made her personal choice in refusing
to sign an advance directive and designating a sister who was involved
in traditional religious practice as her proxy decision maker.

The final phase of the case illustrates the potential contribution of
clinicians and cultural workers in mediating between family members
who subscribe to an elder's traditional values emphasizing noninterference
and family members who want their loved one to receive all life-sustaining treatments. One interpreter/advocate described her role as mediator
between a dying patient and family members as follows:

In speaking with her before she became very, very ill and when
she knew she was going to pass into the next world, she knew
that, and what she wanted the most was to have her children
there. She asked the older sister to ensure that [she] get her
children, because her children were in care, and . . . she wanted
to tell all her children that she loved them and that whatever
happened, that they were to let her go, and so when I spoke
with the older sister, two of the younger brothers did not want
this, [they] did not want to let her go.

The interpreter's narrative affirms Deloria's assertion that acceptance
of death and elements of mystery and the unknown are widely held
and well-integrated values that have an impact on Indigenous peoples'
relationships with care providers and the ethical frameworks they may
apply in making end-of-life decisions (Deloria 1993).

*Community as Hospice: Challenges of Pain Management and
Care Coordination within an Indigenous Setting*

The experience of Mrs. M, her family, and the palliative care providers illustrates how Saunders's requirements for benevolent hospice care emphasize the provision of total pain control. Mrs. M's care experience involved initiatives by all participants to manage both physical pain and engage and mediate the more profound total pain defined in terms of physiological, psychosocial, and spiritual suffering.

Mrs. M's palliative physician and community care providers facilitated pain control in a remote setting removed from the physical space of a hospital or urban hospice. A sustainable care plan involving pain control, home nursing, and personal care services was developed and implemented so that medication could be administered less invasively by primary care providers and family members. One physician described his involvement in flexible care planning to ensure adequate pain control for patients living and dying in remote Indigenous communities:

> However [the patient] wants to approach this, we can make you comfortable. If you want to be in the bush on the . . . trap line, there's meds we can give nasally by spray. So we can adjust to the cultural needs or the individual needs quite easily. It's not a huge challenge. . . . We have these med kits . . . they're kind of like a little tackle box. They have about five of the basic drugs that can rescue someone from a bad situation.

This doctor emphasized that successful palliation in Indigenous communities and individual family households depended on the capacity and commitment of community-based nurse practitioners, community health care workers, and family members to support the care plan by working directly with the patient.

The same physician also recognized the need for mutual respect and dialogue with traditional healers. Collaborative healing relationships involving traditional elders and medicine people may involve communication between the spiritual practitioner and the dying person that may be more directed by the healer and demanding of compliance. These approaches may contrast with contemporary idealized biomedical interpretations of co-participation in doctor/patient relationships. For example, traditional practitioners may require absolute compliance to regimens involving the use of plant medicines or participation in ceremonies.

Physician informants with expertise in Indigenous community care also emphasized that palliative care providers should approach community elders and their traditions as "respectful learners" who can gain knowledge from the elders' expertise in end-of-life care.

Coming Home: Dying within the Context of the Family and Community

Mrs. M wanted to die at home, and home meant her Indigenous community. She wanted to die within her own space; she did not want to experience end-of-life care in an institutional setting. The phrase, "going home," or "coming home," used by many of the Indigenous key informants we interviewed involves nuanced meanings that extend beyond the physical structure of a dwelling. Home is more than a location; it is the locus of kinship connections, family participation in eating traditional foods, and a safe cultural and spiritual space for life and death.

Providing Appropriate Spiritual Care within the Context of "Safe Space"

The composite narrative of Mrs. M reflects the experiences of several terminally ill cancer and end-stage renal patients who returned to their families and home communities to die. The capacity for ensuring their final participation in the spiritual context of traditional Indigenous ceremonies helped them integrate the end of life with the continuing cycles of the spirit world.

Another elder spoke of a dying woman whose return home was celebrated in a four-day sun dance:

> I know a woman who had cancer and that's when we're talking about good death. . . . This is back home. She was a Sun Dance Chief and she had . . . cancer. And she was given so long to live because [this type] of cancer is usually terminal and she accepted it immediately. She got her family together and she told her family that she didn't have very long to live and so she needs to spend time with them and to do the necessary things . . . to organize her family in terms of finances, etc.

The elder described her friend's participation in the sun dance as a central part of her spiritual life:

That year she sun danced for one more time and that was her last sun dance and she dragged the buffalo skulls. And she already had . . . cancer. Yeah, she wanted to do it alone without anyone supporting her. She wanted to walk around and she did that and her daughters stood around the circle of her dragging the skulls, her children waited for her there and she completed the whole sun dance. She went home and she prepared medicine to help her on her journey, not to heal her, but to help her on her journey to the spirit world and all of her family members did that, and she died a very beautiful peaceful death. . . . Many of the sun dancers were with her and that was her request. So that was a good death.

The elder concluded by describing how her friend's leadership in traditional ceremonies and relationships with her family was commemorated at the time of the woman's death:

It was very touching to see that and at the end of the funeral where the burial . . . the sun dance drum went to sing that last song for her. It's called the Traveler's Song. . . . It's a beautiful song, a beautiful, beautiful song and it's her journey back into the spirit world. I think [that kind of] good death . . . helped her family, it helped her children, it helped her grandchildren, it helped her great grandchildren accept death as it is. It's part of our life.

A Bad Death?

In contrast to the case of good death, the case reflecting "bad death" involves situations and experience of barriers that are diametrically opposed to death within a safe cultural, ethical, and spiritual space. Awareness of both is important to understanding death and dying and approaches to hospice among Indigenous people. The following case study is a composite of several stories describing the difficult deaths faced by Indigenous patients dying within the health care system.

Mr. R lived in a remote northern Indigenous community. He had been feeling sick for quite some time, but staffing at his community health clinic was sporadic with high staff turnover, which meant that the diagnosis of his illness was delayed. People with acute or chronic conditions were usually referred to a southern hospital. Although he had noticed blood in his stool, Mr. R delayed telling anyone until his condition worsened. He visited at the local community health clinic. The nurse referred him to a specialist clinic in the city. The diagnostic process took time and required repeated plane trips between his community and the tertiary care center. Finally, he was told that he had bowel cancer, that active treatment via chemotherapy or radiation would be ineffective, and that his care needs and levels of disability would increase. An Ojibwa interpreter who did not know Mr. R provided translation during his consultation with the oncologist. However, no family members were present, and it is unclear whether Mr. R fully understood what the oncologist had told him or engaged the message that he was dying.

Mr. R asked to be sent back to his community, but within a week of his return he started to experience intolerable pain and went back to the community clinic. The nurse practitioner told him the opiate medications recommended by his oncologist for adequate pain control could not be prescribed within the community because of the lack of supervision and other security issues. She contacted his oncologist who recommended that Mr. R should return to the southern urban hospital.

After three days of hospitalization, Mr. R was transferred to a transitional housing unit located close to the hospital where he continued to have treatment. None of his care providers discussed the possibility of a referral to a hospice or palliative care program. Mr. R had agreed to this transfer partly because of his fear of hospitals. He was given a single room in the transitional housing unit and access to home care services, but there were frequent personnel changes among home care workers. He was isolated because no one could speak his language.

Mr. R came from a close-knit family, and his wife, mother, and daughter worried about him not knowing anyone in the city and wanted to be with him. His treaty benefits would only cover the airfare for one family member, but the chief and council agreed to pay for the air flight and accommodation costs of his mother and daughter. The boarding house made available for the family was located about ten kilometers from the transitional housing unit. Transportation to and from the unit was only available in the morning and the evening. The timing of meals was regulated, and there was a strict night curfew. Mr. R's family had no choice but to stay in the boarding house, as the rules governing the transitional housing did not allow family members to stay overnight, even as his condition worsened. The lack of flexible program regulations left

Mr. R and his family feeling that they had little or no control over their lives and minimal capacity to provide social support for their relative. Barriers in the family's access included noninsured benefits (e.g., benefits supporting travel for accompanying family members for First Nations peoples). Other barriers included the patient's and his family's level of knowledge of the urban care system. Both barriers meant that the family were not able to be present or provide support at critical moments in Mr. R's end-of-life care.

Having family members around to support him was very important to Mr. R, but so also was his desire for spiritual guidance from an elder from his First Nation. The hospital spiritual care programs included an Aboriginal services worker and referral to Indigenous spiritual care workers. However, Mr. R refused to be referred to the spiritual care programs because of his negative experience with religious authorities when he was a student in the residential school system. Although the oncologist proposed referral to an elder working within the hospital, Mr. R replied that the person would be unfamiliar with his life and unaware of his personal networks. Several informants identified the problems of role conflicts in defining formal institutional roles for elders and traditional spiritual practitioners within the formal administrative structure of the hospitals.

Mr. R requested to be referred to an Ojibwa elder who lived in his community for counseling and healing. However, his family was not able to arrange for the healer to visit Mr. R, and travel support for the visit was not provided by the First Nation or federal noninsured benefits.

Mr. R's family included members from Catholic and Pentecostal churches, both of whom discouraged traditional religious participation. Before he died, Mr. R was concerned that family involvement around end-of-life decision making might evoke disagreements between them and conflict with other relatives who emphasized traditional Indigenous beliefs. After Mr. R's death family members disagreed over funeral arrangements, and he was buried without either traditional ceremonies or a memorial service.

Mr. R was not able to die in his own community surrounded by family members because oncologists and primary care providers were not able to provide adequate pain control and personal care in his community. He had no other choice than to accept transitional housing, as no offer of hospice care had been made and he did not want to die in hospital in an institution "full of strangers." In urban home palliative care, distance and costs made it impossible for him to be supported by his broader extended kinship networks and community. Members of his family who could come to Winnipeg were unable to stay with him when he needed them most. As his condition worsened, Mr. R and his family became increasingly concerned over the lack of adequate pain control. In the end, he died in pain one night alone and without the spiritual support he requested.

What Is a Bad Death?

Adequate pain control is the first of the three principles laid down by Dame Cicely Saunders for a good death. In the case study of Mrs. M, pain control was well managed through collaboration between the palliative care physician, health care providers in her community, and her family. Adequate pain management was a major problem for Mr. R. His oncologist provided a list of medications for Mr. R before he returned to his community, but did not assure their availability with the nurse practitioner in the health center. The nurse practitioner said that opiates could not be prescribed, citing lack of security and supervision. As a result, he was referred back to the tertiary care hospital and effectively denied access to his family, community, and spiritual mentors.

The reasons given by the nurse for the health center's lack of capacity to provide palliative care may reflect limitations in access to opiate pain medication imposed by policies intended to reduce access to these drugs, involving potential risks of unauthorized use by community members. Barriers to accessing adequate pain management may be related to inflexible legal and medical policies and resource and attitudinal barriers impacting service providers. These barriers continue to limit development of community hospice with a primary commitment to managing total pain in both Indigenous communities and urban home care programs. We know from information collected in the VP NET interviews that access to pain control medication has been a contested area in the relationships between physicians, health workers, and Indigenous patients. Attitudes toward prescribing these drugs are a powerful indicator of trust, but also mistrust, in these relationships. Service workers and advocates described situations in which physicians were reluctant to prescribe any pharmaceuticals with potential street value.

Home-based palliative care programs are increasingly providing portable "kits" containing pain and antinausea medication that can enable patients, and local care providers to noninvasively manage severe pain outside the hospital environment. However, the extension of improved pain management and comfort care and involvement of family and community primary care providers must be accompanied by appropriate policy change, provider training, and commitment to control of pain in whatever setting the individual chooses to live and die in. These challenges are more profound in Northern and First Nations communities where lack of capacity for personal care and pain control often forces individuals out of their own communities and into an urban landscape with few supports for the dying person.

Isolation from Community Environment

Mrs. M was surrounded, supported, honored, and respected by her family and her community, and her dying was accompanied with traditional ceremonies and intense family involvement in personal and spiritual care. Her death met Dame Cicely Saunders's second criterion for a good death. Access to a "family or community environment" was exactly what Mr. R wanted, but was unable to achieve. It is a challenge for many small communities where chronic and palliative care services are only provided in a few regional hospitals and personal care homes. Requisites for a good death are more difficult in remote Northern communities and First Nations with overstretched primary care resources and with inadequate and overcrowded housing. These barriers mean that home-based palliative care programs in these settings may not be able to ensure that dying persons have personal space, quiet, and privacy. Provider interviews also confirmed their limited capacity to provide and monitor the adequacy of pain control.

The choices for those having to leave their community in order to access pain control are also very limited. Some, like Mrs. M, already had a home in Winnipeg with members of family; others can sometimes stay with family members in the city. Many individuals with chronic and terminal illnesses are forced to relocate with their families to urban hospitals to receive specialized treatment. Often this requires the person and family to learn to function in the city and rely on social benefit payments that will only support rental of substandard accommodation. Mr. R had no family in the city and no offer of a place in a hospice setting; his only choice was between transitional housing in an unsafe neighborhood or care on the medical wards of an urban hospital.

Mr. R preferred transitional housing to the hospital because its rules and regulations were less restrictive; however, he was also afraid of the hospital environment and said that he felt too vulnerable and vigilant to let himself sleep in the hospital. To understand his reaction it is important to know that Mr. R, like many of his contemporaries, was a residential school survivor. Memories of this period in their lives have remained very strong and are easily triggered when encountering other institutions with power to regulate and deny. One elder we interviewed in the VP NET study told us that for Indigenous people, the hospital is seen as a "sick house":

> The hospital is a sick house. They call it the sick house not the well house so everyone is a little bit afraid of a hospital because immediately you get classified . . . by white society as a sick person, in a way an incarcerated person.

The image of an "incarcerated" patient echoes their experience in the residential school system. It may also be a reminder of the impact of relocation for treatment in previous epidemics. Treatment for tuberculosis often involved enforced relocation to a distant sanatorium. The residential schools were also a breeding ground for epidemics involving both tuberculosis and other childhood illnesses (Wood 2009).

These memories of residential schools may be one of the reasons why Stienstra and Wiebe reported that emotional security and good physical care for Indigenous patients was not ensured by end-of-life care in urban centers (Stienstra and Wiebe 2004). There are more recent events that have triggered suspicion and mistrust in the Indigenous community and defensiveness on the part of the health care system. The most recent was observed in the response of First Nation leaders and communities to management of the H1N1 epidemic. Several leaders criticized the lack of response reducing environmental risk factors (housing density and quality) and emphasized the inadequacy of the public health and acute care services in Aboriginal communities. Another defining event is the case of Mr. Sinclair, an Indigenous man with double amputations and communication disabilities. The man died unattended and alone in his wheelchair after spending thirty-four hours in the waiting room of a large urban acute care hospital emergency department. Mr. Sinclair's death is currently the subject of a major ongoing review.[3]

Spirituality and Death

The connection between spirituality and death is very important in Indigenous communities, but it is also very complex. Varied and sometimes conflicting beliefs and diverse church affiliations among the members of families can lead to significant conflicts in end-of-life decision making. The impact of spiritual intersection of traditional spirituality and Christianity within families may be profound. Conflicts may occur between family members affiliated with Catholic, Anglican, and United churches and members of churches involved in more recent evangelical mission activity. The survival of traditional spirituality is overlaid with the reemergence of neo-traditional and pan-Indigenous spiritual and healing traditions. Within families and communities, conflict often emerges in the crisis-laden situations that may accompany the impending death of a family member.

Both Mrs. M and Mr. R recognized the impact of diverse religious affiliations among their family members and anticipated the potential tensions that arose around death and dying. Mrs. M was very aware of these tensions, but an elder requested that her family members support her participation in traditional ceremonies and make end-of-life decisions that were consistent with her spiritual beliefs, and she was able to persuade family members holding diverse beliefs to join together in honoring her passing in their own ceremonies and memorial services.

Mr. R also came from a family that included members from several religious/spiritual traditions. Before he died, he was concerned that family involvement around end-of-life decision making might evoke conflict between relatives who emphasized traditional Indigenous beliefs and others who were members of Christian churches. Mr. R had become more involved in traditional spiritual practice before the onset of his illness. Once he had to leave his community, he became very anxious that he would not be able to prepare for his death through working with a traditional Ojibwa elder from his own community. Although the hospital programs included provisions for spiritual care program for Indigenous patients, Mr. R was reluctant to take part in activities offered by the chaplaincy. As a residential school survivor, he emphasized his negative experience with religious authorities and churches. He wanted to either have the elder receive transportation expenses to visit the city or himself receive medical and financial support to enable him to return to the community to meet the elder. He was ultimately unable to receive support for either of these options.

The inability of the system to meet Mr. R's search for spiritual comfort and family support contrasts with the experience of Mrs. M and her commitment to meeting her death in the traditional manner, surrounded by her family and in her community nurtured by trusted family members and elders. Narratives used to develop both cases emphasized that Indigenous people living in either urban settings or their own communities may experience barriers in finding an environment characterized by cultural safety, physical security, and spiritual sanctuary, which must characterize hospice. Within the urban core, barriers to palliative care delivery include the reluctance of home care workers and volunteers to visit persons living in areas that are perceived to be "unsafe neighborhoods."

Our interviews in the study of access issues impacting vulnerable persons also indicated that barriers associated with the representation of Aboriginal people in the care team and gaps in the cultural competence of all care providers exist. Key informants emphasized the impact of cultural and structural barriers related to the predominantly Eurocentric approach to understanding issues of death and dying among palliative care professional providers and volunteers. Despite increasing access to cultural awareness training in their clinical and continuing education, several informants stated that many caregivers still failed to engage and facilitate traditional spiritual practices for Indigenous patients who held these beliefs.

Discussion

The three principles described by Dame Saunders fit so well with our analysis of two case studies of a "good" death and a "bad" death. They represent universal requisites of hospice care. However, it is important not to ignore the wider context of how death and dying occur in a particular place, to a particular people, and at a particular time. Indigenous peoples in Canada experience poverty, lack of safety, isolation from family and community, racism, social disenfranchisement, and disempowerment throughout their lives. This past and present history influences the pattern of their dying. It is difficult, for example, to understand the deep loneliness of Mr. R's death without knowing something of the history of the residential school system. We do not know whether Mrs. M went to residential school, but it is very likely because of her generation. If so, she would have gone through a system determined to erase both her language and culture. Her commitment to traditional spirituality is a testimony to her resilience.

Other barriers in these case studies reflect the impact of government policies, both provincial and federal. They include the long-term failure of both governments to tackle the living conditions of Indigenous people both in urban areas and on the reserves. The health system for Indigenous peoples is also affected by barriers created by the ambiguity in federal/provincial jurisdictional responsibility in terms of payment for care needs, medication, and transportation. At the federal level, the First Nations and Inuit Health Branch is the federal agency mandated to deliver health services to First Nations peoples. At the provincial level, cultural and organizational barriers and resource limitations in urban and tertiary care services also influence end-of-life care for Indigenous people.

Some of our informants argued that an integrated system for end-of-life care for Indigenous people was needed. In VP NET interviews, advocates, and support workers for street-involved Indigenous persons reported that finding adequate end-of-life care for street persons is difficult. One support worker talked about street people and access to palliative care.

> Getting into palliative care, the waits are really difficult. . . . If people are still actively using drugs and alcohol and substances, palliative care refuses them on that basis. I mean, sometimes people have been kicked out of palliative care because of their "lifestyle"! . . . They're still working the street and not being "good dying people." And yes, people are in palliative states, but you know, if they're strong enough to go out and turn tricks on the street, then they shouldn't need palliative care, and then the person dies on the street the next week, right? . . . There are lots of issues around that.

Another advocate for street people commented on the lack of hospice care for those who were dying:

> The hospice movement . . . is a very narrow slice of society. . . . There's not a willingness to consider that unless it's done by the rules of engagement in the medical clinical model—and those

rules are the ones that set up the barriers in the first place, mostly unknowingly—it's a very linear model. For the folks I meet, it is multiple dominoes falling in their lives. It's a collective and not a singular journey, and that's the problem.

If people don't have access to palliative care, what happens to them? A care provider for people living with HIV/AIDS told us:

The hospice palliative care thinking about really low-income people, the street people, is, "You die." There are three deaths a month at the. . . . Hotel, and that's where you find low-income palliative care and hospices.

Conclusion

The primary focus of this chapter has been on individuals, families, and communities who experience obstacles to obtaining end-of-life care that is culturally, spiritually, and physically safe, with appropriate supports and services. Although initiatives over the past three decades have extended more comprehensive access to hospice and palliative treatment, Indigenous peoples living in remote First Nations, Métis communities, and urban centers still face barriers in accessing hospice and palliative care resources.

The two case studies suggest the importance of developing a system that is more participatory and respectful of Indigenous traditions and which better enables a wider spectrum of spiritual and religious practice. Many individuals we interviewed described the need for Indigenous caregivers and cultural advocates to be part of care teams providing end-of-life care. We (Kaufert and Lavallee) have observed that interpreter advocates currently play a critical role in urban hospitals in negotiating access to more appropriate end-of-life care and providing links with community and family support systems (Kaufert et al. 1999). New models of care require a broader concept of "hospice" that encompasses both the settings and the cultural/spiritual contexts in which people are dying. "Hospice" should not refer only to a specific facility and model of service provision, but to any place an individual may choose to live while they are dying—which can offer adequate pain management, family support and safe space for spiritual practice.

The key may lie in finding a "safe place." Thien and Hanlon (2009) recommend that for Northern peoples, it is necessary to think about health issues broadly, with an understanding of place as always integral. They hold that there must be an emphasis on the dynamic aspects of place, including the significance of attending to the imagined places and perceptions of place that Northern people bring with them (Thien and Hanlon 2009). One key informant who had spent much of his life in Indigenous communities talked about how, in Indigenous peoples' sense of a cultural and spiritual safety, place is integrally connected with the concept of open space in traditional life.

> They said, "We don't believe in closing everything off." So you need to stay in touch with your environment around you. It suggests that enclosure is a particular European architectural concept. If you want me to demonstrate it the tent has the flap and most of the living. . . . I was told, "we do most of our living outside. To enclose is to hem us in. So if you wonder why on the reserve most of our doors especially the screen doors get broken down the first week or our windows are broken, we need to have connection with the outdoors and that's how we feel health wise." You can even make a health comment about oxygen and air and stuff, but the enclosure versus non-enclosure is two ways of depicting two different cultures.
> They said, "We do our worship outside. How could you ever enclose your deity? So we're not obsessed with having everything enclosed like you guys are." . . . They don't like to have locked doors . . . the church [is seen] as the locked door place and you had to knock and you wait a long time. They can't understand that. So little wonder that they don't enter those places. They come in the door; they look both ways first. This feels a little bit . . . like the residential school. The jail is like that. Most of the institutions are like that. So how [does] that apply to health care? . . . It's enclosure versus non-enclosure. The people . . . find that very claustrophobic . . . especially if it shuts out their own relatives, their own kinship.

Providing End-of-life Care to First Nations and Métis Peoples: What Health Care Providers Need to Know

Margaret Lavallee, an Ojibwa traditional elder working with Kim Gray, developed a series of guidelines that are used for training health care professionals participating in programs sponsored by the Winnipeg Regional Health Authority. These guidelines provide examples of approaches that palliative caregivers can use for communicating with patients and families who follow a wider range of traditional Indigenous spiritual practices.[4] The successful application of these approaches is reflected in this description of an elder's final practice:

> He said, "Don't cry for me because it's time for me to go. My journey is ready to begin" . . . He assured me he was ready to go home . . . and a month before that, he refused to take his medications, he said, "I'm going to take my traditional medicines, and that's all I'm going to take because it's time for me to go home." He also told me that two weeks prior to that he . . . heard the drums in his room. He said, "I heard drum groups singing and they were, they were calling me home."

This elder's preparation was characterized as supplying appropriate support for traditional spiritual practice by an Ojibwa elder who stated, "The kinds of things that are so important for traditional people are to have their pipe, to have their drum, and to smoke it for one last time."

Acknowledgments

The participation of Joe Kaufert and Rhonda Wiebe and the collection of qualitative data on policymaker, caregiver, family-member, and care-recipient perspectives was supported by the Canadian Institutes of Health Research: Vulnerable Persons and End of Life New Emerging Team (VP NET) Grant 2004–09 (Harvey M. Chochinov, principal investigator; Deborah Stienstra, co-principal investigator; Zana Lutfiyya, co-investigator; Joseph Kaufert, co-investigator). We wish also to thank Dawn Stewart and staff at the Centre for Aboriginal Health Research at the University of Manitoba for their continuing editorial and administrative help.

Notes

1. The term *Indigenous peoples* includes Aboriginal First Nations and Métis with or without treaty status. In 2001, more than 1.1 million people, or

4.4 percent of Canada's total population, reported having Aboriginal ancestry. This represents a 22 percent increase over the 1996 Census figures, while the non-Aboriginal population grew by 3.4 percent. About 62 percent of Canada's Aboriginal people are First Nations, 30 percent are Métis, 5 percent Inuit, and the remaining 3 percent identified themselves with more than one group or as band members not identifying as Aboriginal (Statistics Canada, 2001 Census). People identifying themselves as Aboriginal include 150,000 individuals or 15.5 percent of the population of the Province of Manitoba (Lavallee and Gray, 2009). Thirty-five percent of the Aboriginal population lives in Winnipeg, making it the largest urban Indigenous population in Canada.

2. The availability of palliative and hospice care for Aboriginal people is impacted by multiple levels of authority and by discontinuities in health service provision and eligibility across provincial, federal, and First Nation governments.

3. Mr. Sinclair had taken a taxi from a community health center to the hospital on Friday afternoon and was found dead Sunday morning after someone else in the emergency room alerted the hospital staff. The catheter he had as a result of a bladder infection had been blocked, and the infection spread to his bloodstream. According to the health authority spokesperson, Sinclair appears to have never been assessed by a triage nurse and was not registered as a patient seeking care (CBC News 2009). His death, as indicated by Dr. Thambirajah Balanchandra, the provincial chief medical examiner, was "entirely preventable" (CBC News 2008). Mr. Sinclair died without medical, social, or spiritual support. This case also appears to involve some of the elements identified in our interviews with key informants in describing "bad deaths" among people who died outside acute or palliative care facilities.

4. The following guidelines were provided for care providers communicating with Indigenous patients and families. They are intended to facilitate access to culturally safe spiritual care. Source: Margaret Lavallee and Kim Gray, "Caring for Aboriginal Peoples When Dealing with Dying and Death, Aboriginal Health Programs" (Winnipeg Regional Health Authority 2009).

a. Health care professionals need to ask—what religion does the family follow? If they follow the Native traditional spiritual way, the family will bring their spiritual elder or medicine person to the hospital to be with the family and patient.

b. Health care professionals need to know that there is a process of passing on information. Usually, the one that is the closest relative of the patient will inform other members of the family that their loved one is dying. It is at this time that staff needs to be aware that the family spokesperson will call all family members to the dying person's bedside. You can expect many people to arrive at the hospital.

c. Health care professionals need to know and be prepared to meet family needs. These could include support to accommodate large numbers of visitors to pay their respects; negotiating space for many people to be in one space; a place for traditional smudging ceremonies where sacred items and medicines (sage, sweet grass, tobacco, and hand drum) are used.

d. After the apparent death, another smudging ceremony takes place. The sacred pipe may be brought so all family members can smoke, the drum will be sounded, and the medicine person will sing the end of trail song. At this time people will visit and talk about the person who has passed on as if they were present in the room. This is done because this is the last time they will use the name of the person as if she/he were of this world.

e. Traditional people will not speak the name of the one who has passed on. If one uses that name, it is seen as inviting that spirit to visit, which can be harmful to the ones who remain. Instead, the person who has died is referred to as "the one who passed away," and it is after the burial the relatives may show great sadness.

References

Brant, C. 1990. Native ethics and rules of behaviour. *Canadian Journal of Psychiatry* 35: 534–39.

Deloria, V. 1993. Death and religion. In *God is red: A Native view of religion,* 165–84. Golden, CO: Fulcrum.

Carrese, J. A., and L. A. Rhodes,. 1995. Western bioethics on the Navajo reservation. Benefit or harm? *Journal of the American Medical Association* 274(10): 826–29.

du Boublay, S. 2007. *Cicely Saunders: Founder of the modern hospice movement.* London: SCK.

Ellerby, J., et al. 2000 (Oct. 3). Bioethics for clinicians: 18. Aboriginal cultures. *Canadian Medical Association Journal* 163(7): 845–50.

Freedman, B. 1993. Offering truth: One ethical approach to the uninformed cancer patient. *Archives of Internal Medicine* 153: 572–76.

Gao, S., B. J. Manns, B. F. Culleton et al. 2008. Access to health care among status Aboriginal people with chronic kidney disease. *CMAJ* 179: 1007–12.

George, D. 1982. *My spirit soars.* Surrey, BC: Hancock House.

Hultkrantz, A. 1989. Health, religion and medicine in Native North American traditions. In *Healing and restoring: Health and medicine in the world's religious traditions,* ed. L. E. Sullivan, 327–58. London: Macmillan.

Kaufert, J., and J. O'Neil, 1995. Cultural mediation of dying and grieving among native patients in urban hospitals. In *The path ahead: Readings in death and dying,* ed. L. A. DeSpelder and A. L. Strickland, 59–74. Mayfield, CA: Mountain View Press.

Kaufert, J., R. W. Putsch, and M. Lavallee, 1999. End-of-life decision making among Aboriginal Canadians: Interpretation, mediation and discord in the communication of bad news. *Journal of Palliative Care* 151: 31–38.

Lavallee, M., and K. Gray. 2009. Caring for Aboriginal Peoples when dealing with dying and death. PowerPoint presentation. Aboriginal Health Programs, Winnipeg Regional Health Authority.

Menec, V., L. Lix, and C. Steinbach et al. 2004. *Patterns of health care use and cost at the end-of-life*. Manitoba Centre for Health Policy. University of Manitoba.

NAHO (National Aboriginal Health Organization). 2002. *End of life/ palliative care for Aboriginal Peoples*. Discussion paper. Ottawa: National Aboriginal Health Organization.

Standing Senate Committee on Social Affairs, Science and Technology. 2000. *Quality end-of-life care: The right of every Canadian*. Ottawa: Senate of Canada. http://www.parl.gc.ca/36/2/parlbus/commbus/senate/com-e/upda-e/rep-e/repfinjun00-e.htm.

SPHERU (Saskatchewan Population Health and Evaluation Research Unit). *Improving end of life care for Aboriginal families* 14(1). Saskatoon: Alberta Centre for Active Living and SPHERU.

Stienstra, D., and R. Wiebe. 2004. *Finding our way home: Housing options in inner-city Winnipeg for people with disabilities who are dying, final report*. Winnipeg: Winnipeg Inner City Research Alliance/ Canadian Centre on Disability Studies.

Thien, D., and N. L. Hanlon. 2009. Unfolding dialogues about gender, care, and "the north": An introduction. *Gender, Place and Culture* 16(2): 155–62.

Tinker, G. The rocks shall cry out: Consciousness, rocks, and American Indians. Video excerpt. Counterbalance: New views on complex issues. http://www.counterbalance.org/global/tinker-body.html?b=enviro/index-body.html (Accessed July 22, 2009).

Woods, A. 2009. The health of First Nations children upon entrance to a residential school in a northern Manitoba community. MSc. thesis, Department of Community Health Sciences, Faculty of Medicine, University of Manitoba.

12

Caring for Children in
Hospice and Palliative Care

The Spiritual/Religious Dimension

Betty Davies
Thomas Attig

Introduction

Life-limiting illness in childhood deeply affects the child, parents, and other family members, and those who care for her or him. Infant mortality rates declined dramatically in the last century in many parts of the world due primarily to successes in public health and sanitation, disease prevention, and the development and availability of antibiotics. These developments have made the death of a child seem only more tragic where it occurs relatively less frequently and more unexpectedly. But, no matter where or how often it occurs in a community, the death of a child has always been and always will be out of season and profoundly challenging. And caring for a dying child will always be among the most difficult labors of love.

In many parts of the world, scarce resources are still directed toward reducing high infant mortality rates. Children in these countries die most commonly from infection or starvation (Sumner 2006). The relatively new field of pediatric palliative care began in countries with lower infant mortality and more resources available for specialized health care. The first hospital programs for dying children were established in Montreal and Toronto in the mid-1970s, while the first home care programs were established in the United States about the same time. A pediatric nurse, who was also an Anglican nun, established the world's first free-standing children's hospice, Helen House, in Oxford, England, in 1982. Recognizing the plight of parents of children with life-limiting illness, Sr. Frances Dominica wanted to provide respite for these parents, comfort for their children, and, for both, companionship on their journey to death and grief. Though their goals were similar, when she turned to her friend Cicely Saunders for advice, she was told not to start the hospice because it would be too difficult. Undaunted, Sr. Frances persisted. And today, resulting from her pioneering efforts, forty children's hospices exist in the United Kingdom alone. Canuck Place in Vancouver, British Columbia, became the first free-standing children's hospice in North America in 1995, and the San Francisco Bay Area's George Mark Children's House the first in the United States in 2004. Other children's hospices exist throughout the world, and all are based on the centrality of symptom management, involvement of the family, and spiritual care—though Sr. Frances would prefer the term *holistic care* (personal communication, Sr. Frances Dominica, Dec. 5, 2009).

Even where infant mortality is low, it remains true that more than half of the children who die are neonates or infants (up to twelve months of age). After that critical first year, the most common cause of pediatric death is trauma, where there is little opportunity for palliative care. The disease most often responsible for childhood death is cancer. Other prominent causes include various metabolic and neurodegenerative genetic illnesses (Field and Behrman 2003). In earlier years, children with cancer and these genetic disorders died more quickly. Now, however, with medical developments in diagnosis and treatment, children are living longer with these illnesses, in many cases years longer.

Dealing with uncertainty is a prominent aspect of the experiences of dying children, their families, and their caregivers (Davies et al. 2008). Diagnoses of life-threatening illness in children are rare and therefore often uncertain. Protocols and treatments are hard to develop, given the limited numbers of subjects available for randomized clinical trials. The courses of the illnesses themselves are unpredictable and filled with acute episodes, remissions, and relapses. Uncertainty about what may be next in the course of illness takes a toll on children, family members, and caregivers alike.

The location of care also matters. Even in the Western world, where palliative and hospice care for dying children is most widely available, most children who die still do so in hospitals (Field and Behrman 2003). And most of the hospital deaths occur in intensive care units (over half in neonatal intensive care nurseries) where fully developed palliative care programs do not usually reach children and their families. There is still much to be done to bring the benefits of such care, even where the possibilities are limited, to as many as possible and to train emergency room and intensive care teams in palliative techniques they can use.

Although most children in the Western world die in hospitals, some also die at home or in hospices. At home, families can follow their own practices and routines, as they do where specialized services, or even hospitals, are not readily available. When children die at home, home care hospice personnel are often considered "part of the family" as they become familiar with the family and offer support. This contrasts to not-so-well trained others who can be seen as "invaders" in the home and intruders in family routines and decision making.

Attending to the environment plays a key role in the success of still not widely available freestanding hospice and hospital-based palliative care programs. The hospices provide large, comfortable "home away from home" settings where spaces are created for individuals and families to engage in familiar practices and routines and where they are encouraged to openly express their emotions and concerns. Hospital-based programs do all they can to make the comforts of home available, support families in caring for their children as they would at home, and encourage open communication.

As with adult hospice and palliative care programs, programs for dying children take the family as the unit of care. They are designed to respond not only to the physical needs of the children but to the full range of emotional, psychological, sociological, and spiritual needs of the entire family. A team comprised most commonly of nurses, physicians, social workers, and clergy, and often including physical, art, music, and other therapists, works together with the children and family members in discerning and meeting the full range of these needs.

Here we confine our attention to the nature and means of addressing spiritual and religious need in pediatric hospice and palliative end-of-life care. We discuss the nature and subjects of spiritual and religious needs in these contexts. We examine what respectful caring response to these needs requires. And, as we do, we tell stories that illustrate some of the varieties of challenge that arise in interactions with the children themselves and their families.

We approach this discussion from the perspectives of a nurse who, for the past forty years, has worked in the field of pediatric end-of-life care as a clinician, educator, and researcher, and an applied philosopher who for the past thirty-six years worked in the field of death, dying, loss, and grief as an educator and researcher. Our involvement in the day-to-day lives of families of children with life-threatening illness and the bereaved and in grounded theory and phenomenological research has provided unique opportunities to observe and reflect upon religious and spiritual experiences in pediatric palliative and hospice care.

The Need for Spiritual/Religious Care

We have observed that when a child is dying, parents and families feel profoundly out of tune with reality. Unanswerable questions of Why my child? or Why any child? fill them with anguish. Parents and caregivers alike almost inevitably wonder about matters of life and death: Where did the breath that sustained this child's life come from? Where has it gone? What did this life mean? How has it changed us? Why are we still living? How do we go on? What meaning might our lives still have? Where do our child's and our own lives fit in the vast scheme of things?

These profoundly challenging questions speak of the deep spiritual needs of parents and families for understandings that religions offer. Religions of the world variously provide worldviews, beliefs, scriptures, myths (in the sense of compelling narratives), accounts of mystical experiences, creeds, authority figures, and guidance for personal reflection on questions of the origins and nature of reality, the place of human life in the universe, reasons for living, and the possibilities of an afterlife or reincarnation. These provide a basis for understanding of mysteries of life, death, suffering, the divine, and the order of things.

We have also observed that when a child is dying, parents and families are at a loss as to what to do and how to carry on living. Unwelcome change transforms the world of their experience and brings them into crisis. Their confidence in taken-for-granted ways of living and being with one another is shaken. Their world becomes a frightening place. It can seem as if chaos has broken out. Unprecedented challenges threaten to overwhelm them. They doubt their abilities to meet their child's, their other children's, or even their own needs. Their daily life patterns are shattered. Their future is shrouded in darkness and uncertainty.

These profound life challenges speak of deep spiritual needs of parents and families for behavioral guidance and support that religions offer. Religions of the world variously provide spiritual practices such as worship, formal ritual, sacrifice, meditation, prayer, daily devotion, and service that support parents and families as they search for ways of responding to crisis and sorrow. They also variously endorse ways of life that include such qualities as honesty, humility, gratitude, faithfulness, piety, respect for family and the earth, compassion, love, charity, patience, forgiveness, and harmony. These provide a basis for direction, trust, hope, and courage while living in the shadows of the mysteries of life, death, and suffering.

In practice, many like Sr. Frances prefer not to separate religion and spirituality, seeing the former as an expression of the latter. Unlike St. Christopher's, Helen House "never has had ward prayers or anything remotely resembling that. We have always emphasized that people of all faiths and none are welcome and given equal respect" (personal communication, Sr. Frances Dominica, Dec. 9, 2009). The core value in providing spiritual care in hospice and palliative care for children is respecting the parents and family (including the dying child), no matter their religious or spiritual or religious beliefs or practices. Some family members, or children and adolescents themselves, are very clear about the spiritual/religious practices and beliefs that matter to them and about the support they want. They may find much comfort, for example, in a belief that "everything is in God's hands." Or they may find spiritual/religious support for decisions that they make about continuing or discontinuing medical efforts to cure or halt the progress of disease. Some have no history with and find no comfort or benefit in religious affiliations or teachings. Others are not so clear in their beliefs, but may still seek benefit in religious practices.

One Chinese mother learned of religious practices that she herself did not fully believe in. But she engaged in them in order to "cover the bases" (her words) for her son's benefit and her own peace of mind. Her teenage son was diagnosed with a serious form of cancer and received experimental treatment for several months. When the cancer returned, there was no alternative chemotherapy to try. She had seen a psychologist for depression before her son's diagnosis and continued to see him during his illness. The psychologist introduced her to his Christian church. She attended infrequently and was uncomfortable (as many Chinese are) with group sharing of personal matters with strangers. Her Christian friends told her that baptism was required for going to heaven. If she wanted to see her son after he died, he had to be baptized (and so did she). Because she asked, out of respect her son agreed without hesitation, and both of them were baptized. The mother's Buddhist sister recommended that she pay money to a Buddhist holy person to pray for the son. The mother did this too "just in case" there would be value in doing so for her son. She was greatly comforted by both the baptisms and the prayers offered by the holy person.

Wherever hospice or palliative care are offered to dying children and their families, there is great need for finding means to live well in whatever time remains and for finding understanding in the compelling presence of mystery. Caregivers do their best to support children (as they are capable) and other family members in their efforts to find the trust, hope, courage, and understanding they need. They are trained to offer them compassion in their suffering, to support them in finding time and space for the religious practices they value, and to honor and respect whatever religious beliefs they hold and profess.

The Spiritual/Religious Needs of Dying Children and Adolescents

Sadly, in some cases, especially when children are very young, there is a tendency to think that children themselves have no spiritual or religious needs, and a matching tendency to treat them as islands of innocence in the midst of the chaos that terminal illness brings. Those who work with dying children know better. During my years of pediatric palliative care, I have learned that very ill children, even young ones, are what I consider "spiritual beings" in that they seem to have an awareness or an implicit understanding of situations that escape the rational perspectives of older people. If parents are in the habit of talking about religious concepts (such as God or heaven) then their children will sometimes express thoughts and feelings using these same concepts. But even children without religious training often express ideas about life and death.

Terminal illness intrudes insistently into the lives of children. It shatters their sense of invulnerability as they learn that medicine cannot make everything better. It shatters the taken-for-granted patterns of their daily lives. It truncates their future and changes utterly both the shape and content of the remaining pages and chapters of their lives and the character of their biographies as wholes. And it sometimes threatens children's connections with others, as they find it difficult to continue to participate in their families, friendships, and wider communities. Some come to doubt the safety and security of the world, the fairness of it all, whether it is worth going on day to day, and whether they still belong on this earth.

It is by now well established that terminally ill children regularly acquire awareness and understandings of death that are far in advance of their unafflicted peers. Since the early 1960s with Waechter's study of seriously ill children (Krulik and Holaday 1987), and surely after the publication of Myra Bluebond-Langner's seminal work (1978), the views that children younger than ten do not understand death, do not experience anguish over death, are incapable of coping with the anguish, and should be protected from the truth have been reversed. Children's personal experiences with diagnosis, courses of disease and treatment, the deaths of ill peers and the like are much more significant than age or cognitive development in determining their understandings of illness and its meanings. Terminally ill three- or four-year-olds may know more about illness and dying than healthy nine- or ten-year-olds. And children often come to know and understand despite receiving precious little to no information from parents or health care personnel. Attempts to keep children blissfully unaware in order to preserve their innocence and spare them anguish simply fail.

Existential suffering may be defined as anguish over what is possible in life and about our place in the greater scheme of things. It is not difficult to see how many very familiar childhood fears share features of existential suffering (Attig 1996). Children are at times profoundly fearful of being annihilated or overwhelmed. They are fearful when they sense they are helpless and powerless. They fear abandonment or separation from those who care for and love them. They fear rejection that is a refusal to love them. They fear punishment, especially when they see it as unfair or arbitrary. In fear of the dark, they fear the unknown that may lurk within. If childhood fears are similar in these ways to adult existential suffering in the face of terminal illness and death, it seems not really a leap to think that children experience similar apprehensions when they, too, are terminally ill. Think of the torrents of questions raised by very young children about their surroundings: how the world and things in it work; origins of things including the sun, moon, and stars, animals, the whole world, and themselves; why things are as they are; and what is fair. That children are concerned about the fairness of the differences that terminal illness introduces into their lives is evident in the persistence of the question "Why me?" Concerns about punishment are also transparent. Children are endlessly curious and filled with wonder about things great and small. How remarkable it would be if their wonder and curiosity were to halt abruptly only when they were terminally ill. On the contrary, terminally ill children are filled with questions that cry for honest and clear answers that orient them to present realities and what lies ahead.

Children are also full of answers and speculations about how and why things are as they are and where their lives, illness, and pending death fit into the greater scheme of things. Often they echo their parents, teachers, or peers. Many parents or guardians expose children to early training in the teachings of the world's religions about such things as the divine, heaven and hell, reincarnation, and the meanings of life, death, and suffering. Again, how remarkable it would be if children brought none of their beginning understandings to bear upon their experiences of terminal illness. Mark's story (below) serves as an illustration of how children express spirituality. Scotty's story (also below) shows how a young child thinks about death and the afterlife despite being protected from information about his condition.

Mark and Henry both had leukemia and a long course of treatment. This was in the early 1970s when most children with leukemia died from the disease, unlike today where the five-year survival rate with acute lymphocytic leukemia is 80 percent overall (Field and Behrman 2003). Back then, children also had to be admitted to hospital for chemotherapy—it was before the days of outpatient chemotherapy. Thus, Mark and Henry were both in hospital for many weeks at a time. From their first meeting, they became fast friends. They were diagnosed and admitted about the same time and were about the same age (four and five years old). Neither spoke English but they soon learned. Mark was from a Cree reservation, many miles from the city where the hospital was located. Henry was from a German community also far from the hospital. Henry's parents lived close enough that they could come most weekends and take Henry home for a couple of days. They would arrive on Friday evening, after Mark had gone to sleep. On Saturday mornings, Mark would look for Henry and then remember that "Henry gone home." Sunday night, Mark would be excited knowing that he would awake and find Henry had returned. This pattern continued for some time.

Henry's condition deteriorated, and he was too ill to go home for several weekends. He was in a private room, close to the nursing station, with a window facing the hallway. Each morning and several times each day, Mark would stand on the chair outside the window to wave at Henry. One night, Henry died. The nurses gathered at the station to discuss how to break the news to Mark. Before finishing the discussion, they turned to see Mark climbing up on his chair to greet Henry. He had woken up early. The nurses could only watch in silence as Mark looked into the empty room to see the bed stripped clean and all of Henry's belongings gone from the room. Puzzled, Mark looked at them, back into the room, and back at them. With a worried tone, he queried, "Henry gone home? No!" He turned his eyes once more to the empty room, and with a deep sigh, he announced confidently, "Henry not gone home. Henry gone HOME!"

In his own way, Mark understood that the "home" to which Henry had gone this time was a different one than his usual earthly home. The nurses did not know what teachings Mark had had, nor did they know if he and Henry were aware of their mutual plight. But, they felt that the peace that came over Mark in those few seconds was palpable. His spiritual awareness comforted and inspired them all.

Scotty was an eight-year-old boy with leukemia and a poor prognosis. His parents were adamant that no one should talk to their son about his diagnosis or prognosis. Scotty's grandparents came to pick him up to take him home for the Thanksgiving weekend. Unknown to me, they had just boarded the elevator that I ran to catch. Slipping in between the closing doors, I saw Scotty and his grandparents and commented, "So you are going home for Thanksgiving, Scotty?" And, jokingly, I admonished, "Be careful you don't eat too much turkey!" Without hesitation, Scotty looked directly at me and said, "Why not, I won't be here for the Christmas turkey." His grandmother paled and fell against the wall of the elevator. The doors opened and they quickly left.

Scotty's parents brought him back to the hospital on Monday morning and demanded a meeting with the head nurse and the attending physician. They believed that "someone must have talked to Scotty" against their wishes. They reinforced their desire that no one talk to Scotty for fear of distressing him.

Scotty had returned accompanied by a gift he had received—a stuffed animal, a long snake that he had named Super Salami. Super Salami became his constant companion. When Scotty's white blood count fell and he needed to be in protective isolation, he asked that the second bed in his room remain so that Super Salami also had a place to sleep. When meals were delivered, Scotty insisted that Super Salami also have a meal tray. When the lab technician came to take blood from Scotty, she had to also take blood from Super Salami. Scotty's condition was deteriorating. I was his primary nurse. One morning as I was giving Scotty his morning care, he said to me, "Super Salami is very sick, you know." "He is?" I replied. "Yup . . . he has something wrong with his blood. It can't get better." "No?" I asked. "Nope," he affirmed. A few moments passed during which time I wasn't sure what to say next. Scotty was the one to speak: "What do you think will happen to Super Salami?" I didn't have a clue what to say. My nursing education had not prepared me for this conversation. I took a deep breath and picked up Super Salami. I held him in my arms, and stroked his back. With all honesty, I said, "You know, Scotty, I really don't know for sure. But wherever he goes, there will be someone to love him and take care of him." My heart was pounding. But Scotty simply grinned and chuckled, "That's exactly what I thought!"

The Spiritual/Religious Needs and Desires of Other Family Members

Hospice and palliative approaches to care have always talked about attending to the needs of the entire family, not merely the dying person. The dying child's parents, siblings, grandparents, and quite possibly other members of the family (depending upon how close they are to the child) also have spiritual/religious needs. Time does not allow us to illustrate the full range of cases here. But we do want to note the importance of not assuming that all members of a family practice or believe in the same way. The story of the Chinese mother and son above illustrates how sometimes ways can be easily found to accommodate such differences. Outcomes for mother and son might have been quite different had the son refused baptism.

At other times it can be far more difficult to accommodate such differences. In one instance, parents who were Jehovah's Witnesses refused to authorize a life-saving transfusion for their six-year-old son. Staff were distressed, and discussed among themselves how to approach and try to persuade the parents of the necessity of the transfusion. When the staff did approach them to make their case, the parents persisted in their decision, saying, "You are intent on saving our son's life on earth. But we are determined to save his soul for eternal life." The matter rested there.

In another case, a sixteen-year-old girl had developed a brain tumor and had it removed successfully. Her recovery was difficult, but, on her understanding, progressing well. Her mother and grandmother insisted that their faith was strong enough to ensure that the girl would recover.

When a second, inoperable brain tumor appeared, the teen was not told because her family insisted that if she were told, she would lose hope. Their religious convictions dominated the situation, and the physicians incrementally imposed more and more standard treatments (medications and other therapies) to support her various bodily functions (digestion, elimination, respiration, mobility, speech, even tear production).

The girl's condition deteriorated slowly, inexorably, and horribly. Her spirits were high until she became bedridden and began losing her capacity to communicate. They did not flag through the period when special voice support mechanisms were provided and she eventually lost her voice. While able to communicate only through blinking her eyes, she seemed to be losing hope. Eventually, in order to protect the one eye with which she could still blink from dehydration, cellophane was placed over the eye, and she lost the ability to respond to her environment altogether. The story ends with the girl oblivious to her fate and in limbo, isolated from all interaction with others on a clear trajectory of indefinite duration toward death.

No one attended to the girl's spiritual/religious needs as they would have in a palliative care approach. Nor did anyone reach out to the mother and grandmother, acknowledge their helplessness, or try to counsel with them about alternative ways of understanding the support that faith could provide them and the girl.

In still another case, an African American father's unborn child was diagnosed with hypoplastic left heart. The condition is incompatible with life, although a series of major surgeries can be performed after birth and subsequently to extend the child's life for a time. The father was a pastor in a Christian evangelical church. Given the seriousness of the baby's condition, the parents were advised to consider abortion. The father was adamant that "because of our relationship spiritually with God, abortion is not an option." He and his wife argued about this because she wanted to consider the option and saw her husband as "not being sensitive enough in this area."

A social worker in the hospital who was aware of the family's religious affiliation asked questions that allowed the father to express his questions and needs. The social worker and a senior chaplain were compassionate and listened attentively in conversations with him. Together they explored his religious beliefs and interpretations of God's judgment. These explorations allowed the father to broaden his thinking and come to new understandings of his faith and of his behavior in relation to his seriously ill child and his wife. The father said, "My outlook on God changed drastically." He said he went from seeing God standing in judgment of him and his decision to seeing God as holding both his child and him in his loving arms. He saw God as also suffering and understanding of his predicament. He came to believe that a God of compassion would want him to do the best he could for his child and his marriage. When the baby delivered early, no extraordinary measures were taken to sustain its life. The mother and father took turns holding the child until death came. In this case, optimal caregiving for the parents enabled them to agree on what was best for their child while remaining true to their religious beliefs.

Caregiver Need for Spiritual/Religious Sensitivity

Spiritual/religious traditions often prescribe norms pertaining to end-of-life caregiving, including meanings ascribed to illness or accident, language used to talk of sickness and death (e.g., whether death may be openly acknowledged), symbolic value placed on an individual's life (or death), meanings of pain and suffering, appropriate expressions of suffering, preferences about the intensity of treatment, willingness to make use of hospice and palliative care, differences in access to or use of pain medication and other therapies, styles and assumptions about decision making, concerns about trust in the health care system, appropriate roles for healers and families, care and disposition of the body after death, and mourning behaviors and expressions of grief.

Clearly, caregiver respect for spiritual/religious practices and beliefs of dying children and their families is not only important, but daunting. There are so many ways in which practices and beliefs can support those in their care in living meaningfully and finding understanding. And they may bring so many different traditional expectations about appropriate end-of-life care with them.

The most recent discussions of respecting cultural differences (for example, Hays 2001) distinguish between "competence" and "sensitivity" and can be applied to religious/spiritual differences. *Competence* is a matter of mastering quantities of information about a wide variety of religions and the differences among them pertaining to the broad range of issues identified above. Few will ever have such mastery, given the considerable numbers of religious beliefs, practices, and norms that can easily be represented in contemporary populations. And even those who acquire such mastery may lack understanding of what to do with the information that they have digested. There is a strong tendency among some who have it, for example, to stereotype individuals rather than to appreciate (1) how there are great variations within religious traditions themselves or (2) how individuals vary greatly in the ways in which they experience the religions that have colored their unique life experiences.

Sensitivity, on the other hand, has to do with tuning in to how those in care, as the unique individuals they are, have experienced religion and religious traditions. Some identify very strongly with their religious heritage, while others do not. Some find considerable support in religious beliefs, practices, and norms, while others not. Some are remarkably indifferent, or even resistant, to elements of, or even the entirety of, religious traditions from which they come or which they represent. Caregivers need to inquire respectfully, to enter into dialogue with those in their care, to learn about their unique experiences, and to support them as best they can in finding comfort and meaning in aspects of their religion with which they identify, and possibly in resisting religious influences they do not find supportive. Dying children and their families may have a great deal to teach their caregivers about survival and resilience.

Spiritual/religious sensitivity also requires that caregivers remember that they themselves have spiritual/religious needs, experiences, and predispositions. Part of respectful, sensitive caregiving is resisting temptations to impose one's own beliefs and expectations upon others. Knowing one's own family or communal religious predispositions is essential.

Spiritual/religious sensitivity also requires awareness of how the knowledge, values, methods, and approaches caregivers are disposed to bring to bear in interactions with others are extensions of a broader, predominantly secular, cultural system of health care that may be unfamiliar to those in their care. This medical culture includes emphases on the body (biochemistry and disease), the material versus the spiritual or religious, problem solving and science, and curing versus palliative care. Caregivers must also appreciate the power, influence, and privilege represented in the position they hold in a system that those in their care may distrust or find to be alien and unsupportive.

It is important in hospices or palliative care programs in hospitals to communicate clearly that representatives of all spiritual/religious traditions are welcome and will be served with sensitivity to their particular needs, beliefs, and practices. When Canuck Place Children's Hospice opened in Vancouver, a First Nations medicine man, representing the land on which the hospice was founded, was invited to visit and bless the house. The smudging ceremony included prayer, chanting, and the burning of sweetgrass in the corners of the building and was a model of ecumenical acknowledgment. It communicated to the staff, families, and the broader community that the house is a sacred place where extraordinary things happen. It established an environment that is open, accepting, and inclusive of all religions. The creation of a mourning room or other sacred space in hospitals can convey this same message, as can the availability of reading materials about various religions and their practices in the hospice or hospital. Particularly helpful for adults and children alike is a series of children's books entitled, Religions of the World (for example, *I am Muslim, I am Jewish*).

This openness can at times be seriously challenged when beliefs or practices fall far outside of even the expected ranges. The parents of a young seriously ill child believed in a form of witchcraft. Most of the hospital unit staff members found this to be an "impossible" situation. However, after much discussion, and in an attempt to provide "family-centered care," the staff agreed the family should be allowed to engage in their religious rituals, which included, for example, displaying pictures of the devil and burning black candles. Knowing that these actions would be very distressing to other families on the unit, the staff asked the family to engage in such rituals at specified times when the door to the room could be shut and no one would be coming to do a procedure or a test. If anyone were to ask why the door was closed, the staff would offer the simple explanation that the family had requested some privacy to conduct a religious ceremony. No doubt the staff would have drawn the line had the ceremonies involved anything such as animal sacrifice or ritual infliction of pain.

How Caregivers Can Help

As caregivers, including family, friends, and professional and volunteer staff, we can create a safe and secure environment where children and adolescents can find comfort and freely express their spiritual/religious needs and anguish (Attig 1996). We can show that we are willing to witness and accept whatever they say or otherwise express. We can wonder whether our intense efforts at symptom control may wall them from us, discourage intimacy with terminally ill children, or mute their expressions.

We can offer our simple presence free of any agenda save to be their companions as they live with their illness. Such presence provides a basis for trust that enables them, when they are ready, to face what threatens and frightens them. They can then begin to move into a healing space where they can put their anguish into perspective in lives shaped by illness but no longer dominated by anguish. When existential suffering and spiritual/religious pain are acknowledged and expressed, terminally ill children can begin to seek ways, old and new, in which they can experience the time remaining as still valuable, meaningful, and hopeful.

We can learn to recognize existential suffering and spiritual pain in children's questions, conversation, play, drawings, and behaviors. We can learn of the power of special interventions such as image work, dream work, art therapy, and music therapy. We can ask them what, if anything, they believe about God (or Allah or Buddha as appropriate), how God feels about them or their sickness, or how God is helping them. We can encourage children to use such practices as prayer and meditation to express and process their spiritual/religious anguish.

We can also learn how to minister to terminally ill children's fears. Our presence in itself speaks directly to fears of separation and abandonment. We can support families that find it difficult to offer such presence. We can assure dying children that they need not be alone unless they choose to be so and that someone who cares will always be close. We can also reassure them that, no matter their condition or distress, they will always be worthy of our caring attention. We can ask them what, if anything, frightens them about their illness and what lies ahead. And we can assure them that good care will relieve their physical distress. We can ask them what is hardest for them about being ill and how we can help with it.

We can address helplessness and powerlessness as we include children in decision making about treatment options, symptom control, and where they will live, and seek every opportunity to give them choice and control in shaping their daily lives. We thus assure them that, though none of us has a choice about when illness comes, we can choose how to live in response to its intrusion and in death's shadow. Our confidence and affirmation that the life remaining can be precious can encourage the same appreciation in them and counter feelings that they are burdens on others or failures. We can help them to focus upon remaining opportunities for meaningful experiences, achievements, and expressions. Much of what previously interested them may still be possible, sometimes with assistance. We can also encourage them to explore new possibilities of living with their illness, for example, in interaction with peers who are similarly afflicted. In these and similar ways, we can encourage children to live their days on their own terms and to find value, meaning, and hope that are still within reach.

We can also support terminally ill children as they face the spiritual/ religious challenges of leaving this life and entering the unknown. We can assure them that they will always be in our hearts and that we will not forget them. We can talk with them about how they would like to be remembered. We can ask if, when they think about dying, they have any concerns about us, their close friends, or pets and whether they are trying to help their loved ones get ready for a time when they might not be here any longer. We can answer their questions honestly and in ways that orient them to concrete reality and candidly acknowledge the limits of what we know. Where they are troubled by what may come for them after death, we can invite them to tell us what they believe and hope. We will often find ourselves exploring concepts of heaven, reincarnation, reunion with others who have died, possible reunion with us and the like. We need not dissuade them where beliefs or hopes comfort or console. Where punishment concerns them, we can help them to reality test their feelings of responsibility and provide assurance about forgiveness.

As professional and volunteer caregivers we can also create a safe and secure environment where family members, including parents, siblings, and grandparents, can find comfort and freely express their spiritual/ religious needs and anguish (Davies et al. 2002). We can show that we are willing to witness and accept whatever they express. We can ask parents about what concerns them most about their child's illness or whether they've ever talked with anyone about what might happen if their child were to die. We can discuss how their child's diagnosis has affected their values and priorities and spiritual/religious beliefs or practices and what helps them most in coming to terms with the seriousness of what is happening. Where they profess a religious faith, we can ask whether they have been supported by, or would like the support of, a priest, rabbi, minister, guru, holy person, or chaplain. We can discuss what is most difficult for them from the perspective of their faith and how it supports or helps them. We can assure them we are willing to support them in maintaining spiritual/religious practices in the hospice or hospital setting.

We can ask who is responsible for their child's daily care, including spiritual support. We can ask if their child has ever brought up the subject of death, what the child said, how they responded, and what it was like for the child or them. We can discuss their understandings of their child's spirituality or religious beliefs and practices, if any, and their perspective on how it has been affected by the illness. We can discuss whether they ever pray with their child, what they pray about, and how they feel as they pray. If they are anxious about or would like guidance in understanding, listening to, speaking with, or comforting their child, we can explore alternative ways (including those discussed above) for them to provide spiritual support. We can explore how their child's illness has affected their spouse, other children, or their own parents and their relationships with them. If they need help with those relationships, we can work with them individually or possibly through family counseling.

As with dying children, it is all too easy to treat brothers and sisters as islands of innocence when, in fact, their sibling's serious illness affects them profoundly. Parents are often deeply concerned about them but at the same time deeply absorbed in care and concern for the dying child in ways that make caring for siblings difficult. We can approach siblings, as we do the dying child, in ways appropriate to their age and stage of development, speaking at a level they can understand or using storytelling, drawing, music, or favorite objects as needed. If they are distressed the ways that their dying siblings are, we can help and support them in the ways discussed above.

In order to determine what they are experiencing, we can explore with siblings what they understand about their brother's or sister's illness, what it is like for them, and what is most difficult about it. We can discuss their thinking about why their brother or sister got sick. If they feel that they are somehow responsible for the illness, we can assure them that they are mistaken. We can explore how the illness may have changed life in their family or ways their parents relate to them. We can explore how they are trying to help. We can ask what helps them most in dealing day to day with what is happening.

We can explore if they've thought about what it might be like if their brother or sister dies, ask if they have someone to go to with their feelings, and ask what they would most like to remember about him or her. We can explore their understanding of God (or Allah or Buddha), God's feelings about their brother or sister, God's feelings about them, and whether and how they ever pray. We can wonder together with them about what comes after death. We can explore with them what they understand about funerals and other after-death rituals and whether and how they might want to attend or be part of them.

Grandparents, too, suffer when a grandchild is seriously ill and dying. They anguish not only for the child but for the parents, one of whom is their own child. As with siblings, their needs and anguish can easily be overlooked or neglected. Even when it is recognized, it can be difficult for members of younger generations to know how to reach out to and help them. Where others are unavailable or uncomfortable in supporting grandparents, we can approach them and indicate our willingness to hear their stories, witness their sorrows, and support them in any ways they believe appropriate.

We can ask grandparents what it is like for them to have such a seriously ill grandchild, how they are able to interact with him or her. We can inquire about what concerns them most and what it might be like for them if the child were to die. If they are at a loss as to how to be with, comfort, and speak with the child, we can share with them some of the ideas outlined above. We can explore what concerns them about the child's parents, how the illness has affected their relationship with the parents, and what kind of support they are able to provide. We can inquire about concerns about the child's brothers or sisters and other grandchildren. We can discuss the grandparents' spiritual/religious faith and practices and the meaning and support they find in them. We can ask if they have, or would like to be connected with, a priest, rabbi, minister, guru, holy person, or chaplain. We can inquire whether there are any tensions or conflicts with the parents on spiritual/religious matters, and, if so, whether they would like help in resolving them.

These ideas and guidelines about providing spiritual/religious support for dying children, parents, siblings, and grandparents are intended to be suggestive, not exhaustive. They represent some of the best of what good-quality hospice and palliative care programs for dying children offer in response to the spiritual/religious needs of dying children and their families.

We, like Sr. Frances, believe that the reason it is a privilege to do the kind of work we do has to do with the fact that in the tragedy of a child's death, people so often let the mask drop. The things that frequently keep people apart—race, religion, education, social background, gender—no longer have relevance, because the universal experiences of life and death unite us, even with agnostic or atheist parents. At such times, labels are often unhelpful, but symbols such as the chrysalis and the butterfly can be powerful for children and their families and for those who work in pediatric palliative and hospice care.

References

Attig, T. 1996. Beyond pain: The existential suffering of children. *Journal of Palliative Care* 12(3): 20–23.

Bluebond-Langner, M. 1978. *The private worlds of dying children*. Princeton: Princeton University Press.

Davies, B., S. Sehring, J. C. Partridge et al. 2008. Barriers to palliative care in children: Perceptions of pediatric health care providers. *Pediatrics* 121(2): 282–88.

Davies B., P. Brenner, S. Orloff et al. 2002. Addressing spirituality in pediatric hospice and palliative care. *Journal of Palliative Care* 18(1): 59–67.

Field, M. J., and R. E. Behrman. 2003. *When children die: Improving palliative and end-of-life care for children and their families*. Washington, DC: National Academy Press.

Hays, P. 2001. *Addressing cultural complexities in practice: A framework for clinicians and counselors*. Washington, DC: American Psychological Association.

James, W. 2003. *The varieties of religious experience: A study in human nature*. Centenary Edition. London: Routledge.

Krulik, T., and B. Holaday. 1987. *The child and family facing life-threatening illness: A tribute to Eugenia Waechter*. Philadelphia: Lippincott Williams and Wilkins.

Sumner, L. 2006. Pediatric care: The hospice perspective. In *The textbook of palliative nursing, 2nd edition*, ed. Betty Ferrell and Nessa Coyle, 909–24. New York: Oxford University Press.

13

Interfaith Chaplaincy in Hospice Palliative Care

Kelli I. Stajduhar
Coby Tschanz

Introduction

After almost twenty years of working as nurses and academics in hospice palliative care, we find ourselves wondering why we have not given much critical consideration to the place of religion within this field. We agree with others that religious and spiritual care providers are integral members of the hospice palliative care team (Kernohan et al. 2007; Lloyd-Williams et al. 2006). We have wholeheartedly embraced the modern-day hospice ethos (a focus on pain control, a family or community environment, and religious support) put forward by Cicely Saunders more than four decades ago. And we believe that a good death is best accomplished by paying attention to the "total pain" of those we care for. As nurses, we have consulted chaplain colleagues to address some of the most profound issues facing those at the end of life, and have ourselves sought counsel from them regarding issues arising from that work. How is it, then, that we only now find ourselves giving serious thought to religion? Though we cannot quantify our claim, we suggest that many of our palliative care colleagues might find themselves in a similar position if they were faced with writing a chapter on interfaith chaplaincy, or indeed, editing a book on the religious understandings of a good death in hospice palliative care!

And so, we begin our exploration of interfaith chaplaincy by positioning ourselves not as experts, but as nurses with a renewed interest in and commitment to the provision of religious care.

We first provide a brief history of the development of chaplaincy and interfaith chaplaincy in the West and delineate how chaplaincy is defined today. We then draw on a relatively small base of literature and discussions with religious leaders and scholars to outline the complexities associated with the practice of interfaith chaplaincy. In doing this, we use illustrative examples from our interviews with chaplains and our own practice experiences as we attempt to demonstrate how these complexities play out in the "real-life world" of ministering to the dying and their families. Finally, we offer some concluding thoughts that we hope will compel those in the hospice community to, like us, reconsider the importance of religion and the provision of religious care in our field. We do this in full acknowledgment that we are not chaplains or religious scholars. We are, rather, nurses who are concerned that an increasing emphasis on *spiritual* care in hospice settings may serve to marginalize some people from accessing what hospice has to offer and has the potential to do a disservice to our patients and families for whom *religion* is an important part of their lives.

The Development of Interfaith Chaplaincy

Historically,[1] religion has played an important role in influencing the care of the dying. Most European hospitals and early hospices were run by Christian religious orders (Manning 1984; Stoddart 1978) and were either attached to a church or most certainly had a chapel or altar centrally featured in their architecture (Swift 2009). During this early period (between 1066 and 1540), the church was actively involved in defining the role of physicians and clergy. As Swift[2] (2009) points out, the role of medical doctors was to "warn and persuade the sick to see a priest before medical treatment begins, as sickness may sometimes be the result of sin, and if the priest can remove the 'cause' then the person will respond better to the bodily treatment" (10). Swift maintains that an overriding emphasis on the spirit permeated every detail of a hospital's organization and operation during this time period. Even as hospitals began to develop as separate entities, they still retained the strong religious traditions of the monasteries from which they emerged. The chaplain was a key figure, and the hospital was a place of "religious immersion" (Swift, 12).

Religious and social changes in the latter part of the fifteenth century brought about significant shifts in the role of the chaplain. With
widespread poverty and disease, societal attitudes toward the dying
changed. Death became stigmatized, and those who were careless enough
to become ill were often beaten and enslaved (Stoddard 1978). Support
of Christian religious orders weakened with Protestant reformation. Many
hospitals were closed or suppressed as religious houses and clergy were
either punished or pensioned off.

The needy, ill, and dying were left for the most part unattended
(Campbell 1986). While hospitals eventually reopened and religion and
chaplains continued to have a place, the material artifacts of faith no
longer predominated. Chaplains, now otherwise known as *hospitalers,*
comforted the sick and administered the sacraments of the Church. They
were responsible for contributing to the smooth running of the hospital,
for ensuring no drunkenness or blasphemy occurred, and were required
to reside at the hospital. Yet, these reemerged hospitals were now under
government control, and "the chaplain's centrality to the hospital had
been removed" (Swift 2009, 27).

During the eighteenth and nineteenth centuries, chaplains continued to play important roles, especially in the charitable hospitals in the
United Kingdom (UK). Initiated to provide care for the growing number of poor and destitute, these hospitals were little more than rented
houses, but where both physical and spiritual care featured strongly (Swift
2009). Given space limitations, no dedicated place for religious practice
was available; this time period marked, perhaps, the first time in history
where the chaplain did not reside in the hospital (Swift 2009). During the
Industrial Revolution, and to complement the care provided by charitable
hospitals, workhouses were established to deal with the increasing numbers of sick and poor people. In writing about the role of the workhouse
chaplain, Swift (2009) contends:

> In practice, the chaplain had a broad and ill-defined job descrip-
> tion: to be a friend to the sick and poor, to offer structured
> rites and comfortable words, and to moderate the excesses of
> institutional life. In the conduct of his duties, the chaplain was
> wedded to the *status quo,* required to use his position to ensure
> conformity to social expectation through a particular form of
> biblical and theological understanding. Namely, that God had
> determined the social order and that faithfulness required accep-
> tance of one's circumstances with equanimity.

In the late 1940s religious orders were incorporated into formal hospital structures (Wright 2001). The creation of the National Health Service (NHS) in the United Kingdom appointed paid chaplains of different religious (mainly Christian) traditions to minister to the sick and dying. While chaplaincy roles continued to evolve and professional chaplaincy organizations, standards of practice, and formal educational structures were developed, the creation of the NHS resulted in a significant decline in the influence that the Church had on the provision of health care (Swift 2009). The role and scope of chaplaincy practice continued to shift, influenced heavily by the institutional structures by which they were now bound. Remnants of role confusion continue today. As Jacobs (2008) writes:

> It can be really hard—or really easy—to explain what I do for a living. Chaplains share academic training with clergy, but we complete clinical residencies and work in health care organizations. Our affinities are with the patient and family, but we may also chair the ethics committee or serve on the institutional review board, and we spend a lot of time with staff. We must demonstrate a relationship with an established religious tradition (in my case, United Church of Christ), but we serve patients of all faiths, and of no faith, and seek to protect patients against proselytizing. We provide something that may be called "pastoral" care, "spiritual" care, or just "chaplaincy"—but even among ourselves, we do not always agree about what that thing is. (15)

While there is variation in role and scope of interfaith chaplains, the term *chaplain* is generally used today to designate religious leaders who are commissioned by faith communities to provide religious and spiritual care to a group of people outside of the parish (Garces-Foley 2006; Swift 2009). Most chaplains are ordained, associated with recognized faith traditions, and graduate from seminaries, divinity schools, or rabbinical schools (DeVries, Berlinger, and Cadge 2008). While spiritual care responsibilities are primarily directed toward patients and relatives, health care chaplains in particular also increasingly provide care to staff (Wright 2001). Chaplains are responsible for facilitating appropriate religious practices for people of their own faith, for contacting religious leaders that are not of their own faith to conduct religion specific rituals at the request of the patient and family, and for conducting such rituals if these religious leaders are not available (Walter 1996). In the context of health care, a primary role of the chaplain is also to assess and respond to the spiritual needs of patients and to educate the rest of the team on religious issues.

The positioning of the chaplain in hospice palliative care has not always been clear. It is clear, however, that St. Christopher's Hospice, the first modern-day European hospice, had well-established religious underpinnings (du Boulay 1984). Founded as an ecumenical Christian ministry, St. Christopher's was named for the patron saint of travelers because it was devoted to those whose journey in this life was nearly over (Phipps 1988). When St. Christopher's opened, all staff were practicing Christians. Religious and spiritual care was, as Wright (2001) put it, "a corporate responsibility of the whole team" (229). Chaplains were one group among the HPC team that delivered spiritual care. While religious care featured prominently in conceptualizations of a good death at St. Christopher's, the application of such care became much broader as HPC developed across parts of the industrialized world. Responding to the diminishing role of the church, at least in the developed world, spiritual or religious care of the dying now bears little resemblance to the religious rites once performed in institutions of the past (Walter 1996). In an increasingly pluralistic and multicultural society, inter- and multifaith chaplaincy is taking on renewed prominence. But, as Ballard (2009) warns, "some branches of medicine, notably palliative care and nursing, pressing for a 'holistic' approach to patient care, have responded to the current interest in 'spirituality,' seeing this as a vital dimension, but without a necessary reference to religion" (1). This is but one of many complexities associated with chaplaincy in the twenty-first century.

Complexities of Interfaith Chaplaincy

In developing a beginning understanding of complexities associated with interfaith chaplaincy, we draw on a relatively small body of literature on chaplaincy, particularly in hospice and palliative care. This is supplemented with interviews with chaplains,[3] insights prompted by discussions with religious leaders/scholars, and our own experiences as hospice nurses. We acknowledge that this is a Western Christian approach. Research on chaplaincy tends to use sample populations that are mostly Christian, and the three male chaplains we interviewed[4] all claim familiarity with or primary commitment to Christian traditions. Also, our own positioning as Christians most certainly influences our interpretations of such complexities.

Having situated ourselves as Christians, then, we began our study asking: What is it like to provide interfaith support for people who are dying and their families? Our analysis addresses three questions: (1) Who is responsible for attending to religious needs in hospice palliative care? (2) How do chaplains work with the trend away from religious care to spiritual care? and (3) What is it like for chaplains serving those from diverse religious traditions or no religious tradition?

Who Is Responsible for Attending to Religious Needs in Hospice Palliative Care?

Some scholars have questioned both the role of the hospice chaplain and the degree to which hospice chaplains should act as frontline providers of spiritual care. Walter (1997) argues that free-standing hospices have become increasingly secular, despite their Christian roots; this has meant that spiritual care has become the exclusive responsibility of hospice chaplains. Nurses and doctors have been conditioned to refrain from sharing their religious or spiritual beliefs with patients. Walter makes the case that *all* members of a multidisciplinary palliative team can and should be responsible for the spiritual care of patients. Although chaplains have specific religious knowledge to impart, they cannot be expected to provide total spiritual care. Meador (2006) notes that the onus is on physicians to be both sensitive to the religious needs of patients, as well as informed about the chaplaincy and spiritual care resources available to their patients. In a recent (2009) editorial in the journal *Palliative and Supportive Care,* Breitbart asks: "Who should be spiritual care professionals?" Citing Lloyd-Williams's (2006) and Meador's (2006) studies, Breitbart makes the case that the entire palliative care team should be informed by the concept of "spiritual care"; such an ethos would encompass both patients who are members of mainstream religious groups and individuals who consider themselves to be "spiritual." Like Walter (1997), he concludes that chaplains are not the only professionals who can or should attend to the spiritual health of hospice patients.

Other scholars have suggested that the hospice chaplain's role is central within the multidisciplinary team. Harvey (1996) submits that the hospice chaplain performs many roles including (among others) "shaman," "miracle worker," "Bible answer man," "social worker," "friend," "guide," "student," "healer," "teacher," and "servant" (42). To Harvey, the role of "servant" is the most crucial one: "As Jesus washed the feet of the disciples, the hospice chaplain wipes the tears of the patient. The chaplain sits on the side of the bed as the patient withers and dies in silence and total acceptance" (43). He stresses that hospice chaplains must be able to adapt to new situations and continually learn from patients in order to become better spiritual counselors. Wright's (2001) survey of chaplaincy in hospitals and hospices in England and Wales suggests that the hospice chaplain is increasingly asked to take on the role of a "listener," rather than a minister or religious guide (238).

Garces-Foley (2006) argues that although religious and spiritual care provided by non-chaplain members of the hospice palliative care team is in keeping with the broad-based conceptualization of spiritual care first put forth by Cicely Saunders, such an approach assumed that team members were mature Christians, able and willing to talk about spiritual matters. She contends that hospices that make no faith requirement of care providers cannot assume that their staff know how to or are willing to meet these spiritual needs. Let us consider the following case scenario based on an experience one of us (CT) had as a nurse working in hospice care.

Case scenario: Encounters with patients and families wherein religious concerns are at the fore occur every day but may be unexpected or unrecognized. Sometimes I (CT) don't recognize religious concerns in a timely fashion or I am in "too deep" before a chaplain can be consulted. Indeed, I felt out of my depth the day I visited a man (I'll call him John) who was described as near death and suffering complex symptoms. The plan was to ensure John was comfortable and that he and his family were "on the same page"—everyone knew that John was likely very near death—so that that they could be prepared and make plans. You can imagine how surprised I was when the first thing John said to me was, "I am cured! I am cured! I'm healed!" I literally leaned back and closed my eyes in the force of his claim. Listening to him, he did not sound like a man who was too weak to rise from bed and expected to die in a matter of days. His voice was full and vibrant, exuberant even; I felt a powerful happiness for him. When I opened my eyes to look at him, the disparity between John's voice and his appearance was shocking. He was jaundiced and waxy in complexion, and he was trembling, thin, wasted. Happiness for him melted to a sort of dismay when I remembered why I had been asked to visit him. After all, he was telling me he was cured, healed, and yet others wanted him to realize he was going to die soon. And, it seemed necessary that he realize his nearness to death. How else could he and his family make plans and decisions or be prepared for what was to come? Thus, I was tempted to deny his claim of being healed.

Of course, there were a multitude of approaches to take in this situation. I could have held to an intent to gently help the man see the apparent "reality" of his situation. I could have presented all data pointing to the diagnosis of terminal illness and impending death and encouraged him to prepare for this. I could have proceeded by conducting a thorough assessment in order to identify and address troublesome symptoms. Was he in pain? Was he beginning to suffer from delirium? Could he be considered incompetent? As it turned out, in that instance I resisted the urge to make assessments immediately or make sense of his experience for him. Sitting at his bedside, I learned that the man had had an amazing experience that had transformed his understanding of grace inherent in his relationship with his God and Christ. While it seemed important to witness his transformed understanding, I couldn't help wishing that a chaplain was there *in that moment*. While I understood something of what he had to say, I had a strong sense that I was not able to nurture deeply his understanding or celebrate with and learn from him. In this situation as the man spoke I knew that I had only a vague inkling of what it meant to him to be healed. I was distracted with the agenda to make a nursing assessment and settle decisions about his care. I was tentative, even reluctant, about engaging in conversation about religious experiences for fear of being seen as unprofessional or of being unable to address his particular concerns. It is often only much later and, it seems, somehow *too* late, when a chaplain is consulted. While I realize that all team members are responsible for attending to religious and spiritual care, I'm not sure how we go about meeting that responsibility, especially with regard to religious needs. I wonder, What might have happened if a chaplain was as available as a nurse, counselor, and physician in our hospice community? Is religious counsel as available as a medical consult for symptom management? What might our service to patients and families be like if we more often considered religious/theological perspectives before we feel we are "in too deep"? How many other situations occur when I and others don't recognize or respond to an opportunity to attend to religious concerns of patients, family members, and team members? While it may be common practice to record religious preferences, how is it that I and other HPC team members may not engage in deep conversation about the importance of religion—for good or ill—in a person's life?

The chaplains we interviewed reported that hospice team members may or may not initiate, recognize, or respond to discussion about religious concerns. One chaplain expressed some bafflement as to why on various occasions over his years of service, a chaplain had not been consulted. Yet, he noted other times when team members practiced as if religious and spiritual care was the responsibility of every member of the team and team members freely engaged with such matters themselves and consulted a chaplain as necessary. Differences in comfort and competence related to provision of religious care may be related to how such care is valued or whether staff members are comfortable addressing religious needs. As another chaplain put it, "There is a lot of tip-toeing around religion." Specifically, colonial perspectives and practices have contributed to the association of religion and being religious with dogmatic, autocratic, and destructive tendencies. Walter (1997) writes that "expressing personal views on religion and politics is considered by some likely to ruin a good conversation or even a friendship" (24). Interestingly, we have observed that the name badges of some of our chaplain colleagues display a shortened version of the title *spiritual and religious care coordinator* to *spiritual care coordinator*. Some chaplains no longer wear clerical collars. Similar to the way that HPC nurses or counselors may be asked by family members to avoid mentioning death and dying to a patient, Christian chaplains might be consulted but asked to avoid using the words God or Jesus. Hence, beginning dialogue may be constrained. Religious care or contact with chaplains may not even be offered as an aspect of holistic health care. The chaplains we interviewed suggested that it was generally more acceptable to refer to oneself as spiritual or as belonging to a faith community rather than use the term *religious*.

How Do Chaplains Work with the Trend away from
Religious Care to Spiritual Care?

Cicely Saunders founded the modern-day hospice as an ecumenical Christian ministry. In her biography, it is clear that her original conservative evangelicalism was shaped and broadened based on her care of atheist, Catholic, and Jewish patients (du Boulay 1984). While early hospices were motivated by Christian compassion, current-day hospices, in the main, do not share that original vision (Walter 1996). Hospices, like other health institutions, are increasingly expected to care for a religiously diverse clientele. Garces-Foley (2006) asks: "How should institutions deal with religious pluralism? Must they be strictly secular, or can they make room for or even nurture a religious dimension of life? Will other institutions follow hospice in avoiding religious differences by focusing on a supposedly universal spirituality?" (119).

Garces-Foley (2006) contends that there has been a "discursive shift" (118) in both the literature and practice of hospice care from a discussion of religion to one about spirituality. She argues that an increasing emphasis on spiritual care as independent from religious traditions has essentially stripped the modern hospice of its Christian roots. The literature on hospice palliative care promotes a dichotomy between religion and spirituality, advancing the idea that spirituality, rather than religion, is integral to a good death. This so-called more generic view of providing spiritual care (Engelhardt 1998) does, as Garces-Foley argues, "a disservice to patients and can lead to the alienation of truly religious hospice patients" (133). It can also overly constrain both chaplain and non-chaplain care providers from exploring with patients what it means to provide religious care. Bradshaw (1996) contends that a distancing of religion from spirituality has resulted in hospice providers being taught that spirituality is about exploring personal meaning and that to transcend pain and suffering, a deeper connection within the self is necessary. Spirituality is viewed as expansive, meaningful, and inclusive, whereas religion is viewed as narrow, rigid, and superficial (Garces-Foley 2006). This negative characterization of religion is not one shared among religious scholars and those who practice religion. With a strong emphasis on spirituality of self and the devaluation of religion, at least within some literature, it is not surprising that hospice serves the predominantly white middle class and continues to under-serve others such as Hindus, Muslims, Aboriginal people, and African Americans (Garces-Foley 2006).

A waning attention to religion and growing interest in spirituality have led to significant changes in chaplaincy services. One chaplain remarked that much of the work he does now involves witnessing as people reflect upon their lives. He is less likely to discuss matters of religious belief but continues to focus his practice with an intention of hope and healing. Another chaplain states that his work might more accurately be referred to as "faith work" rather than "interfaith work." This means that the work primarily requires presence and compassion in the midst of suffering and wonder. Faith work means understanding that "life and death goes on in this place." As such, having faith is not about having faith in something but is a matter of "letting things just wash through . . . not questioning . . . or intellectualizing, just being fully aware of what goes on," especially in moments when there are no words. Chaplains, patients, and family members may experience challenges related to a de-emphasis on religious practices however, when there is a desire for dialogue and ritual participation to explore and express pain or comfort related to religion in life.

The chaplains we interviewed remarked that in the past there was a greater repertoire of vocabulary available to people to describe their experiences, explore questions, and express and ease fears and desires. While chaplains do not regret doing away with old language and conceptualizations of sin and guilt in the Christian tradition that obscured original messages of love and forgiveness, it may be that persons want to express the meaning of teachings about sin for their life and relationships. Also lost to a large segment of the population is any spiritually enriching language of religion. Thus, one chaplain suggests there is a need to craft new, vital metaphors about dying and death, "metaphors that metamorphize" and "give words to those things that you feel and you profoundly know" about living and dying.

Likewise, the implications of having fewer established and acceptable comforting rituals available to patients and families near death and during bereavement can be profound. Crafting rituals with family members first requires that opportunities for meeting and commemorating important events or situations be created deliberately or recognized by the patient/family, chaplain, and/or other team members. The details of proceedings involve dialogue and negotiation in planning and performing ceremonies. One chaplain offers the following example. He tells of a time when a woman with several children was dying. Whereas the woman who was dying lay in a coma, her children were scattered apart from her and each other on the hospital unit. Eventually, one daughter came to the chaplain saying that something should be done for her mother and with a desire to bring her siblings together near their mother. After some negotiation, the chaplain offered to perform an anointing. They consulted the nurse about the timing, who advised, "Do it sooner rather than later." When the family gathered to consider various rituals, the chaplain discussed what he had done for others in the past. In this particular situation, he was challenged to ensure that any activities be conducted with solemnity and authenticity without seeming too similar to rituals completed in a church. Initially, the family did not want anything that involved human touch or mention of death or God. After much discussion, they all agreed it was acceptable to sound a prayer bowl, recite a blessing, and perform an anointing with oil. During the ceremony, one of the daughters placed her hand on her mother and her brother followed to place his hand on hers. The chaplain perceived a sense of settling and focus for the family in conjunction with a slowing of the pace of his words. He subsequently improvised a short speech acknowledging the qualities of the woman conveyed as significant by her children, the complexity of family relationships, and the importance of witnessing times of transition. He then left the family to be together. This was an immensely meaningful and challenging situation. Whereas a number of years ago chaplains might have felt more well equipped or more readily prepared to do the work of a chaplain, these chaplains explained that there seems to be less to hold on to these days.

The chaplains we interviewed find that there is now less call for them to provide support for specific religious observances than for questions of meaning and connection. People with strong connections to a religious community are commonly served by that community's chaplain; interfaith chaplains may be consulted by a community chaplain who is ill or living at a distance from where the patient is placed. In such circumstances, chaplains are likely to know very little about the people they are asked to serve. Thus, one chaplain remarks that he carefully crafts the first questions he asks of patients and family members. He wants to convey that he is "not here to tell you anything, [but is] here to hear who you are." In conversation he learns what is important to each person, often starting with work, hobbies, life experiences, and relationships. Learning about what a person enjoys doing, whom a person loves, and who loves them sometimes surfaces memories and regrets about the past and hopes for the future. As such, dreams of longed-for reconciliation and other goals may be achieved imaginatively in the minds of the patient and chaplain or accomplished through the collaborative efforts of family members and the palliative care team.

For many reasons there may be a lack of opportunity and commitment to ensure in-depth consideration of what it means to patients and families to receive religious care and for providers to offer such care. Well-staffed programs that can serve diverse religious needs of individuals and communities are rare. Challenges related to lack of space, strict privacy legislation, and demands of professionalization may restrict abilities to address religious needs of various persons who rely on communal approaches and informal leaders for provision of religious care. There may be only one part-time chaplain in an agency, with no or little peer contact to dialogue about interfaith work and its nuances. The work hours allotted to chaplains may be few or fluctuate depending on program funding, so that opportunities to maintain ongoing and trusting relationships with other team members, become familiar with the needs of patients and family members, and contribute during team meetings are limited. The daily challenges of working out what it might mean to provide religious care seem further compounded by a shifting focus from religious to spiritual care.

What Is It Like for Chaplains Serving Those from
Diverse Religious Traditions or No Religious Tradition?

Chaplains working in interfaith settings minister to patients, family, and staff who practice a wide range of faith traditions or none. In modern-day health settings, we increasingly care for Christians, Muslims, Jews, Aboriginal and Chinese people, Buddhists, Hindus, atheists, and others. Such diversity can make chaplaincy work interesting and provide opportunities for new and enlightening experiences. Honoring religious diversity can also present challenges, particularly when the overwhelming majority of funded chaplains are Christian (Lloyd Williams 2004).

Mellon's (2003) paper addressing the issues confronting hospital (but not hospice) chaplains working within an ecumenical or multifaith framework suggests that chaplains must be grounded in their own theological tradition in order to better serve those whom they minister to. "It is not only important that the chaplain who serves patients of different faiths possess a theological foundation, but he or she must also be able to balance personal convictions with the orientation and faith of those receiving care" (60). He sees the personal faith of the chaplain as a potential source of strength, rather than a hindrance. Delkeskamp-Hayes (2003) criticizes this approach, however, noting that it is nearly impossible for chaplains to be both "ecumenically settled" (74) in their role as a counselor and guide, as well as faithful to their own theological tradition.

De Vries and colleagues (2008) agree, arguing that deploying chaplains outside of their own religious tradition confuses their professional identity; they maintain that this problem is further compounded when chaplains work in faith-based institutions that have their own religious ethos.

Hall (1997) discusses how hospice chaplains can work with respect for and understand religious diversity. He advises (independent) hospice organizations that they should be careful in their selection of potential hospice chaplains. It is important to assess the chaplain's openness to both religious diversity as well as diversity among lifestyles, beliefs, and sexual orientation, among other matters. Notably, Hall does not recommend that potential chaplains undergo specific training to better understand the spectrum of world religions: "A knowledge of religious variety is helpful in chaplaincy work, but should serve as only a guide in dialogue with the patient or family" (223). Instead, the author makes the case that hospice chaplains should seek to understand their patients on a case-by-case basis; chaplains should not assume that their knowledge of a particular religious tradition will be consistent with their patient's understanding of that tradition. "Hospice chaplains must assess the degree or level a patient or family accepts and follows a certain religion or spiritual direction. Asking a patient what being Protestant, Buddhist, etc., means to them and how they practice their beliefs is a way to begin understanding" (223). Further, interfaith chaplains can support other team members in working with respect for diversity and uniqueness in religious expression.

One chaplain recalls a story of a man who was Sikh, and was considered near death and was offered palliative care when he was brought one night to the emergency department. Some staff members had a well-developed awareness of and ability to ask about the religious preferences of the patient and family; however, the presumption by other staff members and even some non-Sikh family members was that a religious leader should be called to deliver a blessing and lead prayers. In this situation, the Sikh family members of the man completed their own prayers and rituals; they had no need or desire to call upon a religious leader, who in their community carried out his duties in the temple and not in hospitals and homes. The chaplain was consulted when various staff members continued to express frustration and anger that a leader would not be called. As such, the age-old question of why it sometimes seems so difficult to consider and honor the beliefs of one another was raised. The role of the chaplain with the patient and family was to learn what it meant to be Sikh and to ensure that community connections were established as they desired. An additional primary role was to educate and support staff members and others who were not aware of, or did not understand or accept, customs. In this case, we can see how chaplains work with/in the team to clarify where support is needed—for patients, family members, and/or staff members—and raise awareness of and capacity to address religious needs.

While religious and spiritual care may require complex negotiations and closer attention to creating opportunities to come together, there may indeed be benefits to the appreciation for religious variety and new understandings of spirituality. Specifically, one chaplain says that he has been wonderfully amazed to glimpse the diversity, mystery, and expansiveness of the Holy, the Divine. Openness to human spirituality and to religious and spiritual care in diverse forms may provide a broad realm to explore and address questions and concerns of faith and connection. The notions of diversity and connection, however, cannot be taken for granted; we suggest that future examination of ideas and experiences related to diversity and commonality, as well as who can and should attend to religious needs, may bring surprising insights.

Conclusion

We began this chapter curious but somewhat puzzled by our apparent lack of thoughtful reflection on the place of religion in hospice palliative care. We end with continued curiosity in what we still have yet to learn, but refreshed in our interest in religion as a profoundly important feature of our field. We have only touched the surface of some of the complexities associated with the practice of interfaith chaplaincy. Thus, our study has become the vehicle by which we have collectively begun to explore larger issues of faith, religion, and spirituality that are, in many ways, so taken for granted in hospice palliative care.

Death, dying, and bereavement are among the most common issues that congregants bring to clergy (Flannelly et al. 2003). Research has shown that gravely ill people value a physician asking about their religious beliefs (Ehman et al. 1999) and that knowing such information can greatly enhance the quality of care given and the possibility for a good death (Hanson, Tulsky, and Danis 1997). It is not only sacramental care, customary prayers, sacred readings, rites, and ceremonies that may be important. Effective religious care "connects an individual with customary sources of faith and hope and surrounds an individual with supportive community" (Cooper 2005, 5). This supportive community is what, we believe, Cicely Saunders envisioned at St. Christopher's Hospice more than four decades ago.

We submit that the current emphasis on spiritual care in hospice care and the reluctance to take up religion as having an equally important place arises perhaps from a place of fear—a fear that religion, with its so-called dogmatic, autocratic, and destructive tendencies will somehow overtake one's individual search for meaning. That the rituals and ceremonies—somehow—dilute or obscure that which is intrinsically important to us. We suggest, too, that a fear of what we may uncover constrains our willingness to explore whatever influences religion may have in a person's life. But if religious care, as Cooper (2005) proposes, is "individually appropriate" (9), and if people who are dying are asked what they want (whether they identify themselves as part of a religious community or not), then perhaps we have a better chance of alleviating some of the isolation that people experience because of their illness. Attending to both the physical and the spiritual/religious, is what Cicely Saunders had in mind when she coined the term *total pain*.

Chaplains pay particular attention to the total pain of patients and family members, knowing that religious care can bring ease. Chaplains also witness suffering that cannot be relieved and choices that may or may not seem reasonable. They see that staff members themselves suffer with the people they care for. One chaplain tells the story of a man who was dying from anorexia and kept removing his feeding tube. After treatment and numerous rounds of replacing the feeding tube, the decision was made to leave out the tube. When the usual bedtime hour arrived, the man asked to be left in his wheelchair where he remained for the night. Each hour of the night when the nurse checked he declined to go to bed or accept pain medication. In the morning when the sun came up, the man rang for the nurse and asked to be put to bed and given his prescribed medication. He slept all day, awakening near suppertime with a new sense of peace. He died four or five days later. The chaplain tells how the nurse supported the man in his choices, having learned from the man that he saw his suffering as a way of making amends with God before death. This is an example of what Cicely Saunders might have envisioned for addressing total pain. In this example and others we also see how interfaith chaplaincy and religious care can honor journeys of living and dying, supporting people to "live until they die." As illustrated and interpreted in the above examples and interviews with chaplains, such living and dying encompasses a multitude of human experiences. Acknowledging such breadth, chaplains we interviewed expressed a desire for and commitment to an ever-deepening engagement with matters of religion, faith, and spirit. Similarly, we hope that nurses, chaplains, and others will continue striving together to provide a supportive environment, minimize physical pain, and tend to the religious and spiritual needs of patients and families, with due regard for the richness of faith traditions.

Acknowledgments

We gratefully acknowledge Lee Blanding for his assistance with the literature review for this study. We are also thankful to Dr. Kathleen Garces-Foley, Stan McKay, our research team, and clinician colleagues Dr. Michael Downing and Ms. Kathy Bodell for their careful consideration and feedback on earlier versions of this chapter. Finally, we thank the three chaplains we interviewed who provided their insights and expertise and helped us to better understand interfaith chaplaincy work in hospice palliative care.

Notes

1. Given that the modern hospice movement emerged out of the United Kingdom (UK) and that much of what is written about chaplaincy comes from the UK, we have focused here almost exclusively on the development of chaplaincy in the UK.

2. In providing a "brief" description of the history of chaplaincy we recognize that we have simplified this historical account and have missed some important details. For a full account of the historical evolution of chaplaincy, see Christopher Swift's (2009) study of hospital chaplaincy in the National Health Service in the United Kingdom.

3. Ethics approval to recruit and interview chaplains for this study was provided by a university-based institutional ethics review board.

4. The chaplains interviewed had varied experiences of working in a mid-size Canadian city in hospice and hospital settings. Their job descriptions are general; although the patient population might be considered relatively homogenous, their work requires the capacity to attend to diverse religious and

spiritual interests and expressions. Their work encompasses times of struggle and celebration, related to the circumstances of the patients and families they meet. Each chaplain recounts human experiences of uncertainty, awkwardness, grief, hope, wonder, antagonism, disillusionment, forgiveness, frustration, despair, and compassion lived in rituals of conversation, communion, transition, and blessing. The moments of irony, humor, and experiences of connecting and learning with others—of "intentionally making space in our day and our time for the Holy"— balance "the harsh . . . times, when you just want to weep; the times . . . when people are dying poorly either in pain or over-sedated." All three chaplains interviewed remark that in the midst of common human experiences, each encounter is somehow unique. Echoing the way that some patients and family members are searching and grappling in a time of transition between everything they've known and have yet to experience, the chaplains too must find their way, moment by moment.

References

Ballard, P. 2009. Foreword. In Swift, C. *Hospital chaplaincy in the twenty-first century: The crisis of spiritual care on the NHS*, xiii–xiv. Cornwall, UK: Ashgate.

Bradshaw, A. 1996. The spiritual dimensions of hospice: The secularization of an ideal. *Soc Sci Med* 43(3): 409–19.

Breitbart, W. 2009. The spiritual domain of palliative care: Who should be "spiritual care professionals"? *Palliative and Supportive Care* 7: 139–41.

Campbell, L. 1986. History of the hospice movement. *Cancer Nurse* 9(6): 333–38.

Cooper, D. Spiritual and religious care of the hospice palliative care client. The Pallium Project. http://www.pallium.ca/infoware/Cooper_24Mar05.pdf.

Daaleman, T. P., and L. VandeCreek. 2000. Placing religion and spirituality in end-of-life care. *JAMA* 284(19): 2514–17.

Delkeskamp-Hayes, C. 2003. The price of being conciliatory: Remarks about Mellon's model for hospital chaplaincy work in multi-faith settings. *Christ Bioeth* 9(1): 69–78.

De Vries, R., N. Berlinger, and W. Cadge. 2008. Lost in translation: The chaplain's role in health care. *Hasting Center Report* 38(6): 23–27.

du Boulay, S. 1984. *Cicely Saunders.* New York: Amaryllis.

Ehman, J. W., B. B. Ott, T. H. Short et al. 1999. Do patients want physicians to inquire about their spiritual or religious beliefs if they become gravely ill? *Arch Intern Med* 159(15): 1803–06.

Engelhardt Jr., H. T. 1998. Generic chaplaincy: Providing spiritual care in a post-Christian age. *Christ Bioeth* 4(3): 231–38.

Flannelly, K. J., A. J. Weaver, W. J. Smith et al. 2003. A systematic review on chaplains and community-based clergy in three palliative care journals: 1990–1999. *Am J Hosp Palliat Me* 20(4): 263–68.

Garces-Foley, K. 2006. Hospice and the politics of spirituality. *OMEGA-J Death Dying* 53(1–2): 117–36.

Hall, S. E. 1997. Spiritual diversity: A challenge for hospice chaplains. *Am J Hosp Palliat Care* 14(5): 221–23.

Hanson, L. C., J. A. Tulsky, and M. Danis. 1997. Can clinical interventions change care at the end of life? *Ann Intern Med* 126: 381–88.

Harvey, T. 1996. Who is the chaplain anyway? Philosophy and integration of hospice chaplaincy. *Am J Hosp Palliat Care* 13(5): 41–43.

Jacobs, M. R. 2008. What are we doing here? Chaplains in contemporary health care. *Hastings Center Report* 38(6): 15–18.

Kernohan, W. G., M. Waldron, C. McAfee et al. 2007. An evidence base for a palliative care chaplaincy service in Northern Ireland. *Palliat Med* 21: 519–25.

Lloyd-Williams, M., M. Wright, M. Cobb et al. 2004. A prospective study of the roles, responsibilities and stresses of chaplains working within a hospice. *J Palliat Med* 18: 638–45.

Lloyd-Williams, M., M. Cobb, C. Shiels et al. 2006. How well trained are clergy in care of the dying patient and bereavement support? *J Pain Symptom Manage* 32(1): 44–51.

Manning, M. 1984. *The hospice alternative: Living with dying.* London: Souvenir Press.

Meador, K. G. 2006. Spirituality and care at the end of life. *South Med J* 99(10): 1184–85.

Mellon, B. F. 2003. Faith-to-faith at the bedside: Theological and ethical issues in ecumenical clinical chaplaincy. *Christ Bioeth* 9(1): 57–67.

Phipps, W. 1988. The origin of hospices/hospitals. *Death Stud* 12(2): 91–99.

Stoddard, S. 1978. *The hospice movement: A better way of caring for the dying.* New York: Stein and Day.

Swift, C. 2009. *Hospital chaplaincy in the twenty-first century: The crisis of spiritual care on the NHS.* Cornwall, UK: Ashgate.

Walter, T. 1997. The ideology and organization of spiritual care: Three approaches. *J Palliat Med* 11: 21–30.

———. 1996. Developments in spiritual care of the dying. *Religion* 26: 353–63.

Wright, M. C. 2001. Chaplaincy in hospice and hospital: Findings from a survey in England and Wales. *J Palliat Med* 15: 229–42.

Conclusion

Harold Coward
Kelli I. Stajduhar

The authors of this book set out to answer the question, "What are the understandings of a good death in the major religious traditions for use in hospice palliative care?" In our chapters on the specific religious traditions (Part I) and on real-life hospice case studies (Part II), we have provided a detailed description and analysis of how scholars of the major religious traditions understand a good death. In this way we have focused on the third of Saunders's three principles of pain control that related to engagement with the dying person's religion. While Saunders's first two principles (pain control and family involvement) have been well studied, the third, engagement with a person's most deeply rooted spirituality or religion, has, to a large degree, been ignored in recent years. The aim of this book has been to fill that gap by foregrounding the knowledge needed by doctors, nurses, administrators, social workers, psychologists, and volunteers in hospice palliative care so that spiritual pain can be engaged along with physical pain in the treatment of persons from the major religious traditions.

We began our explorations of the major religious traditions by examining the Eastern religions of Hinduism and Buddhism and their belief that we are reborn to a new life when our body dies. This understanding of life as *karma—samsara* (birth, death, and rebirth) until an ultimate release from rebirth (*moksha or nirvana*) is realized—has important implications for hospice palliative care practice. In the Hindu case, as Anantanand Rambachan demonstrated in chapter 2, understandings of a good death found in the Vedic teachings focus on the attainment of liberation from rebirth (*moksha*) conceived of as eternal life in the presence of God (described as Vishnu, Shiva, or mother goddess Durga) or identity with the infinite (*Brahman*). *Moksha* is the fulfillment of life (and the end toward which the Hindu life is oriented), whether one dies at home or in a hospice unit. In the Hindu view, one's mental state at the time of death is most important as it needs to be focused on God. Therefore, there is a need for honesty and disclosure, and, although painkillers are welcome, they must not impair one's mental processes. In line with Cicely Saunders, Hindus believe that there is a possibility for religious growth during the final stage of life and especially during one's last days.

In his beautifully written chapter, Rambachan showed that a good death requires turning away from finite realities and fixing one's mind and heart on God. Hospice palliative care providers can facilitate this state by making the patient's room a sacred space with an easily visible altar upon which one's favorite icon or God-image (e.g., Shiva, Vishnu, Krishna, or Kali) is installed, and by allowing for the continuous chanting of sacred sounds or mantras—the person's favorite name for God chanted by family members or on a CD. Arrangements need to be made for priests to visit the dying person every two hours (between eight o'clock a.m. and six o'clock p.m.). In the midst of the family, the priest bends over the dying person with smoking incense sticks inscribing "AUM" in the air while reciting and spooning sacred Ganges water into the mouth of the dying person. In a narrative example, Rambachan showed an instance of health care staff refusing to allow this ritual at a person's last moments, causing the family members considerable grief. Also, some Hindus will want to be placed on the ground (floor) as death approaches in a symbolic return to the earth, which Hindus understand to be God's body. Ideally, the hospice room or space needs to be large enough to hold the whole extended family (including children and relatives) to say farewell words, to receive and extend forgiveness, and to take part in chanted prayers. This can be easily done when palliative care is offered at home, but when the dying person is in an inpatient setting, all of this may pose a challenge. For Hindus, dying is as much a family as an individual event. Hindus will welcome health care institutions, including hospices, having at hand some of the standard ritual God images and material objects. A good death for the Hindu is also informed by attitudes toward the physical body and by norms of purity and cleanliness. The view of the body as a temple of God requires modesty in dress and a preference for caregivers of the same sex. Sacred markings on the face and special jewelry need to be honored. Vegetarian diets are judged conducive to religious deepening and are thus common during the final days of life, as are special fasts for some. Hindu family members traditionally provide physical and spiritual care for dying family members, including bringing in meals prepared at home. Hindus hope for the company of family at their moment of death. Thus, hospice and palliative care institutions will need to demonstrate flexibility in accommodating family during the dying process, recognizing the lasting pain that would be caused by their exclusion.

While not neglecting pain control and the physical comfort that modern medicine offers, a good death for the Hindu is much more focused on detaching oneself from transient material things and keeping one's mental and emotional energy focused on God. Thus, with the support of religious ritual, family, and sacred space, Hindus may be willing to accept some physical pain and a conscious death leading to a better rebirth or the ultimate goal of realizing *moksha* (liberation from rebirth into eternal oneness with God). Rambachan puts it well in his title; death should be "like a ripe fruit separating effortlessly from its vine."

In chapter 3, Anne Bruce showed that, like Hinduism, Buddhism believes in a continuation of the state of mind at the moment of death into the next life. Buddhism is presented as a religion that accepts death as natural—something to think about and prepare for during life. In its broadest sense, death is understood as happening in each moment as one thought passes and the next arises. It is also the end of life and a spiritual opening that, if prepared for properly, may come as a "most glorious moment of life," as the story of Christina and her willingness to prepare for and engage with death directly demonstrates. Christina's story points to the key elements of a good death in Buddhism: (1) having a peaceful and clear mind at the moment of death; (2) having pain managed so that one can consciously focus on the experience of dying; (3) being surrounded by family and spiritual friends; and (4) recognizing the continuity of living, dying, and future rebirth. These key principles were shown to parallel Saunders's teaching on a good death in hospice palliative care. The Buddhist principles are drawn from the Buddha's instruction on how to obtain liberation (*nirvana*) from suffering—a lasting state of happiness free from discontent.

Bruce showed how these teachings are differently developed in hospice case studies in the major denominations of Theravada, Mahayana, and Vajrayana Buddhism. Each denomination is shown to have different hospice bedside needs and practices surrounding the preparation for the moment of death. Among Western Buddhists, death has been increasingly viewed as an opportunity, leading to a strong emphasis on meditation practices in the hospice context. But this is not always the case in the cultural practices and attitudes of Asian Buddhists. In general, for all Buddhists, as the case examples showed, dying well means approaching the end of life and final moments with a calm and virtuous mind. If a dying person is well trained and practiced, then one may be able to rest in the natural state of mind at the moment of death and be liberated (*nirvana*). If not, the dying person's state of mind, whether fearful or peaceful and calm, will determine their transition and next rebirth. Thus, final moments in hospice care (at home or in an institution) are important and require:

A calm, peaceful atmosphere with no loud noises or distractions;

Family, friends, and caregivers to generate mental and emotional states that will support the person's ability to meditate, pray, and chant;

Refusal of opiate medications so that the person can remain lucid and focused; however, severe pain may be relieved with careful titration of medication that still allows for dying meditations and practices;

Recitation of prayers or mantras by lay persons or monks to help the person not become afraid or confused;

An altar with an image of the Buddha at eye level along with a picture of one's spiritual teacher;

Meditations aimed at letting go of thoughts and concentrating on the movement of the breath so as to produce calmness, decrease fear, and control pain;

Reading out over and over again from the *Bardo Thotrol* description (Mahayana tradition) of the experience that happens to body and mind as one dies;

Positioning of the person on the right side, like that of the dying Gautama Buddha.

Regarding the experience of living with cognitive deterioration such as dementia, the Buddhist view is that one should not hold on to an idealized notion of how things should be but practice surrendering to how things are. In the case of children, there are no unique rituals, but the meditation practices of mindfulness and loving kindness are also taught to dying children. Keeping in mind the variety of Buddhist beliefs and cultural practices, Bruce suggests that each person's or family's approach be explored so as to prevent oversimplifying or misunderstanding what is needed at the time of death. Overall, the Buddhist attitude is one of welcoming death as an old friend. Living and dying are intertwined, like breathing in and breathing out.

In chapter 4, Earle Waugh explored Muslim perspectives on the good death in hospice palliative care. Because the Qur'an states that God determines both the time and nature of death for each one, the individual's pathway to God must be respected and not intruded upon by medical care. Preparation for death is critical to ensure a person is in the proper religious frame of mind to pass on to the afterlife which, for a Muslim, is more important than this life. Once death has taken a person, then that individual belongs to God and the other world, and important rituals must be followed for it to be a good death. Furthermore, God plays a key role in the evaluation of sickness, which is seen in Islam as a test. Thus, a terminal illness will be seen as a spiritual test, and consequently one should not complain. Suffering should be borne with fortitude since God is addressing eternal matters through it; for the believer it is a "learning experience." In the view of Islamic traditional medicine, if "spiritual pain" (the result of a religious violation) is dealt with correctly, then physical pain should naturally dissipate, resulting in a peaceful death. A key element for the good death, thus, is avoidance of any religious violation that would cause spiritual pain.

Waugh outlined the following ritual requirements for a good death that need to be observed in hospice palliative care. Most important is the five times daily prayer, even if prone in bed, and the ritual washing required before prayer (here, hospice nurses may need to help). If no water is available, there are provisions for a dry ritual washing. Waugh notes that hospital protocol (even including doctors' rounds) should be suspended during the person's moments of direct connection with God in prayer. Waugh also outlined special food requirements (*halal*). In addition, there are special modesty requirements that affect both women and men in hospice care.

Because death is in the hands of God, no medicine or procedure should prolong the end of life, and for some Muslims even the use of pain medication is controversial. At the moment of death, the body is to be turned in the direction of Mecca. Hospice caregivers need to be aware of the responsibilities of the family and community at the time of death. The oldest males in the family are responsible for funeral arrangements. They must ensure that the body is washed and dressed by members of the same sex, arrange for the burial site, marshal the community for final prayers at the Mosque, and organize the procession to the burial site where the body must be buried facing Mecca on the day of death or the following day.

In view of all the above spiritual and physical requirements, it is evident that, for the Muslim person, a good death requires considerable cultural and religious knowledge as well as flexibility from the hospice caregiver. The various case studies included in the chapter provide help in understanding the key norms and the varieties of Islamic practice concerning hospice and end-of-life care. Awareness by health care professionals of conceptions such as "pain as God's discipline" and the requirements for the family and community will go a long way toward helping Muslims in hospice care experience a good death.

In his chapter on Jewish ideals regarding a good death, Norman Ravvin showed how Torah, Talmud, and *halachan*, or Jewish case law discussions, guide a rabbi's response to end-of-life care. While there are differences between the major denominational groups (Orthodox, Conservative, and Reform), there is a broad agreement against active euthanasia or mercy killing. It is also generally agreed that while nothing should be done to hasten death, at the same time impediments to the natural progress of death are to be removed (e.g., a respirator or other technologies). Traditional Jewish texts and ideals seek to allow death to occur naturally—neither postponed nor brought on by active intervention. The ideal, when it appears that one is very ill and will die soon, is to be in a comfortable setting with family and friends accepting that the power over life and death is in God's hands. If life is granted, that is well and good. If not, the preference is to die not in an active hospital, but in a peaceful hospice setting.

Regarding the Jewish understanding of death, Ravvin describes how, in both the Hebrew Bible and in his own family experience, heaven and hell are not important concerns. Rather, the Jewish response to death is a recognition that the future is not something that will happen to us, but what will come out of the way one is currently living (one's ethical relationship to others within a lived tradition). Ravvin reminds us of the medieval Eastern European institution called *hekdesh*, a longstanding, little-known, independent Jewish version of hospice, which appears in Nobel Laureate Issac Bashevis Singer's story of "Gimpel the Fool." From the thirteenth century, the *hekdesh* was a neglected structure at the edge of a settlement in the vicinity of a cemetery, which housed the ill, the poor, and the homeless—a place where one received some care, medical and otherwise, while waiting to die. Since the mid-sixteenth century, Jewish burial societies spread throughout Eastern Europe with duties that included saying prayers (with the person) in the final stages of dying, cleaning the body, physical burial, and funeral arrangements. In these activities the focus is not so much on care, as we would think of it in modern medical terms, but rather on ritual activities, intimacy, and attentiveness to the dying person. In his concluding case study of B, a family member dying in a Calgary hospital, Ravvin shows how another family member took on these roles as a doorkeeper, preventing distractions of interruptions to the process of a natural death—except for routine feeding and other basic needs. B's care reflected the Jewish principles of pain relief to prevent unnecessary suffering, no unnecessary medical interventions, dying surrounded by loved ones, and being buried in a Jewish cemetery within twenty-four hours of death. In Montreal's larger Jewish community, the Montreal Jewish General Hospital palliative care guidelines include ensuring that the dying person hears the opening line of the *Shema*, the central prayer of Judaism ("Hear, Israel, the Lord is our God, the Lord is One"); and if Orthodox, the opportunity to say a final confessional prayer, the *vidui*, requesting the expiration of sins. As Ravvin makes clear, all of the above activities may be carried out in the hospice context with or without the presence of a rabbi, so long as the dying person and/or the family members are knowledgeable of the tradition.

In chapter 6, Janet Soskice presented an understanding of what it is to die well as a Christian. In its first two centuries following the life and death of Jesus, the Christian movement spread quickly through the Greek-speaking lands of the Mediterranean, across North Africa through Egypt, Libya, and Tunisia, across Syria, Turkey, Iran, and Iraq, and later northward into Europe. Thus, prior to the rise of Islam in the seventh century, there was a great diversity of Christian life and practice that continues today in, for example, the Copts of Egypt, the Syriac-speaking church of the East, the ancient Syro-Malabar Church of South India, and the Greek and the Russian Orthodox communions, not to mention the various Roman Catholic and Protestant denominations of Europe and North America. Each of these groups has their own practices and rituals to do with death and dying. Consequently, there are no universal or obligatory actions or rituals to be observed near or on the death of a Christian. But there are shared core beliefs which inform the Christian understanding of a good death in hospice palliative care.

Through her case studies of the dying Christian monk and her aging Aunt Effie, Janet Soskice drew out the core teachings surrounding a good death as found in the Hebrew Bible and the New Testament. The first is that God cares for everything in creation individually. Thus, each person (along with everything else in creation) is to be given reverence and sanctity. Each person is created "in the image of God" and therefore, no matter how poor, burdened, dissolute, or even demented, is entirely distinctive and worthy of reverence. Physical disability, illness, and death are not seen as a punishment for sin but as part of a disordered world that suffers and groans awaiting its day of salvation. Individual suffering is not attributed to person's wrongdoing, but our individual wrongdoing is seen to contribute to the corporate disorder of the universe. Healing is thought of not only in terms of prayer and miracle (the in-breaking of a new Kingdom of God on earth) but primarily in Jesus' teaching of the parable of the Good Samaritan. In this story, the Samaritan represents Jesus as the true physician who cares for all regardless of kinship. He cares for all—widow, orphan, homeless, or stranger—without regard for merit or gain because each is in the spirit and image of God. This ethos early on led to the creation of Christian hospices (ca. 500 CE) at the time of Bishop Eusebius, a period of drought and plague. In this hospice, hospitality was extended to everyone in need and dying, for anything done for one who is sick is done for God (Matt. 25:34–36); one is to see Christ in each person in need, as St. Francis and Mother Theresa taught and practiced. In the teaching of Jesus, the emphasis is on God as God of the living rather than on life after death (Mark 12:24–26). But God can raise up the dead. The God who creates can save, and the Christian teaching of the resurrection of the body is part of the way one shares in the coming of the Kingdom of God (Rom. 8:22–23).

For a clinician dealing with a Christian person, the above teachings were seen to manifest themselves in the case studies of the monk-brother and Aunt Effie. For a Christian, death is a part of life and not the end of life or of God's love. A good death is not just for the dying but also for the family and those left behind—for all, it is meant to be a time of spiritual growth, a time of living well, as Cicely Saunders taught. A good death is a peaceful death—being at peace with one's family, neighbors, friends, and oneself. To facilitate this, Christian patients may choose to forgo or lessen pain medication in favor of clarity of mind in their last hours. Also there may be a willingness to let go and leave oneself in the hands of God, which should not be interpreted by clinicians as a giving up on life—for many Christians believe in a continuation of life after death as a part of the Christian idea of the resurrection. But, says Soskice, the most important teaching for hospice care—a lesson she takes from Judaism—is the respect and attention to be given to each individual. Each person, whether Christian or not, believer or not, an AIDS sufferer or not, senile or not, is in the image of God and must be respected as such. As is the case with Hinduism and Buddhism, loss of sight and speech is not to be understood as a failure to somehow be present. While extraordinary measures should not be made to keep a dying person alive, a dying person, no matter how frail, silent, and physically or mentally disabled, may still be "living and active" in ways invisible to us but apparent to God. Thus, the importance, as shown in the case of Effie, of continuing to recite scripture and of singing and praying with the dying person, who is still to be regarded as living a life in praise and service to God. From the perspective of family, friends, and caregivers, Christian teaching is that "God has no hands or feet but ours."

In chapter 7, Ed Hui and Danny Leung introduced us to the very different world of Chinese culture and religion—a religious tradition with Confucianism as its basis but with strong influence and shaping from both Buddhism and Daoism. The authors demonstrated how in the Chinese conception of a good death, things good for the bereaved have priority over things good for the deceased. Unlike the modern West, this is a culture based on social, especially filial, obligations rather than individual rights—a big difference when one has to deal with a dying person and his or her family. Even many of today's young Chinese people (who are exposed to modern individualism and rights-based ethics) follow traditional family obligations when faced with death and dying. This is not surprising for, as we learned, in the Chinese tradition personhood is grounded in family and social relation as defined by Confucianism. Consequently, a major "completeness" requirement for a good death is that one should be surrounded by one's family, especially by one's sons, with the eldest son being the most important. Thus, as the Pan case demonstrated, it is crucial that health care providers inform the family in time (to the best of their ability to predict) so that those needing to travel can see the patient alive—otherwise there will be guilt, unhappiness, and disappointment all around. In Hong Kong, ethics protocols give priority to keeping a person alive so that families will have sufficient time to see their loved one before ventilators, for example, are withdrawn. Another difference has to do with truth telling and patient autonomy. In the Confucian view, one should not give bad news to a senior person for this will accelerate deterioration. The doctor should discuss the prognosis and treatment options with the family who make treatment decisions and break the truth to their mother or father step by step. Further, children are to provide around-the-clock care for the parent, including the cooking of special soups to balance the "hot" and "cold" constituents of the body according to traditional Chinese medicine (disease being understood as a disharmony of *yin* and *yang*). Chinese cancer patients will often wish for traditional Chinese medicine treatments along with modern Western biomedicine—and this can pose interesting challenges for health care and hospice staff as the case of Mr. L showed.

Confucian teaching also instills a value in continuing to live as long as one can, worrying that there might still be some unfinished social responsibilities. Giving oneself up to a good death too soon may be seen as an escaping of the social responsibilities that have been delegated by Heaven (*Tian*) to the person. It is by fulfilling one's own social responsibilities that a person can transcend herself and make progress (even while dying) toward the Confucian ideal of "Heaven and Man becoming One." It is in this way that one lives out the good death requirements of compassion and humanness (*ren*) in which one's social obligations to parents, siblings, family, and society are fully satisfied.

In Hui and Leung's chapter, we saw how this Confucian basis for the good death is added to and complicated by Daoist and Buddhist ideas. For example, Daoism holds that an autopsy will cause injuries to the spirit of the deceased, and so Chinese families will resist such requests by physicians. When it comes to tolerance for pain, Daoist and Confucian beliefs taken together lead terminal cancer patients to suffer a moderate level of pain even while being given pain medication. In the Chinese approach, pain endurance is seen as a virtue. Also, taking too much pain medication is not considered good, for it may lessen one's ability to be consciously alert and present with one's family as one dies. Further, in a Confucian context doctors are assigned a high social status, thus Chinese patients may choose to minimize their pain in front of their doctors to avoid appearing as sinful or bad patients. Lastly, in Daoist thought, disease and death are naturally accompanied by pain, and as such, physical pain does not have to be totally eradicated. Also in Buddhist thought, with its adoption of *karma* theory, it is important that one should hold good thoughts front and center in one's consciousness at the moment of death, and therefore the use of pain medication and sedatives should be resisted in one's dying moments. For all of these reasons, then, it is clear that Chinese culture and religion are a complex amalgam of Confucian, Daoist, and Buddhist influences that makes the seemingly simple medical question of hospice pain control exceedingly complicated.

Chinese Buddhist followers, especially of the Pure Land tradition, believe that a habitual chanting of the name of Amitabha Buddha will help them purify their consciousness and be reborn in the Pure Land— and from there realize the goal of final liberation or *nirvana*. If the dying person is too weak to do the recitation, or the family thinks that stronger mental power is needed, a Help Chant Group of devout Buddhists is invited to the bedside to provide a long and continuous chanting that ideally should last for eight hours beyond the moment of death—the period during which the dead person's consciousness will be slowly leaving the body but will still be able to hear and be influenced by the chanting. Once again (as we have observed in the requirements of other religions), a good hospice death in the Chinese context may require that the dying person have a private room set aside for an extended period of chanting following death before the body is moved. If the Chinese Buddhist person is suffering from dementia or Alzheimer's disease, the chanting is seen to be especially important in helping the compromised person to remember their religion in their last moments and still have a good reincarnation.

Having reviewed the understandings of a good death in hospice palliative care of the six major religious traditions in Part I, we are now in a position to consider some common points of concern that hospice palliative caregivers need to keep in mind. The first is that Cicely Saunders's key principle of pain control, which is now such a fundamental part of palliative care, is given a very nuanced and different response in each religious tradition. In almost all cases, there is a strong emphasis placed on an experience of death in which a conscious focus on family and specific religious practice can be maintained. Second, it is essential for a good death that a home or hospice room be made into a peaceful sacred space in which family, friends, and religious practitioners can be with the dying person and engage in rituals, chants, and practices that (as in the Chinese Pure Land Buddhist case) may continue for several hours after death has been medically certified. Third, there are specific dietary requirements in the different traditions from *kosher* and *halal* foods to Hindu/Buddhist vegetarianism and Chinese requirements to balance the *yin/yang* (hot and cold) constituents of the body with special soups that may need to be home cooked. Fourth, rooms need to have an eye-level altar space on which images for use in meditation, prayer, or chanting can be placed. Fifth, in some traditions, there is important disagreement with Western biomedicine's norm of the individual autonomy of the patient when it comes to telling bad news, making treatment decisions, and obtaining consent. In many cultural and religious traditions, the identity of the dying person is collective with the family rather than individual and autonomous (as we assume it to be in the modern West)—and this makes for large differences in the way these most sensitive matters need to be handled so that a good death for all (patient, family, and caregivers) may be realized. This also was a key issue in the chapter on Canadian Aboriginal experiences in accessing palliative care. Finally, there are important religious rituals accompanying the moment of dying in almost all traditions, from the Roman Catholic last rites to turning the body to face Mecca in Islam, to chanting the name of the Buddha for eight hours in Chinese Buddhism. It is essential that hospice care providers be culturally and religiously literate of these requirements and able to help to make their realization possible. In that way, Saunders's hospice goal of caring for spiritual pain as well as physical pain will be achieved.

In writing this book we realized that an increasing problem for hospice caregivers is the need to deal with dementia and Alzheimer's disease while the person is dying. Thus, each author in Part I has included the thinking of each religious tradition on how to provide the possibilities for the good death even under these challenging conditions. These religious responses to dementia and Alzheimer's can be located in each chapter by consulting the index.

Part II of the book moved from the theoretical considerations of a good death in each religious tradition to in-depth consideration of real-life hospice palliative care examples from around the world. We looked first at the hospice care provided by Buddhist monk-healers in monasteries in Thailand. In chapter 8, Robert Florida and Pinit Ratanakul explained how the radiation of loving kindness and chanting are used by Thai monks to help patients die a peaceful good death. Many are dying from HIV/AIDS. Radiation is described as direct transmission of the healing power of loving kindness generated by the meditative mind of the monks to the disturbed mind of the dying person. It is done by touching or sitting close to the patient. Chanting done in Pali by the monks is also very comforting to the dying. Listening to the Buddha's limitless compassion embodied in the verses chanted soothes and calms the mind, enabling the person to experience a good death. Monks visit homes where extended families are providing palliative care for a dying family member. This is typical of villages in the rural areas of Thailand. But in urban areas, families often have to depend more on hospitals where palliative care is rather inadequate. Thus, out of compassion, the monks of many temples have opened their doors to the dying and offer free hospice care. The chapter offered a detailed description of the care provided by the temple Wat Doi Gueng as an example. This care consists of the patients doing daily chanting, learning the *dhamma* or teaching of the Buddha, and practicing morality and meditation to prepare themselves for dying. For meditation they practice mindfulness of breathing to calm the agitated mind and loving-kindness meditations to cultivate love and compassion in place of negative emotions such as ill-will or resentment. The abbot of the monastery offers teaching of the Buddhist method of pain control through meditation so that there is a reduced need for the use of painkilling drugs. Many temples like Wat Doi Gueng give hospice care for cancer patients. Other temples focus on caring for people with AIDS who were often turned away from hospitals and in some cases rejected by their own families. Now, however, more hospitals and families understand more and are beginning to accept and care for those dying of AIDS. But Wat Phrabat is the place where most people with AIDS feel safe to go for hospice care. The monastery also offers hospice care for a large number of AIDS orphans and children of adult AIDS patients. Other Buddhist monasteries focus on outreach and home care for the dying and those with Alzheimer's disease. On their visits to homes, the monks advise family members and the dying on the use of meditation practices to help relieve them of their distress. For Thai Buddhists, apart from the physical and mental contributing factors, disease is understood as the sum of one's demeritorious deeds in this and earlier lives. For them, a good death does not mean a painless or sudden death, but dying with wholesome consciousness leading to a good rebirth or even liberation (*nirvana*).

Chapter 9 shifted our focus to Africa and the Ugandan way of living and dying. The authors, Michael Hadley and Godfrey Agupio, explained how Uganda's population is 90 percent Christian and 10 percent Muslim with a pervasive underlay of Indigenous African traditions. This presents health care workers with a complex challenge made more difficult by the ravages of HIV/AIDS on an economically disadvantaged populace. Responding to this challenge, Hospice Uganda attempts to provide palliative care that is affordable, culturally appropriate, and religiously sensitive. It was founded as a Christian NGO in 1993, uses modern methods to control pain, and focuses on home care as well as day care clinics. Most patients prefer to die at home close to their ancestors where they will be buried. Christian-based hospice care workers closely follow the model of Cicely Saunders. When death is imminent, there is a strong tendency to resort to African "witchcraft" practices or the miraculous healing of incurable illnesses offered by some churches. In the face of these challenges, the chapter demonstrated valiant work done by Hospice Uganda to promote an understanding of good death as one that offers "peace with one's God and one's community," while providing pain control and helping the dying to see meaning in their life journey. Traditional religious rituals such as last rites are carried out along with rituals to the ancestors before death and burial in their ancestral home. Case studies offered in the chapter showed the range of physical, social, cultural, and spiritual challenges engaged by hospice care workers in helping their patients experience good deaths. Emphasis was also given to the huge role played by women and children. In Uganda, most palliative care depends upon them, especially in the many child-headed families where HIV/AIDS has killed the parents. Given all of these challenges, the chapter demonstrated Hospice Uganda's significant achievement of remaining open to patients of all spiritual traditions by praying with them as they seek to end their life journey in a meaningful good death.

We have already mentioned that in some cultures and religious traditions the extended family has traditionally provided hospice palliative care in the home setting. Chapter 10 offers a case study example of Punjabi extended-family hospice care in a Hindu/Sikh context. The author, Kamala Nayar, is the granddaughter of the study subject Durga Devi and had intimate access to her and the whole family. This excellent study provides an in-depth look at the Hindu/Sikh understanding of pain (to be treated with traditional means such as massages and allopathic medicine) and the Punjabi understanding of how the aging and dying ought to be cared for at home. The case study tells of Durga Devi's escape by train from Pakistan to India during partition with four young children while pregnant and ready to give birth. In 1988 at the age of seventy-seven, her health began to deteriorate, and her second son Rajiv, who resided with her, became her main caretaker. In addition, her youngest daughter, a registered nurse, would come to the house at regular intervals to help with her care. Her daughter-in-law prepared vegetarian meals for her, served by her grandchildren. As Durga Devi's health worsened, her eldest son in Canada wanted to take her there to die, but she refused, wishing to remain and die in her own home. There, as matriarch of the family, she would frequently recount the story of her life struggles, especially to her female children and grandchildren, always ending with her devotion to the Hindu god Lord Ram. Her granddaughter, Kamala, also a registered nurse, came from Canada to help with her care. On occasion, the doctor would come to the house to see her. The narrative of the chapter tells how she no longer left her bed, ate little, but remained lucid throughout her dying. She never spoke of death for that would have been unsettling and inauspicious (the author carefully explains the complex Punjabi approach to truth telling), but she would raise her hands in prayer and say, "When it is my time God will take me." The same routine of feeding and bathing her in her room and the cleaning of her wastes continued at home until she died on a cot in her home in December 1999. By Punjabi standards, hers was a good and auspicious death. She died on the cot she had slept on for fifty-two years of her life. She had lived a long and full life and had been able to see her grandchildren and great grandchildren. Although she did not die lying on the floor as the Hindu tradition desires, Durga Devi's family carried out rituals to correct this. The family provided good hospice care at home in that (1) she had been able to practice her religion; (2) she was primarily cared for by one of her sons, albeit not her eldest; (3) she had other family members with her providing her care and company; and (4) she was cared for at her own home. As the narrative concludes, "For a traditional woman such as Durga Devi, it would have been traumatic for her to have been placed in an institutional health care facility in order to die."

Set in a Manitoba, Canada, context, the team of Joseph Kaufert, Patricia Kaufert, Rhonda Wiebe, and Ojibwa elder Margaret Lavallee offered us a clear and helpful comparison of a good death and a bad death in Aboriginal hospice care. The authors demonstrated that respect for Aboriginal, spiritual, cultural, and ethical values are essential for a good death defined in terms of both the act of gathering people to be present and in an actual physical location. A good death is a spiritual journey of "coming home" to one's origins and one's people. Consequently, the care environment of a dying person allows safe physical and emotional space for extended family involvement and ceremonial practices. The case example of a bad death failed to do that, while the good death example showed how the dying person was able to experience end-of-life care within the context of her families, her Indigenous community, and her traditional spiritual practices. The good death of Mrs. M required coordination between palliative care and community-based health care providers and members of her kinship network. Throughout, there was respect for the individual and inclusion of the family in end-of-life decision making. As in the Chinese and Punjabi examples, there was a need for truth telling and the giving of bad news to occur slowly and be mediated through the family. In this connection, the role of the language and cultural translator was shown to be key to a successful outcome of the interaction between the doctor and the dying person. In the bad death example, the system failed because a trusted translator was not present and the challenges of providing pain management and hospice care within the person's Indigenous tradition were not met. Adequate pain management, Cicely Saunders's first principle, was the major problem in the bad death of Mr. R and was the result of inflexible legal and medical policies. These barriers, along with resource and attitudinal problems of health care providers, continue to limit the development of community hospice committed to managing total pain (physical and spiritual) in both Indigenous communities and urban home care programs.

Chapter 12 dealt with the difficult problem of caring for children in hospice and palliative care. The authors, Betty Davies and Thomas Attig, offered the example of Canuck Place in Vancouver, the first free-standing children's hospice in North America. The goal of hospices such as Canuck Place is to create large, comfortable "home away from home" settings where families can engage in familiar practices and routines and openly express their emotions and concerns. Thus, programs for dying children take the family as the unit of care and respond to the physical, emotional, and spiritual needs of the children. The chapter focused on the nature and means of addressing spiritual and religious needs. When a child is dying, parents and families are confronted with unanswerable questions such as "Why my child?" or "Why any child?"—questions that can shatter one's sense of the meaning and purpose of life. The authors find that the core value required in providing spiritual care in hospice for children is respecting the parents and family (including the dying child) no matter their religious or spiritual beliefs or practices. Some are very clear about the spiritual/religious practices and beliefs that matter to them. They may find comfort, for example, in believing that "everything is in God's hands." Such spiritual/religious support may help them make difficult decisions about continuing or discontinuing medical treatment. Others may have no history with and find no comfort in religious teachings and practices.

Case examples offered in the chapter emphasize the spiritual and religious needs of very young children and adolescents. Terminally ill three- or four-year-olds may know more about illness and dying than a healthy nine- or ten-year-old. Any very young children with terminal illness may wrestle with questions such as "Why me?" or have concerns about punishment related to their illness. The case studies offered are sensitive descriptions and explorations of what may help provide for a good death in such situations. In this regard, the special challenges for caregivers are explored in terms of both *competence* (knowledge about the various religions and differences in their understandings of a good death) and *sensitivity* (knowing one's own religious predispositions and "tuning in" to the religion/spirituality, or lack of it, of one's patient and family). The chapter concluded with a most helpful and complete discussion of how caregivers can help with the spiritual/religious needs in the hospice palliative care of dying children.

Our final chapter examined the role of hospital chaplains in hospice palliative care. In chapter 13, Kelli Stajduhar and Coby Tschanz offer a brief history of the development of chaplaincy in the West and describe how chaplaincy is defined in today's interfaith context. Chaplains typically have gone through theological education within a religious tradition and, in addition, may have specialized training in pastoral care. Their role is to provide religious and spiritual care to patients, relatives, and health care staff outside of the parish. In the hospital or hospice context, a primary role of the chaplain is to assess and respond to the spiritual needs of patients and to educate the rest of the health care team on religious issues. Chaplains provide religious practices for people of their own faith, contact religious leaders not of their own faith when requested by the patient and family, and conduct rituals for patients of other faiths if their religious leaders are not available. In St. Christopher's Hospice, the first modern-day European hospice, the chaplain was a full member of the health care team and operated in an ecumenical Christian context. Today's hospice situation is much more pluralistic. In their interviews with chaplains, the authors focused on three questions: Who is responsible for attending to religious needs in hospice palliative care? How do chaplains work with the trend away from religious care to spiritual care?

and What is it like for chaplains serving persons from other faiths or from no religious tradition?

Stajduhar and Tschanz found that while Cicely Saunders's original conception of hospice assumed that all care team members were mature Christians and thus able and willing to talk about spiritual matters with the dying person, in today's hospice situation staff may not have the competence or desire to engage in discussion of religious concerns and thus increasingly need to rely on chaplains. Chaplains interviewed reported a trend away from specific religious traditions toward a generic or undefined spirituality in the way they were asked to deal with the dying. Some chaplains are now called "spiritual care coordinators" rather than chaplains on their name badges. Indeed, in some hospices today, budget cuts and other factors may lead to religious care or contact with chaplains no longer being offered as an aspect of holistic care—a far cry from Saunders's original conception. While St. Christopher's was grounded in Christian ecumenical compassion, current-day hospices in the main do not share that vision. Partly as a response to today's religious pluralism, and partly as a shift from religion to a supposedly universal spirituality, the modern hospice has been essentially stripped of its Christian roots. Thus, hospice professional care literature tends to promote a dichotomy between religion and spirituality, advancing the idea that spirituality, rather than religion, is integral to a good death. This shift, the authors suggest, can constrain both chaplain and non-chaplain care providers from exploring with dying patients what it means to provide care within the context of a religious tradition. The implications of this loss of traditional religious language and rituals, essential for devout followers of the traditional religions, mean that sometimes hospice chaplains and staff may find themselves unable to provide to the dying the third of Cicely Saunders's three principles for hospice care, namely, religious support.

In their interviews, the chapter authors found that funded hospice chaplains, almost always Christian by faith and training, were increasingly caring for people from other faiths—Jews, Muslims, Buddhists, Hindus, Aboriginals, Chinese, atheists, and others. This presents a considerable challenge for the chaplains as well as the doctors and nurses of the hospice palliative care team. While our book may offer help to clinicians in their understanding of a good death in the various religious traditions, the chapters in Part I make it clear that for a hospice chaplaincy to be adequate to today's multicultural and multireligious context, it needs to be truly interfaith in makeup. A Christian-based chaplain, no matter how well-intentioned or well-educated in other religions, simply cannot fill the roles (ritual and otherwise) required by the various religions for a good death to be experienced. In the interfaith chaplaincy chapter, the Sikh example showed that a professional priest, religious leader, or chaplain is not always needed. The Indigenous case study (chapter 11) made clear that a Christian-based non-Aboriginal chaplain may be a significant obstacle to care. Rather, an elder and appropriate rituals in the person's community are required. For Hindus, a priest is needed to provide Vedic rituals every two hours, and for the Buddhist patient, priests or monks may need to help the person maintain continuous chanting as they die so as to ensure a good death. All of these considerations argue for an interfaith hospice chaplaincy with chaplains from each of the major religious traditions operating out of a common hospice office, with all being members of the care team. Such true interfaith chaplaincies currently function in the military, in prisons, and in many universities. Hospice and hospital chaplaincy seem to lag behind in this respect, significantly limiting the opportunities for providing the religious support that Saunders maintained is needed for a good death in hospice care.

The goal of this book has been to examine the understandings of a good death found in the major religious traditions and their applications to care in the hospice palliative context. As we acknowledged in the introduction, there is today an increasing segment of the population who do not identify with a particular religious tradition, yet follow an understanding of life they call "spiritual." Hospice palliative care for the future will have to provide support for dying persons of the "spiritual but not religious" persuasion (of which there are many versions). Consequently, we are already at work on a follow-up volume that will aim at addressing this need along with the needs of atheists and agnostics. In our next volume, we will also examine the notion of a universal or generic spirituality that is common in the North American health care culture and specifically in the training of doctors, nurses, and chaplains. Our working title for this follow-up volume is "Perspectives on Spirituality in Hospice Care: Beyond Traditions."

Glossary of Terms and Abbreviations

Lee Blanding

This glossary comprises terms and abbreviations that the authors felt deserved greater clarification, as well as terms that will be commonly found in clinical situations. These definitions are not standardized, but reflect the way that the authors have used the terms in their respective chapters. Please note that terms italicized in text are defined elsewhere in the glossary.

Aart	A Hindu ritual of waving flame clockwise before icon.
abaya	A full-length dark outer garment worn by some women in Muslim countries for modesty and as a religious sign of their commitment to Islam.
Aboriginal Peoples	The term refers to both status and non-status First Nations, Inuit, and Métis peoples of Canada. (referenced in section 35(2) of the Constitution Act, Canada 1982).
Ahmadiyya	A Pakistani minority religious tradition based on Islam, but also including adherence to a later prophetic-type messenger, Ghulam Ahmad.
akusala	Pali term meaning unwholesome, demerit.
Amitabha Buddha	Amitabha Buddha is a Sanskrit term meaning "Buddha of infinite light" who presides over the Pure Land of the West. Amitabha is important in Mahayana Buddhism.
anatta	Buddhist term meaning no-self or nonsubstantiality.

artha	Wealth; one of the four goals of Hindu life.
ARV	Antiretroviral drug.
asauca	Sanskrit term meaning impure, pollution; (*apavitra/apavitar* = Hindi, Punjabi).
Ashkenazi and Sephardic Jews	Terms used to designate the presumed cultural background of Jews. Those who understand their ancestry to be Central and Eastern European call themselves Ashkenazi (meaning *German* in Hebrew), while those who connect their ancestry with the Spanish exile refer to themselves as Sephardic (*Spanish* in Hebrew).
ashramas	The four stages of Hindu life.
asubha	Sanskrit term meaning inauspicious (*asubh* = Hindi, Punjabi).
atman	The Self; regarded in some Hindu traditions as identical with the infinite (*Brahman*).
bhajana	Hymn in Sikh and Hindu traditions.
bhakti-marga	A Hindu term meaning the way of loving devotion.
Bhavana	Buddhist meditational practice.
bindi	A dot placed in the center of forehead in Sikh and Hindu traditions.
Bitachon	Hebrew, meaning faith or confidence.
bodhisattva	A Buddhist term meaning being destined to enlightenment.
bojjhanga paritta	In Hindu traditions, *Bojjhanga* are the seven factors leading to enlightenment; *paritta* means protection. The two terms are used jointly for protective chanting.
Brahman	A Hindu concept meaning the infinite; source, ground, and end of all creation.
Chasidim	A religious and social movement begun in mid-eighteenth century Poland, which spread throughout the lands of the Russian empire, whose originator was a mystic known as the Ba'al Shem Tov. Belzer Chasidim recognize as their leader the ancestral line of *Rebes* (Chasidic leaders) from the Ukrainian town of Belz.
Chengfu	A Daoist concept meaning if one's seniors of past generations have done something good, one will have good fortune.

By the same token, if one has done something good, this will bring good fortune to one's offspring. In this way the individual is morally tied to his/her family members. (*Cheng* means "to bear" and *Fu* means "to be responsible for").

Communions	Refers to the specific sects of Christianity; the "Russian Orthodox Communion," for instance, or the Anglican Communion.
creatio ex nihilo	The Christian idea that God created all that is, including matter, space, and time, from nothing.
cuti-citta	A Pali term for the last state of consciousness before death.
dadiji	Hindi or Punjabi term for paternal grandmother.
dana	Generosity (in Buddhism).
darshana	Hindu concept meaning seeing the sacred; used especially for seeing an icon.
devi	Divine feminine; mother-goddess in Hindu traditions.
dhamma	The Buddha's teaching.
dhamma osod	The use of Buddhist teaching for therapy.
dharma	Ethics; one of the four goals of Hindu life.
dosa	Pali word meaning hatred, anger; one of the three roots of evil.
dukh	Hindi and Punjabi word for suffering, pain; *dukkha* is a Sanskrit term.
Easter	A Christian holy day that celebrates the day on which Christians believe Jesus rose from the dead.
eid	A special Muslim feast, as at the end of the month of fasting, i.e., Ramadan.
Elder	A spiritual or community leader recognized by an Aboriginal community. Elders are cultural experts with special knowledge of community values, ethical practices, and spirituality. Some elders also play roles as counselors and healers.
False messiah	Two substantial Jewish movements of messianic yearning and activity, which followed the leadership of Sabbatai Zevi (1626–1676) and Jacob Frank (1726–1791), whose pretension to world-changing religious aims ended in disarray.

First Nations People with Treaty Status	Aboriginal people who are registered under the Indian Act of Canada and who can document membership in a *First Nation* that signed a treaty.
Gentiles	Term used in the New Testament to indicate non-Jewish people.
The Gospels	Refers to the four stories of the life of Jesus—Matthew, Mark, Luke, and John—that comprise the first four books of the Christian New Testament.
Guru	In South Asian traditions such as Hinduism and Sikhism, a religious teacher.
hadith	Sayings and reports of the Prophet that became the basis for Muslim norms and laws.
hakim	A practitioner who prescribes therapies based on Muslim spiritual or "commonsense" notions.
Halachah	Religious laws governing the daily life and worship of Jews, understood to derive from an oral tradition, set down in the early centuries of this millennium and resulting in the Talmud.
halal	Meat from lawfully killed animals and birds (under Islamic law).
hekdesh	An institution, not unlike hospice, common in Eastern and Central European Jewish communities up till World War II. It was largely a way of caring for the indigent and those with incurable diseases. The structure known as the *hekdesh* often stood near to the cemetery.
hijab	Head covering worn by some Muslim women as a sign of their Islamic commitment.
hikmat	In Islam, technically the wisdom/knowledge of ancient medical procedures; also known as the Prophet's medicine.
Ibadis	Minority *Shi'a* (Muslim) tradition group based primarily in Yemen.
imago dei	Literally, "the image of God."
Indigenous Peoples	This more inclusive term in the Canadian context includes Aboriginal Peoples, First Nations, and Métis, including individuals with and without treaty status. In Canada the term

	also includes Inuit peoples. The term is used internationally to refer to groups and nations who were living on the land before colonial involvement.
Inuit	Circumpolar Aboriginal people living in Canada, Greenland, Alaska, and Siberia.
Ishtadeva	In Hindu traditions, an individual's or family's favorite form of God.
Isma`ilis	Minority *Shi'a* tradition group with allegiance to the Aga Khan; a significant number of adherents live in India, Pakistan, Afghanistan, Africa, and now Canada.
jidhadist	A small, conservative, reactionary movement that argues for a violent Islamic reaction to modernity and Westernization.
Jnana-marga	The way of wisdom in Hindu traditions.
Kaddish	Jewish prayer for the dead, said as part of a funeral and commemorative ceremonies at certain holidays. The prayer itself is an important part of the weekly liturgy.
kama	Pleasure; one of the four goals of Hindu life.
kamma	A Pali term meaning an action or deed, leading to result (*vipaka*).
karma	A Hindu concept for the results of action; the moral law of cause and effect.
Karma-marga	The way of ritual action in Hindu traditions.
kilesa	The Hindu concept of defilements.
Kirtana	Recitation of the names of God in the Hindu and Sikh traditions.
kusala	A Pali term meaning wholesome or merit.
lobha	A Pali term for greed; one of the three roots of evil.
The Lord's Prayer	A prayer which, according to the Gospels, Jesus taught his disciples to pray. It is thus of central importance to worship, public and private, in all Christian groups and the religion's best-known prayer.
Mangala-sutra	Necklace worn by married women in Hindu traditions to signify wedded state.

Mantra	Sacred words; chanted prayer in the Sikh and Hindu traditions.
masjid	Arabic for mosque, the Muslim building for prayer.
Métis	Métis are distinct peoples who have evolved from the union of European and First Nations or Inuit cultures combining traits and traditions. Twenty-six percent of the self-identified Aboriginal population in Canada identified as Métis, according to the 1996 Canadian census.
metta	Buddhist concept of loving-kindness.
moha	Pali term for delusion; one of the three roots of evil.
moksha	Liberation; the highest goal of Hindu life.
Murti	In Hindu traditions an icon that is a focus of worship.
Mu`tazilism	Rationalist-type school that flourished in the seventh-eighth Muslim century that influenced theological and legal matters.
New Testament	A collection of writings of the early Christian community and judged authoritative by Christians now. Together with the Old Testament (made up of Jewish writings) it makes up the Christian Bible.
NGO	Nongovernmental organization.
nibbana	Complete liberation from *samsara* (in Therava Buddhism).
Pali	Buddhist scriptural language of Therava Buddhism.
panna	Buddhist term for knowledge, insight, or wisdom.
Pikuach Nefesh	Hebrew term meaning saving of human life. This ideal allows one to break laws regarding the Sabbath and other observance in order to save a life.
Pir	A special religious person deemed to provide spiritual guidance for believers; usually associated with the mystical branch of Islam known as Sufism, and of considerable significance to ordinary Pakistani believers; sometimes called a Fakir.
Puja	Ritual worship in Hindu and Sikh traditions.
qibla	Part of mosque structure indicating the correct direction for prayer.

Qur'an	Muslim holy scripture.
Ramadan	Month of daytime fast that takes place in the ninth month of the Muslim lunar calendar; called *ramzan* in South Asia.
Ren	The central character of *Tian*. There is no one-to-one correspondence of this word in English, but it is commonly translated as "benevolence," "compassion," and "love-giving."
salat	Word for prayer by Arabic speakers, or the daily ritual of Muslim mandatory prayers; called *namaz* in south Asia.
samadhi	One-pointed concentration in Hindu traditions.
samatha	In Buddhism, calming meditation to attain tranquility.
samsara	The cycle of birth, death, and rebirth/rebirths; also called *sansar* (Punjabi). This concept is familiar to Hindu, Punjabi, and Buddhist traditions.
sangha	A community of Buddhist monks.
sati	Mindfulness, in Therava Buddhism.
sauca	A Sanskrit term meaning pure, purity; (*pavitra/pavitar* = Hindi/Punjabi).
sharia	Islamic law.
Sharing circle	Originally an Indigenous term denoting a process in which each person has an opportunity to speak in turn. The process is used for seeking consensus in decision-making, resolving conflicts between participants and building community trust.
Sheol	A domain of the dead mentioned in the Hebrew Bible, which refers to a place beneath the earth (Numbers) and under the waters (Job). Those who descend there are understood to never return (from the Hebrew "to dig").
Shi'ism/Shi'a	A numerically smaller community of Muslims who differ in doctrinal matters with other Muslims known as Sunnis; one part of a very ancient religious division within Islam. Its adherents are known as Shi'a Muslims.
sila	Moral precepts in Buddhism.
smudging	A cleansing ceremony using the smoke from plant medicine; this ceremony is used by many Indigenous peoples.

subha	A Sanskrit term meaning auspicious; (*subh* = Hindi, Punjabi).
such	A Sanskrit, Hindi, and Punjabi word for joy or pleasure.
Sun Dance	A ceremony practiced primarily by First Nations groups living in the Prairie regions of Canada and the United States.
sunnatta/ shunyata	A Buddhist word for emptiness, nothingness. *Sunnatta* is Pali, while *shunyata* is Sanskrit.
Sunnism	Comprises about 85 percent of Muslims in the world; a religious differentiation going back to the earliest days of Islamic development.
Svarga	A Hindu term meaning heavenly world.
Talmud	Jewish civil and religious law, derived from key texts to which are attached commentaries by various rabbinic sources. Its contents are both legalistic and narrative in style. Two gatherings of such material were undertaken—one in Babylonia (600 CE), the other in Palestine some two hundred years later.
Temple	The central sanctuary of Jewish worship in Jerusalem. The first Temple was built by Solomon in 960 BCE and was destroyed by the Babylonians. The second Temple, completed in 520 BCE was destroyed by the Romans in 70 CE.
Tian	In Chinese religion, a supernatural force rather than a personified god. *Tian* has intentions and principles to regulate physical events and justice on Earth.
Tianming	The intentions of *Tian*. Humans are supposed to conform to it if they know it.
Tirtha	Sacred place in Hindu traditions.
Torah	Hebrew for teaching or learning; can refer to the Five Books of Moses, known as the Hebrew Bible by non-Jews and Jews, but also includes the full range of Jewish religious literature, including the Talmud.
tulasi/tulsi	Sacred basil plant used in Hindu worship.
Twelvers	The largest minority Shi'a religious group in Islam; based primarily in Iran but with important communities in Pakistan and Afghanistan.
unani	Technically deriving from the Greek word, Ionian, but generally a popular medical system developed by the Greek phy-

sician Hippocrates and found in Egypt and other Muslim countries; related to the Prophet Mohammed's medicine by some.

Upanishads   Final sections of the Hindu *Vedas*; wisdom dialogues between teacher and students.

upapatti   A Pali term for rebirth.

Upavita   Sacred thread worn by Hindu males across left shoulder.

Vedas   Authoritative Hindu scriptures.

vipassana   Insight meditation to gain wisdom in Buddhist traditions.

wudu'   A Muslim term delineating ritual washing rite signaling one's personal preparation to encounter God in prayer.

Yom Kippur   Day of Atonement, the Jewish High Holiday that follows and completes the undertakings of Rosh Hashanah, or the Jewish New Year in the Hebrew month of Tishri.

Contributors

Godfrey Agupio (RN, Dip. PC) is a quality assurance nurse at the Hospice Africa center in Makindye, Uganda. Following twelve years of clinical nursing and palliative care experience, he is now pursuing his principal focus of improving clinical palliative care services through research. He has published articles on patients with HIV/AIDS and cancer in journals such as the *British Medical Journal* and the *Journal of Palliative Medicine*. His international experience includes study at Lancaster University, UK, as well as research-related travel to Canada and other African countries.

Thomas Attig is professor emeritus in the Department of Philosophy at Bowling Green State University. He received his PhD in philosophy from Washington University, St. Louis, in 1973. Dr. Attig is the author of *How We Grieve: Relearning the World* and *The Heart of Grief: Death and the Search for Lasting Love*, both with Oxford University Press. He is a past president of the Association for Death Education and Counseling and past vice chair of the International Work Group on Death, Dying, and Bereavement.

Lee Blanding is a PhD candidate in the Department of History at the University of Victoria. His dissertation deals with the political and ideological origins of multiculturalism policy in Canada during the period 1963–1973.

Anne Bruce is an associate professor in the School of Nursing at the University of Victoria, Canada. She received her PhD from the University of British Columbia in 2002. Her research interests include existential suffering in end of life, Buddhist approaches to hospice palliative care,

contemplative practices in nursing, and interpretive research method-
ologies. She is currently part of a team examining end-of-life care for
non-Western immigrants in Saskatchewan.

David Clark is a medical sociologist and director of the University of
Glasgow Dumfries Campus in southern Scotland. Professor Clark has
wide-ranging interests in end-of-life issues and particularly the global
development of hospice and palliative care. He is the author of numerous
books and publications including *Cicely Saunders, Founder of the Hospice
Movement: Selected Letters 1959–1999* (2002) and, with David Wright,
*Hospice and Palliative Care in Africa: A Review of Developments and Chal-
lenges* (2006).

Harold Coward is founding director and associate fellow of the Centre
for Studies in Religion and Society, University of Victoria, Canada. He
is a fellow of the Royal Society of Canada. A specialist on Indian philosophy and religion, he is the author or co-author of eighteen books,
including *Hindu Ethics: Purity, Abortion and Euthanasia, A Cross-Cultural
Dialogue on Health Care Ethics,* and *The Perfectibility of Human Nature
in Eastern and Western Thought.* His most recent publication is *Acceptable
Genes? Religious Traditions and Genetically Modified Foods,* co-edited with
Conrad Brunk.

Betty Davies is a senior scholar in the School of Nursing, University
of Victoria, Canada, and professor emerita in the Department of Family Health Care Nursing at the University of California San Francisco.
Her research pertains to death, dying, and bereavement in families with
children. She is the author of *Fading Away: The Experience of Transition
for Families with Terminal Illness* and *Shadows in the Sun: Experiences of
Sibling Bereavement in Childhood.* Dr. Davies was the recipient of the
2008 Distinguished Career Achievement Award from the Hospice and
Palliative Nurses Association.

Robert E. Florida was professor of religion and dean of arts at Brandon
University in Manitoba and is currently a fellow at the Centre for Studies in Religion and Society at the University of Victoria, Canada, where
he also teaches in the Department of Religious Studies. His primary
scholarly interests are in ethical issues in contemporary Buddhism. He
is the author of *Human Rights and World's Major Religions: The Buddhist*

Tradition (Westport CT: Greenwood, 2005) as well as a number of articles on Buddhist ethics.

Michael L. Hadley (CD, PhD, FRSC) is professor emeritus of the University of Victoria and an associate fellow at the university's Centre for Studies in Religion and Society. A multidisciplinary scholar, he has made major contributions through books and articles in the areas of naval history, religious studies, religion and criminal justice, and social history. He teaches in Uganda in a program leading to a degree in health care administration under the aegis of the International Christian Medical Institute. He serves on the editorial board of *The Northern Mariner/Le Marin du Nord: Journal of the Canadian Nautical Research Society.*

Edwin Chi-wai Hui, a native of Hong Kong, received his undergraduate degree from UCLA and earned his MD, PhD, and MTS from the University of British Columbia. He was professor of medical ethics at Regent College, University of British Columbia, from 1990 to 2002 and has been a professor of medical ethics and director of the Medical Ethics Unit in the LKS Faculty of Medicine at Hong Kong University since 2003. He has published extensively in both English and Chinese. His research interests are in clinical, cross-cultural, and religious ethics.

Joseph Kaufert is a professor in the Department of Community Health Sciences and the Centre for Aboriginal Health Research in the Faculty of Medicine at the University of Manitoba. His areas of research are in medical anthropology, disability studies, clinical and research ethics, and Indigenous health. His research with urban First Nations and Inuit communities has documented the impact of language interpreters and cultural advocates in urban hospitals. He is currently co-principal investigator in two projects documenting ethical dimensions in end-of-life care for vulnerable persons and the participation of human subjects in health research.

Patricia Kaufert received her PhD from the Centre of West African Studies at the University of Birmingham, England. She is currently professor in the Department of Community Health Sciences in the Faculty of Medicine at the University of Manitoba. Her research interests are in women's health, with a focus on menopause, mammography, midwifery, health policy, and the new genetics. She is currently involved in a project at Centre for Applied Ethics at the University of British Columbia researching the meaning and experience of human subjects in health research.

Margaret Lavallee (BA) is elder-in-residence at the Centre for Aboriginal Health Education at the University of Manitoba. She has served as an Aboriginal awareness facilitator for the Winnipeg Regional Health Authority and is co-owner with Jules Lavallee of Red Willow Lodge, Inc., a training and teaching center for Aboriginal awareness. She is grandmother to twenty grandchildren and an active member of the Grandmothers Council for the Protection of Children. She is a sacred pipe carrier and has participated in the sun dance for the past fourteen years.

Danny Chi-keung Leung is a post-doctoral fellow at the Medical Ethics Unit, University of Hong Kong. He received his MPhil in philosophy of science from Hong Kong University, an MSc in the history of science from Imperial College, and a PhD in the history of medicine from University College London. He is the author of "Thomas Clifford Allbutt and Comparative Pathology" (2008) and co-author of *Twenty Problems in Philosophy* (2006). He is currently involved in two bioethics projects investigating perceptions of medical professionalism and genetic discrimination in Hong Kong.

Kamala Elizabeth Nayar teaches South Asian Studies at Kwantlen Polytechnic University near Vancouver, British Columbia. Her two books, *Hayagriva in South India: Complexity and Selectivity of a Pan-Indian Hindu Deity* (2004) and *The Socially Involved Renunciate: Guru Nanak's Discourse with the Nath Yogis* (2007), are extensive textual studies on Hinduism and Sikhism respectively. She is also the author of *The Sikh Diaspora in Vancouver: Three Generations amid Tradition, Modernity and Multiculturalism* (2004) and several articles on the Sikh community in Western Canada. She holds a PhD in Asian religions (1999) from McGill University.

Anantanand Rambachan is professor and chair in the Department of Religion at St. Olaf College, Minnesota. Rambachan's works include *Accomplishing the Accomplished: The Vedas as a Source of Valid Knowledge in Sankara* (1991), *The Limits of Scripture: Vivekananda's Reinterpretation of the Authority of the Vedas* (1994), and, most recently, *The Advaita Worldview: God, World and Humanity* (2006).

Pinit Ratanakul received his PhD in philosophy from Yale University. He is professor of philosophy and founding director of the College of Religious Studies at Mahidol University in Bangkok. Prof. Ratanakul is recognized for introducing the study of philosophy to the Thai university curriculum in the 1970s and '80s. He is the author of *Bioethics and Buddhism* and a contributor to the *Encyclopedia of Bioethics*. His research interests include bioethics, religion and culture, and religion and psychology.

Norman Ravvin is chair of the Institute for Canadian Jewish Studies in the Department of Religion at Montreal's Concordia University. His publications focus on Jewish literature, Holocaust Studies, ethics, and Yiddish Studies. His books include *A House of Words: Jewish Writing, Identity and Memory*, the novel *Lola by Night*, and, as co-editor with Richard Menkis, *The Canadian Jewish Studies Reader*. In a previous volume produced by the Centre for Studies in Religion and Society he contributed an essay on Canadian Jewish ethnicity, culture, and religious identity.

Janet Soskice is professor of philosophical theology at the University of Cambridge. She is past president of the Catholic Theological Association of Great Britain and of the Society for the Study of Theology. Her publications include *Metaphor and Religious Language* (1984), *The Kindness of God* (2008), *Sisters of Sinai* (2009), *Medicine and Moral Reasoning*, edited with Grant Gillett and K. W. Fulford (1994), and, with Diana Lipton, *Feminism and Theology* (2003).

Kelli I. Stajduhar is associate professor at the School of Nursing and Centre on Aging at the University of Victoria, Canada. She has worked in oncology, palliative care, and gerontology for more than twenty years as a staff nurse, clinical nurse specialist, and academic. Her research has focused on health service needs for those at the end of life and their families and on the needs of marginalized and vulnerable populations. Dr. Stajduhar holds a New Investigator Award from the Canadian Institutes of Health Research and a Scholar Award from the Michael Smith Foundation for Health Research.

Coby Tschanz is senior instructor and PhD student at the University of Victoria School of Nursing. Her master's thesis is titled "Bearing Witness for Nurses in Practice with Persons Living Their Dying" (2006). Her interests include hospice palliative care nursing practice, nursing philosophy, and theory-guided nursing practice and research.

Earle H. Waugh is professor emeritus of religious studies and director of the Centre for the Cross-Cultural Study of Health and Healing in Family Medicine at the University of Alberta. His early research focused on Islamic and Indigenous Studies. In 2005 his promotion of understanding of Muslim and Indigenous cultures was recognized by the Salvos Prelorentzos Award for Peace Education from the Canadian organization Project Ploughshares. He is currently leading a research project on the intersection of culture and health that recently published the *Manual of Cultural Competence for Health Care Professionals*.

Rhonda Wiebe (BA) has extensive experience in spiritual care and research advocacy for persons with disability and Indigenous peoples. Currently, she is a researcher in the Vulnerable Persons New Emerging Team (VP NET) Ethics Theme, interviewing people with disabilities, health care and service providers, Indigenous community advocates, and voluntary palliative care providers. Rhonda co-chairs a national committee on death-making concerns for the Council of Canadians with Disabilities and is appointed by Order-in-Council to the Manitoba Health Review Board.

Michael Wright is a co-founder and senior research fellow of the International Observatory on End of Life Care at Lancaster University, UK. He is a Christian priest and holds a PhD for research on the spiritual dimension of health care. His research interests include hospice history and the global development of palliative care. His most recent book, *Hospice and Palliative Care in Southeast Asia: A Review of Developments and Challenges in Malaysia, Thailand and the Philippines,* was published by Oxford University Press in 2010.

Index

333